TO ADD

- No History of Economic Thoughts, Pl

GW00862893

Not Only an Economist

Not Only an Economist

Recent Essays by Mark Blaug

Mark Blaug

Professor Emeritus, University of London, Professor Emeritus, University of Buckingham and Visiting Professor, University of Exeter, UK

Edward Elgar

Cheltenham, UK • Brookfield, US

Published by
Edward Elgar Publishing Limited
8 Lansdown Place
Cheltenham
Glos GL50 2HU
UK

Edward Elgar Publishing Company
Old Post Road
Brookfield
Vermont 05036
US

A catalogue record for this book is available from the British Library

Library of Congress Cataloguing in Publication Data
Blaug, Mark.
    Not only an economist : recent essays by Mark Blaug / Mark Blaug.
    Includes bibliographical references.
    1. Economics—History.   2. Competition—History.   3. Economics—
Methodology.   I. Title.
HB75.B665   1997
330—dc20   96–26479
                                                                          CIP

Printed and bound in Great Britain by
Biddles Ltd, Guildford and King's Lynn

ISBN   1 85898 455 6

Contents

Figures and tables

FIGURES

TABLES

Preface

This is the fourth collection of my papers: the first was *Economic History and the History of Economics* (1986); the second was *The Economics of Education and the Education of an Economist* (1987); and the third was *Economic Theories True or False?* (1990). Between them they cover the five subject-areas in which I have worked, namely, economic history, cultural economics, the history of economic thought, the methodology of economics and the economics of education. All but the first two of these are represented in this fourth collection of personal papers.

I begin with an autobiographical essay which attempts to account for my life-long interest in the history and methodology of economics as two sides of the same coin. In one sense, this chapter, entitled 'Not only an economist', serves as a fitting preface to this collection that I might have written now, had it not appeared previously. Do such 'confessions' add anything to the ideas and arguments of one's more serious papers? Is biography relevant to the understanding of economic ideas, one's own and those of other economists? I am sure that the answer to that question is affirmative but I have never been sure of the true significance of that affirmative yes. The chapter on 'Recent biographies of Keynes' raises this famous question once again in a specific context, namely, the ongoing assessment of the meaning of Keynes's writings. It was one of the dogmas of 'logical positivism' that biographical information hinders rather than assists the appraisal of ideas. I doubt that dogma now but, in any case, the sheer intellectual fascination of biography has never left me.

Chapter 3 is the preface to the Japanese translation of my first book, *Ricardian Economics: A Historical Study* (1980), previously unpublished in English. *Ricardian Economics* (1958) was my PhD dissertation and, on balance, I am not ashamed of it even after all these years. One reason I am publishing this preface in English is to draw attention to many issues that I got right in this jejune publication. It must rank as one of the most neglected books in the history of world literature, and if I had a pound for every article I have read on the history of English classical political economy in the period 1815–70 that failed even to mention it, I could retire a rich man. I am willing to admit that indifference hurts. There is a Jewish saying: children crave attention; how much more so do scholars. Precisely!

Chapter 4 is a popular exposition of 'the case for Adam Smith' as the one great economist of the past that every well-educated person should read. Biography counts for little with Smith because we know almost nothing about his personal life, but his texts, *The Wealth of Nations* and *The Theory of Moral Sentiments*, are so rich and yet so ambiguous in their message that he more than any of the great economists of the past raises the famous question of precisely what he meant, should have meant, must have meant. This is precisely the central issue in the next chapter on 'The historiography of economics'. It explains why I can no longer applaud Whig history of science. Such 'rational reconstructions' of past thinking have their uses but, when pushed to the limit, they tend to undermine 'historical reconstructions', namely to grasp the ideas of the past 'as they really were'. This is an ideal we can never completely attain, but striving to attain it as nearly as possible is nevertheless what the history of ideas is all about. Lest anyone suggest that we can live quite well without the history of ideas, I give a number of examples in this chapter of a ploy the reader can himself or herself observe in every second paper in one of our five current journals in the history of economic thought: the rational reconstruction of the writings of, say, Adam Smith or David Ricardo or Léon Walras which quickly turn into a historical reconstruction – as if one could have one's cake and eat it too!

Chapter 6 elaborates a theme that has run increasingly through all my thinking in the last few years. After a short lifetime of studying economics, I have come to realize that my own profession was sold long ago (well, actually about 60 years ago) on the value of concentrating almost exclusively on the equilibrium values of economic variables, on the terminal state of the process of competition in an economic model of market transactions. Equilibrium as 'a position of rest' came to be the dominant conception of what an economist aimed to write down about economic relationships. But whenever we pronounce on the merits of markets, of competition, of capitalism as an economic system, what we in fact invoke are dynamic disequilibrium propositions of evolving processes as, for example, that private firms competing in highly contestable and relatively unregulated markets will produce more and better goods at lower costs than any alternative economic arrangement. We sell economics to ourselves as a rigorous discipline capable of delivering precise answers to precise questions in comparative statics but we peddle economics to the world as a subject that can deliver rough-and-ready answers to the Big Question in 'magnificent dynamics'. We must lift our eyes from the contemplation of competition as an end-state in logical time to the consideration of competition as a process in real time even if it means sacrificing some rigour for the sake of acquiring more relevance.

This is a point of view that Friedrich Hayek came increasingly to express in his writings. Chapter 7 on 'Hayek revisited' pays homage to this complex, many-sided figure in twentieth-century economics, not all of whose ideas hang together in a coherent package but whose writings nevertheless are filled with golden nuggets, some of which still await further explanation.

The chapter on entrepreneurship in the history of economics further pursues the theme of the need to explore the working of market processes. Entrepreneurs and entrepreneurship are essential to that process and by excluding disequilibrium price and quantity adjustments from orthodox economic theory, economists have virtually doomed themselves to analyse markets under capitalism as if entrepreneurs were epiphenomena instead of central actors.

Chapter 9 on the quantity theory of money confronts what is, surely, 'the oldest successful theory on economics' with the methodology of falsificationism. How good is the empirical track record of the quantity theory of money? Is it true or false? It turns out that it is more than one theory and that the question whether it is true or false depends critically on which version of the quantity theory is being put forward.

That brings me to Chapter 10 on unemployment and inflation, which is a Child's Guide to the great macroeconomic question of the day: is the cost of inflation in modern industrialized economies really greater than the cost of unemployment as all bankers, financiers and most politicians seem to think? I think not, and in saying that unemployment and not inflation is Public Enemy No.l, I nail my flag to the neo-Keynesian mast.

The first chapter in Part Two is an essay on questions of methodology. It is in fact, an attempt to say what we mean by 'progress of knowledge' in economics and how would we know that we had attained it. Do we mean 'analytical progress', 'empirical progress', or what? This, I am sure, is a paper that will be laughable even to me in another ten years but, nevertheless, the effort to get it down on paper has been good for my soul and it may do as much for those who will improve on it in years to come.

The discussion of methodological issue continues with a postscript on a conference I organized with Neil de Marchi on the application of Imre Lakatos's Methodology of Scientific Research Programmes (MSRP) to economics. The conference came as something of a surprise to me personally because what I thought would prove to be a stimulating occasion on which to extend the applicability of Lakatos's scheme to economics proved in the final analysis to mark the virtual demise of Lakatosianism in economics. The best-laid plans of mice and men 'gang aft a-gley'. I continue my defence of Lakatos in two contributions to the forthcoming *Handbook of Economic Methodology*.

Part Three on the economics of education begins with the text of a lecture on 'The economic value of higher education', in which I argue against the continued subsidization of higher education in both the First and the Third Worlds. This is one of my hobby-horses, as I record in my autobiographical reflections. I take a dim view in this chapter of the so-called externalities of schooling, which figure so prominently as the source of endogenous growth in the 'new' growth theory.[1] It is noteworthy, by the way, that a recent state-of-the-art econometric exercise – cointegration and Granger-causality tests – demonstrates the ambiguous relationship between higher education and economic development: the numbers of students enrolled at higher education institutions was not causally related to real GDP in Italy and Australia over the last 80–90 years and only weakly related in Japan, UK, France and Sweden over the same period. In the longer run, the two were not related at all in any of the six countries.[2] So much for the widespread belief, fondly endorsed by all my academic colleagues, that spending on colleges and universities is good for growth.

Chapter 17 on 'The University of Buckingham after ten years', written jointly with Keith Shaw, was an attempt to evaluate the achievements of the only privately financed university in Britain. It must be difficult for readers from America and Japan, two countries with a vigorous private sector in higher education, to appreciate that the founding of the University of Buckingham in 1976 was greeted by all and sundry in Britain as a fascist plot that marked the end of British higher education as we knew it. It is early days yet, but to date it appears that the University of Buckingham has been a success, albeit a qualified success, because its aim of influencing the rest of British higher education has not so far been realized. I must add that my own years of teaching at the University of Buckingham were among the most enjoyable I have experienced in academic life. 'Small is beautiful' or so it seems at least in institutions of higher education.

Among the most famous of Britain's education institutions are the so-called 'public schools', that is, private secondary schools, the most prestigious of which are also boarding schools. The Labour Party in Britain has long hoped to abolish or at least throttle these schools and there is hardly any better litmus-paper tests of the political convictions of an average British social scientist than to elicit his or her views about public schools. I have long detested these schools, in part because of personal experience of them, but I object strenuously to the notion of eradicating them by political fiat. However, as a economist I cannot help noticing that they are generously subsidized out of public funds, a fact that the friends of public schools never openly admit. My Chapter 18 on independent education is an attempt to provide some evidence about this contentious issue.

Chapters 16 and 17 refer specially to Great Britain and may have only limited interest to readers in other countries. Still, given the world-wide reputation of British higher education, they raise issues that are of greater than local interest. 'The state of the British Economics profession', co-authored with my wife, was the product of a commissioned study of the UK labour market for professional economists.[3] It raised a furore when it appeared if only because it failed to find any evidence of a shortage of professional economists in Britain and criticized our colleagues for teaching economics to undergraduates as if every one of them was destined to become a professional economist. Chapter 19 on 'The "pros" and "cons" of education vouchers' analyses their merits and demerits, which are once again on the political agenda, if not in the USA then certainly in the UK.

Finally, in this Part there is a chapter on 'Education and the employment contract', which puts together my ideas about the economic value of education – just why do employers pay better-educated workers more than less-educated workers? – with my ideas about one of the characteristic features of an industrial society, namely, the impossibility of fully specifying the employment contract between employers and workers; much follows from the incompleteness of that fundamental contract.

Part Four contains three chapters on cultural economics that I wrote in the 1970s but which are still relevant today, details apart. In one way or the other, they all deal with the economic case for subsidies to the arts. I am particularly fond of the last of these three chapters, entitled 'Why are Covent Garden seat prices so high?', in part because it involved more hard work than anything I have ever done, but mostly because it neatly lays bare the nuts and bolts of opera subsidy. It represents a method of analysis that the Arts Council of Britain should long ago have adopted.

I close in Part Five with a selection from more than 100 book reviews I have written over the years. All these are reviews of major books, at least major to my intellectual development. I am afraid that I read books the way a drug addict takes drugs – as if I could not get through the day without them. Even after some 60 years of constant daily reading, I never open a new book without a rush of adrenaline: perhaps this book will prove to be truly exhilarating, revealing some entirely new insights about this or that. Ninety-nine times out of a hundred, of course, I am disappointed. The reviews that follow are of those one out of a hundred books that did not disappoint.

NOTES

1. R.E. Lucas (1988) 'On the mechanics of economic development', *Journal of Monetary Economics*, **22**; 3–42; reprinted in *Growth Theory*, vol.1, ed. R. Becker and E. Burmeister, Aldershot, Hants.: Edward Elgar Publishing, 1991: 81–120.
2. J.-L. de Meulemcester and D. Rochat (1989), 'A causality analysis of the link between higher education and economic development', *Economics of Education Review*, **14** (4), December: 351–61.
3. The Royal Economic Society's *Newsletter*, **69**, March 1990: 16–27, contained critical comments from Austin Robinson, Peter Sloane and Ross MacKay, followed by our reply. Further letters and comments followed in *Newsletter*, **70**, June 1990: 15–26.

Acknowledgements

The author and publisher wish to thank the following who have kindly given permission for the use of copyright material:

American Economic Association for article: 'Recent biographies of Keynes', *Journal of Economic Literature*, **xxxii**, September 1994: 1204–15.

American Economist for article: 'Not only an economist' *American Economist*, **38**(2), Fall 1994: 12–27.

Blackwell Publishers for articles: 'The current state of the British economics profession' with Ruth Towse, *Economic Journal*, **100**, March 1990: 227–36; and 'The University of Buckingham after ten years: a tentative evaluation' with, G.K. Shaw, *Higher Education Quarterly*, **42**(1), Winter 1988: 72–89.

Critical Review for article: 'Hayek revisited', *Critical Review*, **7**(1), 1993: 51–60.

Economic Notes for article: 'Public enemy no. 1: unemployment not inflation', *Economic Notes*, **22**(3), 1993: 387–401.

History of Economics Society for article: 'On the historiography of economics', *Journal of the History of Economic Thought*, **12**, Spring 1990: 27–37.

Institute of Economic Affairs for article: 'Can independent education be suppressed?', *Journal of Economic Affairs*, October 1981: 30–7.

Netherlands Institute for Advanced Study in the Humanities and Social Sciences for arrticle: 'The economic value of higher education', Uhlenbeck-Lecture VIII, 1990.

Routledge for article: 'Why I am not a constructivist; or Confessions of an unrepentant Popperian', in *New Directions in Economic Methodology*, ed. R. Backhouse, 1994: 109–36.

Every effort has been made to trace all the copyright holders but if any have been inadvertently overlooked the publishers will be pleased to make the necessary arrangements at the first opportunity.

PART ONE

History of Economic Thought

1. Not only an economist: autobiographical reflections of a historian of economic thought*

I owe the decision to study economics to the influence of the writings of Henry George and Karl Marx. In 1944 I was 17 years old and attending Peter Stuyvesant High School in New York City. I enrolled for a course in Commerce, and in the last week of the term the teacher took some of the better students, which included me, to a special lecture at a nearby Henry George School. The lecture was an explanation of why the unrestrained growth of land rentals had produced poverty, wars, and all the other ills of modern civilization. Henry George had long ago provided both the diagnosis of the evil and the treatment that would cure it: a single confiscatory tax on ground rent! At the end of the lecture, we were all presented with free copies of Henry George's *Progress and Poverty*, which I duly read without understanding much of it. But years later when I finally studied the Ricardian theory of differential rent, I did have a moment of excitement at discovering the true source of George's theory.

THE INFLUENCE OF MARXISM

I was intrigued by *Progress and Poverty* but I was not entirely convinced. But shortly afterwards, during my first year at New York University, I became friendly with some left-wing students who introduced me first to the pamphlets of Lenin and Stalin and later to the weightier tomes of Marx and Engels. I was completely bowled over by these writings and within a matter of months became a Marxist, that is, an avowed follower of Marx.

When I now try to recall just what it was about Marxist writings that converted me so quickly, I think it was a combination of qualities that says as much about me as about Marxism. Firstly, it was the aura of the absolute conviction of possession of the truth that radiated from every page of the writings of the leading Marxists, accentuated in the case of Lenin and Stalin by their dogmatic and abusive tone towards their intellectual opponents. Secondly, it was the encyclopaedic range of Marxist theory, the sense that here was a universal science

* First published in *The American Economist*, **38**(2), Fall 1994, 12–27.

of society and indeed a philosophy of history as well as a philosophy of nature; whether it was the latest political election result, or the causes of the French revolution, or the overthrow of the matriarchy in ancient Greece, or why Rembrandt was so partial to chiaroscuro, or why Beethoven's last piano sonata Op. 102 consisted of only two movements, or what Goethe meant by the end of *Faust*, it could all be explained by Marxism. I was always a bit of a smart alec when I was young and Marxism was made to order for me: it allowed me to pontificate on every subject with a cocksureness that suited me perfectly.

Marxism taught me economic determinism, that is, the idea that economic interests and economic forces are the foundations of all social and political conflicts. It followed that economics is the queen of all social sciences because everything is ultimately reducible to economics. Within six months of becoming a Marxist, I had therefore decided that I had to master economics. I took my first course in economics in my second year of university and I keenly remember finding it a rather taxing subject. I am glad that I can still remember my own difficulties in learning economics because it has made me a better teacher as a result.

Even all this does not fully account for my attraction to Marxism. The real appeal of Marxism for me was its conceptual apparatus, its intricate jargon of special terms and categories, its endless Talmudic distinctions between 'base' and 'superstructure', between 'modes of production' and 'relations of production', between 'strategies' and 'tactics' of social action, between the 'contradictions' and the 'unity of opposites' of social and economic systems, etcetera, etcetera. Once one had commanded the technical language, adherence to Marxism created an entire subculture of discourse in which, literally, one could only be understood by other Marxists. In short, Marxism gave me my first glimpse of the culture of scholarship, an intellectual community that feeds upon itself.

I did not remain a purely intellectual Marxist. I joined the American Communist Party, attended political meetings and participated in party demonstrations. I did this reluctantly because I was never much of a joiner but, nevertheless, I went through a brief period of genuine political activity. It was brief because my natural rebelliousness soon got me thrown out of the Communist Party. As the war drew to a close in 1945, the question of the continued occupation of Germany by Allied troops came to the fore as a political issue. Earl Browder, the President of the American Communist Party, endorsed President Roosevelt's recommendation of post-war military conscription so as to allow American troops to be stationed permanently in Germany. This was regarded as heresy by some members of the Communist Party, and when Stalin came out against Roosevelt's policy, Browder's fate was sealed; he was deprived of his presidency and expelled from the Party. In a flash, he became *persona non grata*. A few of the communist students at college collected a petition on Browder's behalf, which I signed after due consideration. I was called before a Party tribunal and, having failed to repent, was promptly expelled. From that moment on a large number of friends and acquaintances in the Party refused, not just to speak to me, but even to recognize me when they met me in the street. To those who have never been a member of a conspiratorial or quasi-conspiratorial group, the speed with which party members will ostracize a heretic is hard to believe. In retrospect, and given the total political insignificance of the American Communist Party in 1945, the experience seems ludicrous but at the time it proved to be a harrowing awakening to the realities of left-wing politics.

Although I ceased to be a card-carrying member of the Communist Party in 1945, it took me at least another seven to eight years to shake off all the blinkers that Marxism leaves behind. Between 1945 and 1952 I travelled gradually but irreversibly away from communism. I well remember the effect of reading *The God That Failed: Six Studies in Communism* (1950) by Arthur Koestler, Ignazio Silone, André Gide, Richard Wright, Louis Fischer and Stephen Spender, all writers who had at one time been 'fellow-travellers'. Even after all these years, I can still recall the awful feeling of having shared the disillusionment of these famous communist converts. It is curious how far one can go in abandoning previous beliefs without making the final jump to non-belief. The movement for me was the abortive East German 'revolution' in the summer of 1952 when the people of East Berlin came close to throwing off the Soviet-imposed government of East Germany. I had visited East Berlin as a tourist in May 1952 and had seen evidence of seething resentment against the regime. When I returned to London, I read accounts of the outbreak and its suppression by Soviet tanks in the communist press. I had always recognized that communist papers are capable of telling lies but I had previously closed my eyes to the extent to which they carry their lying. The disillusionment of a 'true believer', such as I had been, comes in the final analysis like a cold shower after a hot bath.

When I think of some of the things that I believed when I was a communist and that I expounded passionately and with a sense of total conviction, I blush to the roots of my hair. I can remember, for example, how I defended the Stalinist version of the Moscow Trials, namely that Trotsky, living in Paris and Mexico City, had orchestrated a vast conspiracy of sabotage inside the Soviet Union that even infected the Soviet military hierarchy – and this despite reading Arthur Koestler's *Darkness at Noon*, which I brushed aside as bourgeois propaganda. It has made me suspicious ever since of beliefs strongly held and has helped me to be more tolerant than I am naturally inclined to be. Whenever I now pronounce that so-and-so is absolutely true, I always say quietly to myself: 'Yes, just like the Moscow Trials.'

I dropped communism like an old coat thrown off but Marxism took longer to discard. In some sense, the great themes of exploitation, alienation and inequality haunt me still. Of course, the more economics I learned, the less

Marxian economics I believed in. I could soon see that Marx's grasp of the economic problems of running a socialist society was ludicrous: he really thought that it would present no more than an accounting problem rather like a corner grocery store writ large. Moreover, most of Marx's economic predictions were palpably awry and it was perfectly clear that he himself was deeply disappointed at the time of his death by the failure of the proletariat to overthrow capitalism. But it still took me many years to perceive the profound, central fallacy at the core of Marxian economics, a fallacy which even today is not acknowledged by Marxists and even ex-Marxists. It is a most interesting fallacy and it is so cleverly hidden away in *Capital* that not one in a thousand readers ever notices it. It is the idea that there is a uniform rate of surplus value in every industry in the economy, that, in short, every dollar of wages paid out yields capitalists an identical number of dollars of profit, irrespective of whether these wages are earned in agriculture digging ditches or in the oil industry refining oil. This is a most improbable assumption but there is no way of demonstrating that it is false because the rate of surplus value is neither an observable nor a behaviourable variable in a capitalist economy: no one strives to minimize or maximize it; it is truly a ghost-in-the-machine. Marx was well aware of this phenomenon but, in the eagerness to disguise the arbitrariness of his assumption he reified value and surplus value and spoke repeatedly of the capitalist system striving to increase the rate of surplus value; this is something that individual capitalists cannot do and in any case have no incentive to do. Nevertheless, Marx simply had to assume a uniform rate of surplus value because without it his claim that labour alone creates surplus value would have fallen to the ground.

Many modern Marxist economists, at least in Western countries, no longer believe in the labour theory of value and its corollary, the labour theory of surplus value. Even so, to the extent that they remain Marxists they continue to believe that capitalism is grounded on the exploitation of labour. By 'exploitation', they mean simply that workers do not own the means of production and hence are denied the profits that result from employing labour in the production of saleable goods. Their argument is therefore that there is a fundamental injustice in capitalism, an injustice residing in the fact that workers do not own and owners do not work. It is fascinating to me to see how far such 'analytical Marxists', as they call themselves, have abandoned all varieties of consequentialism in appraising capitalism and have instead opted for more moral judgements based on the ethical meaning of social relationships in a capitalist system. In other words, they ask: is it fair that most of us have to work for a living, while a small minority can live without working? (to which of course the only answer is that it is exceedingly unfair), instead of asking whether the consequences of capitalism in generating unprecedented economic growth could be obtained without an unequal and hence unfair distribution of private property. In other words, we can agree that capitalism is not an edifying system: it is crass, brutal and morally reprehensible but it does deliver the goods and in the final analysis it is the goods that we want!

THE McCARTHY EXPERIENCE

I doubt whether it would have taken me so many years to throw off the weight of Marxism if it had not been for an encounter in 1952 with the spectre of McCarthyism. McCarthy was riding high in 1952, the product of the anti-communist hysteria that held America in its grip at the height of the Cold War. And it was a hysteria, as the following story will show. I had graduated from Queens College of the City University of New York in 1950 and was in the midst of my preliminary year for the PhD at Columbia University when Arthur D. Gayer, the chairman of the economics department at Queens College, was killed in an automobile accident. The department looked around for someone to take over his courses in the middle of the semester and since I had worked for him as a research assistant, I was asked whether I would have a go. And so I suddenly found myself teaching a full load of courses in microeconomics, consumer economics and marketing, a subject I had never studied. I can remember being so nervous about my first lectures that I literally memorized them in their entirety the night before giving them.

I was just getting on top of all this teaching when the Un-American Activities Committee, chaired by Senator Joseph McCarthy, arrived in New York City to investigate communism in the New York City college system. They called on three well-known professors to appear before them in order, no doubt, to ask them the familiar questions: 'Are you now or have you ever been a member of the Communist Party?' All three refused to co-operate with the committee, pleading the First and Fifth Amendment to the Constitution, which prohibits witnesses from incriminating themselves. Despite the fact that all three were tenured professors, they were promptly and summarily dismissed by their employer, the City University of New York. One of these three professors was Vera Shlakman, Professor of Labour Economics at Queens College, a former teacher of mine and, at that point in time, a colleague. She was the president of the Teacher's Union, a left-wing professional union of college teachers in the New York City area, and was herself left-wing and, for all I knew, a fellow-traveller. But having been taught by her, I knew that she was scrupulously impartial and leaned over backwards not to indoctrinate her students. A number of students organized a petition to the President of Queens College demanding Vera Shlakman's reinstatement but, by the by-laws of the college, student petitions could not be submitted to a higher authority without an endorsing signature of at least one faculty member. The students went right through the economics department, which then numbered 40 professors, associate professors, assistant professors, and lowly tutors like myself, without encountering one person willing to endorse the petition. At the end of the line, they came to me and because of my personal regard for Professor Shlakman, and because I could not bear the thought of being pusillanimous, I signed the petition. Within 24 hours, I received a curt note from President Thatcher of Queens College (odd that I should remember his name after 40 years!) informing me that, unless I resigned forthwith, I would be dismissed, and black-listed for future employment.

For a day or two, I contemplated a magnificent protest, a statement that would ring down the ages as a clarion bell to individual freedom, that would be read and cited for years to come by American high school students – and then I quietly sent in my letter of resignation.

I was now at my wits' end. I had planned to apply for a scholarship to begin working on my doctoral dissertation and had been relying on my teaching salary from Queens College to carry me through the application period. I was broke and depressed by the entire experience when suddenly the telephone rang to inform me that I had been offered a grant by the Social Science Research Council to enable me to go abroad to write my PhD thesis: clearly, there were people here and there behind the scenes lending assistance to victims of McCarthyism.

In the curious way that every disaster in my life has always in due course turned into a blessing, there now began what I quickly realized were the best two years in my life. I had picked a topic, the rise and fall of the school of David Ricardo in nineteenth-century economic opinion, that turned out to be even more promising than I had imagined.[1] I also discovered that scholarly research was my true *métier*. I took a room within a stone's throw of the British Museum Reading Room in London and lived the life of a mediaeval monk, reading and writing as much as 18 hours a day, seven days a week. My early efforts were sent off to my doctoral supervisor, George Stigler, then at Columbia University, whose acerbic but accurate comments were just what I needed to spur me on. Two years later I was back in New York with a completed thesis and the undeniable pleasure of witnessing the final downfall of Senator McCarthy on television.

In the summer of 1954, I was interviewed for a post as Assistant Professor at Yale University. On my interview committee was William Fellner, who later became one of my mentors. In the course of the interview, I felt impelled to explain how I lost my previous teaching position at Queens College. I always remember how Fellner cut me off, saying: 'We don't want to hear about that. This is a private college and what transpired at a public university a few years ago is of no concern to us.' I never had a better demonstration of Milton Friedman's thesis that a free market, by multiplying the number of probable employers, is more likely to secure liberty for the individual than a socialist system in which the state is a monopsonist.

It is difficult nowadays to convey the extraordinary atmosphere of the McCarthy era in which one was likely to be stabbed in the back by one's best friends and in which everyone was literally looking for 'reds under their beds' every night. In my youth I had innocently believed that intellectuals would always stand up for ideas against the powers that be but, as a result of the McCarthy experience, I lost whatever respect I ever had for intellectuals and academics. With enough social pressure, they will capitulate to McCarthy, Hitler, Stalin, Sadam Hussein or anyone else with the power of the army and police behind them.

By the time I started teaching at Yale in 1954 I had shaken off almost all of my old communist beliefs, and when Kruschev delivered his famous anti-Stalin speech in 1956, I had the quiet satisfaction of having all my new beliefs confirmed out of the horse's mouth. In the next few years, I moved steadily to the right but I never became as maniacally anti-communist as many ex-communists. I remained, and probably still remain, politically schizophrenic: rather right-wing on questions of economic policy, such as privatization, deregulation, trade union legislation and the like, but fiercely left-wing on questions of social policy such as welfare payments, unemployment compensation, positive discrimination in favour of women, blacks and gays, the right to abortion, legalization of soft drugs and so forth. My rightward journey was halted by Reagan and Thatcher. Living in England in the 1980s, I was increasingly appalled by the blatant use of mass unemployment to counter inflation and was amazed that the persistence of double-digit unemployment was tolerated by the British electorate for a decade or more. I was struck by the way Mrs Thatcher managed to persuade voters, financial journalists and even many economists that the costs of inflation are always greater than the costs of unemployment. I believe this to be blatantly false for single-digit inflation but double-digit unemployment rates, which indeed was the prevailing scenario throughout most of the 1980s.[2] The Falklands War was bad enough but her failure to attack the unemployment problem, or even to admit that it was a problem, made me as left-wing on macroeconomic questions as I had long been on social questions. Thanks to Mrs Thatcher I came back to a more or less consistent belief in capitalism, yes, but capitalism tempered by Keynesian demand management and quasi-socialist welfarism.

THE FLIRTATION WITH FREUD

Even as I fell under the spell of Marx, I also succumbed to the siren call of Freud. In the summers of 1944, 1945 and 1946, I worked as a waiter in upstate New York hotels – the so-called 'Borsht Belt' – and many of my guests were psychiatrists and psychoanalysts. It didn't take long before I was deeply immersed in the writings of Freud and Freudians and thrilled by the power of Freudian theory to explain everything, a power which of course reminded me of the style of Marx. I still recall vividly being absolutely entranced by Freud's *Interpretation of Dreams*, the sense that something as inherently mysterious as dreams could be accounted for in a rational manner. I yielded too, to the enormous rhetorical power of Freud, who, whatever one may think of him as a scientist, was a great literary artist. Freudianism stayed with me insidiously much longer than Marxism. But, gradually over the years, I became increasingly aware of how self-fulfilling and self-justifying were many of the key concepts of psychoanalytic theory and how characteristic was the unwillingness of analysts to submit Freudian ideas to an empirical test. I now think that virtually the whole of Freudian theory is a tissue of mumbo-jumbo and that psychoanalysis as a therapeutic technique is not very different from Chinese brain-washing. But this was a view that came to me only slowly and not without a certain measure of personal experience with psychoanalysis.

In the wonderful poem, 'In Memory of Sigmund Freud', every line of which I ought to quote, W.H. Auden concludes:

> If often he was wrong and at times absurd
> To us he is no more a person
> Now but a whole climate of opinion,
> Under whom we conduct our differing lives.
> Like weather he can only hinder or help

Not so: he can only hinder and does!

WHY BOTHER WITH THE HISTORY OF ECONOMICS?

Ever since my childhood, I have been a voracious reader. When I was young, I read to escape, and later, reading a book a day became a habit which I could not shake off. A non-stop reader has a comparative advantage in a subject like the history of economic thought and in that sense intellectual history is, at least for me, a form of self-indulgence. Within a year of arriving at Yale University in 1954, I was asked to take over William Fellner's graduate course in the history of economic thought for no better reason than that I was the only person on the faculty anxious to teach it. And so, at the tender age of 27, I found myself teaching a compulsory course in the history of economics to postgraduate students at one of America's foremost institutions of higher education. Yale in those years admitted some 20 to 30 hand-picked graduate students in economics and in the next few years my students numbered at least a dozen or so names who later became well-known academic economists. I was so nervous about teaching the course that I over-prepared myself: within a few years I had collected thousands of pages of notes, notes that were eventually to become my only well-known book, *Economic Theory in Retrospect* (1962).

In the introduction of the book, I claimed that all historians of economic thought are either 'relativists' or 'absolutists': they either believe that all past doctrines are more or less faithful reflections of the historical circumstances in which they are created or that past ideas are largely the result of the internal logical development of the subject, being almost always mistaken in the light of later thinking. I announced myself an unapologetic absolutist and poked fun at relativists throughout the book. This is not a point of view I now hold, having been upstaged over the years by even more strident upholders of the 'Whig interpretation of history'. When I witness the attempt of many commentators in recent years to reproduce the great ideas of the past in modern dress, particularly in one or another mathematical model, I realize that absolutism carried to its logical extreme deprives the history of ideas of all *raison d'être*: far from imparting an appreciation of the past, it actually destroys historical understanding by condemning all thinkers down the ages to live now and to think as we do.

Be that as it may, my youthful absolutism was the product of three forces. Firstly, the discipline of economics was never so confident as it was in the late 1950s and early 1960s: we *knew* that general equilibrium theory was the last word in theoretical elegance, that input–output analysis and linear programming would soon make it not just elegant but operational, and that 'the neo-classical synthesis' had successfully joined Keynesian macroeconomics to Walrasian microeconomics; in short, that true economics was one church and that the full truth was at any moment to be revealed to us. If ever one were going to take an absolutist view of the history of economic ideas, 1960 was just the right date to bring it off. Secondly, I was deeply influenced by Schumpeter's *History of Economic Analysis* (1954), and Schumpeter was of course a peculiar but nevertheless adamant absolutist. Reinforcing the influence of Schumpeter was the influence of both the writings and the personality of George Stigler, my doctoral supervisor.[3] He had a reputation of destroying students but I always got along very well with him. I like aggressive, assertive people and when George Stigler said that something you had written was nonsense, he produced so many crushing reasons to back up his judgement that you could not but be grateful that he had condescended to criticize you. Also he was one of the few really funny men that I have ever known: his sense of humour was wicked and even vicious and I loved it. I found myself imitating his lecture style and of course his writing style but I have never been able to match his biting footnotes.

Whenever I met him in later years, I regressed immediately to the status of a young graduate student ingratiating himself to a senior figure. In fact, I was a bit scared of him, particularly as our political views were a thousand miles apart and I once or twice inadvertently expressed opinions that were abhorrent to him.

My most touching memory of him is a day in 1960 when he introduced me in Chicago to Frank Knight, his doctoral supervisor in the 1930s. I watched him talking to Frank Knight with the same deference that I showed him and I suddenly realized that he too could not address an elderly teacher of Knight's renown as an equal, no more than I could relate to him as an equal. There is something very stirring in the idea of the successive generations of teachers and pupils passing down 'the lamp of knowledge'.

But apart from Schumpeter and Stigler, it was my students at Yale who would have driven me to absolutism whatever its intellectual merits. The history of economic thought was a compulsory graduate course in the 1950s but these students were typical American graduate students: they wanted to learn the tools and techniques of modern economics and to hell with such scholarly subjects as economic history and the history of economic thought. I was aware from the moment the course began that I had to sell the history of economics as somehow relevant to these young Turks. No wonder then that I taught the subject of emphasizing the filiation of purely analytical concepts and continually emphasizing the modernity, and sometimes lack of modernity, of the ideas of the past.

The very task of working so hard to put over the history of economics as a legitimate subject for intellectual inquiry eventually soured me on the subject altogether. By the time I left America in 1962, I was more or less determined to work instead in applied economics. But eventually, after a holiday from the history of economic thought for a decade, I came back to it again in the 1970s as my first and ultimately last love. In the final analysis, I find nothing as intellectually satisfying as the history of ideas. I have never been able to grasp how one can understand any idea without knowing where it came from, how it evolved out of previous ideas. As soon as I learned calculus, I had to find out how Newton invented it, how Liebniz invented it independently, how they argued over the right calculus notation and just what was meant by the concept of a derivative. And one reason I have never really understood Einstein's general theory of relativity, despite repeated attempts to learn it, is that late nineteenth-century physics is too difficult for me, so that I can't follow how Lorenz almost got as far as Einstein did. Great theories, in economics as in other subjects, are path-dependent, to use popular recent jargon in economic history; that is, it is not possible to explain their occurrence without considering the corpus of received ideas which led to the development of that particular new theory; had the body of received ideas been different we would have arrived at a different theory at the culmination of that development. In other words, without the history of economics , economic theories just drop from the sky; you have to take them on faith. The moment you wish to judge a theory, you have to ask how they came to be produced in the first place and that is a question that can only be answered by the history of ideas.

I understand very well why historians of economic thought figure so little in the pecking order of economists. But it does mean that economics is for most economists an almost wholly unintellectual subject. In the face of ideas, many economists are simply philistines, like troglodytes listening to a Beethoven quartet and asking why the four players seem to be unable to bow in unison.

THE ECONOMICS OF EDUCATION

In 1962, I left America to spend a year in Paris on a research scholarship to continue my investigations of the nineteenth-century cotton industry. At the end of that year I reached the promotion barrier at Yale: after six years as an assistant professor an American university must either promote you to an associateship, which carries tenure, or dismiss you. Yale refused to promote me on the grounds that they had no need of a senior professor specializing in the history of economic thought, and I therefore found it necessary to look elsewhere for a new appointment. When I now thought of returning to the United States, my heart sank. I realized that despite 20 years in America, I had never ceased to think of myself as a European. America was too crass, too commercialized for me and I had never entirely given up the condescending feeling of a cultured European for those vulgar Americans: a nation in which 'the life of the whole of one sex is devoted to dollar-hunting, and of the other to breeding dollar-hunters', as John Stuart Mill put it, or, in Oscar Wilde's words, 'A country that has passed straightway from barbarism to decadence without the intervening phase of civilization'. I made up my mind to move to Britain, a country in which I had lived as a boy during the Second World War and had lived in again as a student working on my doctoral dissertation.

I began making applications for a number of vacancies at British universities, but there was little expansion in the academic job market in 1962 and I soon realized that I might well fail to find a job before the year was out. By a fluke I bumped into Lionel Elvin, the Director of the University of London Institute of Education, who told me that they had been unable to fill a vacancy in the economics of education because this was a new field in Britain. I had never heard of something called 'the economics of education' and decided to inform myself. This did not take long because the subject was indeed little researched in 1962. I took the bull by the horns and wrote to Lionel Elvin, admitting that I was a novice in the economics of education, but asking whether the Institute would hire me on a temporary basis for a year or two. They agreed to do so and those two years turned, much to my amazement and theirs, into 23 years! I mention all this only to emphasize the role of accident in life. I have read dozens of involved explanations of how people make occupational choices, or marital choices for that matter, but when investigated closely and in detail it often appears that it was pure chance that A became a chemist and B a lawyer, or that A married B and C married D.

The Institute was a post-graduate teacher training college and the bulk of my students were teachers seeking to upgrade themselves. My teaching load at the Institute was light; my administrative duties were equally light because the department of economics at the Institute numbered only two or at most three; and for the first time I was able to give myself almost wholly to writing and research. The lack of economists to talk to would have been painful but for the fact that the London School of Economics was just down the street. I soon became a visiting lecturer at LSE and divided my time between the two institutions.

The world of education was a wholly new milieu for me: it was much softer than the world of economics; very few educationists paid much attention to empirical evidence in supporting their assertions and many arguments degenerated into a clash of value judgements. I was not at first prepared for the unmitigated hostility with which educationists viewed all economists, who they regarded at best as cost-cutters and at worst as fascist swine. The sway of fashion was even worse in education than in economics and, while the centre of gravity of the political spectrum in education was well to the left of what it was in economics, when educationists were right-wing they made Milton Friedman look like a loony left-winger.

It did not take me long to become an enthusiastic advocate of human capital theory and I was certainly the first to venture to make rate-of-return calculations for educational investment in Britain. For about a decade, roughly from 1965–75, I proselytized on behalf of human capital theory and I, like all enthusiasts, outperformed my adversaries at least quantitatively. But then this god failed as had Marxism and Freudianism before. In 1976, I published a long post-mortem whose title says it all: 'Human Capital Theory: a Jaundiced Survey'. It said, not that human capital theory is wrong, but that it is thin and unproductive despite its early promise, and unable to vanquish its principal competitor, the screening hypothesis, credentialism, the diploma disease, call it what you will. I came in the end to think that human capital theory vastly exaggerates the role of cognitive knowledge in the undoubted economic value of education. What really accounted for the economic and even the social and political role of education in the modernization process was what educational psychologists call 'the affective behavioural traits' that formal education imparts, that is, the effect of schools in shaping the values and attitudes of students; what employers really value about education is not such much what educated workers know than how educated workers behave. This insight has far-reaching implications for questions of vocational training, for aspects of educational planning and even for problems in the financing of education. Eventually, I married up my notions of the incomplete contract, requiring the monitoring of human effort and the screening and signalling problem that characterizes the hiring and promotion of workers, with my new conception of the economic value of education. But by the late 1970s, I found myself repeating this message over and over again in different contexts without the slightest visible effect on either educational circles or the treatment of education by economists and, as a consequence, became bored by the very topic.

Indeed, it seemed to me then, and it still seems to me now, that education is more plagued than most subjects by a sense of *déjà vu*, an endless merry-go-round in which every question or argument recurs every ten or twenty years, frequently in identical form. I could give many examples of this phenomenon but let me cite just one: I began advocating student loans in higher education, preferably financed by a graduate tax throughout working life, in the late 1960s; although this was already old-hat in the USA by then, it remained right up to the 1980s in Britain an outrageous and extremely unpopular idea. I came very close to the centres of power in British education, first under Labour in the early 1970s and then under the Tories in the early 1980s, but was never successful in selling the idea to those who could have implemented it. I gave it up in disgust around 1982 but since then the argument has been carried on more ably by other British economists but again to no real avail! When the Conservative government under Mrs Thatcher in 1988 finally adopted a very modest student loan scheme, conceived as a personal debt repayable in 15 years, no reference whatsoever was made to 20 years of writings on the subject and the British economic profession swallowed the proposal without a murmur or criticism. To this day it is not generally recognized by politicians that the finance of higher education is an economist's issue *par excellence.*

I spent a good deal of time during my years at the Institute of Education on leave in Asia and Africa as an educational consultant for various UN agencies, such as UNESCO, UNECAFE, ILO and the World Bank. I participated in economic missions to six underdeveloped countries in tropical Africa, South and South-East Asia. I lived in India for six months writing a book on graduate unemployment and worked in Thailand and Indonesia for a year, working for the Ford Foundation. At first, I learned a lot about development economics and the role of economic advice to Third World governments, but diminishing returns to learning soon set in and I found myself repeating more or less everything I had said in the last country I had worked in. I started out as a do-gooder, anxious to help lift the downtrodden masses of the Third World from the squalor in which they lived. But as time passed, I found myself more and more inclined to agree with Peter Bauer that aid to developing countries does more harm than good. The whole business of UN aid missions and advice to Third World governments on what to do or not to do in economic policy was a gigantic charade. The governments in question simply wanted aid or World Bank loans but could not get it unless they could show they had consulted the best advice they could obtain. Instead of buying that advice from the international consultancy industry, which did in fact happen in technical fields like oil drilling or hydraulic engineering, they went to the UN agencies to secure the services of freelance consultants like myself, who soon learned which side their bread was buttered on – always the underside, of course – and did well by doing good at least for a while until the song they were singing at that moment went out of fashion.

I became more and more cynical about the Third World ministers and politicians I had to work with who exploited me and other economists like myself to get the aid they wanted, whilst lining their own pockets with the leavings of that aid. The amount of corruption and political hypocrisy that I witnessed in every country I worked in eventually turned me against the entire development consultancy business. Getting out was easy: all one did was to say something that Third World governments did not want to hear; by saying it often enough, one could be assured of not being rehired.

The bee in my bonnet was simple enough: down with higher education and up with primary schooling! In my view, all these countries, and particularly those in Africa, overspent outrageously on free higher education, which the government officials of the moment had of course themselves enjoyed, and underspent equally outrageously on the primary schooling of the rural poor. Another bee in my bonnet was the wastefulness of formal vocational schooling at the secondary level, not to mention the vocationalization of the primary and secondary school curriculum, which was simply the old fallacy that the cognitive knowledge of students was what made education so economically valuable. Underlying both these mistaken policies was a technique of educational planning called the manpower-requirements approach, which was input–output analysis inappropriately applied to the matching of educated workers to different occupational slots in individual industries. I spent ten years or more attacking the manpower-requirements approach to educational planning but to no avail, at least in the Third World. The fact of the matter is that the approach, being entirely in terms of physical quantities and involving no prices – 'priceless economics' as someone called it – is so easy to understand and hence so politically irresistible that the manpower-requirements approach remains to this day the principal technique for the planning of education and training in the Third World.

One of the great lessons imbibed from my years as a Third World advisor was the hopeless inconsistencies involved in marrying the objective of socialism with that of development and modernization. Every government I ever worked for was to some extent committed to socialism but also wanted to modernize and to imitate America, Japan, Britain, etcetera. They would wax eloquent about the need for indigenous entrepreneurship but would stamp on everyone who made money, particularly by selling shoddy goods to ordinary people in the so-called 'informal sector'. In short, they never could accept the rugged individualism and the consequent inequalities that rapid economic growth inevitably entails but, nevertheless, they could not abandon the objective of growth and development. They utterly failed to understand the 'causes of the wealth of nations', which, whatever they are, are not the immediate eradication of unearned incomes and perfect equality in the distribution of earnings.

It is ironic that practically every one of the economic mission reports that I helped to write in the 1970s was commissioned by a government headed by a dictator who was overthrown either as soon as the report was delivered or shortly thereafter: a UNESCO World Experimental Literacy Project mission to Iran headed by the Shah in 1964 and 1976; an ILO World Employment Programme Mission to Ethiopia headed by Haile Selassie in 1972; an ILO World Employment Comprehensive Mission to the Philippines headed by President Ferdinand Marcos in 1973; an ILO World Employment Comprehensive Mission to the Sudan headed by President El Nimeiry in 1975; an ILO World Employment Programme Mission to Lesotho headed by King Moshoeshoe in 1976; a UNDP Mission to Buthan headed by King Wanghuk in 1981; UNDP Mission to Brunei headed by Sultan Bolkiah in 1983; and a World Bank Mission to China headed by Dang Xiao Ping in 1983. With the exception of Buthan, Brunei and China, all the other countries are now governed by other leaders, often in violent opposition to those to whom I and my team-mates delivered our reports. So much for the notion that economists have an influence on the policies of foreign governments.

THE METHODOLOGY OF ECONOMICS

As the 1970s passed by, I turned increasingly towards the methodology of philosophy of economics as a subject of abiding interest. Actually, this had been my interest all along but I had never realized it. It started of course with my early infatuation with Marxism or rather with my gradual disillusionment with Marxism. In my last year as a undergraduate at Queens College I took a seminar course in the philosophy of social sciences with Donald Davidson (who, I learned later, was an eminent philosopher of science). Davidson knew that there were a number of young Marxists in the class (remember this was 1949) and his way of dealing with Marxism was gently to ridicule it. Thus, when I trotted out the three laws of Hegelian dialectics (the change of quantity into quality, the unity of opposites, the negation of the negation) as the master-key to unlock all doors, he topped it with Herbert Spencer's 'law' of evolution: evolution is a change from a state of relatively indefinite, incoherent homogeneity to a state of relatively definite, coherent heterogeneity. 'That neatly explains absolutely everything,' Davidson said, and with a shock I realized that was just as true of the laws of dialectics: they explained everything, which was just like explaining nothing.

Davidson asked us to read Carl Hempel's *The Function of General Laws in History* (1942), which argues that any valid explanation of a historical phenomenon like, say, the French revolution, must necessarily invoke some universal empirical hypothesis of which this is said to be a particular instance; if it fails to do so, it is merely a pseudo-explanation. This is what later came to be called 'the covering-law model of scientific explanation': to explain a thing is to 'cover' it under some universal law. I can still recall more than forty years later how this article hit me like a thunder-clap; it is probably one of the dozen or so essays that has left a permanent mark on my thinking. I suddenly realized that I had been employing pseudo-explanations for years without realizing that they were untenable because they involved alleged covering laws of which I nor anyone else had any knowledge. A covering law for revolutions? Yes, we had all read Crane Brinton's *Anatomy of Revolution* (1938), which collected some general features of revolutions, based on a sample of three, but these hardly amounted to universal laws or even universally applicable characteristics. In short, no one had ever really explained the French revolution or the Russian revolution except in a purely *ad hoc* way.

By the time I had come to work on my doctoral dissertation, I had somehow absorbed Popperian falsificationism without ever reading Popper. Some of it I acquired from Milton Friedman's classic essay 'The Methodology of Positive Economics' (1953), which, without mentioning Popper, represents a sort of vulgar, Mickey Mouse Popperianism. Some of it filtered down from remarks and asides in Stigler's essays on the history of economic thought. When I started teaching in Yale in 1954, I soon became friendly with Tjalling Koopmans, partly because he was an amateur composer and I had just started playing the cello, so we talked about music, and partly because we were both Dutch and enjoyed speaking Dutch together. Our interests in economics were totally different, but when he started working on the second of his *Three Essays on the State of Economic Science* (1957), which is all about methodology, we talked about Friedman's essay and then for the first time I became entirely persuaded by predictionism, that is, the idea that theories must ultimately be judged by the accuracy of their prediction. When I published my first professional paper in 1956, 'The Empirical Content of Ricardian Economics', it was shot through by predictionism, but, nevertheless, I still had read no Popper. Indeed, I can remember like yesterday the first moment I finally decided to read Popper.

In 1962, while living in Paris, I strolled into a bookshop one Friday afternoon and saw a copy of Karl Popper's *The Open Society and Its Enemies* (1945) which, as everyone knows, is a study of Plato, Hegel and Marx as three great enemies of the open society. I went home and started reading it as soon as I had finished dinner. I read all night, all day Saturday, and after falling asleep reluctantly, finished the book on Sunday. I can safely say that no book before and no book since has excited me more. It was literally like drinking a whole bottle of champagne at a single sitting.[4] Not only did it slay Plato and Hegel, both of whom I had always regarded as monsters of the right, but it made short shrift of Marx for committing the 'apocalyptic fallacy', the game of predicting doomsday some day in the indefinite future. At the same time, it offered a philosophy of science, falsificationism, and a convincing argument against political revolutions, on the grounds that we lack the knowledge totally to transform society, but that we can and should reform society on a piecemeal basis.

I then sat down and read everything that Popper had ever written. I became a through-and-through Popperian and although I now think that there are exaggerations in Popper – there is no such thing as induction; there is a fundamental asymmetry between verification and falsification; methodology is normative and has nothing to do with the history of science – I remain to this day an unregenerative Popperian. I think that I learnt from Popper how to write about complex issues in clear, unadorned, Saxon English and indeed found myself almost copying his style word for word.[5] When I arrived in London in 1952 to work on my doctoral thesis, I was thrilled to learn that Popper was teaching a weekly seminar at London School of Economics in the philosophy of science. I was given permission to audit the course but imagine my surprise when I soon saw that Popper was a Prussian-style teacher of the old school, a walking embodiment of all the arrogant intolerance that he preached against in his books. There was a cruel joke about Popper that went around the London School of Economics invented apparently by one of his students: '*The Open Society by One of Its Enemies* is what he should have called his book. *The Open Society by a Closed Mind* would have been an even better title.' Ah well, Beethoven, the greatest composer that ever lived, was a dreadful man and so was Wagner, and Goethe, and Tolstoy – and I am not very nice myself!

BEFORE ECONOMICS THERE WAS PHILOSOPHY

I have never regretted my youthful decision to become an economist but there have been moments when I wished I had studied philosophy. In one sense philosophy is where I started and philosophy seems to be where I am ending up. But where I started was not so much philosophy in general as a particular kind of philosophy, namely, theology. The question of the existence of God was the first philosophical question I ever asked, and answered, and it interests me still. I was brought up as an orthodox Jew, achieved pantheism by the age of 12, agnosticism by the age of 15, and militant atheism by the age of 17, from which I have never wavered. Indeed, I seem to become more militant about my atheism the longer I live and it taxes all my tolerance nowadays to keep a civil tongue in my head when I argue with arch believers, which I am afraid I love to do, love too much to do.

It all started when one of my uncles gave me a Bible at the age of 12, not noticing that it included the New as well as the Old Testament. Being a non-stop reader, who devoured any book that I could lay my hands on, I naturally read the New Testament of whose very existence I had never heard. I was immediately enthralled by the story of Jesus and reinforced it by reading Ernest Renan's *Life of Jesus*, a romanticized nineteenth-century biography of Jesus as a humanized prophet of old. This account I thought had to be true but all my relatives told me that it was not true. I argued with them and was sent to a rabbi to be corrected. He soon persuaded me that Jesus could not be the son of God, because the central intelligence that created the universe does not have children nor could he be the Messiah because when the Messiah has come to this world, the lamb will lie down with the lion, swords will be turned into ploughshares, and nations shall no longer war with one another. Have swords turned into ploughshares? Have nations ceased to war with one another? Well then. That struck me as a thoroughly convincing argument.

Perhaps the beautiful story of Jesus as set down in the gospels was false, but what about the story of the Buddha, the next account of a god that I read? That struck me as an equally beautiful story. But again, I was told, by relatives and friends, that the story of Buddha could not be true. All these beautiful stories, the story of Moses and Joseph and David in the Old Testament, the story of Jesus in the New Testament, the story of Buddha in the Mahayama texts of Buddhism, must all be true, I thought, because they were so beautiful, and yet equally they must all be false because they contradicted each other. In one leap, I ceased to believe in any authorized religion and became a Spinozean pantheist, without of course ever having heard of Spinoza. When we fled Holland after the German invasion of 1940 and my parents sent my elder brother and me to a boarding school in England, the headmaster of the school was a Christian Scientist and he tried to convert me to Christian Science. This introduced me to authorized deviant religious sects, and for several years I was a regular little pest to adults because I never left off asking them questions about their religious beliefs, not to learn but to persuade them to drop the argument of design, or the argument of first cause, or the argument of ultimate purpose as fallacious arguments for the existence of God. As for the historicity of Jesus, I had a dozen clever reasons for demonstrating that his existence was no better established than that of King Arthur or Robin Hood. I am afraid that this is a weakness I have never really learned to overcome. To this day I cannot resist trying to argue with a fundamentalist, whether Christian, Jewish, Islamic or Hindu, even though I know it to be a hopeless undertaking. I am an infernal optimist and always believe, against all evidence, that rational argument will eventually win out.

I like to describe myself as a religious person, meaning that not a day goes by but I ponder the great questions: is there order in the universe? does it mean anything? are we here for a purpose? These are good questions but to answer them by God or Church is to insult the profundity of the questions. One reason that I took to Marxism in my teens like a duck takes to water is that its atheism suited me down to the ground. One reason that I took to the writings of Popper, when I eventually read them, is not that Popperianism equals atheism but that Popperian falsification is perfectly suited to atheism. Show me what events, if they occurred, would imply that God does not exist? None, of course, the existence of God is a matter of faith. Well, then, it makes no difference whether we believe or do not believe in the existence of God. A difference that makes no difference is no difference! QED.

FROM POPPER TO LAKATOS

Sometime in the late 1960s, while I was teaching regularly at LSE, I met Imre Lakatos, Popper's successor to the professorship in logic and philosophy of science at LSE. Imre, in the few years that I knew him (he died in 1974), was someone of whom I became extremely fond. In the course of the student troubles at LSE in 1968, he emerged as a fearless and yet sympathetic critic of the students, making merciless fun of their radical chic, which he was entitled to do as someone who had spent years in a Hungarian prison as a 'right-wing deviationist' before escaping to the West in 1956. He had a marvellous sense of humour[6] and we took to each other almost as soon as we met. He knew no economics but was becoming interested in economics as a field of application for his methodological views, inspired by one of his PhD students, Spiro Latsis, who was indeed the first to apply Lakatos's ideas to economics. In 1974, Imre organized a conference in Greece, which was to bring together physicists, economists, and philosophers of science in the attempt to develop some case studies in his own 'methodology of scientific research programmes'. A month before the conference was to take place, he died suddenly. Spiro Latsis went on to hold the conference as a memorial to Imre, and it proved to be, for me and for many others, the conference of a lifetime. In economics, there were great men like Lionel Robbins, John Hicks, Terence Hutchinson, Herbert Simon and Axel Leijonhufvud. In philosophy, there were giants like Carl Hempel, Adolf Grünbaum and Paul Feyerabend. It was intellectually exciting; it was held in Nafplion, a beautiful site in Greece; and it was lavishly financed by John Latsis, Spiro Latsis's father, who gave us all a glimpse of the style to which we would have loved to become accustomed.

Arguments about the relationship between Popper and Lakatos have raged on ever since 1974. I regard Lakatos as, say, 80 per cent Popper and 20 per cent

Kuhn, emphasizing different things but conveying essentially the same methodology as that of Popper. When Neil de Marchi and I organized a second Nafplion conference in Capri in 1989, I was taken aback by the hostility that so many of the economists at the conference expressed for the ideas of Lakatos and Popper. Much of that hostility was directed at Lakatos's insistence that scientific research should ultimately be judged by the number of novel predictions that they generate. This criterion proved to be too much to stomach for most of the participants, who realized that its implication was to cast doubt on virtually the whole of what passes nowadays as neoclassical economics.

Gradually, since the 1950s, and at an accelerating rate in recent years, economics has become ever more formalistic, that is, almost exclusively concerned with analytical rigour at the expense of policy relevance, taking on ever more the appearance of a kind of social mathematics rather than an empirical social science. Economists have sometimes been accused of physics-envy but that is an utterly misleading accusation. Anyone who knows modern physics will testify that physicists care about experimental evidence, about bringing their theories into conformity with the experimental evidence, and very little about rigorous theorems and analytical lemmas. What economists really suffer from is mathematics-envy. Consider general equilibrium theory, the most prestigious type of economic theory, practised only by the professional front-runners of the subject. Here is a theory with absolutely no empirical content. Having 'proved' the existence, uniqueness and local stability of multi-market, general equilibrium, what have we learned about the economy? Absolutely nothing. No physicist would ever think that general equilibrium theory raised interesting questions but a mathematician would of course find it perfect grist for his mill. Some modern practitioners of general equilibrium theory even justify it as fulfilling Adam Smith's age-old promise of demonstrating the tendency of 'the invisible hand' of competition to harmonize private and social interests. This assertion is not only a travesty of intellectual history but an utter misunderstanding of the significance of competition as a social process occurring in real time and ensuring technical dynamism and cost minimization in an economy based on private enterprise; an end-state theory like Walrasian general equilibrium theory is simply irrelevant to it.

What strikes me most about economics after 45 years of studying the subject is the high regard that general equilibrium theory continues to enjoy, despite its failure to realize its own objectives, and the persistent neglect of technical progress as a topic of economic investigation. Economic historians have in recent years finally begun to open the black box of technical change but economic theorists continue to study economic growth as if it were all the result of increases in capital and labour, mere quantitative increments in the factors of production. There is a central figure in twentieth-century economics that perfectly reflects this overemphasis on Walrasian general equilibrium theory combined with an underemphasis on technical progress, namely, Joseph Schumpeter. The curious fact about him is how much he himself admired Walrasian theory as the pinnacle of intellectual achievement in economics and, on the other hand, how his own original contributions to economics owed little if anything to the Walrasian inspiration; indeed, if truth be told, it clashed with it. In my younger days, I did not rate highly Schumpeter's theory of entrepreneurship and its associated treatment of innovations, but since then I have come to regard *The Theory of Economic Development* (1911), the product of a 28-year-old economist, as one of the seminal works of twentieth-century economics, on a par with Fisher's *Theory of Interest* or Keynes's *General Theory*. The insight that process innovations are only one kind of innovation and probably much less important in economic growth than product innovations or organizational innovations, was an insight of genius.[7] And so was Schumpeter's recognition that bank credit played an essential role in the promotion of entrepreneurship and was not just a financial appendage to machine-driven factory production. It is true that Schumpeter glamourized entrepreneurship and almost reduced it to the heroism of outstanding individuals but, nevertheless, he said more about economic progress under capitalism than any economist since Marx. (What a sad comment on the last hundred years of economics theorizing!) He also recognized that Pareto optimality, perfect competition, static efficiency, and all that – the much-praised first and second Fundamental Theorems of Welfare Economics, inspired by general equilibrium theory – have no practical import because we actually appraise market structures by means of the standards of workable competition, dynamic efficiency, and technical dynamism: that's what Adam Smith meant by the invisible hand of competition, not the equality of the marginal rate of substitution in consumption with the marginal rate of transformation in production.

An alarming manifestation of sterile formalism in much current economics is the popularity of post-modernist strictures on the very idea of methodology as a set of prescriptive norms. Economics, Donald McCloskey has told us, is nothing more than a species of persuasive rhetoric, not really different from literary criticism and aesthetics. Certain 'thick' methodological rules – speak softly, listen to your opponents, give reasons for your conclusions – are all right but the 'thin' methodology of Popper and Lakatos is somehow ruled out as illegitimate. That this is a hopelessly inconsistent position seemed never to have occurred to him or his acolytes.

Without turning Popper or Lakatos into gurus whose writings may not be questioned, I would insist that the valid core of their contribution is the notion that economics must aspire to address real-world economic problems and that this aspiration is best satisfied by the production of theories with empirically refutable implications. That is not to say that every analytical concept that fails to meet that requirement must be instantly discarded, but simply that we must strive to make falsifiable predictions and certainly must never rest satisfied with an economic theory until it has been confronted by empirical evidence. Technical puzzle-solving as a game to be played for its own sake is not to be held out as an ideal to students, the way it is at the moment.

Throughout my professional career as an economist, I have admired Milton Friedman's style of doing economics while detesting his political views, and admired Paul Samuelson's political views while disliking the type of economics he practises. Between that Scylla and Charybdis, I seem condemned forever to remain.

NOTES

1. When I published my thesis as *Ricardian Economics* (1958), I thought that Ricardo, the rigorous theorist, was an admirable figure, so much that I named my eldest son after him. But over the years I came to identify Ricardo's 'telescopic' tendency to collapse the long run into the short run as it there was no transition period as the abiding vice of orthodox economics.
2. The economics of inflation has interested me ever since my days as a graduate student at Columbia University. One of my teachers was Arthur F. Burns, who taught me macroeconomics tinged with great scepticism about the theories of John Maynard Keynes. Burns was one of the four examiners in my doctoral oral examination (the other three being Abram Bergson, John Maurice Clark and Karl Polanyi). Burns asked me what was wrong with inflation, a strange question in 1952 when the American inflation rate was 1 per cent. Whatever answer I gave him – unfair to creditors, costly to wage earners and pension receivers, a tax on saving, and the like – he refuted with a counterexample. Within ten minutes, he reduced me to gibberish and made me feel two feet tall. My heart sank as I realized that I had certainly failed his part of the oral. When I was finally told that I had passed overall, I apologized to him for my poor performance on the inflation question. He patted me on the shoulder familiarly, saying: 'That's all right, my boy, better men than you have flunked the question.' I ran home and read myself blue in the face on the question of inflation, swearing that I would never fail that question again.
3. Of all my Columbia University teachers, James Angell, Arthur Burns, William Vickrey, John Maurice Clark, Abram Bergson, Ragnar Nurkse and Karl Polanyi, I recall vividly only the latter because he introduced me to general economic history, made me read books I had never heard of (like Malinowski's *Argonauts of the Western Pacific*) and taught me how easy it is to concoct 'laws' of history – Polanyi's categories were 'reciprocity' and 'redistribution' and in these terms he described just about all pre-market economies in history. I did not believe the central thesis of *The Great Transformation* (1944) but it was congenial 'bourgeois Marxism' and immensely stimulating.
4. *Favourite books.* This is a Victorian parlour game which I love to play: (1) favourite novel: Homer's *Odyssey*; (2) favourite poem: Stephen Spender's 'I Think Continually of Those Who Were Truly Great'; (3) favourite drama: Arnold Strindberg, *The Father*; (4) favourite military history: William Prescott, *The Conquest of Mexico*; (5) favourite history of ideas: Arthur Koestler, *The Sleepwalkers*; (6) favourite philosophical work: Alfred Ayer, *Language, Truth and Logic*; (7) favourite anthropological study: Malinowsky as above; (8) favourite political study: Popper's *Open Society*; etcetera, etcetera: this is a game without end; it is made difficult because second choices are not allowed.
5. A similar stylistic inspiration nearer to home was Joan Robinson, whose economic writings I first encountered as a student; they continued to fascinate me in later years. I read every word that she ever wrote and her language – verbal algebra peppered with homely colloquialisms – attracted me as much as her political views repelled me . She was always very rude to me when we met – after the Cambridge controversies on capital theory she regarded me as an enemy

– but I did not mind. It's hard enough to be a brilliant woman in a male-dominated profession like economics but to be a brilliant woman in the homophilial atmosphere of the Cambridge economics department must have been maddening.

6. One of my favourite Lakatos stories has all the flavour of a great Jewish joke. He told us that he was brought up in a small Hungarian village. When he came home at the age of seven with his first report card, he had As in all subjects except physical education in which he received a C. His mother beat him black and blue in punishment and the next year, he brought home a report card with As in all subjects including physical education (this was already funny enough, half way through the story, because he was a physical runt and unlikely ever to have excelled in sports). His mother always told him that she hoped that he would one day be a professor at the University of Cambridge, a university that for some unknown reason she regarded as a pinnacle of academic achievement. Imre escaped from Hungary in 1956 and fled to England, and, lo and behold, obtained a scholarship to study the history of mathematics at Cambridge. He completed his doctorate (later published as *Proofs and Refutations*) and was appointed on the strength of it as a temporary lecturer at Cambridge. He wrote to his mother still living in Hungary to tell her the news and she wrote back: 'Yes, but why didn't they make you a professor?'

7. I have personal reasons for appreciating the importance of product innovations. My father manufactured raincoats in Holland in the 1930s. A Swede transformed the business in 1932 by inventing the poplin raincoat; before that, raincoats were always made of artificial rubber. My father found himself with thousands of unsaleable rubber raincoats in 1933, the depth of the Great Depression in the Netherlands, and faced bankruptcy. Everyone in the industry thought that the new fad of poplin raincoats would not last but my father, being a pessimist, was convinced that rubber coats would never again be demanded, so he offered his entire stock at a penny a piece to C&A, the leading clothing store in Amsterdam. They were so impressed by his boldness that they gave him an order for poplin raincoats if he could learn to manufacture them. He went to Sweden, poached a tailor and a cutter, and filled the order. That led to more orders and still more orders, and, by 1935, he was the Raincoat King of the Netherlands and a self-made millionaire. His good fortune did not last very long, because in 1940 the Germans invaded Holland and we lost it all. When this rags-to-riches story started, I was six years old; when it ended, I was twelve. In short, I have good reasons to think that new products can make a difference.

2. Recent biographies of Keynes*

There are now four book-length biographies of Keynes: there is Roy Harrod's authorized *Life of John Maynard Keynes* (1951), now over 40 years old; there is Charles Hession's *John Maynard Keynes: A Personal Biography of the Man Who Revolutionized Capitalism* (1984); there is *Maynard Keynes: An Economist's Biography* (1992) by Donald Moggridge, one of the editors of Keynes's *Collected Writings* and author of the Fontana Modern Masters volume of Keynes (1976); finally there is Robert Skidelsky's multi-volumed *John Maynard Keynes*, of which two volumes have so far appeared covering the years 1883–1937, with a third volume on the years 1937–46 promised for 1994. There are also two excellent histories of the Keynesian Revolution, the old *Economics and Policy* (1969) by Donald Winch and the more recent *Keynesian Revolution in the Making: 1924–1936* (1989) by Peter Clarke. And, of course, there is literally an endless list of books about 'what Keynes really meant' and indeed about 'what Keynes should have meant', not to mention the ever-growing number of writings on Keynes's juvenilia. My central concern in this review will be the recent biographies but we shall occasionally touch on the rest of the Keynes industry.

Let me say at the outset that Harrod is now so out-of-date as to be worth reading only as a historical document of how one of Keynes's leading disciples attempted to package Keynes five years after his death so as to maximize the spread of his ideas.[1]

Likewise, Hession's account is so coloured by certain psycho-biographical preoccupations and so replete with factual errors as to put him out of court for serious historians.[2] Moggridge, on the other hand, is scholarly, authoritative and in full command of the entire range of primary and secondary sources. It is fundamentally an intellectual biography but with many hints of the purely personal. However, I cannot suppress the feeling that it is slightly dull and fails sufficiently to rouse the reader's enthusiasm about its subject. For me, Moggridge is surpassed by Skidelsky, which is written with an eloquence and verve that Moggridge cannot match. Skidelsky is not a professional economist but one would never notice that. He places Keynes squarely in his intellectual context, which of course includes that of the development of monetary economics in the inter-war period, and his grasp of the theoretical issues, particularly in the

* First published in *Journal of Economic Literature*, **32**, September 1994, 1204–15.

central second volume of his work, is unerring. Moreover, in his account one comes to know Keynes almost as a personal friend. On this ultimate criterion of quality in biography, Skidelsky is the clear winner.

Before we begin, however, we must raise the question how it is that two scholars simultaneously came to the decision to write a biography of Keynes, using much the same secondary and virtually the same primary sources? The cloistered atmosphere of Cambridge, the almost religious protection of the reputation of Keynes by his coterie (many of whom have only recently died), plus the fact that Moggridge was the privileged insider and Skidelsky the importunate outsider,[3] probably accounts for his blatant example of scholarly redundancy. Competition in biography is no doubt preferable to monopoly but it secures its best results if the two authors approach their subject from radically different angles or if each emphasizes different aspects of the subject's life and works, neither of which is true in this case. Still, the co-existence of Moggridge and Skidelsky does provide the reader with the bonus of being able to compare two versions of just about every *significant* event in the life of Keynes.

THE ROLE OF BIOGRAPHY

Economics is not well served by biographies and this despite the fact that Keynes himself showed how one might combine mastery of economic theory with mastery of the biographical essay. One reason for the small stock of biographies of great economists is that so little is known about the private lives of some of them that no truly personal biography is possible. Thus, Adam Smith's works present us with the same baffling anonymity as the plays of Shakespeare.[4] Sometimes, there is biographical data but it's too sparse to allow more than a purely intellectual portrait. That applies to such masterful studies of second-rate classical economists as Robert Torrens (Robins 1958) and Ramsay McCulloch (O'Brien 1970). Sometimes what material there is has never been fully exploited. That is true of Ricardo[5] and, until someone takes up where the late Bill Jaffe left off, it remains true of Walras.[6] Academic economics, to be sure, rarely lead exciting lives and that is no doubt one explanation for the paucity of economists' biographies. But there are striking counterexamples, such as Knut Wicksell, the subject of an admirable biography by Torsten Gardlund (1958),[7] and Thorsten Veblen (Dorfman 1934; Diggins 1978). Nevertheless, it is difficult for academic scholars to provide much grist for the mill for a biographer. It is easier to write about non-academic 'activists', such as John Stuart Mill, Henry George, Frederick List, Pierre-Joseph Proudhon, Karl Marx and Philip Wicksteed.[8] Perhaps Peter Groenewegen's (forthcoming) biography of Marshall will show that there is life after all in the Groves of Academe.[9] Jevons, Menger, Böhm-Bawerk and Cassel are likely subjects awaiting potential biographers. In the meanwhile, Robert Allen (1991, 1993), with his startlingly revealing life of Joseph Schumpeter[10] and the more recent life and works of Irving Fisher, demonstrates the extent to which there is still much unexplored archival material about the great economists.

THE CONTEXT OF DISCOVERY VERSUS THE CONTEXT OF JUSTIFICATION

But so what? Although it is fun to read biographies, is it really true that a knowledge of the lives of the great economists adds anything to our understanding of their economic ideas? Jaffe (1970) thought so and tried to make a case for biography as an aid to the understanding of an author's work. George Stigler (1982: ch. 8) would have none of this, arguing that personal biography was irrelevant to the interpretation of a scientific work because it related to the individual scientist's intentions, which had little of anything to do with the impact of the work. 'Science is a good social enterprise', Stigler argued (1982: 91), 'and those parts of a man's life which do not affect the relationships between that man and his fellow scientists are simply extra-scientific.' He agreed that biography contributed to the science of science, the so-called sociology of science, dealing with questions such as why some intellectual innovations are accepted or rejected in one country rather than another, and at some time rather than another, but he doubted that even such questions were much illuminated by biographical data. His final knock-down objection to biography was that the history of science was itself a scientific subject, that is, capable of providing falsifiable hypotheses, and biography was typically characterized by anecdotal and specially selected examples which defied falsification.

This debate between Jaffe and Stigler on the relevance of biography to the history of economic thought was reviewed by Walker (1983b) and again by Moggridge in the preface to his biography of Keynes. Walker awards the debate to Stigler but Moggridge understandably favours Jaffe over Stigler. Without referring to the philosophy of science, Jaffe seems to have been familiar with the distinction between the 'context of discovery' and the 'context of justification', which derives from Hans Reichenbach (1938), a leading logical positivist. The logical positivist believed that the 'logic of discovery' belongs to the psychological realm, unlike the 'logic of justification', which is a matter of empirical validation. Jaffe conceded fatally that biography has little if any relevance to the 'context of justification', but that is in fact the $64,000 question. Is there really a watertight distinction between the context of discovery and the context of justification, between genesis and scientific validity? The origins of a theory, the intentions of the creator of that theory, the biases and unexpressed ideological underpinnings of a writer's thoughts, may influence the way in which the theory is expressed and these rhetorical over- and undertones of a theory may well influence its acceptance or rejection by contemporaries, in which case the context of discovery spills over into the context of justification.[11]

As an author who once wrote a history of economic thought 'undiluted by entertaining historical digressions or biographical coloring' (Blaug 1985: vii) I am hardly the right person to argue that the genesis of a theory may well influence the evolution of the discipline to which that theory belongs. But I also wrote *Great Economists Before Keynes: An Introduction to the Lives and Works of One Hundred Great Economists of the Past* (1986), which is evidence either of schizophrenia or of different objectives. If we want to explain the Keynesian Revolution, the astonishing speed with which Keynesian economics won professional approval, it would be difficult to deny that Keynes's personal biography was extremely relevant. The fact that he was a world-famous financial journalist, editor of the *Economic Journal* and a Fellow of King's College, Cambridge, lent authority, and perhaps decisive authority, to his pronouncements even on esoteric issues of economic theory. Clearly, if Keynesian economics lacked analytical coherence and empirical support, it would have failed despite Keynes's prestigious location in the professional hierarchy of economics. Nevertheless, there remains scope for the influence of purely personal factors and, to that extent, the sociology and even the psychology of science cannot be as neatly separated from the philosophy of science as Hans Reichenbach (and, incidentally, Karl Popper 1934: 31) claimed.

The importance of biographical data for the history of economic thought therefore depends critically on the questions we are asking. The more technical the subject matter, the less likely is biography to be relevant for establishing its meaning. If we want to know why the numerical value of the instantaneous multiplier played such a central role in the construction of *The General Theory*, it won't help to know that Keynes was bisexual. But if we want to account for the Keynesian Revolution, it might well be relevant by way of explaining his highly charged relationship with certain colleagues, such as Dennis Robertson and A.C. Pigou. Certainly, Keynes's siren-like charisma had much to do with his professional success, and to deny it is just puritanism of an intellectual sort.

Books such as the two biographies under review may be read for their intrinsic interest but also as case studies of the true value of biographical knowledge. As we read them we should be continually asking ourselves whether it was Jaffe or whether it was Stigler who was right in the assessment of the relevance or irrelevance of biography.

THE YOUNG KEYNES AND EARLY BELIEFS

Skidelsky is at his best in painting the early years of growing up in Cambridge when Keynes acquired what Harrod called 'the presuppositions of Harvey

Road', the ingrained confidences of being a member of an intellectual elite that
was designated and indeed duty-bound to guide human affairs. Falling under
the influence of G.E. Moore's ethical beliefs, according to which beautiful objects
and enduring friendships are the only absolute values in life, Keynes forged a
personal philosophy that to some extent lasted him all his life. Edmund Burke,
the father of British conservatism, was another early influence and both
Skidelsky and Moggridge raise the question whether this was a momentary or
lasting influence. Keynes's relationships with Lytton Strachey and Duncan
Grant, and the aesthetic homophilial atmosphere of the Bloomsbury set, served
him as a backdrop to his increasing fame as a journalist after the publication of
The Economic Consequences of the Peace (1919). He was, as Skidelsky says,
a 'partitioned' man who combined Whitehall and Bloomsbury because neither
religion nor tradition any longer provided moral guidance. Skidelsky is a
signed-up member of the tell-it-all school of biography virtually invented by
Michael Holroyd's biography of *Lytton Strachey* (1967), and we are not spared
a blow-by-blow discussion of Keynes's sexual adventures in the 1910s and 1920s.
But even Moggridge cannot resist printing Keynes's sexual engagement diary
in an appendix to his book. And why not? It may have made Keynes more
inclined to intellectual heterodoxy, although neither Skidelsky nor Moggridge
spend any time indulging in such psycho-biographical speculations.

   The Economic Consequences of the Peace was not only Keynes's most
carefully constructed and persuasive book but one that made him a household
name. There are some modern parallels among economists, for example, John
Kenneth Galbraith and Milton Friedman, but even they pale in comparison to
the popular fame and instant recognition that Keynes achieve with *The Economic
Consequences*, not just in Britain but all over Europe and in the United States.

   But was Keynes right to argue that Germany simply could not have paid the
reparation exacted at Versailles? Skidelsky (1992: 31–4) exonerates Keynes
although he condemns the arguments of *The Economic Consequences* as having
been technically defective: the reparation problem was a budgetary, not a
transfer, problem, and Germany could have paid war reparations if she had been
politically willing to do so. Moggridge (1992: 341–46) is just as cogent as
Skidelsky and perhaps even more acute in discussing the lasting questions
raised by *The Economic Consequences*.

   Keynes's *Treatise on Probability*, published in 1921 but written in the years
before the First World War, figures heavily in all discussions of the early
beliefs of the young Keynes. It is a most perplexing book that was traditionally
regarded as an unconvincing attempt to defend the subjective theory of
probability. It is perplexing because it rejected the standard frequency conception
of probability, treating probability instead as expressing degrees of belief in
propositions rather than the frequency of occurrence of events, but nevertheless
retained the notion that such subjective probabilities are 'objective'; they are

objective because they dictate what it is 'rational to believe in the light of evidence' independently of what people choose to believe. Unfortunately, Keynes also argued that such subjective probabilities are frequently non-numerical and even undefinable; moreover, he conceded that some individuals are 'irrational' in the sense that they lack the ability to detect the logical relationship between a proposition and the evidence that should cause them to believe in it. In short, Keynes seems to have argued at one and the same time for an 'objective' theory of epistemic probability and something like a Knightian conception of non-measurable, irreducible uncertainty.[12]

To make matters even more confusing, Keynes is said to have capitulated in 1928 to Frank Ramsey in adopting the betting-quotient method for converting apparently incommensurable degrees of belief into numerical form, thus abandoning not only his own earlier view that subjective probabilities can be objective but even the very notion of incalculable Knightian uncertainty.

Such was the received view of what was wrong with *The Treatise on Probability* when Skidelsky published the first volume of his autobiography in 1983. Harrod had devoted an opaque appendix in his book to the *Treatise of Probability* and Skidelsky barely mentioned it in his Volume 1. But the 1980s witnessed the growth of a veritable cottage industry in the interpretation of Keynes's views on probability and now, in the second volume of his biography, Skidelsky (1992: 58–89) devotes three appendices to the origins, meaning and significance of *The Treatise on Probability*. Moggridge (1992: 144–65, 364–6, 623) gives a whole chapter to it and is no less convinced than is Skidelsky (1992: 61) that

> Keynes's concern with the rationality of judgement and behaviour under conditions of uncertainty was lifelong; it gives a distinctive flavour, or style, to his utterances; it is the intellectual motif of his life.

Nevertheless, neither of the two authors is prepared to defend Keynes's objective theory of subjective probability as tenable and neither is willing to follow O'Donnell, Ann Carabelli and Athol Fitzgibbons, to mention only the leading writers on the early 'philosophic' Keynes, in the view that all the epistemic roots of Keynes's discussion of expectations in *The General Theory* are to be found in *The Treatise on Probability*. There is a further unresolved question whether Keynes had indeed capitulated to Ramsey between the writing of the two books. O'Donnell and Carabelli deny it, although on different grounds, but Bradley Bateman, in an influential contribution to the debate,[13] confirms it. Moggridge (1992: 623) expresses agreement with Carabelli but Skidelsky (1992: 70–2) states the issues and leaves the reader to decide. There is little doubt, however, that Skidelsky (1992: 86) is not inclined to attribute great consistency to Keynes's public and private utterances on probability.

Keynes did have a determinate theory of economic behaviour despite the presence of pervasive Knightian uncertainty but never quite managed to explain just what it was.[14]

FROM FINANCIAL JOURNALIST TO ECONOMIC THEORIST

The success of *Economic Consequences of the Peace* led Keynes in the 1920s to substitute journalism and currency speculation for work in the civil service. These activities were eventually to make him a very rich man and possibly one of the richest economists who has ever lived. His personal fortune fluctuated from a high in 1924 to a low in 1929 – he failed utterly to predict the 1929 crash – to a new high in 1936, when he was worth somewhere around half a million pounds (about ten million pounds in today's money; Skidelsky, 1992: 24–9, 42–3, 339–42, 524; Moggridge, 1992: 345–52, 408, 585–6). He continued to lecture at Cambridge one term a year, continued to edit the *Economic Journal* single-handedly,[15] became Bursar of King's College, Cambridge, established himself as principal economic spokesman for the Liberal Party, and, last but not least, married Lydia Lopokova with whom he lived happily ever after.

Keynes's next book, so slim as to be almost a large pamphlet, was *A Tract on Monetary Reform* (1923). It reveals him as thoroughly steeped in what we would now call 'monetarism', the doctrine that a government can steer the economy solely by monetary policy. All through the 1920s he fought against the policy of dear money, attacked the overvalued pound created by the return of the gold standard at the pre-war parity, and emerged as Britain's leading advocate of public works to reduce unemployment. Deeply influenced by the writings of Robertson, he refined and developed the macroeconomic reasoning inherent in the old classical quantity theory of money, finding a definite relationship between the equality of saving and investment and the policy objective of price stability. Such concerns were to result in the *Treatise on Money*, published in 1930, a flawed book but one which nevertheless contained many of Keynes's most striking lifelong ideas.

Both Skidelsky and Moggridge are masterful on the 1920s, this busiest of all decades in Keynes's life. Moggridge's unrivalled knowledge of the financial history of the period gives him something of a comparative advantage in the debates on the return to gold and the German Transfer Problem but only by a small margin.

By 1931 Keynes had served as a member of the pivotal Macmillan Committee on Finance and Industry, had testified to the Committee in respect of the causes of the slump and how to remedy it, and had begun to move away from the analysis of the *Treatise on Money* to what was to become five years later *The General Theory of Employment, Interest and Money.*

THE MAKING OF *THE GENERAL THEORY*

Keynes's intellectual journey from the *Treatise on Money* to *The General Theory* has spawned an enormous literature, detailing on a month-to-month basis the 'context of discovery' of Keynesian economics. As Moggridge (1992: 557) puts it: 'Although scholars will always hope for more, it is probably the case that with the *General Theory* they have the most voluminous record surrounding the creation of any classic work in economics.' Don Patinkin has written an entire book about it, so has Robert Dimand; and Patinkin (1993) has recently returned to the chronology of the making of *The General Theory* in the light of recent evidence on Keynes's lectures to Cambridge students (Rymes, 1989). They all agree that the breakthrough came in the autumn of 1932 or at the latest in the spring of 1933 (Skidelsky, 1992: 443, 459–66; Moggridge, 1992: 563–5). Of course, agreement on the date of discovery implies agreement on the nature of what it is that is being discovered, that is, the essence of Keynesian economics as set out in *The General Theory*.

Given the customary difficulties of exegetical interpretation in any subject and certainly in a subject like economics, and given the fact that *The General Theory* is 'the least clear of Keynes's contributions to economics' (Moggridge, 1992: 557), it is gratifying to learn that Patinkin has now convinced everyone that the central message of the book is the equilibrating role of output changes with investment being the active and saving the passive factor in the process (Skidelsky, 1992: 461–2; Moggridge, 1992: 558–9). Once this step had been taken, it followed that the rate of interest had to be explained as determined by something else than saving and investment. Thus, the liquidity preference theory interest was in place almost as soon as Keynes had seized on the central output-adjustment framework.

Both Skidelsky (1992: 416–17, 419–20, 464–5) and Moggridge (1992: 563) note that Keynes may have been stimulated to express his theory in the way that he did by reading Malthus: in preparing *Essays in Biography* for publication in the winter of 1932, Keynes updated his earlier biographical essay on Malthus and reread the Ricardo–Malthus correspondence. Both conjecture that what Keynes took from Malthus was a name for a new concept – effective demand – in the effort to invent a pedigree for his own ideas. However, Steve Kates (1994) has argued that the influence of Malthus on *The General Theory* extended beyond language to matters of substance. Be that as it may, the strongest evidence that reading Malthus indeed left a mark on Keynes's thinking is the fact the Keynes attached so much importance to Say's Law, which he alleged was held by virtually all economists before him. Yet he could find no examples of that belief other than John Stuart Mill's *Principles* and Marshall's *Economics of Industry*. In point of fact, Say's Law is rarely mentioned by any economist after Mill; it would be difficult to find more than two or three places in the 1848–1936 literature in which Say's Law of Markets or the thesis of 'the impossibility of general gluts' is even mentioned, much less defended. In short, it would appear that at least the rhetoric of *The General Theory* was decisively influenced by Keynes's reading of Malthus. This is an aspect of the making of *The General Theory* that deserves further consideration by his biographers.

WHAT DID KEYNES MEAN?

I have said that there is general agreement with Patinkin on the central message of Keynesian economics but that is not to say that there is agreement on all the associated messages attached to the central theory of effective demand, nor on the manner in which Keynes obtained his results. Moggridge (1992: xvi, 592–607) spends a short chapter describing the early reactions to *The General Theory* but declines to enter into a discussion of the what-Keynes-really-meant literature. But such literature emerged almost as soon as the book was published and within a year Keynes answered at least some of his critics in print. It is striking that in all he wrote in defence of his theory, he gave pride of place to his theory of the rate of interest and indeed, in the years before the war, arguments about the meaning of Keynesian economics centred more on the liquidity preference theory of interest than on any other feature of Keynesianism. However, the real controversies about interpretation began in the 1940s, increased in the 1950s, and reached a crescendo in the 1960s.

Skidelsky (1992: 536ff) devotes a whole chapter to the vision that colours *The General Theory* and to the analytical structure of the book. He follows this with a chapter on the reactions to the book, the furious debates with Dennis Robertson and Ralph Hawtrey, and Keynes's replies to his critics. He does not of course review all the subsequent, conflicting interpretations of Keynes's meaning but they are clearly in his mind in writing these pages.

Patinkin (1990) has recounted the history of the conflicting attempts to discern Keynes's intentions in writing *The General Theory*. Meltzer (1988: ch. 6, 249ff), in an otherwise questionable book,[16] provides a useful classification of the various interpretations of *The General Theory*[17] that brings home at the same time the technique of overkill that makes *The General Theory* the influential book that it is. He delineates six possible interpretations: (a) wage and price stickiness; (b) intertemporal co-ordination failures; (c) elasticity pessimism, or what Coddington called 'hydraulic Keynesianism'; (d) irrational expectations and persistent dynamic disequilibria; (e) denial of gross substitution between money and other assets; and (f) miscellaneous factors. The first is identified with Modigliani, appearing as early as 1944 when Keynes was still alive, but it is also found in Haberler, Hicks and Johnson. The second is associated with Clower and Axel Leijonhufvud and consists of co-ordination failures exacerbated by quantity adjustments, volatile long-term expectations and informational asymmetries. The third, leaning heavily on the liquidity trap and interest-inelastic investment, is primarily associated with Hansen. The fourth is found in Patinkin and Leijonhufvud; an extreme variety of this fourth version involving irrational and unstable expectations is most prominently argued by Robinson and Shackle. The fifth interpretation is found in Shackle and Robinson but is most vehemently advocated by Davidson and might perhaps be described as *the* post-Keynesian interpretation of Keynes's economics.[18] Finally, the sixth interpretation weaves elements of all the previous five together in various combinations.

The striking feature of virtually all these interpretations is that they typically adopt one or another chapter of *The General Theory* as the essential chapter bearing the central message of the book. Modigliani, Hicks and Patinkin all attach great significance to Chapter 19, the chapter in which Keynes finally relaxes the assumption of wage and price stickiness adapted in the previous 18 chapters of the book. Hansen finds the main point of *The General Theory*, namely elasticity pessimism, in Chapter 3, 'The Principle of Effective Demand', coupled with Chapter 10, 'The Marginal Propensity to Consume and the Multiplier'. Shackle and Joan Robinson argue that the key to the book is to be found in Chapter 12 on 'The State of Long-term Expectations' and the 1937 *Quarterly Journal of Economics* paper. Davidson chooses Chapter 17 on 'The Essential Properties of Interest and Money' as his favourite chapter, and Meltzer himself reads much significance into Chapter 24, 'Concluding Notes on the Social Philosophy Towards Which the General Theory Might Lead'. Perhaps only Clower, Leijonhufvud and Patinkin are exceptions to this tendency of hanging a definite interpretation of Keynes on one or more chapters of the book. Clower and Leijonhufvud disclaim any attempt to provide a 'historical reconstruction' and opt explicitly for a 'rational reconstruction' of Keynes's system.[19] Pantinkin claims to be fundamentally concerned with authorial intention and yet interprets *The General Theory* as an analysis of an economy in dynamic disequilibrium without offering any warrant for this interpretation in Keynes's text; there is nothing wrong with such a 'rational reconstruction', and indeed it is perhaps the most cogent interpretation of what it should have meant, but it is clearly not a 'historical reconstruction', in which case the author's intention is either irrelevant or just another interpretation, no better or worse than anyone else's.

Many puzzles about the composition of *The General Theory* remain despite Skidelsky's and Moggridge's fine-tooth-combing of Keynes's correspondence. To give just one example: why did Keynes fail to link his own macroeconomic analysis to the theories of imperfect or monopolistic competition when this would have strengthened his own conclusions and made the analysis even more persuasive than it already was? The standard explanation for Keynes's failure to make even so much as a reference to imperfect competition was that he was more concerned with establishing a purely theoretical proposition – that unemployment can occur in equilibrium under perfect competition – than with the development of an analytical model based on realistic assumptions (Sawyer 1992). But Robin Marris (1991: 181–7) has another explanation: dislike of Joan Robinson and sexual jealously because of her love affair with Richard Kahn made Keynes reluctant to use the insights of the *Economics of Imperfect Competition*.[20] Moggridge makes one or two references to the affair between Joan Robinson and Kahn but that is not to endorse the Marris thesis. The mystery of why the Keynesian Revolution and the Imperfect Competition Revolution took place simultaneously in the same country and in the same university without in any way connecting up together lies unsolved to tantalize our historical imagination.

THE KEYNESIAN REVOLUTION

There were two Keynesian Revolutions: the revolution in economic policy and the revolution in theoretical opinion within the economic profession. The revolution in policy refers to the slow conversion of the Treasury to fiscalism, the deliberate unbalancing of the budget to secure full employment. Clark (1988) has recounted the revision of the 'Treasury View' of the 1920s from an argument about crowding out to one more concerned with administrative impediments to public-works spending. By 1939 or thereabouts even these objections were largely set aside and the war brought wholesale surrender of the Treasury to the Keynesian canon.

But some revisionist economic historians have wondered whether Whitehall officials may have been right after all. Keynes estimated the value of the British expenditure multiplier in 1936 at 1.5 but recent research has shown that the true figure may only have just exceeded unity. Given the low value of the impact multiplier and the structural rigidities of the pre-war British economy, economic historians have increasingly expressed doubts that Keynes's remedies could ever have worked in the circumstances of the late 1930s: the fiscal stimulus designed to produce full employment would have had to have been so large as to virtually imply physical planning on a wartime scale (Skidelsky, 1992; 467, 475, 631; Collins, 1988).

It is worth noting that Keynes himself would not have been as startled by such historical revisionism as we are. He was perfectly aware that government budgets in the 1930s were so small that any likely budgetary deficit could have had only a minuscule effect on national income. For example, the fall in income experienced by the United States and the United Kingdom between 1929 and

1933 was so great that public expenditure would have had to have increased by 50–70 per cent to have filled the gap. However, that is only to say that Keynes, at least in *The General Theory*, did not actually advocate budgetary deficits as a tool of stabilization policy, but rather monetary policy in conjunction with the stabilization of investment by means of a permanent rise in the proportion of income spent by governments; that is what he meant by the famous plea for 'the socialisation of investment' in the closing pages of his book.

But all this is only about half of the Keynesian Revolution. The other Keynesian Revolution is the revolution in economic thought, namely, the unprecedented speed at which the vast majority of economists throughout the Western world were converted to the Keynesian way of thinking within the space of about a decade, 1936–46. The precise details of this remarkable success story has never been fully set out[21] and it is a pity that neither Skidelsky nor Moggridge have taken the opportunity to fill in the blanks; Skidelsky's study stops in 1937 and of course it may be that he will do precisely that in his third volume. This success story is more than a matter of the reviews of *The General Theory* and Keynes's reactions to them; it is a matter of issue after issue of the leading economic journals in the five to eight years after the publication of *The General Theory* succumbing to the Keynesian steamroller. A recent study (McCormick, 1992) has labelled it 'the Keynesian avalanche' and that is just what it was. Until this story is fully told, we have not done justice to the Keynesian legacy. And I contend that it has never been fully told.

THE WAR YEARS

Skidelsky, as I have said, stops around 1937, by which time Moggridge still has 200 pages to go in a book of over 800 pages. Despite his heart attack in 1937, Keynes continued to edit the *Economic Journal* and to publish articles on economic policy in the pages of *The Times* and elsewhere. When war broke out he re-entered the Treasury, not as a civil servant but, as he himself put it, a 'demi-semi-official' – that is, an unpaid adviser to the Chancellor of the Exchequer. Six months after the outbreak of hostilities, he published his recommendations on war finance, *How to Pay for the War* (1940). Although the details of his proposals for compulsory saving were never accepted, the general principle of paying for the war by deliberately deferred consumption became the foundation of British war finance. Moreover, the 1941 Budget was couched in *The General Theory* language of macroeconomics accounting and so marked the more or less official endorsement of Keynesian economics, a mere five years after the appearance of *The General Theory*. Has any great economist ever succeeded as Keynes did?

As the war drew to a close, Keynes, now Baron Keynes of Tilton, became increasingly involved in post-war international economic policy centred around the creation of the IMF and the World Bank. The story of Keynes's role in obtaining the US wartime loan to Britain and his participation in the Bretton Woods Conference of 1944 and the Savannah Conference of 1946 has been told many times before but Moggridge nevertheless takes us expertly through this familiar territory. He pays particular attention to Keynes's fascinating last paper which appeared posthumously in June 1946 under the title 'The Balance of Payments of the United States', which contained those oft-quoted ominous passages about 'modernist stuff, gone wrong and turned sour and silly' (Moggridge, 1992: 822–5). But he is not any more successful than others have been in pinning down what Keynes had in mind when writing those sentences.

IN CONCLUSION

These two biographies tell us much about Keynes that we never knew beforehand – his mild anti-Semitism, so typical of educated people in the interwar years (Skidelsky, 1992: 238–9; Moggridge, 1992: 609, 728); his insensitivity about Hitler and indeed indifference to the Nazi experience (Skidelsky, 1992: 486–8, 581; Moggridge, 1992: 609–11) – but even old topics frequently canvassed by others – his abrasive dismissal of Marx and Marxism (Skidelsky, 1992: 514–23, 538–9; Moggridge, 1992: 469–70); his almost equally abrasive dismissal of Tinbergen and of any and all varieties of econometrics (Skidelsky, 1992: 618–20; Moggridge, 1992: 620–3) – are here re-examined afresh. There are striking portrait-sketches in both books of all the leading personae in the Keynesian Revolution – Pigou, Kahn, Robertson, Robbins, Hayek, Harrod and Hawtrey – but there is more of this in Skidelsky than in Moggridge. Moggridge writes well but Skidelsky writes superbly. Some of Skidelsky's set pieces are almost as elegantly penned as Keynes's own in, say, his *Essays of Persuasion*. For example, his discussion of the role of *Zeitgeist* in explaining Keynes's thought, the qualities Keynes most admired in other economists, the pre-analytic vision that underlies *The General Theory*, and Keynes's conception of long-term historical trends in Western capitalism (Skidelsky, 1992: 406–10, 410–18, 537–48, 606–10); in all these and many other miniature essays Skidelsky dazzles even as he instructs. Having read him, it is difficult to agree with Stigler that biography is irrelevant to the meaning of a great text: the 'context of discovery' is forever spilling over into the 'context of justification'.

What makes Keynes's career so rewarding to study in its entirety is that, despite the sheer number of publications and total words written (even 30 volumes of the *Collected Writings* amount to only about half his private papers), he was wedded all his life to four for five leitmotifs to which he returned time and again in endless variations: the way expectations are formed under conditions of pervasive ignorance and uncertainty as if they were calculable numbers even though they clearly are not; the flight to money as a haven from uncertainty; the belief that rationality, in the sense of deliberate and carefully calculation action, was not only rare – it was seldom the motor force of action; the chronic tendency towards oversaving throughout human history in contrast to the feebleness and volatility of the inducement to invest; the deceleration of population growth and the imminent saturation of capital leading to secular stagnation in the foreseeable future; and the conviction that it is vested ideas and not vested interests that stand in the way of solving all social and economic problems. A popular essay like 'Economic Possibilities for Our Grandchildren' (1930) contains all of these strands but they appear just as incessantly in his technical writings.

Economists, as we all know, are still divided about Keynes. Either he was a hero who forged a new type of economics capable of dealing with the perennial problems of unemployment and inflation, or he was a villain who attempted to seduce his fellow economists down a dirigiste path in which the market mechanism would take second place to the visible hand of government. There is ammunition for both views in these books. Those of you who find biographies tedious and suitable only for diversion on planes and trains might take these books along on your next trip. They might prove surprisingly thought-provoking of serious economic analysis and of course wonderfully suggestive of the possible links between personality and creativity.

NOTES

1. The introduction to Skidelsky's first volume consists entirely of a scornful dismissal of Harrod's biography and the way Harrod covered up evidence that he thought would reflect badly on Keynes's reputation.
2. Hession (1984) attributes Keynes's genius to his androgynous personality, which he argues is always the hallmark of creativity. Nevertheless, Hession is always very good for what it is: a popular and fairly brief biography for the good reader. I say nothing of Mini (1991), which is an intellectual portrait of Keynes rather than a biography. It is a suggestive but somewhat fanciful attempt to treat Keynes's iconoclasm in economics as just another manifestation of Bloomsbury's assault on every aspect of Edwardian intellectual and cultural life.
3. As late as 1960, Moggridge (1992: 258) tells us, some members of 'the committee then responsible for the *Collected Writings of John Maynard Keynes*' wanted to suppress evidence of Keynes's objections to conscription in World War I. This incident serves to convey the way Keynes was protected by the Cambridge keepers of the flame.
4. See Rae (1895) and Campbell and Skinner (1982). A full-scale biography of Smith by I.S. Ross, incorporating new material that has recently come to light, has been promised since 1976. Another example of the phenomenon of the anonymity of the great is Richard Cantillon; see Murphy (1986).
5. See Weatherall (1976), which does not begin to make use of all the evidence Sraffa provided. James (1979) on Malthus demonstrated what could be done with source materials that were long known and which even Keynes in his famous essay on Malthus failed fully to utilize.

6. Jaffe wrote but never published the first chapter of a projected biography of Walras, which subsequently appeared as a number of papers on aspects of Walras's life: see Walker (1983a: chs 2–4).

7. Gardlund's book, which I vote my favourite biography of a great economist, is even better (I am told) in the longer Swedish version, published in 1953 under the title *Knut Wicksell, Rebell i det nya riket*.

8. On Mill, see Packe (1954). On George, see Barker (1955). On List, see Henderson (1983). On Proudhon, see Hyams (1979). On Wicksteed, see Herford (1931). On Marx, there are a half-dozen biographies; I prefer Seigel (1978) to the more standard McLellan (1973).

9. It will be interesting to see how it will improve on Keynes's own 70-page memorial on Marshall, published in 1924 a few months before his death, which Schumpeter judged 'the most brilliant life of a man of science I have ever read' (quoted in Skidelsky, 1992: 182).

10. In the peculiar way that everyone thinks of the same idea at the same time, Allen's life of Schumpeter appeared in the same year as Richard Swedberg (1991).

11. As Karin Knorr-Cetina (1981: 7), a sociologist of science, expressed it: 'Whether a proposed knowledge claim is judged plausible or implausible, interesting, unbelievable or nonsensical, may depend upon *who* proposed it and *how* it was accomplished ... Thus the scientific community itself lends crucial weight to the context of discovery in response to a knowledge claim.'

12. It is curious that Knight's language of 'risk' versus 'uncertainty' has survived so much better than Keynes's contrast between cardinal and ordinal, numerical and non-numerical, and definable and undefinable probability. That may be because Knight's argument is, I think, more sharply focused than is Keynes's. Rod O'Donnell (1989: 262–3) notes that historical priority belongs to Keynes but does not otherwise compare Knight's position to that of Keynes.

13. I find Bateman (1987) the most illuminating exposition of Keynes's *Treatise on Probability* in the literature; see also Bateman (1991) and Gerrard (1992), reviewing O'Donnell, Carabelli and Fitzgibbon. A useful single book on the entire controversy is the collection of essays edited by Bateman and Davis (1991).

14. It was Alan Coddington (1983: 94–9, 113) who first pointed out that Keynes's famous 1937 article on 'The General Theory of Employment', invariably cited by 'fundamentalist Keynesians' like George Shackle and Joan Robinson as testifying to Keynes's ultimate reliance on uncertainty and ignorance affecting all economic expectations, ends up deploying concepts like the consumption function and the marginal efficiency of capital as if aggregate economic behaviour is determinate after all. O'Donnell (1989: 375) strenuously denies that there is a contradiction between the two halves of the 1937 article but Coddington still seems to me to have the best of the argument.

15. Keynes was a great editor, but it is gratifying to learn that even he could make mistakes. And what mistakes! In 1923, he rejected a paper by Ohlin containing the Heckscher–Ohlin theorem. In the following year, he rejected an essay by Wisksell on Ricardo and the Machinery Question. And in 1931, he rejected Harold Hotelling's classic 1931 article on 'The Economics of Exhaustible Resources' as 'too mathematical' (Moggridge, 1992: 210; Gans and Shepherd, 1994).

16. The book is full of good things but some of its arguments ring false, e.g. that Keynes favoured policy rules rather than fine-tuning to avoid destabilizing effects on expectations (Meltzer 1988: 8, 200). In view of Keynes's activist political philosophy, this seems doubtful, but in any case Keynes had never encountered the Friedmanite distinction between rules and discretion: see Patinkin (1990: 225–33) and Meltzer (1992: 156–9).

17. Coddington (1983) was the first commentator to classify interpretations of Keynes into several mutually exclusive categories.

18. Skidelsky (1992: xi) notes that 'Don Patinkin has reproached me with having adopted a post-Keynesian interpretation of Keynes's economics' and pleads guilty to the charge. But all that this seems to mean is that Skidelsky treats Keynes as having been obsessed throughout his entire life by the problem of economic behaviour under uncertainty; if this is a post-Keynesian interpretation, we are all post-Keynesians now.

19. For those unfamiliar with this distinction in the historiography of ideas, see Blaug (1990a). Leijonhufvud (1988) has recently claimed that his interpretation is in fact an implicit 'historical

reconstruction' as well as a 'rational reconstruction'; the newly discovered discarded introduction to *The General Theory* contrasting a 'Co-operative' and an 'Entrepreneur economy', reprinted in Vol. XXIV of *The Collected Writings of John Maynard Keynes*, contains the central notion of 'co-ordination failure'.

20. Hession (1984: 287) reports that *The Economics of Imperfect Competition* was not in Keynes's well-stocked library but it is difficult to know whether we should count this as serious evidence.

21. I say this despite Winch (1969), Mehta (1974) and Fletcher (1987). I have made a stab at it myself (Blaug, 1990b: ch. 4) but it is only a stab.

REFERENCES

Allen, Robert L. (1991) *Opening Doors: The Life and Work of Joseph Schumpeter*, 2 vols, New Brunswick, NJ: Transaction Publishers.

Allen, Robert L. (1993) *Irving Fisher: A Biography*, Oxford: Blackwell

Barker, Charles A. (1955) *Henry George*, New York: Oxford University Press.

Bateman, Bradley W. (1987) 'Keynes's changing conception of probability', *Economic Philosophy*, **3**(1): 97–119

Bateman, Bradley, W. (1991) 'Das Maynard Keynes problem: review article', *Cambridge Journal of Economics*, **15**(1): 101–11.

Bateman, Bradley W. and John B. Davis (1991) *Keynes and Philosophy: Essays on the Origin of Keynes's Thought*. Aldershot, Hants.: Edward Elgar.

Blaug, Mark (1985) *Economic Theory in Retrospect*, 4th edn. Cambridge: Cambridge University Press.

Blaug, Mark (1990a) 'On the historiography of economics', *Journal of the History of Economic Thought*, **12**(1): 27–37.

Blaug, Mark (1990b) *Economic Theories, True or False?* Aldershot, Hants.: Edward Elgar.

Campbell, Roy Hutheson and Andrew S. Skinner (1982) *Adam Smith*, London: Croom Helm.

Clarke, Peter (1988) *The Keynesian Revolution in the Making*, Oxford: Clarendon Press.

Coddington, Alan (1983) *Keynesian Economics: The Search for First Principles*, London: Allen & Unwin.

Collins, Michael (1988) 'Did Keynes have the answer to unemployment in the 1930s?', in *J.M. Keynes in Retrospect*, ed. John Hillard, Aldershot, Hants.: Edward Elgar, pp. 64–87.

Diggins, John P. (1978) *The Bard of Savagery: Thorstein Veblen and Modern Social Theory*, Brighton: Harvester Press.

Dorfman, Joseph (1934) *Thorstein Veblen and His America*, New York: Viking Press; reprinted New York: Augustus M. Kelley, 1961.

Fletcher, Gordon A (1987) *The Keynesian Revolution and its Critics: Issues of Theory and Policy for the Modern Production Economy*, London: Macmillan.

Gans, Joshua and George B. Shepherd (1994) 'How the mighty are fallen: rejected classic articles by leading economists', *Journal of Economic Perspectives*, **8**(1): 165–79.

Gardlund, Torsten (1958) *The Life of Knut Wicksell*, Stockholm: Almqvist & Wiksell, reprinted 1985.

Gerrard, Bill (1992) 'From *The Treatise on Probability* to *The General Theory*', in *The Philosophy and Economics of J.M. Keynes*, ed. Bill Gerrard and John Hillard, Aldershot Hants.; Edward Elgar, 80–95.

Groenewegen, Peter (forthcoming) *The Soaring Eagle: Alfred Marshall, 1842–1924*, Aldershot, Hants.: Edward Elgar.

Henderson, William O. (1983) *Frederich List: Economist and Visionary*, London: Frank Cass.

Herford, Charles H. (1931) *Philip Henry Wicksteed: His Life and Work*, London: Dent.

Hession, Charles H. (1984) *John Maynard Keynes: A Personal Biography of the Man who Revolutionized Capitalism and the Way We Live*, London: Collier Macmillan.

Hyams, Edward (1979) *Pierre-Joseph Proudhon: His Revolutionary Life, Mind, and Works*, New York: Taplinger.

James, Patricia D. (1979) *Population Malthus: His Life and Times*, London: Routledge & Kegan Paul.

Kates, Steve (1993) 'The Malthusian origins of *The General Theory*: or, How Keynes came to write a book about Say's Law and effective demand', Working Paper, Confederation of Australian Industry.

Knorr-Cetina, Karin D. (1981) *The Manufacture of Knowledge*, Oxford: Pergamon Press.

Leijonhufvud, Axel (1988) 'Did Keynes mean anything? Rejoinder to Yeager', *Cato Journal*, **8**(1): 209–17.

Marris, Robert (1991) *Reconstructing Keynesian Economics with Imperfect Competition: A Desk-top Simulation*, Aldershot, Hants.: Edward Elgar.

McCormick, Brian J. (1992) *Hayek and the Keynesian Avalanche*, Hemel Hempstead, Herts.: Harvester Wheatsheaf.

McLellan, David (1973) *Karl Marx: His Life and Thought*, London: Macmillan.

Mehta, Ghanshyam (1974) *The Structure of the Keynesian Revolution*, London: Martin Robertson.

Meltzer, Allan H. (1988) *Keynes's Monetary Theory: A Different Interpretation*, Cambridge: Cambridge University Press.

Meltzer, Allan H. (1992) 'Patinkin on Keynes and Meltzer', *Journal of Monetary Economics*, **29**(1): 151–62.

Mini, Piero V (1991) *Keynes, Bloomsbury, and 'The General Theory'*, London: Macmillan.

Murphy, Antoin E. (1986) *Richard Cantillon: Entrepreneur and Economist*, Oxford: Clarendon Press.

O'Brien, Denis P. (1970) *J.R. McCulloch: A Study in Classical Economics*, London: Allen & Unwin.

O'Donnell, Rod M. (1989) *Keynes: Philosophy, Economics and Politics*, London: Macmillan.

Packe, Michael St John (1954) *The Life of John Stuart Mill*, London: Secker & Warburg.

Patinkin, Don (1990) 'On different interpretations of *The General Theory*', *Journal of Monetary Economics*, **26**(2): 205–43.

Patinkin, Don (1993) 'On the chronology of *The General Theory*', *Economic Journal*, **103**(418): 647–63.

Popper, Karl R. (1934) *The Logic of Scientific Discovery*, London: Hutchinson; 6th revised impression of the 1935 English translation, 1972.

Rae, John (1895) *Life of Adam Smith*, London: Macmillan; reprinted New York: Augustus M. Kelley, 1977.

Reichenbach, Hans (1938) *Experience and Prediction: An Analysis of the Foundations and the Structure of Knowledge*, Chicago: University of Chicago Press.

Robbins, Lionel (1958) *Robert Torrens and the Evolution of Classical Economics*, London: Macmillan.

Rymes, Thomas K. (1989) *Keynes's Lecturers 1932–35: Notes of a Representative Student*, Ann Arbor, Mich.: University of Michigan Press.

Sawyer, Malcolm (1992) 'The relationship between Keynes's Macroeconomic analysis and theories of imperfect competition', in *The Philosophy and Economics of J.M. Keynes*, ed. Bill Gerrard and John Hillard, Aldershot, Hants.: Edward Elgar, pp. 107–28.

Seigel, Jerrold E. (1978) *Marx's Fate: The Shape of a Life*, University Park, Penn.: Penn State Press.

Skidelsky, R. (1983, 1992) *John Maynard Keynes*. Vol. 1: *Hopes Betrayed, 1883–1920*; Vol. 2: *The Economist as Saviour, 1920–1937*, London: Macmillan.

Stigler, George J. (1982) *The Economist as Preacher*, Oxford: Blackwell.

Swedberg, Richard (1991) *Opening Doors: The Life and Work of Joseph Schumpeter*, 2 vols, New Brunswick, NJ: Transaction Publishers.

Walker, Donald A. (1983a) *William Jaffe's Essays on Walras*, Cambridge: Cambridge University Press.

Walker, Donald A. (1983b) 'Biography and the study of the history of economic thought', in *The Craft of the Historian of Economic Thought*, Vol. 1: *Research in the History of Economic Thought and Methodology*, ed. Warren J. Samuels, Greenwich, Conn.: JAI Press.

Weatherall, David (1976) *David Ricardo: A Biography*, The Hague: Matinus Nijhoff.

Winch, Donald (1969) *Economics and Policy: A Historical Study*, London: Hodder & Stoughton.

3. Preface to a Japanese translation of *Ricardian Economics: A Historical Study* (1980)*

Ricardian Economics was my first book. It appeared over 20 years ago, and those 20 years have seen an enormous outpouring of books and articles on English classical political economy, most of which have perhaps only added detail to our previous knowledge of Ricardian economics.[1] There have been some major studies, however, which have significantly altered our perspective on the entire period.[2] All of which is to say that if I were writing this book today, it would be a somewhat different book.

Re-reading it (for the first time) after all these years, I was both depressed and elated in equal measure: depressed because it clearly falls short of providing a satisfactory historical explanation of both the rise and fall of the school of Ricardo in England; and elated because much of it does survive unscathed in the face of subsequent research. In short, naive as it undoubtedly is, I am not altogether ashamed of *Ricardian Economics* even now and, if pressed, might be willing to agree that it is still worth reading.

I suppose the pages that most need revising are those dealing with Ricardo's 'invariable measure of value' and 'the fundamental theorem of distribution' (pp. 15–29), which eluded even Frank Knight (in a characteristically tetchy but not unkind review, he said: 'there is much [here] I cannot follow'; *Southern Journal of Economics*, January 1959: 365). My views on that subject (along with those of everyone else) have been fundamentally affected by the subsequent publication of Piero Sraffa's *Production of Commodities by Means of Commodities* (1960). When I wrote *Ricardian Economics*, I was convinced that Ricardo's quest for a measure of value that would be invariant to changes in wages and profits was, as Edwin Cannan once said, 'chimerical'. My object was not to defend Ricardo, but to explain what he meant. Sraffa has shown, however, that Ricardo was at least half right. Ricardo was looking for an invariant yardstick by which to express relative prices, and he hoped to find a yardstick that would be invariant, not just to changes in wages and profits, but also to changes in technology. It is possible, under certain assumptions, to define an 'invariable measure of value', or 'standard commodity' as Sraffa calls it, that will measure prices regardless of

---

* Previously unpublished in English.

the ratio of wages to profits, but it is not possible, even under the most stringent assumptions, to define a measuring rod that will not itself change when there is a change in the techniques of production. Thanks to Sraffa, it is now so much easier than it was in 1958 to give a coherent account of Ricardo's lugubrious and obscure discussion of the need for an invariable measure of value. Fortunately, I had the opportunity to restate the argument afresh in later years (M. Blaug, *Economic Theory in Retrospect*, 4th edn, Cambridge: Cambridge University Press, 1992, ch. 4).[3]

If *Ricardian Economics* had a single theme, it was that Schumpeter was altogether wrong to deny the dominance of the Ricardian school in Britain throughout the half-century that followed the death of Ricardo. I argued that the essence of Ricardo consisted of the doctrine that the rate of profit depends on the costs of producing wage goods, which in turn depend critically on the costs of producing agricultural produce. It is the presence of this element, rather than the labour theory of value or Say's Law of Markets, which defines a 'Ricardian economist'. Most British economists of the period, including most of those who explicitly rejected Ricardo, subscribed to the view that the rate of profit and hence the accumulation of capital is fundamentally governed by the efficiency of labour in agriculture, and to that extent they produced Ricardian conclusions on all the outstanding economic problems of the day. In other words, without following Ricardo in all respects, their theoretical and applied work did conform to the type of analysis of which Ricardo's writings are the archetype. It is in this sense that Ricardo may be said to have dominated the economic thinking of his day.

I still think that this is the right view to take of what Ricardo meant to his contemporaries, despite the opinions expressed by some of my reviewers (e.g. J.R. Hicks in *Economic History Review*, August 1960: 130; and R.L. Meek in *Kyklos*, 11(3), 1958: 558), but I now realize that I glided over all sorts of difficulties in that line of argument. How do we decide whether something like Ricardian economics held sway over early nineteenth-century economics in Britain? Do we simply count the number of economists who regarded themselves as disciples of Ricardo? And if we reject the method of counting heads, do we find the essence of Ricardianism in a 'technique of thinking' or in a substantive 'body of conclusions'? The same difficulty arises, for example, in judging the influence of Marxian economics or Keynesian economics in the twentieth century. It is *the* major conceptual problem in studying the rise and fall of any intellectual school of thinkers and I am now much more acutely aware than I was in 1958 of the necessity to face this problem before pronouncing on the question of whether the Ricardian system did or did not decline shortly after Ricardo's death.

In other respects, there is little or nothing that I would revise if I were writing today: the emphasis on the short-run, optimistic character of Ricardo's model, in spite of its superficial appearance of long-run pessimism (pp. 31–3); the insistence that Ricardo adhered to what Professor Stigler has aptly labelled an 'empirical' rather than an 'analytical' labour theory of value (pp. 33–7); the belief that Ricardo was basically concerned with 'Marxian' rather than 'Keynesian' unemployment (pp. 75–9); the interpretation of Malthus's theory of gluts as a fallacious theory about secular stagnation, not periodic slumps,[4] motivated by the desire to make a 'physiocratic' case for the landed classes (pp. 83–97); the demonstration of the sudden, and hitherto unsuspected, eclipse of the Malthusian theory of population in the 1830s (pp. 111–17); the explanation of why Senior's *Outline of the Science of Political Economy* (1836), a remarkably original book, made so little stir at the time (pp. 157–9); the analysis of the failure of Ricardo's followers, particularly John Stuart Mill, to test the accuracy of Ricardo's predictions even though they were in possession of statistical data that would have been perfectly adequate to the task (pp. 182–8);[5] the discovery that the Manchester School, which finally secured the repeal of the Corn Laws in 1846, actually repudiated Ricardo and instead hailed Adam Smith as the hero of free trade (pp. 202–9); the sceptical treatment of Marx's belief that 'scientific bourgeois economy' somehow came to an end in 1830, when in fact the decade of the 1830s marked the high point of classical economics in terms of vigour of debate and the appearance of new ideas (pp. 224–6);[6] and, finally, the denunciation of Marx's critique of Ricardo as a muddled forerunner of himself (pp. 231–7).

Summing it up, I myself would venture the opinion that the book lost sight of the wood for the trees: many of the individual items are well drawn and yet the main outline is somehow not quite right. Part of the deeper failure is due to the fact that I bit off more than I could chew and the rest is due to the fact that I was 28 years old when I wrote it. It should have been my last book, not my first.

NOTES

1.   See for example, S.A. Meenai, ' Robert Torrens and classical economics', *Federal Economic Review*, October 1955, July 1956, July 1959, January 1960; L.G. Johnson, *General T. Perronet Thompson* (London: Allen & Unwin, 1957); W.F. Kennedy, *Humanist versus Economist: The Economic Thought of Samuel Taylor Coleridge* (Berkeley, Cal.: University of California Press, 1958); L. Brown, *The Board of Trade and the Free-trade Movement, 1830– 42* (London: Oxford University Press, 1958); F.W. Fetter, 'The economic articles in the *Quarterly Review* and their authors, 1809–52', *Journal of Political Economy*, February–April 1958; D.F. Gordon, 'What Was the Labor Theory of Value?', *American Economic Review*, May 1958; M. Blaug, 'The classical economists and the Factory Acts: a re-examination', *Quarterly Journal of Economics*, 1958, reprinted in A.W. Coats (ed.), *The Classical Economists and Economic Policy* (London: Methuen, 1971); G.J. Stigler, 'Ricardo and the 93% Labor Theory of Value', *American Economic Review*, 1958, reprinted in his *Essays in the History of Economics* (Chicago: Chicago University Press, 1965); H. Myint, ('The "Classical Theory" of international trade and the under-developed countries', *Economic Journal*, June 1958; R. Torrens, *Letters on Commercial Policy*, ed. L. Robbins (London: London School of Economics, 1958); B. Belassa, 'John Stuart Mill and the Law of Markets', *Quarterly Journal of Economics*, May 1959; D.E. Eversley, *Social Theories of Fertility and the Malthusian Debate* (London: Oxford University Press, 1959); L.C. Hunter, 'Mill and Cairnes on the rate of interest', *Oxford Economic Papers*,

February 1959; H.G. Vatter, 'The Malthusian model of income determination and its contemporary relevance', *Canadian Journal of Economics and Political Science*, February 1959; M. Mann, 'Lord Lauderdale: underconsumptionist and Keynesian predecessor', *Social Science*, June 1959; H. Barkai, 'Ricardo on factor prices and income distribution in a growing economy', *Economica*, August 1959; B.A. Belassa, 'Karl Marx and John Stuart Mill', *Welwirtschaftliches Archiv*, 83(2), 1959; J.J. Spenger, 'John Rae on economic development: a note; *Quarterly Journal of Economics*, August 1959; B.A. Corry, 'Malthus and Keynes: a reconsideration', *Economic Journal*, December 1959; William D. Grampp, *The Manchester School of Economics* (Stanford, Cal.: Stanford University Press, 1960); G.S.L. Tucker, *Progress and Profits in British Economic Thought, 1650–1850* (London: Cambridge University Press, 1960); R.K. Webb, *Harriet Martineau: A Victorian Radical* (London: Heinemann, 1960); L.C. Hunter, 'Mill and the Law of Markets: comment', Quarterly *Journal of Economics*, February 1960; F.W. Fetter, 'Economic articles in *Blackwood's Edinburgh Magazine* and their authors, 1817–53', *Journal of Political Economy*, June–November 1960; M. Paglin, *Malthus and Lauderdale: The Anti-Ricardian Tradition* (New York: Augustus M. Kelley, 1961); H.G. Grubel, 'Ricardo and Thornton on the transfer mechanism', *Quarterly Journal of Economics*, May 1961; R.V. Clements, 'British trade unions and popular political economy, 1850–1875', *Economic History Review*, August 1961; G.S.L. Tucker, 'Ricardo and Marx', *Economica*, August 1961; I. Adelman, *Theories of Economic Growth and Development* (Stanford, Cal.: Stanford University Press, 1961); R.M. Rauner, *Samuel Bailey and the Classical Theory of Value* (London: G. Bell, 1961); P. Bloomfield, *Edward Gibbon Wakefield* (London: Longmans, Green, 1961); B.A. Corry, *Money, Saving and Investment in English Economics, 1800–1850* (London: Macmillan, 1962); F.W. Fetter, 'Robert Torrens: Colonel of Marines and political economist', *Economica*, May 1962; J.T. Ward, *The Factory Movement, 1830–55* (London: Macmillan, 1962); S. Hollander, 'Malthus and Keynes: a reconsideration', *Economic Journal*, June 1962; A.B. Cramp, *Opinion on Bank Rate, 1822– 60* (London: G. Bell, 1962); F.W. Fetter, 'The economic articles in the *Westminster Review* and their authors, 1824–51', *Journal of Political Economy*, December 1962; G. Sotiroff (ed.), *John Barton's Economic Writings* (Regina, Sask.: Lynn, 1962); Earl of Lauderdale, *An Inquiry into the Nature and Origin of Public Wealth*, ed. M. Paglin (New York: Augustus M. Kelley, 1962); R.N. Ghosh, 'Malthus on emigration and colonisation: letters to Wilmot-Horton', *Economica*, February 1963; M. Blaug, 'The myth of the old poor law and the making of the new', *Journal of Economic History*, June 1963; B. Semmel (ed.), *Occasional Papers of T.R. Malthus* (New York: Burt Franklin, 1963); T.R. Malthus *Definitions in Political Economy*, ed. M. Paglin (New York: Augustus M. Kelley, 1963); L. Robbins, *Bentham in the Twentieth Century* (London: Athlone Press, 1963); J. Hamburger, *James Mill and the Art of Revolution* (New Haven, Conn.: Yale University Press, 1963); D. Russell, *Fréderic Bastiat: Ideas and Influence* (Irvington-on-Hudson, N.Y.: Foundation for Economic Education, 1963); M. Blaug, 'The Poor Law report reexamined', *Journal of Economic History*, June 1964; F.W. Fetter (ed.), *Thomas Attwood's Economic Writings* (London: London School of Economics, 1964); R.N. Ghosh, 'The colonisation controversy: R.J. Wilmot-Horton and the Classical Economists', *Economica*, November 1964; E.G. West, 'Private versus public education: a classical economic dispute', *Journal of Political Economy*, 1964, reprinted in A.W. Coats (ed.), *The Classical Economists and Economic Policy* (London: Methuen, 1971); H. Barkai, 'Ricardo's static equilibrium', *Economica*, February 1965; M.A. Hudson, 'Ricardo on forced saving', *Economic Record*, June 1965; J.S. Chapman, 'A survey of the theory of international trade. Part 1: The classical theory', *Econometrica*, July 1965; D.P. O'Brien, 'The transition in Torrens' monetary thought', *Economica*, August 1965; D.P. O'Brien, 'McCulloch and India', *Manchester School*, August 1965; G.J. Stigler, 'Textual exegesis as a scientific problem', *Economica*, November 1965; B. Gordon, 'Say's Law, effective demand, and the contemporary British periodicals, 1820–1850', *Economica*, November 1965; F.W. Fetter, 'Economic controversy in the British reviews, 1802–1850', *Economica*, November 1965; E.R. Kittrell, 'The development of the theory of colonization in English classical political economy', *Southern Economic Journal*, 1965, reprinted in A.G.L. Shaw (ed.), *Great Britain and the Colonies, 1815–1865* (London: Methuen, 1970); J.S. Mill, *Collected Works*, vols II, III, IV, V, ed. John M. Robson, with the Introductions by V.W. Bladen and L. Robbins (Toronto: University of Toronto Press, 1965); R.W. James, *John Rae, Political Economist*, 2 vols (Toronto: University of Toronto Press,

1965); H. Bydedarken, *Die Interpretation der Theorie David Ricardos als geschlossenes nichtarbeitswert-taxiomatisches Gleighgewichtssystem* (Berlin: Duncker & Humblot, 1965); J. Hamburger, *Intellectuals in Politics: John Stuart Mill and the Philosophic Radicals* (New Haven, Conn.: Yale University Press, 1965); E.R. Kittrell, 'Bentham and Wakefield', *Western Economic Journal*, Fall 1965; J. Barkai, 'Ricardo's second thoughts on rent as a relative share', *Southern Economic Journal*, January 1966; P. Lambert 'Lauderdale, Malthus et Keynes', *Revue d'économie politique*, January–February 1966; D.P. O'Brien, 'Torrens on wages and emigration', *Economica*, August 1966; R.H. Timberlake, 'The classical search for an invariable measure of value', *Quarterly Review of Economics and Business*, Spring 1966; D. Winch (ed.), *Selected Economic Writings of James Mill* (Edinburgh: Oliver & Boyd, 1966); S. Moore, 'Ricardo and the state of nature', *Scottish Journal of Political Economy*, November 1966; T.R. Malthus, *The Travel Diaries*, ed. P. James (London: Cambridge University Press, 1966); B. Gordon, *Non-Ricardian Political Economy: Five Neglected Contributions* (Boston, Mass.: Harvard Graduate School of Business Administration, 1967); R.D.C. Black, 'Parson Malthus, the General and the Captain', *Economic Journal,* March 1967; A. Skinner, 'Say's Law: origins and content', *Economica*, May 1967; W. Breit, 'The wages fund controversy revisited', *Canadian Journal of Economics*, 1967, reprinted in I.H. Riema (ed.), *Readings in the History of Economic Thought* (New York: Holt, Rinehart & Winston, 1970); H. Barkai, 'The empirical assumptions of Ricardo's 93 per cent labour theory of value', *Economica*, November 1967; A.W. Coats, 'The Classical Economists and the labourer', in *Land, Labour and Population in the Industrial Revolution*, ed. E.L. Jones and G.E. Mingay (London: Arnold, 1967); G.W. Wilson and J.L. Pate, 'Ricardo's 93 per cent labour theory of value: a final comment', *Journal of Political Economy*, January–February, 1968; J.M. Robson, *The Improvement of Mankind: The Social and Political Thought of J.S. Mill* (Toronto: Toronto University Press, 1968): L. Robbins, *The Theory of Economic Development in the History of Economic Thought* (London: Macmillan, 1968); S. Hollander, 'The role of fixed technical coefficients in the evolution of the wages-fund controversy', *Oxford Economic Papers*, November 1968; F.W. Fetter, 'The rise and decline of Ricardian economics', *History of Political Economy*, Spring 1969; O. Johnson, 'The "last hour" of Senior and Marx', *History of Political Economy*, Fall 1969; S. Hollander, 'Malthus and post-Napoleonic depression', *History of Political Economy*, Fall 1969; B. Gordon, 'Criticism of Ricardian views on value and distribution in the British periodicals, 1820–1850', *History of Political Economy*, Fall 1969; J.R. Poynter, *Society and Pauperism* (London: Routledge & Kegan Paul, 1969); B. Semmel, *The Rise of Free Trade Imperialism* (London: Cambridge University Press, 1970); J.L. Cochrane, 'The first mathematical Ricardian model', *History of Political Economy*, Fall 1970; Hans Brems, 'An attempt at a rigorous restatement of Ricardo's long-run-equilibrium', *History of Political Economy*, Fall 1970; J.S. Mill, *Principles of Political Economy*, ed. D. Winch (London: Penguin Books, 1970); J.L. Cochrane, *Macroeconomics before Keynes* (Glenview, Ill.: Scott, Foresman, 1970); L. Robbins, *The Evolution of Modern Economic Theory* (London: Macmillan, 1970); D.A. Reisman, 'Henry Thornton and classical monetary economics', *Oxford Economic Papers*, March 1971; K.V. Shastri, 'The Ricardian theory of factor-shares', *Explorations in Economic History*, Summer 1971; D. Ricardo, *Principles of Political Economy and Taxation,* ed. R.M. Hartwell (London: Penguin Books, 1971); W.L. Miller, 'Richard Jones: a case study in methodology', *History of Political Economy*, Spring 1971; A. Walker, 'Karl Marx, the declining rate of profit and British political economy', *Economica*, November 1971; G. Kootman, 'Say's conception of the role of the entrepreneur', *Economica*, August 1971; R.D.C. Black (ed.), *Works of Mountifort Longfield* (New York: Augustus M. Kelley, 1971); D.P. O'Brien (ed.), *The Correspondence of Lord Overstone*, 3 vols (London: Cambridge University Press, 1971); E.F. Beach, 'Hicks on Ricardo and machinery', *Economic Journal*, December 1971; J.R. Hicks, 'A reply to Professor Beach', *Economic Journal*, December 1971; H.W. Spiegel, *The Growth of Economic Thought* (Englewood Cliffs, N.J.: Prentice-Hall 1971); H.S. Gordon, 'The ideology of laissez-faire', in *The Classical Economists and Economic Policy*, ed. A.W. Coats (London: Methuen, 1971); G. Chiodi, 'Note sull' andamento delle quote distribute nel sistema Ricardiano', *Revista di Politica Economica*, 12, 1972; J.S. and R.H. Deans, 'John Rae and the problem of economic development', *Review of Social Economy*, March 1972; T. Sowell, *Say's Law: An Historical Analysis* (Princeton, NJ: Princeton University Press, 1972); S. Hollander, 'Ricardo's Analysis of the profit rate, 1813–15', *Economics*, August 1973; R.D.C. Black, A.W. Coats and C.D.W. Goodwin (eds.), *The Marginal Revolution in Economics* (Durham, NC.: Duke University Press, 1973); N.B. de Marchi, 'The noxious influence of authority: a correction of Jevons' charge', *Journal of Law and Economics*, August 1973; M. Bowley, *Studies in the History of Economic Theory before 1870* (London: Macmillan, 1973); E.R. Kittrell, 'Wakefield's scheme of systematic colonisation and classical economics', *American Journal of Economics and Sociology,* January 1973; T. Sowell, *Classical Economics Reconsidered* (Princeton, NJ: Princeton University Press, 1974); C.J. Dewey, 'The rehabilitation of the peasant proprietor in nineteenth-century economic thought', *History of Political Economy*, Spring 1974; N.B. de Marchi, 'The success of Mill's *Principles', History of Political Economy*, Summer 1974; R.V. Eagly, *The Structure of Classical Economic Theory* (New York: Oxford University Press, 1974); V.W. Bladen, *From Adam Smith to Maynard Keynes: The Heritage of Political Economy* (Toronto: University of Toronto Press, 1974); J. Eatwell, 'The Interpretation of Ricardo's *Essay on Profits', Economica*, May 1975; S. Hollander, 'Reply to Eatwell', *Economica*, May 1975; M.J.. Gootzeit, *David Ricardo* (New York: Columbia University Press, 1975); M.A. Akhtar, 'The "classical dichotomy" in Ricardian economics', *History of Political Economy*, Fall 1975; J.H. Thompson, 'Mill's fourth fundamental proposition: a paradox revisited', *History of Political Economy*, Summer 1975; J.C. Whitaker, 'John Stuart Mill's methodology', *Journal of Political Economy*, October 1975; M.D. Bordo, 'John Cairnes and the effects of the Australian gold discoveries 1851–73', *History of Political Economy*, Fall 1975; R.P. Sturges (ed.), *Economists' Papers, 1750–1950* (London: Macmillan, 1975); M. Blaug, 'The economics of education in English classical political economy: a re-examination', *Essays on Adam Smith*, eds. A.S. Skinner and T. Wilson (Oxford: Clarendon Press, 1975); J.R. McCulloch, *A Treatise on the Principles and Practical Influence of Taxation*, ed. D.P. O'Brien (Edinburgh: Scottish Academic Press, 1975); D. Weatherall, *David Ricardo: A Biography* (The Hague: Martinus Nijhoff, 1976); R.B. Ekelund Jr, 'A short-run classical model of capital and wages: Mills's recantation of the wages fund', *Oxford Economic Papers*, March 1976; W.O. Thweatt, 'James Mill and the early development of comparative advantage', *History of Political Economy*, Summer 1976; G.S.L. Tucker (ed.), *William Huskisson: Essays on Political Economy* (Canberra: Australian National University, 1976); S. Hollander, 'Ricardianism, J.S. Mill, and the neo-classical challenge', in *J. and J.S. Mill*, ed. E. Laine and J.M. Robson (Toronto: Toronto University Press, 1976); D. Levy, 'Ricardo and the Iron Law: a correction of the record', *History of Political Economy*, Summer 1976; B. Gordon, *Political Economy in Parliament, 1819–1823* (New York: Barnes & Nobel, 1977); D.P. O'Brien, 'Torrens, McCulloch and Disraeli', *Scottish Journal of Political Economy*, February 1977; W.J. Baumol, 'Say's (at least) eight laws; or, what Say and James Mill may really have meant', *Economica*, May 1977; S. Hollander, 'The reception of Ricardian economics', *Oxford Economic Papers*, July 1977; J. Hicks and S. Hollander ' Mr Ricardo and the Moderns', *Quarterly Journal of Economics*, August 1977; S. Maital and P. Hanwell, 'Why did Ricardo (not) change his mind', On money and machinery?, *Economica*, November 1977; T.W. Hutchison, *On Revolutions and Progress in Economic Knowledge* (London: Cambridge University Press, 1978); C. Casarosa, 'A new formulation of the Ricardian system', *Oxford Economic Papers*, March 1978; C.F. Peake, 'Henry Thornton and the development of Ricardo's economic thought', *History of Political Economy*, Summer 1978; S. Rashid, 'David Robinson and the Tory macroeconomics of *Blackwood's Edinburgh Magazine'*, *History of Political Economy*, Summer 1978; J.M. Pullen, 'The editor of the second edition of T.R. Malthus' *Principles'*, *History of Political Economy*, Summer 1978; A. Hirsch and M.D. Bordo, 'J.E. Cairnes' methodology on theory and practice', *History of Political Economy*, Summer 1978; E.G. West and R.W. Hafner, 'J.S. Mill, unions, and the wages fund recantation', *Quarterly Journal of Economics*, November 1978; A.I. Bloomfield, 'The impact of growth and technology on trade in nineteenth-century British thought', *History of Political Economy*, Winter 1978; P.A. Samuelson, 'The canonical classical model of political economy', *Journal of Economic Literature*, December 1978.

2. See, in particular, L. Robbins, *Robert Torrens and the Evolution of Classical Economics* (London: Macmillan, 1958); E. Stokes, *The English Utilitarians and India* (London: Oxford University Press, 1959); P.A. Samuelson, 'A modern treatment of the Ricardian economy: I and II', *Quarterly Journal of Economics*, 1959, reprinted in *The Collected Scientific Papers*

of Paul A. Samuelson, ed. J.G. Stiglitz (Cambridge, Mass.: MIT Press, 1966); R.G. Link, *English Theories of Economic Fluctuations, 1815–1848* (New York: Columbia University Press, 1959); L. Pasinetti, 'A mathematical formulation of the Ricardian system', *Review of Economic Studies*, 1960, reprinted in his *Growth and Income Distribution* (London: Cambridge University Press, 1974); R.D.C. Black, *Economic Thought and the Irish Question, 1817–1870* (London: Cambridge University Press, 1960); C.S. Shoup, *Ricardo on Taxation* (New York: Columbia University Press, 1960); D. Winch, *Classical Political Economy and Colonies* (London: G. Bell, 1965); F.W. Fetter, *Development of British Monetary Orthodoxy, 1797–1875* (Cambridge, Mass.: Harvard University Press, 1965); W.J. Samuels, *The Classical Theory of Economic Policy* (Cleveland: World Publishing Co., 1966); D.P. O'Brien , *J.R. McCulloch: A Study in Classical Economics* (London: Allen & Unwin, 1970); N.B. de Marchi, 'The empirical content and longevity of Ricardian economics', *Economica*, August 1970; P. Schwartz, *The New Political Economy of J.S. Mill* (London: Weidenfeld & Nicolson, 1972); R. Findlay, 'Relative prices, growth and trade in a single Ricardian system', *Economica*, February 1974; W.J. Barber, *British Economic Thought and India, 1600–1858* (London: Oxford University Press, 1975); D.P. O'Brien, *The Classical Economists* (London: Oxford University Press, 1975); L.S. Moss, *Mountifort Longfield: Ireland's First Professor of Political Economy* (Ottawa: Green Hill Publishers, 1976).

3. The third edition of this book (1978) has been translated into Japanese.
4. I remain unpersuaded by T. Sowell's arguments to the contrary (*Classical Economics Reconsidered*, Princeton, NJ: Princeton University Press, 1974: 46–8; see also M. Paglin, *Malthus and Lauderdale*, New York: Augustus M. Kelley, 1961: 115–8).
5. N.B. de Marchi, 'The empirical content and longevity of Ricardian economics', *Economica*, August 1970, provides a sophisticated defence of J.S. Mill but only by an ultra-permissive interpretation of the length of time required to reach a Ricardian equilibrium – 50 years!
6. The rejections of Marx's famous 'Afterword' to the second German edition of Volume I of *Capital* went down badly with M. Dobb (review in *Science and Society*, Winter 1960: 264–5), who quotes me out of context in his *Theories of Value and Distribution Since Adam Smith*, Cambridge: Cambridge University Press, 1983: 98n, 111, to make me say the exact opposite of what I intended (see also T.W. Hutchison, *On Revolutions and Progress in Economic Knowledge*, London: Cambridge University Press, 1978, 225–30).

4. 'Not quite the patron saint of capitalists'*

Yesterday afternoon a group of Nobel economics laureates made their way from Canongate Kirk in Edinburgh down the Royal Mile to view the gravestone of an eighteenth-century Scotsman. There they paid homage to Adam Smith, author of *The Wealth of Nations* and widely regarded as the patron saint of market capitalism, on the two-hundredth anniversary of his death.

The ideological tug of war between planners and advocates of free markets is as old as economics itself. Despite the traditional association between individual freedom and the workings of markets, until recently most economists were not unsympathetic to some element of planning in what was called the mixed economy. For example, economists never denied that a socialist economy could function more or less coherently, and could even achieve rapid economic growth in the early stages of industrialization. But even this concession now seems excessively generous. The economic collapse of the Soviet empire has drawn attention once again to the inherent inefficiencies of the command economy. Market capitalism appears – for the time being at least – to have triumphed, and today any economists advocating even a tiny element of central planning invites ridicule.

Adam Smith was born in 1725 in Kirkcaldy, a small fishing and mining town across the Firth of Forth from Edinburgh. He was the only son of a controller of customs who died shortly after he was born. Smith lived with his mother whenever he was in Scotland until her death in 1784. He did not marry nor, as far as we know, was he ever amorously involved with a woman. After graduating from the University of Glasgow at the age of 17, he spent six years at Balliol College, Oxford, on a fellowship. This experience left him with a lifelong disdain for the Universities of Oxford and Cambridge, a disdain that he was to elaborate amply in *The Wealth of Nations.*

On his return to Scotland he gave several sets of public lectures, on the strength of which he was elected to the professorship of logic at Glasgow in 1751, followed almost immediately by election to the more prestigious professorship of moral philosophy.

He resigned his Chair in 1763 to accompany and tutor the young Duke of Buccleuch on a Grand Tour of the Continent. He spent three years in France and

* First published in the *Independent*, 18 July 1990.

met all the leading figures of his day including Voltaire, Rousseau and the French 'physiocrats', whose economic ideas profoundly shaped his own. Returning to Britain in 1766, he retired to Kirkcaldy to work on *The Wealth of Nations* (financed by a life pension awarded by the duke) and published it in 1776. Two years later he was appointed a commissioner of customs for Scotland and promptly undertook to suppress smuggling, although he had extolled it in *The Wealth of Nations* as a legitimate protest against 'unnatural' legislation. Smith died in Edinburgh on 17 July 1790, after supervising the burning of almost all his unpublished manuscripts, said to run to 15 folio volumes.

To describe him as the patron saint of market capitalism is a historical cliché, and like all clichés it does not tell the whole story. For instance, he was famous in his own lifetime as the author of a book about standards of ethical conduct, *The Theory of Moral Sentiments*, while *The Wealth of Nations* came to be regarded as his principal contribution only years after his death. *The Wealth of Nations* is hailed by modern economists as the first effective treatise on the subject in any language, firmly establishing economics as an autonomous subject capable of standing on its own feet independent of the philosophical and political doctrines in which it was previously embedded. At the same time, *The Wealth of Nations* launched the concept of free enterprise upon a world still steeped in government regulation.

Smith argued that a 'commercial society' (as it was then called – now a 'capitalist economy') in which people are allowed to pursue their narrow self-interests without any central direction or management, produced not chaos and anarchy as might be expected, but a definite spontaneous order; an order, moreover, that was capable of generating wealth and raising living standards to levels undreamed of in traditional societies. Smith conceded that selfishness was no doubt a vice but 'the invisible hand' of the market, he contended, was capable of transmuting these private vices into 'public virtues'.

He expressed this thought in the most frequently quoted words of the entire book:

> Every individual necessarily labours to render the annual revenue of the society as great as he can. He generally, indeed, neither intends to promote the public interest, nor knows how much he is promoting it. By preferring the support of domestic to that of foreign industry, he intends only his own security; and by directing that industry in such a manner as its produce may be of the greatest value, he intends only his own gain, led by an invisible hand to promote an end which is no part of his intention.

Never mind that this metaphor of the invisible hand securing unintended consequences is mentioned by Smith only once; it is nowadays regarded as the central message of the book.

Adam Smith insisted that markets, the price system, *laissez-faire*, capitalism – call it what you will – is the cause of the wealth of nations, as much for their poorer citizens as for the richer ones. This was a radical, even startling, proposition for its day. But that is not because businessmen or capitalists would have it so. On the contrary: it comes about as a result of competition and businessmen are everywhere the enemy of competitive process. Thus the invisible-hand paragraph continues with these equally characteristic comments:

> By pursuing his own interest he [the individual] frequently promotes that of society more effectually than when he really intends to promote it. I have never known much good done by those who affected to trade for the public good. It is an affectation, indeed, not very common among merchants, and very few words need be employed in dissuading them from it.

And again

> People of the same trade seldom meet together, even for merriment and diversion, but the conversation ends in a conspiracy against the public, or in some contrivance to raise prices.

Finally, in the closing pages of a chapter on rent in which he confronts the question of whether the interests of workers, landlords and manufacturers are necessarily the same as those of society as a whole, he concludes:

> The interest of the dealers in any particular branch of trade or manufactures, is always in some respects different from, and even opposite to, that of the public. To widen the market and to narrow the competition, is always the interests of the dealers. To widen the market may frequently be agreeable enough to the interests of the public; but to narrow the competition must always be against it.

It follows, Smith added, that

> the proposal of any new law or regulation of commerce which comes from this order ought always to be listened to with great precaution ... it comes from an order of men, whose interest is never exactly the same with that of the public, who have generally an interest to deceive and even to oppress the public, and who accordingly have, upon many occasions, both deceived and oppressed it.

In short, Smith was a spokesman for capitalism but he was not a spokesman for capitalists or the bourgeoisie. Indeed, he took a cynical view of the self-interested motives of businessmen, legislators and politicians, and in that sense is a genuine forerunner of public choice theory and the theory of economic regulation associated with such twentieth-century names as James Buchanan and George Stigler.

As these passages indicate, Smith was a complex thinker who never gave with one hand without taking something away with the other. Thus, he spent a large part of *The Wealth of Nations* attacking the existing system of government intervention in the economy which he labelled the 'mercantile system' and held out for free enterprise, free trade, and the free movement of people and goods within and between countries.

Nevertheless, he reserved for government the provision of those social services which he thought would not or could not be provided by private action, such as a judicial system, a monetary system, a standing army and certain 'public works' such as highways, bridges, canals, harbours and 'institutions for promoting the instruction of the people'. In arguing this case he opened a door through which virtually every proposal for government interference could enter, and he made a number of recommendations, for example an enforced ceiling on the rate of interest, that were clearly contrary to his own precepts. If we want a *consistent* argument in favour of markets and against government action, we shall not get it from Adam Smith.

There is also the problem of how to relate *The Theory of Moral Sentiments* to *The Wealth of Nations*. According to *Moral Sentiments*, people judge their own actions and treat others in terms of feelings of 'sympathy', namely the capacity to empathize. According to *The Wealth of Nations*, however, people are selfish and only competitive rivalry ensures that their selfishness does not harm others. Smith failed ever to relate the two books to each other.

He also wrote, but did not publish, a number of essays on philosophical and literary subjects, including a remarkable history of astronomy, and his lecture notes on jurisprudence suggest that he may have been looking towards a comprehensive system of social science. The publication of the *Complete Works and Correspondence of Adam Smith* by the University of Glasgow in the 1970s strengthened this impression, indicating that he was no mere economist but an aspiring system-builder on a grand scale. Furthermore, he was a thinker steeped in eighteenth-century traditions, much less 'modern' than he is usually made out to be. To call him the Milton Friedman or Friedrich Hayek of the eighteenth century is misleading: a socialist will find Smith unpalatable, but libertarians and right-wing Tories will also find much in his writings to make them squirm.

The Wealth of Nations should be read by every well-educated person. For one thing, it is a treatise on economics that stretches the bounds of economics to encompass history, political theory and even anthropology. For another, it is superb prose. The work is organized in five books but it is only the first two that succeeded in creating a distinct school of English classical political economy, grounded on Smith's discussion of the theory of 'value and distribution'. The general reader will be more intrigued by the last three books. They are full of material one would hardly hope to find in an economic treatise, such as an account of the economic and political development of Europe since the fall of Rome, a criticism of the colonial policies of European nations, a history of the growth and decline of the temporal power of the Church, and a diatribe against the English system of higher education and in particular its failure to reward individual members of staff in proportion to the number of students they attract by their lectures. That, of course, is one idea of Adam Smith never mentioned in university lectures on the great man.

5. On the historiography of economics*

Economists suffer badly from what we might call 'Cliophobia'. Why bother with the history of economic thought? they ask. Why not just *do* economics? What is the point of constantly recalling the inadequate economics of yesterday instead of improving the economics of today and tomorrow?

This sort of questioning deserves an answer. How indeed do we justify the history of economics as a speciality within the broad stream of economic studies? A second question arises as soon as this one is answered. What kind of history should we be writing? Should we be trying to determine what the great economists 'actually said'? Or instead, should we be occupied with discovering what they really 'meant to say'? which of course is not necessarily the same thing as what they 'actually said'. There is a third possibility, however. Perhaps we would be asking 'what they should have said', given the kind of questions they posed. Again, that is by no means necessarily the same as what they 'actually said' or what they 'meant to say'.

Historians of economic thought have often disagreed about which of these three questions they should be trying to answer.[1] It may be useful to remind ourselves that such diversity of opinions on historiographical matters is not confined to historians of *economic* doctrines. For example, the philosopher Richard Rorty (1984) distinguishes four different genres in the history of philosophy that are identical to recognizable styles in the history of economic thought: (a) '*Geistesgeschichten*'; (b) 'historical reconstructions'; (c) 'rational reconstructions'; and (d) 'doxographies'. He claims that the first three are all legitimate modes of intellectual inquiry but he deplores the fourth.

The first, *Geistesgeschichten* (literally, 'history of the spirit'), tries to identify the central questions that past thinkers have posed and to show how they came to be central to their systems of thought. If, for example, we traced Ricardo's obsessive interest in the cause of the falling rate of profit to the dramatic effects of the Napoleonic wars on the price of corn and the rent of land in Great Britain in the first two decades of the nineteenth-century, we would be practising *Geistesgeschichten*.

The second, 'historical reconstructions', attempts to give an account of past thinkers' systems of thought 'in their own terms', that is, in terms these thinkers would have accepted as a correct description of what they had done. That is,

* First published in *Journal of the History of Economic Thought*, **12**, Spring 1990.

when we assert that Ricardo traced the tendency of the rate of profit to decline
to the growing cost of producing corn in consequence of the 'law' of diminishing
returns, we are practising the art of writing a 'historical reconstruction'.

'Rational reconstructions' in contrast to 'historical reconstructions' treat the
great dead thinkers of the past as contemporaries with whom we can exchange
views. Rational reconstructions analyse their ideas in *our* terms in order to locate
their 'mistakes' and to verify that there has been rational progress in the course
of intellectual history. 'We need to imagine Aristotle studying Galileo and
changing his mind', Rorty remarks; 'we need to think that, in philosophy as in
science, the mighty mistaken dead look down from heaven at our recent
successes, and are happy to find that their mistakes have been corrected. Such
enterprises are of course, anachronistic. But if they are conducted in full
knowledge of their anachronism, they are unobjectionable' (Rorty, 1984: 33).

Finally, the fourth of the genres, 'doxography' (literally, 'the writing of
hymns of praise'), is the attempt to fit all texts into some recent orthodoxy to
show that all those who have ever worked in the field have in substance treated
exactly the same deep, fundamental questions. Rorty totally rejects doxography,
resting as it does on the notion of absolute truth as possessed by the present
generation. I once contrasted an 'absolutist' and a 'relativist' approach to the
study of the history of economic doctrines. I defined the former as the tendency
to judge past economic theories by the standards of modern economic theory,
as if Truth with a capital 'T' is always concentrated in the very last increment
of economic knowledge, and the latter as the view that every past theory is a
more or less faithful reflection of contemporary conditions (Blaug, 1985: 1–2).
If one must choose between two polar opposites, I hold that 'absolutism' is more
defensible than 'relativism', particularly as strict 'relativism' is logically
impossible. But is absolutism the method of rational reconstruction or is it in
fact doxography? Suffice it to say that the distinction between the two is at best
a subtle one. Absolutism can easily degenerate into omniscience, in which
case there really is no point to the history of economic thought; why study what
Pigou once contemptuously called 'the wrong opinions of dead men'?

Although we can never forget what we now know, so that some version of
'absolutism' is implied in every attempt to examine some text of the past, we
are still left with the distinction between 'historical reconstructions' and 'rational
reconstructions' or 'moderate relativism' and 'strict absolutism'. I wish now to
argue that however much there is a genuine distinction to be made between these
two styles in the historiography of economics, they tend invariably to shade into
one another: what is in principle separable is in practice almost inseparable.

I take as my first example Paul Samuelson's famous article on the
Transformation Problem in Marxian economics, which caused a controversy that
raged on for years. The purpose of Samuelon's paper (1971) was to demonstrate
the spurious nature of Marx's transformation of labour values into relative

prices. Although the exercise was feasible from a mathematical point of view, Samuelson argued, it was pointless because it failed to establish the priority of labour values and was simply an arbitrary operation on a set of prices determined by technology on the one hand and consumer preferences on the other. Although this repudiation of the Marxian theory of value was less devastating than of Ian Steedman's *Marx After Sraffa* (1977), which argued convincingly that labour values simply cannot be calculated independently of competitive prices, it was sufficiently destructive to have raised the hackles of Marxists and anti-Marxists alike. After an initial volley of replies and counter-replies, William Baumol (1974) attempted to bring the discussion to a close by re-examining the intention of Marx in constructing *Das Kapital* in the peculiar way that he did. Baumol's argument was simply that Marx regarded the transformation of surplus values into profits as more fundamental than the transformation of values into prices and indeed was simply not interested in explaining the determination of relative prices.

Now, interpreted as a 'historical construction', there is simply no doubt Baumol is absolutely correct. However, if this is what Marx intended, he was simply straining to accomplish the impossible. As any reader of Piero Sraffa's *Production of Commodities by Means of Commodities* (1960) can prove in the twinkling of an eye, it is impossible to determine the magnitude of the rate of profit in the sort of linear production model that Marx employed without at the same time determining the set of market-clearing prices. In other words, Marx could not have 'transformed' surplus values into profits without simultaneously having 'transformed' values into prices. If one of these operations is meaningless, so is the other. In short, Baumol's 'historical reconstruction' will not stand up as a 'rational reconstruction', a point on which Samuelson immediately seized (1974a: 64). Baumol in reply (1974b) professed to be puzzled by Samuelson's failure to recognize that 'the only objective of my paper was to determine that Marx had set out to accomplish and how *Marx* believed he had accomplished his objective', as if it were possible simply to ignore the fact that this objective was actually misguided. At no point in his original article or in his reply did Baumol intimate that Marx's belief in the importance of explaining the average rate of profit on capital and the unimportance of explaining the determination of relative prices was a fundamental misunderstanding of the nature of his own model.

Replying to Baumol, Samuelson (1974b) provided a perfect statement of the method of rational reconstruction which is worth quoting in full:

> There is a school in the history of science whose practitioners are concerned primarily with how earlier scientists perceived their own problems. In caricature, we can say it is all one to them whether Newton wrote on gravitation, alchemy or the Secret Number of the Beast in Deuteronomy. They would never dream of grading earlier writers for error of fruitfulness ...

> I begrudge no one his pastime. But, in the realm of cumulative knowledge, I
> believe there is a place for what might be called Whig History of Science. In it we
> pay past scholars the compliment of judging how their works contributed (algebraic)
> value-added to the collective stock of knowledge. Economics, I know, is not a hard
> natural science. Still I have thought it valuable to treat Marx not as an historic deity
> or oddity, but to appraise his transformation problem in the way a journal referee would
> treat any serious contribution.[2]

I conclude that rational reconstructions are perfectly legitimate, although
whether they are illuminating depends on the case in question. As for historical
reconstructions, they are inherently problematic. Strictly speaking, they are
impossible because they presume that the past can be recalled without knowledge
of the present; not adult can be expected to recall his childhood as if adulthood
had never happened. A rational reconstruction may remain a mere rational
reconstruction but a historical reconstruction must at some point lapse into a
rational reconstruction for the simple reason that there *is* progress in economics
– progress in the tools and analytical techniques of the trade and, occasionally,
even progress in our understanding of the workings of the economy. *We* can at
best struggle to grasp what a past author really meant to say in terms *he* would
have accepted but we can never fully recapture *his* theoretical innocence.

There are some who would deny that it is even important to determine what
an author really believed or meant. If we want to understand the role played by
the ideas of some great economist in the past on the history of our subject, Stigler
(1976: 60) has argued, what is relevant is not what he intended but how those
ideas were perceived by his contemporaries because 'science consists of the
arguments and the evidence that leads *other* men to accept or reject scientific
views'. In other words, what we should be doing is, not 'personal exegesis', but
'scientific exegesis' (Stigler, 1965). Be that as it may, it is certainly true that
the principle of scientific exegesis helps to sort out those cases in which the central
message of an ancient text is difficult to detect because different passages
suggest different messages. Patinkin (1982: 16–17) contends that the history of
doctrine is an empirical science in the sense that the historical reconstructionist
is like an econometrician fitting a regression line to a scatter of empirical
observations to determine the central tendency of a relationship between
variables. In the same way, historians of doctrine are trying 'to pass a regression
line through a scholar's work that will represent its central message'. But that
simile may be less helpful than appears at first glance if the author in question
displays a high 'ratio of noise to signal' as is surely the case with, say, Smith
and Ricardo.

Thus, in another of Samuelson's famous rational reconstructions, 'The
canonical classical model of political economy' (1978), he argued that all of
classical economics from Smith through Ricardo to J.S. Mill revolved around
the central doctrine that increasing land scarcity would inevitably bring about

a declining rate of profit and so usher in the stationary state. That may have been true for Ricardo, Samuel Hollander (1980) objected, but not for Adam Smith and this despite the fact that the chapter on colonies in Book IV of *The Wealth of Nations* refers to the principle of diminishing agricultural returns as choking off the growth process. The point is that all of Smith's contemporaries, including Ricardo, failed to recognize the presence in Smith's book of diminishing returns and its implications for distribution. Thus, Hollander concludes, the canonical classical model is a Ricardian construction both in terms of analytical logic and intellectual indebtedness and should not be attributed to Adam Smith. Samuelson's (1980) reply agreed that Ricardo might well have read it into Smith – it is almost there – but as a matter of logic it *is* there. In other words, Samuelson seemed to be saying, my rational reconstruction is virtually a historical reconstruction as well. He gave much the same response to Cigdem Kurdas (1988) who criticized him for ignoring Smith's heavy emphasis on the phenomenon of increasing returns in the first three chapters of *The Wealth of Nations*. Smith started the book with an optimistic scenario of increasing returns and ample technical progress, Samuelson (1988) concedes, but this gave way in a later portion of the volume to the gloom of diminishing returns and limited investment opportunities. Again, it is not easy to discern this argument in Samuelson's reply because the distinction between 'what Smith should have said' and 'what Smith actually said' is continually obscured.

Despite Samuelson's insistence on the merits of a Whig History of Science, he sometimes lacks the courage of his own convictions in insisting on a rational reconstruction that resists even a whiff of historical reconstructionism. His critics, on the other hand, seem to deny any merit in something like rational reconstruction in the sense of Rorty. In their eyes, what Samuelson is doing is doxography, detecting in earlier writers only what hints at modern neoclassical economics.

It is not easy to see how anyone can deny the value of rational reconstructions as such. Ricardo added a new chapter in the third edition of his *Principles* in which he announced that he had changed his mind about the effects of new machinery: it could reduce employment, wages and even the size of national income in both the short and the long run. For over 160 years this proposition has been denied by every leading economist except John Stuart Mill, and even his endorsement of Ricardo's thesis was severely qualified as a short-run friction. In more recent times, it was regarded as a complicated fallacy by no less a theorist than Knut Wicksell. Nevertheless, Samuelson (1989) showed recently that Ricardo was right: all the three negative effects of the introduction of new machinery may occur under perfect competition as a result of purely automatic forces. This leaves aside the validity of Ricardo's own numerical example or what impelled him to pursue it, but the latter issue will never be posed in the same way now that Ricardo's basic intuition has at long last been vindicated.

One of Samuelson's critics is Samuel Hollander. It is amusing to note that Hollander, despite his vehement insistence on the virtues of historical reconstruction, is himself a master of the art of rational reconstruction. In a number of books and articles summed up in his *Classical Economics* (1987), he has argued that there never was a 'marginal revolution' in the 1870s, no fundamental break in the history of economic thought between classical and neoclassical economics. Instead, he contends, the works of Smith, Ricardo, Mill and Marx contain a fundamental core of general equilibrium theory on Walrasian lines with resource allocation analysed in terms of the rationing function of relative prices and wages and profits treated as simply the prices of factors of production, determined by the same forces that determine the prices of final goods and services (e.g. Hollander, 1987: 6–7). Although no one is fonder than Hollander of quoting primary sources, his interpretation of these primary sources in support of his 'continuity thesis' continually walks the thin dividing line between what the great economists of the past said in so many words and what they must surely have meant. Phrases like 'it cannot be excluded that Ricardo believed ...', 'there is nothing to stop us from inferring that Marx ...', 'what Mill said is fully compatible with ...', abound in his exegetical tutorials in which the giants of the past are invited to reconsider the logical implications of their arguments in the light of subsequent doctrine.

There is nothing wrong with this as rational reconstruction. If we water down the meaning of general equilibrium theory to the dictum that everything depends on everything else, there is simply no doubt that even the economic ideas of Aristotle or Saint Thomas Aquinas can be reconstructed as primitive general equilibrium theory. It is only objectionable because Hollander righteously insists that he alone truly immerses himself in the primary sources. Needless to say, his reinterpretations of what has long been regarded as settled issues in the history of economic thought have met with outcries of protest for other commentators, sometimes bordering on rage (see, for example, O'Brien, 1981; Blaug, 1986; and Peach, 1988). In any case, Hollander is as guilty of historical reconstructions that are really disguised rational reconstructions as Samuelson is guilty, at least on occasions, of passing off rational reconstructions as if they were for all practical purposes historical reconstructions.

Another telling example of the hair's breadth that sometimes separates a rational from a historical reconstruction, consider Sraffa's discovery as editor of Ricardo's works of something called a 'corn model' in Ricardo. In this model, according to Sraffa, Ricardo managed to determine the rate of profit in his 1815 *Essay on the Profits of Stock* in purely physical terms without entering into the question of valuation. Sraffa did not claim that Ricardo actually formulated the corn model but rather that he 'must have formulated' it, either in lost papers or in conversation, for nothing else makes sense of Ricardo's belief that the rate of profit in the economy as a whole is determined by the rate of profit in agriculture. It is certainly true that we can read the corn model into early Ricardo, but on balance it is doubtful that Ricardo really committed himself to the corn model, which involved too many assumptions that he regarded as patently unrealistic (Peach, 1987: 108; Blaug, 1985: 92).

Once again, the corn model is a valid rational reconstruction of Ricardo but it is probably not a sound historical reconstruction. In much the same way, we could provide a rational foundation for may of Ricardo's and Marx's strong conclusions if we could suppose that they frequently assumed identical capital–labour ratios in different industries. Thus, to give only a simple example, the labour theory of value is safe from virtually all criticisms traditionally levelled against it if capital–labour ratios indeed are everywhere the same. Throughout his *Economics of David Ricardo* (1979), Hollander repeatedly declares that Ricardo procured many of his results by the assumption of identical capital structure in all lines of industry. Not only is there zero textual support for such a declaration (Peach, 1988: 116), however, but Ricardo had laid so much stress in his writings on the problem on unequal factor proportions that he never could have swallowed the 'heroic' assumption that Hollander attributes to him.[3]

There is space for only one more illustration of the distinction between a historical and a rational reconstruction of past ideas. Rational reconstructions of the history of economic thought are particularly appealing to mathematical economists because the mathematization of economic ideas abounds in striking exemplars of the improvements in analytical techniques that have been so marked a feature of economics in, say, the last 50 years. No wonder then that a mathematical economist like Paul Samuelson has frequently turned to the history of economic thought to demonstrate the progress of economic thought. But another (and in some ways an even more typical) instance of the same phenomenon is the work of Michio Morishima, who has written three major interpretative studies on Ricardo, Marx and Walras.

Morishima's first book on *Marx's Economics* (1973) appeared to be a rational reconstruction of Marx in the light of the contemporary theory of economic growth, being a dynamic aggregated version of Walrasian general equilibrium theory. Nevertheless, the text is peppered with references to what Marx 'perceived', 'clearly recognized', 'clearly saw', etcetera, with copious references to *Das Kapital*. This must give us pause as to whether we are being furnished with another version of 'it is all in Marx'. What certainly is studiously avoided is *Geistesgeschichte*, because Morishima (1973: 40, 42) is not above claiming that Marx would have accepted the utility theory of value and present-day demand theory if it had been known to him, and this despite the fact that Marx always ruled out price-induced substitution in consumption. The difficulty of figuring out Morishima's intention in writing the book is that Marxian economics is defended throughout 13 chapters as perfectly valid on its own grounds,[4] and then in the fourteenth and last chapter of the book is admitted to be theoretically untenable because of joint production, heterogeneous labour and unequal rates of surplus value in different industries. Rather it is the labour theory of value that is abandoned in the last chapter (Morishima, 1973: 193), so that what survives is Marxian economics without the labour theory of value. By Marxian economics is meant, apparently, the so-called Reproduction Schema of Volume 11 of *Capital*. At any rate, the 'law' of the falling rate of profit, the jewel in the crown of Marxian economics, is virtually ignored in the 200 pages of Morishima's book.

Similarly, Morishima's study of *Walras' Economics* (1977) is deliberately constructed as a reinterpretation of the true significance of Walras's contributions to economics. According to Morishima, these were not, as some have thought, the first correct exposition of the marginal utility theory of value or the demonstration of the possibility of multi-market equilibrium, but rather certain theories of money and growth usually identified with a number of twentieth-century authors. Apart from ignoring all Walras's writings except the *Elements of Pure Economics*, and even there every portion of that book except Part VII, Morishima's examination and revision of Walras's theory of *tâtonnement* in exchange and production, followed by his formulation of Walras's theory of economic growth, becomes progressively less connected with the actual content of Walras's *Elements*. Walras rigorously preserved the static character of his general equilibrium edifice even when considering the use of money and credit, and treated Part VII of this book, entitled 'Conditions and consequences of economic progress', as a sketch suggesting uses to which his model might be put in passing from static to dynamic analysis. However, Morishima considers it to be an integral part of Walras's general equilibrium modern and in so doing suggests that Walras was as interested in dynamics as in statics, and indeed anticipated not just von Neumann but also Keynes. On the other hand he concedes that 'not a chapter or even a paragraph discussing the time structure of production can be found in the *Elements*', but on the other hand von Neumann's capital theory, which is all about intertemporal choices of techniques, is described as a Walrasian theory (Morishima, 1977: 198–9). This is only one example of many others in which the reinterpretation of Walras's place in the history of economic thought gradually gives way to an original extension of general equilibrium theory into areas that Walras himself never dreamt of. Similarly, Morishima's *Ricardo's Economics* (1989) repeats the peculiar style of his books on Marx and Walras in which as much is given with the one hand as is taken away with the other.

There is a striking difference, we may conclude, between Samuelson's and Morishima's approach to the history of economic thought. Samuelson always insists that his own concern is with rational reconstruction. It is only in occasional moments of weakness that he appeals to a historical reconstruction to support his rational reconstruction. Morishima, however, disguises his rational reconstruction as historical reconstruction and indeed is not above the strident claim that other commentators have totally misunderstood Marx, Walras, Ricardo, etcetera (e.g. Morishima, 1977: 2–8). But in so far as Morishima is ever concerned with the actual words employed by the great figures of the past, what is striking about his treatment is its *a*historical character: in his books, Ricardo, Marx, Walras and von Neumann all seem to be living at the same time in an instructive seminar ably conducted by himself.

I hope that I have now demonstrated that *Geistesgeschichten*, historical reconstructions and rational reconstructions are each perfectly legitimate ways of writing the history of economic thought but that confusion is inevitably created when these distinct ways are not kept apart. In point of logic they cannot be kept entirely apart but we can at least try to be explicit about what we are doing when they are run together.

I turn now at long last to the great question with which we began this discussion: how can one justify *the history of doctrines* as a specialization within economics? Many economists denigrate the history of economic thought as mere antiquarianism, constituting an embarrassment to the claims of economics as a hard science akin to physics or biology. Nevertheless, the heads of these very same economists are stuffed with fallacious ideas about the history of their own subject. And every time anyone has a new idea in economics, every time anyone hankers to start a new school of thought, what is the first thing they do? Naturally, it is to rummage in the attic of past ideas to establish an appropriate pedigree for the new departure. All the great economists of yesterday did exactly that: Smith, Ricardo, Marx, Marshall, Keynes – they all drew on the history of economics to show that they had predecessors and forerunners. Even Milton Friedman, when he launched the monetarist counter-revolution against Keynes, could not resist the temptation to quote David Hume as an ancestral ally.

In short, the history of economic thought is irrepressible and if it were declared illegal to study it, there is little doubt that it would be carried on in basements behind locked doors. Like the writings of books banned in the future society described by Ray Bradbury in *Fahrenheit 451*, it would survive in secret underground organizations.

If I am right that history of economics, like intellectual history in general, cannot be stamped out, there may be something to be said for people who do it as a full-time activity, acquiring in the course of it some professional competence in talking and writing about it. This surely is the justification for a tribe of scholars called 'historians of economic thought'.

I am tempted to add a final argument, namely, that economic knowledge is itself historically determined, that what we know today about the economic system is not something we discovered this morning but is the sum of all our insights, discoveries and false starts in the past. Without Pigou, no Keynes; without Keynes, no Friedman; without Friedman, no Lucas; without Lucas, no ...

T.S. Eliot (1919) expressed it perfectly: 'Someone said: "The dead writers are remote from us because we *know* so much more than they did." Precisely, and *they* are that which we know.'

NOTES

1. See the references in Blaug (1985: 8–9).
2. See also Samuelson (1987).
3. It is also noteworthy that not a single contemporary classical economist ever interpreted Ricardo as assuming identical capital–labour ratios. In criticizing Samuelson's reading of Smith, Hollander, as we saw earlier, involved Stigler's principle of scientific exegesis: what interpretations did Smith's contemporaries place on *The Wealth of Nations*? However, this principle is constantly violated in Hollander's own readings of Ricardo.
4. Thus, Morishima (1973: 6, 53) takes great pains to expound the 'fundamental Marxian theorem', according to which the rate of profit in a capitalist economy is positive if and only if Marx's 'rate of surplus value' is positive. But this fundamental theorem turns out, on Morishima's own admission, to carry no causal implications about the nature of profits because it is equivalent to the proposition that the capital system normally produces a positive net product (see Blaug, 1980: 24–6).

REFERENCES

Baumol, W.J. (1974a) 'The transformation of values: what Marx "really" meant (an interpretation)', *Journal of Economic Literature*, **12**(1): 51–62.
—— (1974b) 'Comment', *Journal of Economic Literature*, **12**(1): 74–5.
Blaug, M. (1980) *A Methodological Appraisal of Marxian Economics*, Amsterdam: North-Holland.
—— (1985) *Economic Theory in Retrospect*, 4th edn, Cambridge: Cambridge University Press.
—— (1986) 'Review of S. Hollander, *The Economics of John Stuart Mill*', *History of Economic Thought Newsletter*, no. 36.
Eliot, T.S. (1919) 'Tradition and individual talent', *Egoist*, September–December.
Hollander, S. (1980) *Classical Economics*, Oxford: Blackwell.
—— (1987) 'On Professor Samuelson's canonical classical model of political economy', *Journal of Economic Literature*, **18**(2): 559–74.
Kurdas, C. (1988) 'The Whig historian on Adam Smith: Paul Samuelson's canonical classical model', *History of Economics Society Bulletin*, **10**(1): 13–23.
Morishima, M. (1973) *Marx's Economics*, Cambridge: Cambridge University Press.
—— (1977) *Walras' Economics*, Cambridge: Cambridge University Press.
O'Brien, D.P. (1981) 'Ricardian economics and the economics of David Ricardo', *Oxford Economic Papers*, **33**(3): 352–86.
Patinkin, D. (1982) *Anticipation of the General Theory?*, Oxford: Blackwell.
Peach, T. (1988) 'David Ricardo: a review of some interpretative issues', in *Classical Political Economy*, ed. W.O. Thweatt, Boston, Mass.: Kluwer.
Rorty, R. (1984) 'The historiography of philosophy', in *Philosophy in History*, ed. R. Rorty, J.B. Schnewind and Q. Skinner, Cambridge: Cambridge University Press.

Samuelson, P.A. (1971) 'Understanding the Marxian notion of exploitation: a summary of the so-called transformation problem between Marxian values and competitive prices', *Journal of Economic Literature*, **9**(2): 399–431.

—— (1974a) 'Insight and detour in the theory of exploitation: a reply to Baumol', *Journal of Economic Literature*, **12**(1): 62–70.

—— (1974b) 'Rejoinder: Merlin unclothed, a final word', *Journal of Economic Literature*, **12**(1): 75–7.

—— (1978) 'The canonical classical model of political economy', *Journal of Economic Literature*, **16**(4): 1415–34.

—— (1980) 'Noise and signal in debates among classical economists: a reply', *Journal of Economic Literature*, **18**(2): 575–8.

—— (1987) 'Out of the closet: a program for the Whig history of science', *History of Economics Society Bulletin*, **9**(1): 51–60.

—— (1988) 'Keeping Whig history honest', *History of Economics Society Bulletin*, **10**(2): 161–7.

—— (1989) 'Ricardo was right!', *Scandinavian Journal of Economics*, **91**(1): 47–62.

Stigler, G.J. (1965) 'Textual exegesis as a scientific problem', *Economica*, N.S., **32** (November): 447–50.

—— (1976) ' The scientific uses of scientific biography, with special reference to J.S. Mill', in *James and John Stuart Mill: Papers of the Centenary Conference*, ed. J.M. Robson and M. Laine, Toronto: Toronto University Press.

6. Competition as an end-state and competition as a process*

What I have to say in this paper will waiver uneasily between the obvious and the incredible, between platitudes which will instantly win your assent and rather similar assertions which you will instantly disavow. My central point is this: the oldest concept in economics is the concept of competition: how does it work and does it work for the good? But throughout the development of economics as far back as Adam Smith or even William Petty, there have always been two very different notions of what is meant by competition: competition as an *end-state* of rest in the rivalry between buyers and sellers and competition as a *process* of rivalry that may or may not terminate in an end-state. In the end-state conception of competition, the focus of attention is on the nature of the equilibrium state in which the contest between transactors is finally resolved; if there is recognition of change at all, it is change in the sense of a new stationary equilibrium of endogenous variables defined in terms of a different set of exogenous variables; but comparative statics is still an end-state conception of competition. However, in the process conception of competition, it is not the existence of equilibrium that is in the foreground of analysis but rather the stability of that equilibrium state. How do markets adjust when one equilibrium is displaced by another and at what speed will these markets converge to a new equilibrium?

But surely, it will be said, all theories of competition do both? Surely, existence and stability are tied up together and to address one is to address the other? Isn't it what Samuelson called 'the correspondence principle'? By no means, however, is it easy to show that the history of economic thought is in fact marked by centuries in which competition meant an active process of jockeying for advantage, tending towards but never actually culminating in an equilibrium end-state. Only in 1838, in Cournot's *Mathematical Principles of the Theory of Wealth* was the process conception of competition totally displaced the end-state conception of the properties of market-clearing equilibria. At first this did not succeed in wiping the slate entirely clean of an interest in competitive processes but in the decade of the 1930s – those 'years of high

* Forthcoming in *Trade, Technology and Economics: Essays in Honour of Richard G. Lipsey*, ed. Curtis B. Eaton and Richard G. Harris, Aldershot, Hants: Edward Elgar Publishing.

theory', as George Shackle (1967) called them – the Monopolistic Competition Revolution and the Hicks–Samuelson rehabilitation of general equilibrium theory, fortified by its corollary, the New Welfare Economics, succeeded in enthroning the end-state conception of competition and enthroning it so decisively that the process view of competition was virtually forgotten.

Having raised your hackles, I shall not spend a little time supporting this bold assertions before drawing from them some surprising implications.

A LITTLE HISTORY OF IDEAS

It was George Stigler (1957) who first drew attention to the great divide that marked Cournot's entry into the history of the theory of competition, and the argument has since been endorsed and elaborated by others (McNulty, 1967, 1968, 1987; Dennis 1977; Stigler, 1987; Backhouse, 1990). It is striking that the term 'competition' invariably appears in *The Wealth of Nations* with a definite or indefinite article attached to it: '*a* competition between capitals', '*the* competition with private traders', and so forth. For Smith, competition is not a state or situation but a behavioural activity; it is a race between two or more persons to dispose of excess supplies or to obtain goods available in limited quantities; it is a regulatory mechanism which forces prices and profits to their lowest sustainable levels. What we nowadays call competition was for him 'the obvious and simple system of natural liberty', meaning an absence of restraints and, in particular, restraints on free entry into industries and occupations. Neither competition nor monopoly was a matter of the number of sellers in a market; monopoly did not imply a single seller but a situation of less than perfect factor mobility and hence inelastic supply; and the opposite of competition was not monopoly but co-operation. In short, competition denoted that pattern of business behaviour which we conjure up by the verb 'to compete': to invade profitable industries, to expand one's share of the market by price cutting, in short, to jockey for advantage by any and all possible means.

Producers in *The Wealth of Nations* treat price as a variable in accordance with the buoyancy of their sales, much like enterprises in modern theories of imperfect competition. This was not a conception invented by Smith because, by the time *The Wealth of Nations* appeared, competition had long been analysed by a whole series of eighteenth-century authors as a process which brings temporary 'market' prices into line with underlying cost-covering 'natural' prices. Those 'natural' prices were indeed 'the central prices, to which the prices of all commodities are continually gravitating', and in saying that Smith invoked Newtonian language to dignify the conception that had of course nothing to do with mechanical attraction. Thus, the end-state of competition in classical economics was one in which market price equalled natural price, goods sold at cost-covering prices including profit at the going rate, and capital and labour ceased to flow between industries.

In other words, there had to be a considerable number of rivals to secure the results of the competitive process; they had to possess some knowledge of market opportunities; they had to be relatively free to enter the activity in question; but that was all and even that much was never spelled out explicitly as necessary prerequisites for competition – only once did Smith ever mention the number of rivals involved in competition. It was Cournot who first had the notion of sellers facing a horizontal demand curve when their numbers became so large that none can influence the price of their own product. Competition, which once meant the way in which firms take account of how their rivals respond to their actions, now meant little more than the slope of the average revenue curve depriving firms in the limit of any power to make the price. Thus was born, decades before the Marginal Revolution of the 1930s, what one Marxist writer has wittily called 'the quantity theory of competition' (Weeks, 1981: 153).

Edgeworth's *Mathematical Physics* (1881) followed Cournot in providing all the trappings of the modern definition of perfect competition in terms of a large number of sellers, a homogeneous product, perfect mobility of resources and perfect knowledge on the part of buyers and sellers (Stigler, 1957: 245–51). However, Marshall's treatment of competition labelled as 'economic freedom' was much closer to that of Adam Smith's 'simple system of natural liberty' than to that of Cournot and Edgeworth's perfect competition (Loasby, 1989: ch. 4; O'Brien, 1990). And even Walras's conception of static equilibrium was that of 'an ideal and not a real state' because 'a regime of free competition' tended, according to him, to evolve continually toward an end-state of rest without ever reaching it (Backhouse, 1990: 67–8). Indeed, it was not until the 1920s that the concept of perfect competition was finally received into the corpus of mainstream doctrine, largely due to the impact of Frank Knight's *Risk, Uncertainty and Profit* (1921) (Stigler, 1957: 256). But it is doubtful whether the lesson was in fact learned as early as 1921 and a good case can be made for the thesis that it was Robinson and Chamberlin who created the theory perfect competition in the course of inventing imperfect and monopolistic competition theory (O'Brien, 1983; Moss, 1984).

The replacement of the process conception of competition by an end-state conception, which was finalized by 1933 or thereabouts, drained the idea of competition of all behavioural content, so that even price competition, the very essence of the competition process for Adam Smith, David Ricardo and John Stuart Mill, now had to be labelled and analysed as 'imperfect' or 'monopolistic' competition. Indeed, every act of competition on the part of a businessman was now taken as evidence of some degree of monopoly power, and hence a departure from perfect competition, and yet pure monopoly ruled out competitive behaviour as much as did perfect competition.

COMPETITION, THE UNATTAINABLE IDEAL

All I have said so far merely reiterates Hayek's (1949: 92) conclusion in a famous essay, 'The meaing of competition': 'what the theory of perfect competion discusses has little claim to be called "competition" at all and its conclusions are of little use as guides to policy'. He emphasized instead the dynamic process of competition in which imperfect knowledge of an uncertain future serves to form severely dispersed expectations of prices and quantities: 'competition is in large measure competition for reputation and good will'; 'competition is essentially a process of the formation of opinion' (Hayek, 1949: 97, 106). But his message, delivered almost a half-century ago, fell on deaf ears and the end-state theory of perfect competition is more firmly in the saddle today than it ever was in the 1940s when Hayek was writing. Likewise, Schumpeter (1942: 106) long insisted that 'perfect competition is not only impossible but inferior, and has no title to being set up as a model of ideal efficiency'. But although Schumpeter's characterization of competition as a 'perennial gale of creative destruction' is widely hailed, it failed utterly then and now to displace the view that business behaviour should be judged in terms of the standards laid down in the theory of perfect competition.

And why? The answer is simple and obvious. It is that most of us hold the view that although perfect competition is never attained, nearly-perfect or almost-perfect competition is frequently observed, and these approximations to the state of perfect competition somehow replicate many of the desirable characteristics of perfect competition; in a word, second-best is so nearly first-best that we may indeed employ first-best as a standard.

Open any textbook and what do we find? The concept of perfect competition is said to be like the assumption of a perfect vacuum in physics: descriptively inaccurate, to be sure, but nevertheless productive of valid hypotheses about actual economies. Thus, Samuelson and Nordhaus (1992: 295) concede that 'a perfect and absolutely efficient competitive mechanism has never existed and never will', but the oil crisis of the 1970s is only one of their examples of how an empirically empty, perfectly competitive model can produce the right answers to a concrete, imperfectly competitive situation. Similarly, Stiglitz (1993: 31, 397) dubs the model of perfect competition ' a convenient benchmark', 'a useful jumping-off point'; 'by observing the difference between its predictions and the observed outcomes [economists] know what other models to employ'. Similarly, Sloman (1994: 217–19, 224–5), insists that non-existent perfect competition nevertheless furnishes us an 'ideal type', 'a standard against which to judge the shortcomings of real-world industries' – and Parkin (1990: 281, 283) agrees. But the best and certainly the longest textbook treatment of this subject that I know of is Chapter 23 of Lipsey's *Introduction to Positive Economics* (1989: 376–98; also 1984).

After building up 'the formal case' of Pareto-optimality in a model of perfect competition, as behooves any writer of an introductory text, he notes that this is a far cry from the layman's case for competition, which in my language is the difference between the end-state and the process conception of competition. He takes due notice of Schumpeter's defence of big business and deplores the fact that economists have generally failed to produce an effective answer to Galbraith's *American Capitalism* with its claim that 'oligopoly may be the most competitive system that is available in the real world' (Lipsey, 1989: 397).

Needless to say, the co-inventor of second-best is unlikely to claim great scope for piecemeal welfare economics, concluding that the case for the free market therefore has to be an informal, qualitative judgement (Lipsey, 1989: 390). But the problem is not simply that we cannot employ welfare economics to rank two states of the very imperfect world in which we live but also that we cannot generally tell how near or far we are to the observable features and predicted outcomes of a perfect competitive market structure.[1] Nevertheless, Lipsey adds, such is 'the political appeal of perfect competition' that many people still cling tenaciously to the belief that the perfectly competitive model does in fact describe the world in which we live.

This is precisely what Reder (1982: 12) called the notion of 'tight prior equilibrium', which he thought was characteristic of the Chicago School of economics: 'one may treat observed prices and quantities as good approximations to their long-run competitive equilibrium values'. Call this the 'good-approximation assumption'. But whereas this is one way to justify the use of the model of perfect competition, it is not the only way. For example, Harold Demsetz (1982) is perfectly aware that the notion of perfect competition precludes consideration of entrepreneurship, risk-taking behaviour, non-price rivalry, transaction costs, firm governance, and the like, but nevertheless defends it as a conceptualization of an economy in which no agent has any control over the plans of others; in that light, he prefers to call it 'the perfect decentralization model' rather than the model of perfect competition (Demsetz, 1982: 8). Instead of defending it, as Milton Friedman (1982: 120) does because so much of the real world approximates to it, he prefers to argue for it as yielding answers to a limited set of questions, relating to the passive effects of an exogenous shock, such as a change in a tax, a tariff, or a technological change. This is indeed a better defence of the end-state conception of perfect competition and it is curious that so many textbooks resort instead to the much weaker grounds of the 'good-approximation assumption'.

But why is there such widespread failure to address questions of active competition and instead to fall back uncritically on a model of perfect competition as an 'ideal type'? I believe that the answer to that question lies deep in the ascendancy of Walrasian general equilibrium theory in modern economics, and the acute and unresolved difficulties of stability analysis in that tradition. Let us spend a moment explaining why modern price theory is so strong on the nature of the competitive equilibrium state and so weak on the issue of how competition drives a market towards a final equilibrium.

WALRAS VERSUS MARSHALL ON STABILITY

Walras's genius lay not so much in seizing upon multi-market equilibrium as a central problem for economic theory as in hitting upon the algebra of simultaneous equations as the appropriate metaphor for tackling that problem. Just as partial equilibrium means solving a single demand and a supply equation for the equilibrium price and quantity, so does general equilibrium means solving a large set of *n* demand and supply equation for *n* prices and quantities. In the use of that metaphor is embodied all the strengths but also all the weaknesses of Walrasian general equilibrium (GE) theory.

Firstly, it led Walras to demonstrate the existence of general equilibrium in ways that were exactly analogous to a mathematical solution of a system of *n* simultaneous equations in *n* independent variables: he wrote down a set of perfectly general demand and supply equations on the assumption of perfect competition, perfect factor mobility and perfect price flexibility and then showed that he had just enough known equations to solve for the unknown prices and quantities. This was all there was to his so-called 'existence proof' for general equilibrium. But he did much more than prove existence. He briefly discussed the question whether the equilibrium price vector was unique, although he never attempted to prove that it was so, and he entered into a lengthy explanation of how competition establishes an equilibrium in practice, namely by automatic price adjustments in response to the appearance of excess demand and supply. Walras labelled these adjustments *tâtonnement*, that is, 'groping' by trial and error on the part of independently acting buyers and sellers.

Since disequilibrium trading at other than market-clearing prices alters the distribution of goods among buyers and sellers before equilibrium is reached, there is little reason to believe that a final equilibrium will always emerge in a real-world competitive process. Walras hankered after a realistic description of the temporal sequence of price adjustments by which actual markets reach a final equilibrium solution and he was persuaded by studies of the operation of the Paris Bourse that disequilibrium transactions were not allowed to occur there. But changes in the formulation of the *tâtonnement* process in successive editions of his *Elements of Pure Economics*, particularly in the pages on production theory and the role of money, show that Walras gradually abandoned this aim of descriptive realism; by the fourth edition of his book in 1900, he had settled for the view that *tâtonnement* was at best an abstract model of how actual markets *may* move to equilibrium without necessarily being the only plausible model of that process (Walker, 1987, 1980, 1993).

Although Walras never mentioned the concept of a fictional auctioneer announcing and changing prices until an equilibrium price is agreed upon – this is one of those historical myths that subsequent generations invented – it is difficult to avoid the conclusion that he simply gave up the effort to provide a convincing account of how real-world competitive markets achieve simultaneous multi-market equilibrium. Such an account has in fact never been provided even to this date. By the 1950s, Arrow and Debreu had demonstrated the existence of general equilibrium by methods infinitely more elegant that those employed by Walras but, in so doing, nevertheless found themselves having to make some severely unrealistic assumptions in order to dispose of the difficulties created by disequilibrium transactions, such as the absence of any medium of exchange and the existence of forward markets for all goods and services in the economy, including all conceivable contingent states in which these goods and services might be produced and consumed. In other words, the entire exercise became even more patently idealized than it had been in Walras.

Even so, Arrow and Debreu never managed to prove that such a general equilibrium would be stable, either locally or globally, in the sense that if the equilibrium price vector is displaced by a demand or supply shock, markets will automatically converge to a new general equilibrium. Walras saw the problem but was too cavalier in dealing with it and it remains to this day a thorn in the side of GE theory. Much hangs on grasping why stability is so difficult to prove.

It is well known (Blaug, 1985: 405–8; Williams, 1987: 108–21) that Marshall and Walras differed in respect of the stability conditions of a competitive market. The now standard Walrasian approach treats demand and supply curves as end points of horizontal lines corresponding to the quantity demanded or supplied at a given price. But Marshall typically viewed the schedules as end points of a set of vertical lines, each corresponding to the price at which a given quantity is produced or consumed; Marshall should have called his schedules 'bid curves' and 'sales curves', not demand curves and supply curves, since they depict the highest price an invididual would be willing to pay or to accept for a certain amount of commodity. On Walras's criterion, an equilibrium price is stable if the excess demand (ED) curve is negatively inclined and unstable if ED is positively inclined; on Marshall's criterion, an equilibrium quantity is stable if the excess demand price (EDP) curve is negatively inclined and it is unstable if EDP is positively inclined (see Figure 6.1). But so what? Surely, in any normal market with negatively inclined demand curves and positively inclined supply curves, we shall get the same price – quantity answers on either criteria? Indeed we shall, but it is perfectly possible to encounter markets in which the two criteria lead to opposite results, that is, stability in the sense of Walras but instability in the sense of Marshall, and conversely.

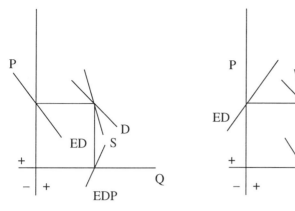

Walras-stable/Marshall-unstable   Marshall-stable/Walras-unstable

Figure 6.1   Two concepts of stability

Both Walras and Marshall recognized that there are two possible types of disequilibrium adjustment in a competitive market and that they may contradict each other, but each illustrated his own adjustment process diagrammatically and left the other to a verbal description. Marshall usually had in mind the case of a long-run forward-falling supply curve exhibiting external economies, and that can produce either of the two diagrams in Figure 6.1; in any case, in the context of the long-run theory of production, it seems perfectly reasonable to think of sellers adjusting output in response to a change in demand. Walras, on the other hand, was thinking of a backward-rising supply curve (really an 'offer curve') in a market period when stocks of goods are given, and that too can produce either of the two diagrams; again, in this context it is perfectly reasonable to assume that buyers adjust prices in response to changes in demand. Neither Walras nor Marshall recognized why their approaches led to directly opposite results and neither realized that the question whether buyers or sellers in disequilibrium adjust output or adjust prices cannot be decided by *a priori* reasoning. In the short run, when output can be varied from existing plant and equipment, the output-adjuster model is just as plausible as the price-adjuster model, even though the latter is generally the only one mentioned in textbooks. Only empirical investigation can reveal just how buyers and sellers actually behave when the price departs from its equilibrium value.

Having said that much, I can add that the argument does not in any way depend on the somewhat perverse case of negatively sloped supply curves. If one believes that long-run negatively inclined supply curves are peculiar in any case because they are not reversible – which is what Marshall himself believed – or that backward-bending supply curves are oddities that are rarely encountered even in labour markets, there is absolutely nothing to exclude output-adjusting competitive behaviour in markets with normal demand and supply functions, such that prices never converge on equilibrium or at any rate too slowly to be taken into account by buyers and sellers; as Hicks (1974: 23–8) used to say, it is simply the case that there are 'fixprice' markets and there are 'flexprice' markets, the former typified by labour markets and goods markets for specialized producer goods and the latter by most commodity and financial markets.

There is of course no reason why the two adjustment processes cannot take place simultaneously as expressed by simultaneous differential equations, and several authors have written down adjustment models that involve such simultaneous reactions (see Takayama, 1985: 301). But there is no escaping the point that the two types of adjustment involve different behavioural responses and these cannot be deduced from abstract principles of rational conduct. But time and again, different authors have tried to settle the matter by armchair deductive reasoning. Thus, Newman (1965: 106–8) argues that Marshallian quantity-adjusting stability conditions are explicitly designed for the theory of production, whereas the Walrasian price-adjusting mechanism is more suited to the theory of exchange, so that to juxtapose them, as I have done, is to commit 'a serious substantive error muddling up exchange with production'. But Okun (1981: 138–55) has long familiarized us with the distinction between personal 'customer markets' and impersonal 'auction markets' in terms of the frequency of search relative to the frequency of purchase, frequent price changes encouraging customers to search for cheaper alternatives. Hotel rooms are his favourite example of a customer market; here is an exchange economy which adjusts in terms of quantity rather than price (see also Stiglitz, 1987). And what of labour markets in which wages are sticky and it is employment and not wages which performs the equilibrating function when demand expands or contracts? Are not labour markets much like exchange economies in the sense that the potential supply of labour services is for all practical purposes a given quantity in any relevant time-period? Are labour markets not characterized by Marshallian rather than Walrasian stability conditions?

Similarly, Takayama (1985: 297–301) asserts that the dispute between Marshall and Walras regarding the stability properties of a competitive market turns on the time period involved in the adjustment process, with consumers adjusting prices long before produces are able to adjust quantities; but 'so long as the price is the sole independent variable in a competitive market', he adds, 'it may be natural to emphasize the price adjustment process'. This conclusion, however, smacks too much of fitting the facts to the theory, rather than the theory to the facts, and in any case pretends that there are no facts to take into account. Curiously too, the view that prices typically adjust faster than quantities is expressly denied by a now well-established tradition in modern macroeconomics in which Keynesian economics is reconstructed in terms of a Marshall ranking of price- and quantity-adjustment velocities, quantities adjusting before and faster than prices, not just in labour markets but in consumer goods markets as well (Leijonhufvud, 1968: ch. 2; see also Gordon, 1981).

Be that as it may, my basic point is that the matter cannot be settled by *a priori* theorizing but requires years, perhaps decades, of patient work monitoring and recording the behaviour of markets out of equilibrium in order to build up a body of empirical knowledge that would finally put non-Walrasian economics on its feet (see Bhaskar *et al.*, 1993). It is true that recent years have seen considerable developments of what is called 'non-Walrasian disequilibrium analysis' or 'fixed-price, quantity-constrained equilibrium analysis' but, alas, it too is thoroughly imbued with the end-state concept of competition that is the invidious legacy of Walras's influence. It started with Clower's dual-decision hypothesis of household consumption, distinguishing notional from effective demand, and was carried forward by Leijonhufvud's reinterpretation of Keynes. Patinkin (1956: chs. 13, 14) had already provided a disequilibrium analysis of a firm's employment plan under constrained demand for its product, and Barro and Grossman (1971) now formulated the on-Walrasian approach to macroeconomics by integrating Patinkin's and Clower's treatment of dual-decision hypotheses of firms and households.

Malinvaud (1977) and Benassy (1986) subsequently refined the non-Walrasian approach into a classification of all possible cases of dual-decision hypotheses when labour and goods markets are in excess demand or supply: in each case the actual volume of transactions in disequilibrium is equal to the short-side of supply of demand, that is, either off the supply curve or off the demand curve. We now get 'classical unemployment' or 'Keynesian unemployment' or 'repressed inflation' as three possible disequilibrium regions with a possible Walrasian general equilibrium as the union of all three.[2] I am not concerned with the exegetical question whether this is a valid reading of Keynes's *General Theory* – a question that much agitates Kahn (1977) – but rather whether this is not once again end-state theorizing. Nothing is said in this literature about how households or firms reach the three disequilibrium regions but merely that the representative household and representative firm do not change their quantities of demand and supply with respect of consumption goods and labour services once they have arrived in the region in question. In other words, this is a curious kind of disequilibrium analysis in which there is no process of rivalry between unrepresentative individual households and firms, no real contest between economic agents, but rather various end-state equilibrium points *called* disequilibria, the entire exercise differing from standard analysis only in that non-clearance of at least one of the sub-sectors of the economy is possible. In short, this is at best truncated or half-hearted disequilibrium economics and at worst another example of armchair equilibrium theorizing.

GENERAL EQUILIBRIUM PERSPECTIVE

To sum up: GE theory has been concerned from its very outset with three aspects of multi-market equilibrium: can it exist? Is that existence unique? And is it both locally and globally stable? The theory has had some success with respect to the first of these questions: the existence of general equilibrium in all markets of the economy can be demonstrated under very general assumptions, some of which, however, do not accord with any observed economic system (such as the absence of money held in preference to other interest-bearing assets, the absence of market-makers holding inventories, the absence of bank credit, and the existence of forward markets for all goods and services). However, as far as uniqueness and stability are concerned, but assumptions required to obtain definite results are so restrictive and patently *ad hoc* (for uniqueness, all commodities must be gross substitutes) as to be unacceptable even to those deeply enamoured of GE theory. In short, after a century or more of endless refinements of the central core of GE theory, an exercise which has absorbed some of the best brains in twentieth-century economics, the theory is unable to shed any light on how market equilibrium is actually attained, not just in a real-world decentralized market economy but even in the toy economies beloved of GE theorists. As Franklin Fisher (1987: 26) candidly admitted: 'we have no rigorous basis for believing equilibrium can be achieved or maintained if disturbed'. The set of equilibria in a real economy is almost certainly path-dependent and it may suffer from hysteresis, equilibrium depending not only on the current state of the system but also on its past history. We do not know that such path-dependent or hysteresis effects are small and we certainly have not proved that they are small. 'What we economists have yet to explain', as Clower (1993: 806) has rightly observed, 'is the workings of the *fingers* of the invisible hand'.

We may conclude that GE theory a such is a cul de sac: it has no empirical content and never will have empirical content. Moreover, even regarded as a research programme in social mathematics, it must be condemned as an almost total failure (Blaug, 1992: 161–9; Ingrao and Israel, 1990: 359–62).[3] That is not to say that highly aggregated computable GE *models*, such as IS–LM, are pointless or that a GE formulation of an economic problem may not prove illuminating (e.g. Shoven and Whalley, 1992) but simply that Walrasian GE *theory* – the notion that the problem of multi-market equilibrium may be studied in a way that is analogous to solving a set of simultaneous equations – has proved in the fullness of time to be an utterly sterile innovation. The real paradox is that the existence, uniqueness and stability of general equilibrium should ever have been considered an interesting question for economists to answer: a complete satisfactory proof would no doubt have been an intellectual feat but it would not in any way have enhanced our understanding of how actual economic systems works.

We have noted that *tâtonnement* for Walras is convergence to equilibrium without disequilibrium trading and this conjuring trick of appearing to analyse the process of competition by peering long and hard at its final end-state – like a geographical map of the towns in a country without a map of the roads between towns – has been a constant feature of GE theory ever since. In view of that fact, the tendency in both undergraduate and graduate textbooks to claim that GE theory is merely a rigorous formulation of what Adam Smith meant by the metaphor of the invisible hand is not just a historical travesty but an almost deliberate attempt to gloss over the fundamental difference between a process and an end-state conception of competition (Blaug, 1992: 163).[4]

THE SOCIALIST CALCULATION DEBATE

That brings me to a final point about GE theory which is intimately connected with my central argument about competition. It is a point about the strange fall-and-rise history of GE theory in connection with the socialist calculation debate of the 1930s. The story, quickly told, goes something like this: in the years before the First World War, GE theory was generally greeted with unmitigated hostility from the economics profession because it was thought to be too mathematical, too abstract, too impractical; as late as 1923 it was only the bowdlerized version of Walras laid down in Gustav Cassel's *Theory of Social Economy* (1918) that conveyed the essence of GE theory to English-speaking economists (without mentioned Walras by name). I doubt if by 1930 there were more than a half-dozen economists in the world who had ever looked at Walras's *Elements*. And then from this virtual state of oblivion began the rise which has brought GE theory to the front ranks of economic theory in our own times. It was (Henry) Schultz, Hicks, Hotelling, Lange and Samuelson who were responsible in the golden decade of the 1930s in bringing about this revival of GE theory. Of all these, the most influential was probably Oskar Lange whose little book *On the Economic Theory of Socialism* (1936–7) taught an entire generation to appreciate the supposed practical relevance of Walrasian GE theory. One of the striking features of Lange's book is that it discussed GE theory exactly as Walras had done, namely, as a realistic although rarified, abstract description of price-setting in a market economy, whether capitalist or socialist. This is striking because by the time we get to Debreu's *Theory of Value* (1959) or Arrow and Hahn's *General Competitive Analysis* (1971), GE theory is explicitly defended as a purely formal representation of the determination of economic equilibrium in a decentralized competitive economy, having no practical value except to exclude propositions that are sometimes advanced about private enterprise economies. All this is a simply remarkable gestalt-switch in the interpretation of GE theory over a period lasting but 25 years.

The socialist calculation debate, of which Lange's book was the centrepiece, was one of the most significant controversies in modern economics – and that in a decade when so much else was controversial in economics.[5] It was significant in the first place because it popularized GE theory. It was significant in the second place because it reconciled many pre-war economists to a sentimental belief in socialism. Ludwig von Mises was said to have argued that socialism was literally impossible but Lange, with the aid of the then standard theory of competition, had apparently refuted Mises, and so one could believe in both markets and socialism. Finally, it was significant because it acted as a catalyst in stimulating Hayek (1978) to go beyond Mises in reformulating the notion of economic co-ordination as an information problem, competition acting as a discovery process.

Hayek was ignored at the time if only because he was on the losing side in the debate. The overwhelming consensus of professional opinion in the 1930s, and even in the 1950s and 1960s, was that Mises was just confused and that Lange had triumphantly vindicated what Schumpeter used to call 'the bourgeois theory of socialism', namely, public ownership of all non-human factors of production combined with free markets in labour and consumer goods; in short, socialism was economically feasible. Since about 1980 or thereabouts, this consensus has been completely reversed and now the difficulty is to understand how anyone could have read Lange as a serious proposal for pricing resources under socialism, not to mention pricing them efficiently (Vaughn, 1980a; Murrell, 1983; Lavoie, 1985; Tenkin, 1989; Steele, 1992; Keizer, 1994). The Lange idea of managers following marginal-cost pricing rules because they are commanded to do so, while the central planning board in imitation of Walras's fictional auctioneer continually alters prices so as to reduce excess demands to zero, is so administratively naive as to be positively laughable. Only those drunk on perfectly competitive end-state equilibrium theory could have swallowed such nonsense, but most economists, certainly then and perhaps even now, were so inebriated.

Hayek always granted that the problem of socialist calculation was logically solvable – '*If* we possess all the relevant information if we start out from a given system of preferences, and *if* we command complete knowledge of available means, the problem which remains is purely one of logic' (Hayek, 1945: 77, original emphasis) – but the real question was whether it was practically solvable. This fundamental point was lost in the shuffle because there was nothing more characteristic of the mainstream tradition against which Hayek was struggling than the contention that if a problem is solved logically, it is solved practically: the conflation of logical rigour and practical relevance is the hallmark of formalism.[6]

But if Hayek was ignored it was in part because he too remained convinced that Walrasian GE theory was an appropriate framework discussing the question of resource allocation under socialism. If only he had insisted that *any* end-state conception of competition is no way of assessing the practical possibility of economic calculation in a socialist society, he might have been attended to. In short, the Austrian case against socialism was not a computational but an informational argument: for Mises and Hayek the question was never that of solving the million equations once they were written down but of formulating them so as to write them down in the first place: for them there simply is no unique price vector that is determined by all the individual demand and supply equations aggregated into market demand and supply equations.

PRICE THEORY OR INDUSTRIAL ECONOMICS?

By now, the reader's patience must be at an end. Very well, you will say, competition really is a process and not just an end-state but are you seriously proposing that we abandon the concept of perfect competition, the theory of general equilibrium and the New Welfare Economics associated with perfectly competitive general equilibrium? Yes, that is precisely what I am proposing.

Perfect competition is a grossly misleading concept whose only value is to generate examination questions. It is misleading because it breeds the view that economics is a subject like Euclidean geometry whose conclusions may be rigorously deduced from fundamental axioms of behaviour plus some hard facts about technology. In order to rid economics of the very notion of perfect competition, we have to get it out of the textbooks. Our task, therefore, is literally to rewrite the textbooks.

Having expunged perfect competition and Walrasian existence proofs, we must also jettison the First and Second Fundamental Theorems of welfare economics, to wit that every competitive equilibrium in a decentralized market economy is Pareto-optimal and every optimum can be achieved via perfect competition if lump-sum taxes and transfers are feasible. First of all, everyone admits that these beautiful theorems are mental exercises without the slightest possibility of ever being practically relevant: first-best optima are never actually observed and Lipsey–Lancaster showed almost 40 years ago that in second-best circumstances it is not in general desirable to fulfil any of the first-best optimum conditions; in other words, piecemeal welfare policies are based on good or bad qualitative judgements but they are not based on rigorous analytical theorems. Secondly, lump-sum taxes and transfers are politically infeasible (as Mrs Thatcher found out) and, in any case, almost always violate the ban on interpersonal comparisons of utility which motivates the whole of the New Welfare economics (Blaug, 1985: 602–3).

Second-best is an idea that is usually dismissed as a 'counsel of despair' (e.g. Scherer and Ross, 1990: 33–8). But once first-best, end-state competition is discarded as irrelevant, as precisely and rigorously wrong, and replaced by process-competition as imprecisely and loosely right, second-best has to be thrown away alongside first-best.[7]

But what are we then left with? We are left with the content of every chapter in every textbook on imperfect or monopolistic competition, on oligopoly, duopoly and monopoly, in short, one industrial organization as a sub-discipline in economics. In those chapters, firms jostle for advantage by price and non-price competition, under-cutting and out-bidding rivals in the market place by advertising outlays and promotional expenses, launching new differentiated products, new technical processes, new methods of marketing and new organizational forms, and even new reward structures for their employees, all for the sake of head-start profits that they know will soon be eroded. In these chapters, there is never any doubt that competition is an active process, of discovery, of knowledge formation, of 'creative destruction'. Now, of course, in this area there are no precise answers but that does not mean that are no quasi-operational criteria of conduct and performance in particular markets. John Bates Clark (1941; 1961; also Downie, 1958) long ago wrote down some of these criteria of 'workable competition' and, while his list has been criticized, experts on business behaviour are not willing to remain silent just because their conclusions lack the rigour of their colleagues in price theory. Thus, the leading textbook in this field (Scherer and Ross, 1990: 52–3), after a lengthy review of first-best and second-best considerations, opts for a third-best pro-competitive policy as a broad judgement.

> The competitive model does display great responsiveness of product supplies to consumer demands and generates a more potent set of incentives for the frugal use of resources than does the monopoly model. This rather than the satisfaction of all optimal conditions in a general equilibrium system of 43 quadrillion equations, may be the core of the case for competition.[8]

It is striking how many economists resist informal, consequentialist appraisals of market structures, preferring the spurious exactitude of the perfect competition model or its near-neighbour, the theory of perfectly contestable markets (Baumol, 1982; Baumol *et al.*, 1982). All in all, and despite a promising switch from demand conditions facing firms towards conditions of entry and exit, contestability theory appears to be little more than the perfectly competitive model with a dash of realism about limit-pricing (see Scherer and Ross, 1990: 374–7).

I come back, then, to what we may now call 'the Austrian view of competition' as a constant, endogenously driven process of rivalry because it is most firmly enshrined in the writings of such Austrian economists as Hayek, Schumpeter and, more recently, Israel Kirzner (see Boettke and Prychitko, 1994). It is no accident that it is associated in the last two thinkers with an interest in entrepreneurship because the entrepreneur only comes into his/her own disequilibrium (Blaug, 1986). The notion that demand conditions facing the firm and the costs of producing various levels of output are objective data that the firm can somehow obtain is one of those convenient fictions that facilitate exposition of the perfectly competitive model. In reality, the preferences of consumers must be explored and so must the production function; a firm is never actually subject to the constraints of exogenously specified demand and production functions. It is the task of the entrepreneur to manipulate these constraints to create new markets, to stretch old ones, and to discover new processes by R&D expenditures. Buchanan (1969) has argued that all costs are subjective, varying from one decision-maker to another even in the same industry, and he is quite right in circumstances out of equilibrium, that is, most of the time. It is only in first-best, end-state competitive equilibrium that subjective and objective costs coincide (Vaughn, 1980; Kirzner, 1986). In other words, whenever we imply that there are objective data in any economy, whether capitalist or socialist, on which to base prices and outputs, we have already committed ourselves to the trappings of end-state equilibrium analysis.

IN CONCLUSION

This is not a clarion call for a new paradigm for economists but merely a plea for a new emphasis, promoting industrial organization and downgrading traditional price theory of the either-perfect-competition-or-pure-monopoly variety. But while we are on the subject of sea-changes, I would welcome more of the 'New Institutional Economics', 'evolutionary economics', neo-Austrian economics, or call it what you will, with its emphasis on bounded rationality, norms of behaviour, and evolving processes (see Langlois, 1986; Witt, 1993; and Hodgson, 1993). I am not alone in sensing that the days of end-state theorizing are over. Books like Nelson and Winter (1982), with its radical use of computer simulation models of firm behaviour, or Penrose (1980), a recently reissued classic study of the growth of firms over time, are leading examples of a renewed interest in the dynamics of the 'invisible hand' (see also Klein, 1977; Brenner, 1987; Best, 1990). The end-product of these developments will be a different brand of economics from what we are used to. So long as we continue to demand the standards of rigour that we have come to accept from the highly stylized, logically tight, choice-theoretic models of mainstream microeconomics, we never will explore an alternative to end-state competitive theory. Empirical science frequently proceeds on the untidy basis of what is plausible rather than what can be formally demonstrated beyond any shadow of doubt. As Tom Mayer (1993) has argued, empirical science is precisely what characterizes much of modern physics and biology, not to mention medicine, chemistry and geology, and not the sort of mathematical formalism that is so highly praised by modern economists, which is one of the methodological legacies of general equilibrium theory and its core concept of perfect competition.

NOTES

1. When Hicks (1939: 83–4) in *Value and Capital* warned that the abandonment of the assumption of perfect competition would 'wreck' much of economic theory, he immediately went on to claim that economic theory might be saved 'if we can assume that the markets confronting most of the firms with which we shall be dealing do not differ very greatly from perfectly competitive markets'. 'Greatly' is a quantitative term but Hicks provided no way of deciding whether such an assumption is justified.
2. For an excellent exposition, see Snowdon *et al.*, 1994: 117–23.
3. It is extraordinary that the failure of Walrasian stability analysis, a failure on its own terms, is hardly mentioned by Weintraub (1991) in his detailed history of writings about economic dynamics in the period 1930–65.
4. Thus Samuelson and Nordhaus (1992: 296, 376) invoke Adam Smith as somehow foreshadowing the model of perfect competition but then chastise him gently for failing 'to prove the essence of his invisible-hand doctrine'. Of course, they really know better and immediately add that *The Wealth of Nations* is 'a practical handbook that might be entitled *How to Make the GNP Grow*'. See also Parkin (1990: 308). It is Frank Hahn who has most loudly proclaimed the Arrow–Debreu model of GE theory as the culmination of a tradition founded by Adam Smith. Loasby (1989: ch. 8) has traced Hahn's gradual disillusionment over the years with GE theory.
5. It is curious that Shackle (1967) should have failed even to mention the socialist calculation debate in his kaleidoscopic history of economic thought in the 1930s; but then he also missed the New Welfare Economics and Knight's destruction of Austrian capital theory.
6. When Hayek (1940: 188) published his final paper on the debate in 1940, he argued that the major reason Dobb and Lange had been misled was their 'excessive preoccupation with the concept of perfect competition'. We now know that Lange actually wrote to Hayek after reading his article in which he made an extraordinary admission: 'I do not propose price fixing by a real central planning board, as a practical solution. It was used, in my paper, as a methodological device to show how equilibrium prices can be determined by trial and error even in the absence of a market in the institutional sense of the word. Practically I should, of course recommend the determination of the prices by a thorough market process whether this is feasible' (Kowalik, 1994: 298). If this admission had been widely known in 1940, the notion that Lange somehow disproved Mises would never have gained currency (see Tenkin, 1989: 220n).
7. A case in point is the standard Harberger-triangle argument, seeking to measure the welfare loss of monopoly by comparing two firms, one competitive, one monopolistic, using the same marginal cost curve for both. In the first place, production costs are never the same for a competitive price-taker and a monopolistic price-maker even when they produce the same good. In the second place, a successful monopolist will invest resources in the activity of monopolizing; this adds the Tullock (1993) rectangle of 'rent-seeking' to the Harberger triangle of dead-weight loss, adding up to a much larger welfare loss from monopoly (Scherer and Ross, 1990: 661–79). This is a typical piece of competitive process reasoning.

REFERENCES

Backhouse, R.E. (1990) 'Competition', in *Foundations of Economics Thought*, ed. J. Creedy, Oxford: Blackwell, pp. 58–86.

Barro, R.J. and H.I. Grossman (1971) 'A general disequilibrium model of income and employment', *American Economic Review*, **51**(1): 82–93.

Baumol, W.J. (1982) 'Contestable markets: an uprising in the theory of industrial structure', *American Economic Review*, **72**(1): 1–15.

Baumol, W.J., J.C. Panzar and R.D. Willig (1982) *Contestable Markets and the Theory of Industrial Structure*, San Diego, Cal.: Harcourt Brace Jovanovich.

Benassy, J.P. (1986) *Macroeconomics: An Introduction to the Non-Walrasian Approach*, New York: Academic Press.

Best, M.H. (1990) *The New Competition: Institutions of Industrial Restructuring*, Cambridge: Polity Press.

Bhaskar, V., S. Machin and G.C. Reid (1993) 'Price and quantity adjustments over the business cycle', *Oxford Economic Papers*, **45**(2): 36–48.

Blaug, M. (1985) *Economic Theory in Retrospect*, 4th edn, Cambridge: Cambridge University Press.

—— (1986) 'Entrepreneurship before and after Schumpeter', in *Economic History and the History of Economics*, Brighton: Harvester Press: pp. 219–30.

—— (1992) *The Methodology of Economics*, 2nd edn, Cambridge: Cambridge University Press.

Boettke, P.J. and D.L. Prychitko (1994) *The Market Process: Essays in Contemporary Austrian Economics*, Aldershot, Hants.: Edward Elgar Publishing.

Brenner, R. (1987) *Rivalry in Business, Science, Among Nations*, Cambridge: Cambridge University Press.

Buchanan, J.M. (1969) *Cost and Choice,* Chicago: Markham.

Clark, J.M. (1949) 'Toward a concept of workable competition', *American Economic Review*, **30**(2): 241–56.

—— (1961) *Competition as a Dynamic Process*, Washington, D.C.: Brookings Institution.

Clower, R.C. (1994) 'Economics as an inductive science', *Southern Economic Journal*, **60**(4): 805–14.

Demsetz, H. (1982) *Economic, Legal, and Political Dimensions of Competition*, Amsterdam: North Holland.

Dennis, K.G. (1977) *Competition in the History of Economic Thought,* New York: Aruo Press.

Downie, J. (1958) *The Competitive Process,* London: Gerald Duckworth.

Fisher, F.M. (1983) *Disequilibrium Foundations of Equilibrium Economics*, Cambridge: Cambridge University Press.

—— (1987) 'Adjustment processes and stability', in *The New Palgrave: A Dictionary of Economics*, ed. J. Eatwell, M. Milgate and P. Newman, New York: Macmillan, **1**: 26–9.

Friedman, M. (1982) *Capitalism and Freedom*, Chicago: University of Chicago Press.

Gordon, R.J. (1981) 'Output fluctuations and gradual price adjustments', *Journal of Economic Literature*: **19**(2), 493–503.

Hayek, F.A. (1940) 'The competitive solution', *Economica*, May: reprinted in *Individualism and Economic Order*, London: Routledge & Kegan Paul, 1949: 181–208.

—— (1945) 'The use of knowledge in society, *American Economic Review*, September: reprinted in *Individualism and Economic Order*, London: Routledge & Kegan Paul, 1949: 77–91.

—— (1949) 'The meaning of competition', in *Individualism and Economic Orders*, London: Routledge & Kegan Paul, 92–106; reprinted in *Austrian Economics*, 3rd edn, ed. S. Littlechild, Aldershot, Hants.: Edward Elgar Publishing: 169–84.

—— (1978) 'Competition as a discovery of procedure', in *New Studies in Philosophy, Politics, Economics and the History of Ideas*, London: Routledge & Kegan Paul: 179–90; reprinted in U. Witt (ed.) *Evolutionary Economics*, Aldershot, Hants.: Edward Elgar, 1993, 399–410.

Hicks, J. (1974) *The Crisis in Keynesian Economics*, Oxford: Blackwell.

Hodgson, G. (1993) *The Economics of Institutions*, Aldershot, Hants.: Edward Elgar Publishing.

Ingrao, B. and G. Israel (1990), *The Invisible Hand: Economic Equilibrium in the History of Science*, Cambridge, Mass.: MIT Press.

Kahn, R. (1977) 'Malinvaud on Keynes: review article, *Cambridge Journal of Economics* **1**(4): 375–88.

Keizer, W. (1994) 'Hayek's critique of socialism', in *Hayek, Co-ordination and Evolution*, ed. J. Birner and R. Van Zijp, London: Routledge: 207–32.

Kirzner, I.M. (1986) 'Another look at the subjectivism of costs', in *Subjectivism, Intelligibility and Economic Understanding*, ed. I.M. Kirzner, London: Macmillan: 140–56.

Klein, B.H. (1977) *Dynamic Economics*, Cambridge, Mass.: Harvard University Press.

Kowalik, T. (ed.) (1994) *Economic Theory and Market Socialism: Selected Essays of Oskar Lange*, Aldershot, Hants.: Edward Elgar Publishing.

Langlois, R.N. (1986) *Economics as a Process: Essays in the New Institutional Economics*, Cambridge: Cambridge University Press.

Lavoie, D. (1985) *Rivalry and Central Planning: The Socialist Calculation Debate Reconsidered*, Cambridge: Cambridge University Press.

Leijonhufvud, A. (1968) *On Keynesian Economics and the Economics of Keynes*, New York: Oxford University Press.

Lipsey, R.G. (1984) 'Can the market economy survive?', in *Probing Leviathan: An Investigation of Government in the Economy*, ed. G. Lerner, Vancouver: Fraser Institute: 3–37.

—— (1989) *An Introduction to Positive Economics*, 7th edn, London: Weidenfeld & Nicolson.

Loasby, B.J. (1989) *The Mind and Method of the Economist*, Aldershot, Hants.: Edward Elgar Publishing.

Malinvaud, E. (1977) *The Theory of Unemployment Reconsidered*, Oxford: Blackwell.

Mayer, T. (1993) *Truth Versus Precision in Economics*, Aldershot, Hants.: Edward Elgar Publishing.

McNulty, P.J. (1967) 'A note on the history of perfect competition, *Journal of Political Economy*, **75**(4), Pt 1, August: 395–9; reprinted in *The History of Economic Thought*, ed. M. Blaug, Aldershot, Hants.: Edward Elgar Publishing, 1990: 14–18.

—— (1968) 'Economic theory and the meaning of competition', *Quarterly Journal of Economics*, **82**, November: 639–56.

—— (1987) 'Competition: Austrian conceptions', in *The New Palgrave: A Dictionary of Economics*, ed. J. Eatwell, M. Milgate and P. Newman, London: Macmillan, **1**: 536–7.

Moss, S. (1984) 'The history of the theory of the firm from Marshall to Robinson and Chamberlin: the source of positivism in economics, *Economica*, **51**, August: 307–18.

Mueller, D.C. (1986) *Profits in the Long Run*, Cambridge: Cambridge University Press.

Murrell, P. (1983) 'Did the theory of market socialism answer the challenge of von Mises? A reinterpretation of the socialist controversy', *History of Political Economy*, **15**(1), March: 92–105; reprinted in *The History of Economic Thought*, ed. M. Blaug, Aldershot, Hants.: Edward Elgar Publishing, 1990: 291–304.

Nelson, R.R. and S.G. Winter (1982) *An Evolutionary Theory of Economic Change,* Cambridge, Mass.: Harvard University Press.

Newman, P. (1965) *The Theory of Exchange*, Englewood Cliffs, NJ: Prentice-Hall.

O'Brien, D.P. (1983) 'Research programmes in competitive structures', *Journal of Economic Studies*, **10**(4); reprinted in *Methodology, Money and the Firm: The Collected Essays of D.P. O'Brien*, Aldershot, Hants.: Edward Elgar, 1994: 277–99.

—— 'Marshall's industry analysis', *Scottish Journal of Political Economy*, **37**(1), February; reprinted in *Methodology, Money and the Firm: The Collected Essays of D.P. O'Brien*, Aldershot, Hants.: Edward Elgar, 1994, 277–99.

Okun, A.M. (1981) *Prices and Quantities: A Macroeconomic Analysis*: Oxford: Blackwell.

Parkin, M. (1990) *Economics*, Reading, Mass.: Addison-Wesley.

Patinkin, D. (1956) *Money, Interest, and Prices*, New York: Harper & Row.

Penrose, E. (1980) *The Theory of the Growth of the Firm*, 2nd edn, Oxford: Blackwell.

Reder, M.W. (1982) 'Chicago economics: permanence and change', *Journal of Economic Literature*, **20**(1): March: 1–38.

Samuelson, P. and W.D. Nordhaus (1992) *Economics*, 14th edn, New York: McGraw-Hill.

Scherer, F.M. and D. Ross (1990) *Industrial Market Structure and Economic Performance*, 2nd edn, Boston, Mass.: Houghton Mifflin.

Schumpeter, J.A. (1942) *Capitalism, Socialism, and Democracy*, 2nd edn, New York: Harper.

Semmler, W. (1984) *Competition, Monopoly, and Differential Profit Rates*, New York: Columbia University Press.

Shackle, G.L.S. (1967) *The Years of High Theory: Invention and Tradition in Economic Thought 1926–1939*, Cambridge: Cambridge University Press.

Shoven, J.B. and J. Whalley (1992) *Applying Central Equilibrium*, Cambridge: Cambridge University Press.

Sloman, J. (1994) *Economics,* New York: W.W. Norton.

Snowdon, B., H. Vane and P. Wynarczyk (1994) *A Modern Guide of Macroeconomics*, Aldershot, Hants.: Edward Elgar Publishing.

Steele, D.R. (1992) *From Marx to Mises: Post-Capitalist Society and the Challenge of Economic Calculation*, La Salle, Ill.: Open Court Publishing.

Stigler, G.J. (1957) 'Perfect competition, historically contemplated', *Journal of Political Economy*, **65**, February; reprinted in *Essays in the History of Economics*, Chicago: Chicago University Press, 1965: 234–67.

—— (1987) 'Competition', *The New Palgrave: A Dictionary of Economics*, ed. J. Eatwell, M. Milgate and P. Newman, London: Macmillan, **1**: 531–5.

Stiglitz, J.E. (1987) 'The causes and consequences of the dependence of quality on prices', *Journal of Economic Literature*, **25**(1): 1–48.

—— (1993) *Economics*, New York: W.W Norton.

Takayama, A. (1985) *Mathematical Economics*, 2nd edn, Cambridge: Cambridge University Press.

Tenkin, G. (1989) 'On economic reforms in socialist countries: the debate on economic calculation under socialism revisited', *Communist Economics*, **I**(1): 31–59; reprinted in *Markets and Socialism*, ed. A. Nove and I.D. Thatcher, Aldershot, Hants.: Edward Elgar Publishing: 196–224.

Vaughn, K.L. (1980) 'Does it matter that costs are subjective?', *Southern Economic Journal*, **46**(3), January: 702–15.

—— (1980) 'Economic calculations under socialism: the Austrian contribution', *Economic Inquiry*, **18**(4), October, 535–54: reprinted in *Austrian Economics*, III, ed. S. Littlechild, Aldershot, Hants.: Edward Elgar Publishing: 332–51.

Walker, D.A. (1987) 'Walras's theories of tatonnement', *Journal of Political Economy*, **95**(4), August: 758–74.

—— (1988) 'Iteration in Walras's theory of tatonnement', *De Economist*, **136**(3): 299–316.

—— (1993) 'Walras's models of the barter of stocks of commodities', *European Economic Review*, **37**: 1425–46.

Weeks, J. (1981) *Capital and Competition*, Princeton, NJ: Princeton University Press.

Weintraub, E.R. (1991) *Stabilizing Dynamics: Constructing Economic Knowledge*, Cambridge: Cambridge University Press.

Williams, P.L. (1978) *The Emergence of the Theory of the Firm: From Adam Smith to Alfred Marshall*, London: Macmillan.

Witt, U (ed.) (1993) *Evolutionary Economics*, Aldershot, Hants.: Edward Elgar Publishing.

7. Hayek revisited*

There were many Hayeks: Hayek, the political scientist; Hayek, the economist; Hayek, the philosopher of social science; Hayek, the psychologist. Even in these different roles, he played many parts. As a political scientist, he was both the leading 'liberal' or libertarian thinker and one of the outstanding 'conservative' thinkers of the twentieth century because of his emphasis on the concept of 'spontaneous order' and his relentless attacks on 'constructivism', the idea that no human institution is viable unless it is deliberately designed. As an economist, he was the principal pre-war advocate of the Austrian 'overinvestment' theory of business cycles, in which all interest has now ceased, and a major opponent of what has been aptly called 'the Keynesian avalanche' (for even the common term 'Keynesian Revolution') amounts to an understatement of what actually happened to economic opinion after 1936).

But while the Keynesian avalanche was descending, a less publicized but equally significant discussion was taking place in respect of the economic merits of socialism. In that famous 1930s debate on 'economic calculation under socialism', set in motion by an earlier article and book by Ludwig von Mises, Hayek played a leading role that influenced the nature of the debate as much as it influenced his subsequent views about both capitalism and socialism. In the meanwhile, he continued to refine the Austrian theory of capital that underpinned his theory of business cycles, but by the time he published his long-awaited *Pure Theory of Capital* (1941), the attention of economists had turned elsewhere. Hayek then abandoned pure economic theory and turned instead to writing *The Road to Serfdom* (1944), a best-seller which for some years made him a household name with the general public.

Although some of his greatest papers in economics were still to come, the next few decades saw more work in the philosophy of science and psychology than in economics proper. Hayeks's interest in monetary economics, however, returned after the Nobel Prize of 1974, in particular with reference to the theory of free banking or the denationalization of money. Nevertheless, the great work of the 1970s was the four volumes of *Law, Legislation and Liberty*, which summed up a lifetime interest in the political constitution of modern society.

But even all this was not the sum total of Hayek's efforts. If he had never written a word on the topics listed above, he would be remembered as a

* First published in *Critical Review*, 7(1), 1993: 51–60.

historian of ideas. Fritz Machlup's survey of Hayek's contributions to economics, commissioned by the Swedish Academy of Sciences on the occasion of Hayek's joint Nobel Prize in Economics in 1974, listed the following publications in the area of the history of economic thought: 24 articles and essays on individual writers; six comprehensive surveys of schools of thought and intellectual movements; one book (on *John Stuart Mill and Harriett Taylor*); and five books by major economists of the past edited or introduced. In addition, several of Hayek's topical books contact large chunks devoted to presentations of the history of some particular stream of ideas.[1]

Hayek's career raises many puzzles and sometimes takes on the appearance of an endless trail of unresolved or only partly resolved issues. Was Hayek truly 'Austrian' in his approach to the philosophy of economics, or did the influence of Karl Popper eventually overwhelm those of Menger and Mises? Why did Hayek abandon technical economics during the Second World War and in particular why was he silent after 1935 about the rising tide of Keynesian macroeconomics? Similarly, why did he become increasingly critical of general equilibrium theory, and indeed of any version of equilibrium economics, in the course of the socialist calculation debate? Finally, why did his interest in the concept of spontaneous order and the history of the doctrine of unintended social consequences undergo very little development after the 1960s? All of his political writings are in fact amazingly repetitious, exploring a small number of big themes which, however, are not further refined or extended in new contexts. As organizing concepts, they held, I am convinced, enormous potentialities but nevertheless Hayek himself failed to realize them.

THE BATTLE WITH KEYNESIAN ECONOMICS

Let us begin with the most obvious puzzle: Hayek's withdrawal from technical economics in the 1940s and his earlier refusal to go on battling against Keynes. Let us remind ourselves that Hayek and Lionel Robbins, both at the London School of Economics, were Keynes's most conspicuous opponents in the 1930s. It is a signal fact, crucial to the unprecedented speed with which the Keynesian Revolution conquered mainstream economics, that its two principal critics quit the battlefield in the crucial years 1936–9. Hayek having published *Prices and Production* (1931) and *Monetary Theory and the Trade Cycle* (1933) and Robbins having published *The Great Depression* (1934), neither of them made any further statement on the nature of the trade cycle (apart from one or two journalistic pieces) until the 1940s.

Hayek explained his own silence in those critical years as a reluctance to repeat his earlier experience of criticizing Keynes's *Treatise on Money*. Keynes simply capitulated and sat down to write a new book, *The General Theory*; Hayek thought that Keynes would eventually change his mind about this book as he had changed his mind about the earlier one, so all he had to do was to wait. I think that this account offered in 1966,[2] is disingenuous, a rationalization after the fact. What Hayek was really doing in the late 1930s was writing *The Pure Theory of Capital* (1941), which proved much longer in the making than he had imagined and which he had hoped would finally establish Austrian business cycle theory on a firm foundation.[3] But the book failed to make any impact, in part because wartime circumstances turned the attention of economists away from purely technical problems in economic theory and in part because Hayek offered no solution to the *pons asinorum* of Austrian business cycle theory, the measurability of 'the average period of production'; indeed, he even went so far as to reject the very concept of the period of production or its corollary, the 'period of investment'.

The Austrians' theory of business cycles attributed slumps to over-investment in the previous boom financed by credit expansion, or what they called the 'undue lengthening of the period of production'. Capital in Austrian theory is always a thing of two dimensions, magnitude and duration, and the investment of capital always means either more capital or the same amount of capital left in existing processes for a longer period of time. Now, as every clever student in the history of economic thought knows, Böhm-Bawerk, the inventor of the concept of the average period of production, never succeeded in defining the average period of production independently of the rate of interest; as Wicksell showed, it was itself a function of the interest rate and hence could not be employed to explain the determination of the latter.[4] In short, the average period of production is not an adequate measure of the capital intensity of an economy; hence we never can say unambiguously that there is an increase of capital in a boom – and even if we could, we never can say that this implies a longer period of production in response to a fall in the rate of interest. In the absence of an adequate metric of capital, reducing it effectively to the time taken to transform inputs into output via production, the Austrian theory of business cycles is simply empty at its very centre. I believe that Hayek failed to engage Keynes after the publication of *The General Theory* because he could not formulate an Austrian counter-theory of the slump that was proof against purely technical objections to the standard Austrian measurement of capital.

His last effort to do so came in 1939 with the introduction, in *Profits, Interest and Investment*, of 'the Ricardo Effect' – Hayek's term for the tendency to shift to shorter and less roundabout methods of production as real wages fall and the rate of interest rises in a boom, and vice versa in a downswing. That formulation received a savage criticism from Nicholas Kaldor in 1942, who ridiculed it as 'the concertina effect', after which it disappeared into the underworld of 'curious doctrines once believed long ago'. But Hayek never abandoned his theory and made one or two efforts in the 1960s to restate it without, however, rousing much interest in it. It has been persuasively argued in recent years that Hayek's arguments fell on deaf ears because he employed a method of analysis that was foreign to the contemporary style of economic reasoning: whereas contemporaries emphasized the comparison of static equilibrium states of income and expenditure flows, Hayek was trying to develop a dynamic theory of business cycles that involved tracing out the 'traverse' adjustment path of the capital stock of an economy from one equilibrium state to another.[5]

But quite apart from speaking a different language from his peers, not just in the 1930s and 1940s but even in the 1960s, there was the further difficulty that the underlying notions of periods of production lengthening and shortening in the process of upswings and downswings in economic activity remained hopelessly ambiguous and utterly non-operational. Most economists after 1936, including Keynes himself, were more or less convinced by Frank Knight's campaign again Austrian capital theory, which Knight based on the argument that capital could not be reduced to time, as the Austrians claimed, and that in any case the length of the period of production did not much matter.[6] The Austrian theory of business cycles failed therefore because it contained a fatal logical flaw, a flaw that is even more apparent today after the switching of the two Cambridges than it was in the 1930s.[7]

It was not only Hayek who failed to take the Keynesian Revolution seriously. Lionel Robbins likewise held back in attacking Keynes, hoping perhaps that Hayek's *Pure Theory of Capital* would soon rehabilitate the Austrian theory. A glance at the pages of the *Economic Journal* in the years 1936–9 should have revealed the extraordinary interest that *The General Theory* had aroused, particularly among younger economists, and of course Robbins was only too aware that several of the most prominent members of the department at the LSE, such as Hicks, Kaldor, Lerner, Scitovsky and Shackle, had become converted to the new economics of Cambridge.[8] Both Hayek and Robbins badly miscalculated the swiftness of the Keynesian Revolution and hence never did succeed in mounting any attack, much less a successful attack on the house that Keynes had built.

THE SOCIALIST CALCULATION DEBATE

The reputation of Austrian economics in the inter-war period rested as much on the economic theory of socialism as on capital or business cycle theory. To most economists in, say, 1935, the name of Ludwig von Mises would have conjured up not so much the monetary overinvestment theory of business cycles as the proposition that economic calculation under socialism is not just irrational, but literally impossible without markets in which to price capital goods – which otherwise simply cannot be priced. The story of the socialist calculation debate has been told by Vaughn, Murrell, and at greatest length by Lavoie.[9] Oskar Lange's brilliant *On the Economic Theory of Socialism* (1936) was judged in its day to have provided a definitive answer to Mises – the Planning Bureau could mimic 'market socialism' by following appropriate price-adjustment rules – but in retrospect it is evident that Lange won the battle only in strictly formal terms. Mises and Hayek had the better case, but it was a case that they never managed to express convincingly. Be that as it may, Lange's book not only buried the Austrian critique of socialism but also promoted Walrasian general equilibrium theory as the appropriate framework for thinking about such issues as capitalism versus socialism. Hicks's *Value and Capital* (1939) was only a few years off, but already general equilibrium theory was becoming the standard of theoretical sophistication in microeconomics, in terms of which Austrian price theory stood condemned as antediluvian.

Hayek's appreciation of the learning and discovery aspects of the dynamic *process* of competition – as distinct from the static properties of the *end-state* of competitive equilibrium emphasized by mainstream neoclassical economics – displayed in his *Collectivist Economic Planning* and the seminal essay on 'Economics and Knowledge' (1937), strike us nowadays as remarkably original and perceptive.[10] At the time, however, they passed by without notice and even Hayek himself may not have realized how close he was to charting a wholly different territory from the 'Walrasian-inspired orthodoxy' that was beginning to emerge in the late 1930s. In two celebrated papers, 'The uses of knowledge in society' (1945) and 'The meaning of competition' (1946),[11] Hayek went on to crystallize the modern Austrian position on the pivotal role of entrepreneurship in the competitive process, 'entrepreneurship' being a constant alertness to unrealized profit opportunities. Israel Kirzner, the outstanding exponent of this modern Austrian theme, has demonstrated by close textual analysis how much both Mises and Hayek learned from the great debate with Oskar Lange in the 1930s.[12] But I contend that they did not learn in equal measure. Let anyone compare Mises's 1920 essay on 'Economic calculation in the socialist commonwealth' with the treatment of the same issue in Mises's *Human Action* (1966), written after the publication of Hayek's papers, and the point is made; there is a sophisticated awareness of disequilibrium adjustments of prices, quantities and, above all, knowledge in the later Mises that is missing in the earlier versions. In short, it is Hayek, not Mises, who deserves to be the patron saint of Austrian economics.

MISES VERSUS HAYEK

Mises and Hayek are usually paired together as exponents of Austrian economics but in fact they differed in a number of ways, in particular on methodological questions. Mises was an apriorist, someone who believed that all economic hypotheses can be inferred from fundamental postulates of economic behaviour, which are Kantian 'synthetic *a priori* propositions' in the sense that they are about reality but nevertheless are known to be true independently of any experience of reality. Mises denied the need to test economic theories by confronting them with empirical evidence because to do so would logically contradict Kantian apriorism. Hayek, on the other hand, always welcomed the empirical verification of the 'trends' or 'patterns' predicted by theoretical reasoning. He insisted that economic systems display powerful and pervasive economic regularities and certainly believed that we ought to observe these regularities so as to check that they do indeed conform to the implications of our theories.[13] Kirzner insists that Mises and Hayek really saw eye-to-eye on the validation of economic theories,[14] but a reading of Hayek's various reviews of Mises's books immediately dispels this complacent view of the two greatest third-generation Austrian economists. 'Considering the kind of battle he [Mises] had to lead', Hayek wrote in 1977, 'I understand that he was driven to certain exaggerations, like that of the *a priori* character of economic theory, where I could not follow him.'[15]

One might well ask why it matters whether Mises agreed with Hayek or not. It matters, however, a great deal to both the recent and the future evolution of Austrian economics. Until very recently, pious obeisance to the heritage of Mises imparted a powerful anti-empiricist stance to all Austrian economics and suggested to young Austrians that statistical and (God forbid) econometric testing of economic theories was *pas de rigeur*. The result was an unhealthy deductive style of economic reasoning in which the great truths of Austrian economics were derived without getting out of one's armchair.

Nevertheless, even Hayek is prone to a form of apriorism. In his great 1934 essay on Cark Menger, Hayek wrote:

> Microeconomic theory at least apart from such instances [in] which it could operate with a fairly plausible *ceteris paribus* assumption, remains thus confined to what I have called elsewhere 'pattern predictions' – predictions of the kinds of structures that could be formed from the available kind of elements. This limitation of the powers of specific prediction, which I believe is true of all theories of phenomena characterised by what Warren Weaver has called 'organised complexity' ... is certainly valid for large parts of microeconomic theory.[16]

Confronted with such a 'limitation theorem', one would appreciate examples to clarify its import and significance. What is it that we are unable to predict in microeconomics? The failure of a tax on butter to raise the price of butter, but by less than the amount of the tax? The lack of response of investment to a fall in interest rates? The ability of unemployment compensation to increase the level of unemployment via its effect on the supply of labour? The tendency of wages to be sticky downwards even in the face of unemployment? In the roughly 10,000 pages that Hayek wrote after 1934, I do not recall a single page in which we are told what we can or cannot predict in economics, in consequence of which I am still not convinced that the forecast of 'patterns' or 'trends' is the best that we can do in economics.

The publisher of *The Collected Works of F.A. Hayek*[17] has told us in the dust-jacket blurb that 'F.A. Hayek's forceful predictions of the inevitable failure of socialism and central economic planning are now rendered irrefutable by the recent collapse of the Eastern bloc', and this is certainly an example of 'pattern prediction' that comes easily to mind. But is the prediction valid? What Hayek predicted in 1935 was the imminent collapse of socialism in the USSR; even then there was the unmentioned fact that it had already survived, for better or for worse, for 18 years. From 1935, it survived for another 53 years. So, the 'inevitable failure of socialism and central economic planning' took nearly three-quarters of a century to reveal itself! Perhaps this is just another example of the limitations of predictions in economics, but I would have thought that we need to rethink the Mises–Hayek thesis about economic calculations under socialism in the light of recent events in Eastern Europe. It would appear that socialism is perfectly viable at low levels of economic development and only becomes positively unworkable when consumers begin to demand a more sophisticated mix of products. To put it another way, socialism appears to be the economics of a wartime, command economy, which begins to break down only under peacetime conditions in which there is once again the possibility of a choice between guns and butter. Socialists throughout the history of socialism always imagined that socialism was tailor-made for an economy of abundance. Instead, it seems that it makes sense only in an economy of acute scarcity and indeed is not workable in an affluent economy.

All of this is to say that the recent economic breakdowns in Eastern Europe do not in fact confirm the concrete predictions of Mises and Hayek; they have merely confirmed their intuition that socialism is a grossly inefficient economic system. We must admire their intuition because many of their contemporaries argued otherwise, but in retrospect it is clear that even they failed to recognize the precise weaknesses of socialism. Hayek went on of course to write about socialism almost to the day he died, and the political case against socialism came in time to weigh more heavily with him than the economic arguments he had earlier employed. But the fact remains that he never foresaw just how and just why the socialist economies of Poland, Hungary, the USSR and Eastern Germany would collapse in the way they did.

NOTES

1. Fritz Machlup (ed.), *Essays on Hayek*, New York: New York University Press, 1976, 43.
2. Frederick A. Hayek, 'Personal recollections of Keynes and the "Keynesian Revolution"', *Oriental Economist*, January 1966; reprinted in Friedrich A. Hayek, *New Studies in Philosophy, Politics, Economics and the History of Ideas*, London: Routledge & Kegan Paul, 1978.

3. As he testified in 1963: '[After] *Prices and Production* ... I soon became aware that the theory of capital on which I had built was much too oversimplified to carry the burden of the superstructure I had tried to build on it. The result was that I had to devote most of the next decade to providing a more satisfactory theory of capital than that I had to work with. I am afraid it still seems to me the part of economic theory which is in the least satisfactory state' (*The Collected Works of Friedrich Hayek*, vol. IV, Chicago: University of Chicago Press, 1992, 37).
4. For an explanation of this point, see Mark Blaug, *Economic Theory in Retrospect*, 4th edn, Cambridge: Cambridge University Press, 1985, 512–15.
5. Laurence S. Moss and Karen I. Vaughn, 'Hayek's Ricardo effect: a second look', *History of Political Economy*, **18**(4), 1986; reprinted in *The History of Economic Thought*, ed. Mark Blaug, Aldershot, Hants.: Edward Elgar, 1990, 328–48. I tried to criticize the Ricardo Effect in the first edition of my *Economic Theory of Retrospect* (1962) as a formally correct but totally unrealistic theorem in comparative statics – in short, I misunderstood it. I spent an hour in a Paris hotel lobby with Friedrich Hayek in 1967 explaining my criticism; he gently reproved me, but not in the terms employed by Moss and Vaughn. This is not an argument against their interpretation but merely an explanation of my lifelong fascination with the Ricardo Effect.
6. See Blaug, *Economic Theory in Retrospect*, 519–21; S. Ahmad, *Capital in Economic Theory*, Aldershot, Hants.: Edward Edgar, 1991, 438–41; Barry J. McCormick, *Hayek and the Keynesian Avalanche*, New York: Harvester Wheatsheaf, 1992, ch. 5, 99–134.
7. See Blaug, *Economic Theory in Retrospect*, 523–8. Even sympathetic commentators on Hayek's business cycle theory concede something like this, e.g. Roger W. Garrison, 'Hayekian trade cycle theory: a reappraisal', *Cato Journal*, **6**(2), 1980: 437–53; Gottfried Haberler, 'Reflections on Hayek's business cycle theory', *Cato Journal,* **6**(2), 1980: 421–35. However, other Austrian commentators simply glide over the difficulty as if this would make it go away: Mark Skousen, *The Structure of Production*, New York: New York University Press, 1990, chs. 3, 4.
8. Denis P. O'Brien, *Lionel Robbins*, London: Macmillan, 1988, 106–17.
9. Karen I. Vaughn, 'Economic calculation under socialism: the Austrian contribution', *Economic Inquiry*, **18**(4), 1980: 535–54; Peter Murrell, 'Did the theory of market socialism answer the challenge of Ludwig von Mises? A reinterpretation of the socialist controversy', *History of Political Economy*, **15**(1), 1982: 52–105; both reprinted in *Harold Hotelling, Lionel Robbins, Ludwig von Mises*, ed. Mark Blaug, Aldershot, Hants.: Edward Elgar, 1992; Don Lavoie, *Rivalry and Central Planning: The Socialist Calculation Debate Reconsidered*, Cambridge: Cambridge University Press, 1985.
10. Friedrich A. Hayek (ed.), *Collectivist Economic Planning*, London: Routledge & Kegan Paul, 1935, 201iff; 'Economics and knowledge', *Economica*, **4** (new ser.) 1937: 33–54; reprinted in Friedrich A. Hayek, *Individualism and Economic Order*, London: Routledge & Kegan Paul, 1949, ch. 2.
11. Reprinted in ibid.
12. Israel Kirzner, *The Meaning of Market Process: Essays in the Development of Modern Austrian Economics*, London: Routledge, 1992, ch. 6, 100–18.
13. On Hayek's by-no-means-unambiguous empiricism, see Terence W. Hutchison, *The Politics and Philosophy of Economics*, Oxford: Blackwell, 1981, ch. 7, 203–32; Bruce Caldwell, 'Hayek the falsificationist? A refutation', in *Research in the History of Economic Thought and Methodology*, vol. 10, ed. W.J. Samuels, Greenwich, Conn.: JAI Press, 1992.
14. Kirzner, *The Meaning of Market Process*, ch. 7, 119–36.
15. *The Collected Works of Friedrich A. Hayek*, vol. IV, 158; see also 142, 147–8, and the comments of the editor, Peter G. Klein, 9–13, who leaves no doubt that in his opinion there was a wide methodological gulf between Hayek and Mises.
16. Ibid., 103.
17. Ibid.

8. The concept of entrepreneurship in the history of economics*

Capitalism is usually defined as an economic system in which the means of production are privately held. Private ownership of the means of production involves a number of separate functions: the provision of financial capital, the employment and co-ordination of the factors of production, the administration of the entire enterprise and the ultimate power of strategic decision-making. The existence of capital markets and the invention of the principle of limited liability make it possible to separate completely the supply of financial capital from all the other functions. Likewise, the hiring of inputs and the functions of routine management and administration can be almost completely delegated to salaried employees. That leaves the power of making the fundamental decisions to invest or not to invest, to enter a new market or to leave an old one, as the only function that cannot be transferred: a businessman need not be a 'capitalist' or 'manager' but he must be a decision-maker, whether he likes it or not. It is this function and this function alone that deserves the title of 'entrepreneurship'.

Given the vital role of entrepreneurs in a private enterprise economy, the analysis of entrepreneurship must, surely, occupy a central role in the investigations of economists? Or so one might have thought before studying economics. However, when one opens any current textbook in economics, one discovers that entrepreneurship is hardly ever mentioned, or mentioned only in passing. Is this some sinister conspiracy of silence, or are economists so confused about the workings of the capitalist system as to ignore what is absolutely central to it?

It was not always thus: have been recognized in the eighteenth century as performing a definite economic function, the entrepreneur virtually disappeared from economic literature throughout most of the nineteenth century, emerging once again at the beginning of the twentieth century in the writings of certain American economists, only to disappear a second time for new and quite different reasons. It is this extraordinary coming and going of the concept of entrepreneurship in the history of economic thought that is the subject of this paper.[1]

* First published in *Liberty Fund Conference on Entrepreneurship*, ed. P. Boettke and M. Rizzo, New York: Liberty Fund, 1996.

THE CLASSICAL PERIOD

Richard Cantillon writing in the 1730s was the first economist to use the term 'entrepreneur' in the modern sense and indeed to imbue it with much of the content of later mature theories of entrepreneurship. Hitherto, it had meant simply someone who undertakes a project, a master builder, an adventurer. For Cantillon, however, the 'entrepreneur' was a merchant who engaged in market exchange for the sake of profit, that is, someone willing 'to buy at a certain price and to sell at an uncertain price', irrespective of whether the transaction involved the employment of labour in a productive process or whether it made use of funds borrowed from someone else. In short, Cantillon left no doubt of the fundamental difference between the function of the entrepreneur and that of the capitalist as an owner of capital finance.[2]

Adam Smith clearly read Cantillon but took no notice of his analysis of entrepreneurship. In *The Wealth of Nations* (1776), Smith did separate the functions of the capitalist from those of the manager and he insisted that the 'profits' of the capitalist exclude the 'wages' of management as payment for 'the labour of inspection and direction'. However, he did not distinguish in any way between the capitalist as provider of the capital 'stock' of an enterprise and the entrepreneur as the ultimate decision-maker. He made use of the terms 'projector' and 'undertaker' as the English equivalent of the French word 'entrepreneur' but only as a synonym for the business proprietor.[3]

This failure to isolate the entrepreneurial function from that of the pure ownership of capital became the standard practice of all the English classical economists. Thus, the term entrepreneur or any of its English equivalents is totally absent in the writings of David Ricardo, and so is the concept of the businessman as the very pivot of the process of production and distribution. Schumpeter (1954: 250) was quite right when he observed that 'Ricardo, the Ricardians and also Senior ... almost accomplished what I have described as an impossible feat, namely the exclusion of the figure of the entrepreneur completely. For them – as well as for Marx – the business process runs substantially by itself, the one thing needful to make it run being an adequate supply of capital.'

The absence of the entrepreneur in Marx is even more startling than its absence in Smith and Ricardo. Marx was undoubtedly the first economist in the history of economic thought to give technical progress a central place in the analysis of 'the laws of motion' of capitalism and, as I have shown elsewhere (Blaug, 1986: ch. 9), he was also the first, and for a half-century or more, the only economist to have appreciated the significance of capital-saving innovations in the process of economic growth. Despite his emphasis on the constant accumulation of capital, on the relentless pressure of competition to induce both labour- and capital-saving improvements to keep ahead of rivals, Marx too treated the running of a business as a simple adjunct to the provision of capital funds.

The only aspect of production that was problematic for Marx was what he called 'the labour process', the control and direction of the work-force so as to secure the quality of effort that could never be properly specified in a written employment contract. According to Marx, squeezing the work-force to work longer hours or to work more intensely is one of the two principal sources of extra profits for capitalists, the other being the introduction of new machinery. But there is never any problem in Marx about which new machines the capitalist is forced to introduce; likewise, in Marx there appear to be no choices to make about the size of the business, the type of products to manufacture or the sort of market to penetrate. Marx knew perfectly well that the first capitalist to introduce a novel improvement is likely to reap extra, head-start profits, but this did not lead him to single out the capacity to innovate as the feature that distinguishes one capitalist from another.

So profound was Marx's conviction that only physical production generates a surplus of output over the cost of inputs that marketing and retailing were dismissed as involving a mere redistribution of 'surplus value' created in factories. In consequence, he reduced technical progress to process innovations and lost sight altogether of product innovations and, even more importantly, of organizational innovations, which have actually loomed as large in the evolution of capitalism as new machines, new products and new means of transportation and communication. Marx, for all his acute awareness of the changing nature of capitalist development, failed to notice the great wave of organizational changes that swept the capitalist world in the 1840s and 1850s, such as the corporate form of business enterprise characterized by the limited liability of its owners, the department store, the mail-order house, the chain store and the discount house (Williamson, 1983: 101–2).

Marx recognized the fact that capitalists can borrow all their capital from banks, which is why he regarded 'interest' on capital as a deduction from the 'profits' of enterprise. He also understood that the special skills of managers, including the skills of monitoring and supervising the work force, can be hired on the labour market. But he never considered whether the residual income left over after paying the wages of management and the interest on borrowed capital corresponded to any particular economic function. He must have thought either that decision-making under uncertainty entails no risks, or that if it does, there is an unlimited supply of people in a capitalist economy willing to take such risks. At any rate, Marx simply conflated the functions of the capitalist and the entrepreneur, and in that sense carried on where Adam Smith and David Ricardo had left off. In a word, Marx, who claimed to be alone in analysing the 'laws of motion' of capitalism, had no explanation to give of the actual source of the acknowledged technical dynamism of capitalism (Rosenberg, 1994).

For the first entirely adequate statement of the entrepreneurial role, one must go not to Marx or even to Cantillon or Say, but to the nineteenth-century German economist, Heinrich von Thünen.[4] His remarkable but hopelessly obscure book, *The Isolated State*, volume 2 (1850), defined the gains of the entrepreneur as that which is left over from the gross profits of a business operation after paying (a) the actual or imputed interest on investment capital, (b) he wages of management, and (c) an insurance premium against the calculable risk of losses. The rewards of the entrepreneur, Thünen went on to say, are therefore the returns for incurring those risks which no insurance company will ever cover because they are unpredictable. Since novel action is precisely the condition under which it is impossible to predict the probability of gain or loss, the entrepreneur is 'inventor and explorer in his field' *par excellence*. This masterful grasp of the entrepreneur as the residual income claimant of a risky, unpredictable income, typified by but not confined to the innovative entrepreneur, predates the publication of the first volume of Marx's *Capital* by 17 years! Moreover, we know that Marx had read Thünen's *Isolated State*. In short, let us not say that Marx confused the role of the entrepreneur with that of the capitalist because he could not have known better.

Similarly, Marx could have read Mangoldt's *Lehre von Unternehmergewinn* (1855) whose pointed title would have taught him almost as much about entrepreneurship as Thünen. Mangoldt treated entrepreneurial profit as a rent of differential ability and emphasized, virtually for the first time, the marketing of products as an innovative activity quite distinct from the allocation of productive factors or the choice of techniques for the production of goods and services.

John Stuart Mill's *Principles of Economics* (1848) popularized the term 'entrepreneur' among English economists but nevertheless endorsed the Smith–Ricardo–Marx tradition of the entrepreneur as simply a multifaceted capitalist variously directing, co-ordinating and supervising the productive process. This disappearance of true entrepreneurship from economic theory in the classical period 1776–1870 despite Cantillon, Thünen and Mangoldt is our first historical puzzle crying out for some explanation. It has been argued (Kirzner, 1979) that the English classical economists failed to distinguish the functions of the capitalist and entrepreneur for good historical reasons. It is true that the corporate form of business organization, in which the capitalist role of the stockholders is sharply distinguished from the decision-making role of managers and entrepreneurs, had been invented centuries before. Nevertheless, until the railway mania of the 1840s, trading on the British stock exchange was largely confined to government bonds and public utility stocks, and the prevalent form of business ownership in the heyday of the Industrial Revolution was the small to medium-sized family firm, the capital funds being provided by the owner, his relatives or his friends. No wonder then that the classical economists failed to highlight the distinctive character of the entrepreneurial function.

On further reflection, however, this explanation of the neglect of entrepreneurship in English classical political economy appears unconvincing (Demsetz, 1983: 272). First there is the fact that still earlier and more primitive financial markets did not prevent Cantillon from discerning an entrepreneurial function quite distinct from that of either the capitalist or the manager. There is the further point that the classical economists clearly distinguished the wages of management from the profits of capitalist owners, on the one hand, and the ground rent of landowners from the profits of tenant-farmers, on the other, and this despite the fact that managers and owners, or landlords and farmers, were sometimes the same person. In other words, classical economists were perfectly familiar with the distinction between a pure economic function and its confused representation in an actual person.

The absence of any notion of entrepreneurship in English classical political economy remains an unsolved puzzle in the history of economic ideas. But perhaps this puzzle is a minor one compared to the relative neglect of technical progress in classical economics: in a century or so characterized by the onward march of the Industrial Revolution, the classical economists from Smith to Mill remained preoccupied by the land-using bias of economic growth and the ever-present threat of Malthusian overpopulation. Has any succession of economic thinkers before or since so utterly misjudged the prevailing historical forces of their own times?

THE NEOCLASSICAL PERIOD

The Marginal Revolution of the 1870s did not in itself make a jot of difference to the treatment of entrepreneurship. Jevons hardly mentioned the behaviour of the individual firm and never raised the question of entrepreneurship. Walras drew attention to the way the English classical economists had conflated the functions of the capitalist and that of the entrepreneur but nevertheless confined an active role for the entrepreneur to states of competitive disequilibrium; since his basic interest was in the nature of end-state equilibrium, he concluded that the entrepreneur played no lasting role in the determination of prices. When perfect competition has done its work, when we have reached short-run and long-run equilibrium, labour receives 'wages' in accordance with the marginal product of labour, capital receives 'interest' in accordance with the marginal product of capital goods, but 'profits' have been eroded, thus eliminating the entrepreneur.[5] Only Menger of the triumvirate that launched the Marginal Revolution found room for the role of the entrepreneur but he essentially reproduced the reasoning of Mangoldt and Thünen.[6]

By the turn of the century, then, the concept of entrepreneurship, while still present in the corners of received economic doctrine, had certainly faded into the background. Even Marshall gave more attention in his *Principles of Economics* (1890) to the routine activities of managers and supervisors than to the innovative activities of the entrepreneur; his discussion of entrepreneurship is, to say the least, thin and anaemic (Pesciarelli, 1992). The next chapter in the history of entrepreneurship came entirely from American writers, chiefly John Bates Clark, Frederick Hawley and, finally, the jewel in the crown of two centuries of writings on entrepreneurship, Frank Knight's *Risk, Uncertainty and Profit* (1921). Knight began by elaborating on Thünen's distinction between 'risk' and 'uncertainty'. Many uncertainties of economic life are like the chances of dying at a certain age: their objective probability can be calculated, and, to that extent, can be shifted via insurance to the shoulders of others; such risks thus become an element in the costs of production, a deduction from and not a cause of profits or losses. There are other uncertainties, however, that can never be reduced to objective measurement because they involved unprecedented situations. 'The only "risk" which leads to a profit', Knight remarked, 'is a unique uncertainty resulting from an exercise of ultimate responsibility which in its very nature cannot be insured nor capitalised nor salaried' (quoted by Hébert and Link, 1988: 71).

The beauty of Knight's argument was to show that the presence of true uncertainty about the future may allow entrepreneurs to earn positive profits despite long-run equilibrium and product exhaustion in accordance with marginal productivity. Production takes place in anticipation of consumption and since the demand for factors of production is derived from the expected demand of consumers for output, the entrepreneur is forced to speculate on the price of his/her final product. But it is impossible to determine the price of the final product without knowing what payments are being made to the factors of production. The entrepreneur resolves this dilemma by guessing the future price at which output will sell, thereby translating the *known* marginal physical products of the factors of production into their *anticipated* marginal value products. Although the factors are hired on a contractual basis and therefore must be paid the full value of their anticipated marginal value product, the entrepreneur may make a windfall gain as a residual, non-contractual income-claimant if actual receipts prove greater than forecasted receipts.

Knight denied that this uncertainty theory of profits provides some sort of social justification for profits as a personal income. We cannot describe this non-contractual, windfall gain as a necessary price that must be paid for the performance of a specific service, he argued, for that would imply a definite connection between the level of profit and the burden of bearing uncertainty. But no such definite connection exists; if it did exist, uncertainty-bearing would have all the characteristics of a productive factor and marginal productivity theory would apply to it: profits would equal the marginal product of entrepreneurship and would therefore constitute a standard charge on production. But profits are the windfall difference between the expected and realized returns of an enterprise and as such would cease to exist in a stationary economy in which all future events could be perfectly foreseen. So, it is not that profits are 'justified' under capitalism but that the capitalism is one way of ensuring that someone, anyone, is willing to assume the gamble of undertaking production under uncertainty. This gamble can be socialized by collective ownership of the means of production, and we can then ask: which system is better at generating successful gambles? What we cannot do is to deny that production in any economic system necessarily involves a gamble.

Knight's book, although published over 70 years ago, has withstood criticism remarkably well. There was little problem in assimilating his contributions to orthodox ideas because Knight did not question static economic analysis so far as it went. Unfortunately, he failed to persuade orthodox economics that the uncertainty theory of profits was anything more than a footnote to mainstream analysis, tying together some loose ends that had been left lying around ever since Adam Smith. Economics was now provided with a satisfactory explanation of profits and entrepreneurship but, of course, the main focus of analysis continued to be the pricing of factors of production in accordance with marginal productivity principles under stationary conditions.

Ten years before the appearance of Knight's book, the young Schumpeter had contributed a wholly different view of *the* economic problem in *The Theory of Economic Development* (1911). In this book, entrepreneurship and its connection with dynamic uncertainty is placed at the centre of economic enquiry.[7] As is well known, Schumpeter developed his argument by constructing a model of an economy in which technical change of any kind is absent by assumption. Such an economy, he contended, would settle down to a repetitive and perfectly routine steady-state growth path. Since the future is known with perfect certainty, in such an economy there would be no profits and, moreover, even the rate of interest would fall to zero. In short, competitive long-run stationary equilibrium as visualized in traditional theory rules out both profit and interest. Schumpeter's claim that only technical innovations and dynamic change can produce a positive rate of interest has been hotly disputed (see Böhm-Bawerk, cited by Streissler, 1994: 34; Haberler, 1951; Samuelson, 1981) but at the expense of considering his associated views on innovation and enterprise. Distinguishing between 'invention' and 'innovation' – the discovery of new technical knowledge and its practical application to industry – and defining 'innovations' broadly as the introduction of new technical methods, new products, new sources of raw materials and new forms of industrial organization, Schumpeter traced all disrupting economic change to innovations and identified the innovator with the entrepreneur. The entrepreneur is the source of all dynamic change in an economy, and accordingly, the capitalist system cannot be understood expect in terms of the conditions giving rise to entrepreneurship.

No doubt, all these distinctions are now perfectly familiar but, I emphasize again, they were first enunciated in German in 1911 and even when repeated in English in 1934 they were startlingly original and radical in the emphasis they gave to the subject of technical progress.[8] Let us add that for Schumpeter, as for all previous theorists of entrepreneurship, the entrepreneur represented a functional role that was not necessarily embodied in a single physical person and certainly not in a well-defined group of people. The entrepreneur might also be a capitalist or even a corporate manager, but whether all these different functions were combined in one or more persons depended on the nature of capital markets and on the forms of industrial organization. 'The entrepreneur *is* what the entrepreneur *does*' is the way one modern commentator (Casson, 1995: 104) puts it. But Schumpeter went even further than his predecessors in recognizing that the same person may be an entrepreneur when he/she is innovating, only to lose that character as soon as he/she has built up the business and settled down to running it along routine lines. Thus, the actual population of entrepreneurs in a capitalist economy is conceived as constantly changing because the function of entrepreneurship is typically mixed up with other kinds of activity.

Schumpeter's influence on entrepreneurial theory has been overwhelming and subsequent writers on entrepreneurship have usually defined their own position by contrasting it with his. Did I say: subsequent writers on entrepreneurship? Yes, Israel Kirzner in the 1970s, Mark Casson in the 1980s and William Baumol in the 1990s; but, nevertheless, mainstream economics continues to ignore entrepreneurship. Having surfaced in Knight and Schumpeter in the inter-war years, the concept of entrepreneurship has once again faded into the background. Consult any elementary textbook of economics in the last 60 years and it will prove to be rich in the treatment of consumer behaviour, the profit-maximizing decisions of business firms, the theory of wages, the theory of interest, the theory of international trade, and so forth, but poor in the analysis of technical change, the growth of big business, the causes of wealth and poverty of nations – and the theory of entrepreneurship.

THE DISAPPEARANCE OF ENTREPRENEURSHIP

We are now at the heart of the central question that is raised by any history of the theory of entrepreneurship: why has modern neoclassical economics consistently neglected entrepreneurship? In one sense, the answer is obvious: so long as economic analysis is preoccupied with the nature of static equilibrium under conditions of perfect competition, as it has been for a half-century or more, there is simply no room either for a theory of entrepreneurship or for a theory of profits (Baumol, 1968; Leff, 1979; Kirzner, 1979, ch. 7). Precisely how economic theory came to be so exclusively concerned with comparative statics, perfect competition, perfect certainty, etcetera, is a complicated story and we can only sketch that story here in very general terms. It is made up, I believe, of three strands: (a) the triumph of an end-state conception of competition after a century or more of a dominant process-conception; (b) the rediscovery and eventual ascendancy of Walrasian general equilibrium theory; and (c) the increasing mathematization of economics in something like a 'formalist' revolution after the Second World War.

Let me briefly explain each of these in turn. Somewhere in the 1930s, largely as a result of the writings of Edward Chamberlin and Joan Robinson on monopolistic or imperfect competition, there occurred a veritable sea-change in the way economists conceived of competition. Until then, in Adam Smith, in Alfred Marshall, in virtually every great economist you can think of, competition was conceived of as a process of rivalry between consumers for a limited supply of goods and between producers for a limited volume of demand, involving on the part of firms not just price adjustments but also various forms of non-price competition, including quantity-adjustments. Cournot as far back as 1838 had already conceived of something called 'perfect competition' in which the number of sellers is so large that each seller must take the price as given, but no one regarded this as anything more than a hypothetical model of business behaviour under extreme conditions, unlikely ever to be observed. But this notion of competition as the end-state of a process taking place in real time – what one author has wittily called 'the quantity theory of competition' – came to be the dominant conception of competition in the pre-war and immediate post-war literature on price theory (Blaug, 1995). With this exclusive concentration on the nature of the end-state equilibrium produced by competition came the further idea of perfect knowledge of the production function as a complete specification of the technological constraints on the quantity-responses of a business firm. Now, whatever is meant by entrepreneurship, whether it is the arbitrage function *à la* Cantillon, or the co-ordination function *à la* Say, or the innovation function *à la* Schumpeter, or the uncertainty-bearing function *à la* Knight, there is no room for entrepreneurship in the neoclassical theory of the firm. There is no arbitrage because all adjustments are instantaneous; there is no co-ordination because all the constraints on the use of inputs are fully known; there is no innovation because novelty of any kind would imply some uncertainty about the future, and there is perfect knowledge of the future. In short, we can have either entrepreneurship or the neoclassical theory of the firm but we cannot have both (Barreto, 1989: 132–3).[9]

This tendency in neoclassical economics to emphasize equilibrium at the expense of disequilibrium was immensely strengthened by the strange decline and rise of Walrasian general equilibrium theory. Walras had invented general equilibrium theory in the 1870s but the questions he raised – does multi-market equilibrium exist? is it unique? is it stable? – were perhaps too new to his fellow economists to gain him an audience. In any case, by 1900 or even 1930, there were not more than a dozen economists in the world who had ever read Walras and not more than three or four who had really understood what he was saying. In short, by 1930 Walrasian general equilibrium theory seemed moribund if not actually dead.

And then, in the decade of the 1930s, it began its slow upward march which brought it eventually to the forefront of economic debates in the 1950s – and it has never looked back since. This remarkable reinvention of an almost defunct tradition of economic thought was the result of the writings of four prominent economists of the pre-war period, namely, Harold Hotelling, John Hicks, Oskar Lange and the young Paul Samuelson (Blaug, 1995). Of all these, the most influential was probably Lange who little book *On the Economic Theory of Socialism* (1938) taught an entire generation to appreciate the supposed practical relevance of Walrasian general equilibrium theory. One of the striking features of Lange's book is that it discussed general equilibrium theory exactly as Walras had done, namely as a realistic, although rarefied, abstract description of price-setting in a market economy, whether capitalist or socialist. This is striking because by the time we get to Gerard Debreu's *Theory of Value* (1950) or Arrow and Hahn's *General Competitive Analysis* (1971), general equilibrium theory is explicitly defended as a purely formal representation of the determination of multi-market equilibrium in a decentralized competitive economy, having neither descriptive nor practical value, expect perhaps to undermine the logical cogency of extreme propositions that are sometimes advanced about private enterprise economies. All this is a simply remarkable *Gestalt*-switch in the interpretation of the meaning and significance of Walras's message over a period of less than a generation.

Let us remember that Walras had posed three great questions about general equilibrium: does it exist? is that existence unique? and is it both locally and globally stable? The Walrasian research programme had some success with respect to the first of those questions: Arrow and Debreu in the 1950s rigorously demonstrated the existence of multi-market equilibrium under very general assumptions, some of which, however, did not accord with any observed economic system (such as the absence of money held in preference to other interest-bearing assets, the absence of market-makers holding inventories, the absence of bank credit, and the existence of forward markets for all goods and services in all conceivable contingencies). However, as far as uniqueness and stability were concerned, the assumptions required to obtain definite results were so restrictive and patently *ad hoc* (e.g. all commodities must be gross substitutes for all other commodities) as to be unacceptable even to those deeply enamoured of general equilibrium theory. In short, after a century or more of endless refinements of the central core of general equilibrium theory, the theory has made no substantial progress on Walras's own theorizing and is even now unable to shed any light on how market equilibrium is actually attained, not just in a real-world decentralized market economy but even in the blackboard economies beloved of general equilibrium theorists. Walras himself had eliminated disequilibrium trading by assumption because he was unable to establish even the existence, much less the uniqueness and stability of general equilibrium once out-of-equilibrium trading was allowed. And today, the leading study of the *Disequilibrium Foundations of Equilibrium Economics* (1983) by Franklin Fisher is perforce driven to the conclusion that 'we have no rigorous basis for believing that equilibrium can be achieved or maintained if disturbed'. Economics is sometimes described as a study of the working of 'the invisible hand'. But 'what we economists have yet to explain', as Robert Clower (quoted in Blaug, 1995) has rightly said, 'is the workings of the *fingers* of the invisible hand'.

We have said enough about the role of the entrepreneurship in the history of economics to show that, whatever entrepreneurship is, it comes into play only when markets are in a state of disequilibrium. But modern economics, in going down the road of Walrasian general equilibrium theory, has made it impossible to consider competition as anything other than an end-state of fully realized equilibrium. Is it any wonder then that entrepreneurship in modern economics is conspicuous by its absence?[10]

RECENT THEORIES OF ENTREPRENEURSHIP

As we said earlier, mainstream economics has continued to neglect Schumpeter's writing on entrepreneurship as it continues to neglect Knight's theory of profits because neither fits in with static equilibrium analysis. The theory of entrepreneurship has, however, been given a new lease of life by the modern Austrian School, descending from Ludwig von Mises to Friedrich Hayek. In two closely reasoned books, *Competition and Entrepreneurship* (1973) and *Perception, Opportunity and Profit* (1979), Israel Kirzner has sought once again to persuade his fellow economists that the properties of disequilibrium states deserve as much attention as those of equilibrium states. Disequilibria are due to interspatial and intertemporal differences in demand and supply and hence give rise to unrealized profit opportunities. Therefore, the essence of entrepreneurship for Kirzner consists in a personal alertness to such potential sources of gain. There is a subtle change of emphasis in Kirzner's discussion of entrepreneurship from that of Schumpeter: Schumpeter always portrayed the entrepreneur-innovator as a disequilibrating force disturbing a previous equilibrium, whereas Kirzner depicts him/her as seizing upon a disequilibrium situation and working to restore equilibrium.

The Kirznerian theory of entrepreneurship, like that of Cantillon, reduces entrepreneurship to either arbitrage or speculation, that is, to either interspatial or intertemporal transactions, and that has struck some as watering down entrepreneurship to a pale reflection of the real thing. Both Loasby (1983: 223) and Ricketts (1992; 1994: 57–8, 61) criticize Kirzner for treating entrepreneurial profit as an income waiting to be discovered – a serendipitous return, so to speak – rather than an income at least partly created by the entrepreneur. Moreover, it may not be easy to distinguish 'rent-seeking' as the socially costly, unproductive pursuit of transfer incomes, from productive, value-added profit-seeking, a point Buchanan (1980) has made against Kirzner. Is the alertness of the shop-lifter rent-seeking or entrepreneurship? asks Ricketts (1992), echoing Buchanan. Indeed, Baumol (1993) has tried to write down a general theory of entrepreneurship entirely in terms of the allocation of venturesome effort between productive profit-seeking and unproductive rent-seeking. As typical examples of rent-seeking, he cites takeover bids, patent litigation, tax evasion efforts, and the like, but he too emphasizes the difficulty of drawing a line between, say, a financial merger between two companies as an instance of rent-seeking and the production and sale of narcotics as an instance of profit-seeking. An activity such as political lobbying may be rent-seeking or profit-seeking depending on whether from a social point of view it is a negative or positive sum game (Tullock, 1996). Nevertheless, the rent-seeker who lowers the national product is just as alert as the entrepreneur-cum-profit-seeker who adds to it.

This idea that profit in Kirzner, being a windfall return to alertness, is a costless 'unearned' income has struck a number of commentators as inherently objectionable. Theodore Schultz (1990: 130–4), defining entrepreneurship as 'the ability to deal with disequilibria', attacks Kirzner for denying that there is such a thing as a supply curve for entrepreneurship as if 'alertness' required no investment and hence involved no identifiable costs. Although this particular criticism is somewhat confused,[11] it is true that entrepreneurs in Kirzner never seem to make mistakes and never seem to suffer losses. Kirzner (1992b, 1994a, 1994b) has defended himself against the criticism that the alertness theory of entrepreneurship abstracts from uncertainty or the possibility of entrepreneurial losses; moreover, he conceded that entrepreneurship requires the creation, and not simply the recognition, of exploitable profit opportunities.

The very fact that Kirzner has no real difficulty in granting every objection to his theory of entrepreneurship indicates what may be wrong with it.[12] Flesh-and-blood entrepreneurs are variously co-ordinators, supervisors, contractors, risk-taking innovators, ultimate decision-makers, employers of labour and even legal owners of enterprises, and yet all these functions are to be reduced to either arbitrage or speculation, according to Kirzner. At a high level of abstraction, all the functions associated with entrepreneurship do indeed boil down to arbitrage and speculation in states of disequilibrium and, yes, entrepreneurship might be construed as a label for all the forces that bring markets into equilibrium.

But that is not to say that entrepreneurship is nothing more than the process by which markets are cleared. Entrepreneurship may be a functional rather than a personal role but the functions of entrepreneurship are necessarily mingled in one or more persons. Furthermore, the person carrying out the entrepreneurial function does incur opportunity costs in terms of time, mental effort, anxiety at the danger of losses and the risk of a damaged reputation. Who can deny that 'if the political system allows persons to retain a larger fraction of the profit created by being alert to lucky events there will be more alertness – a response difficult to reconcile with a belief that alertness requires no cost in terms of resources' (Demsetz, 1983: 279)?

In all these criticisms of Kirzner, much confusion is created by the assumption that the equilibrating theory of entrepreneurship in Kirzner is not essentially different from the disequilibrating theory of entrepreneurship in Schumpeter. But in fact these involve strikingly different conceptions of the purpose of a theory of entrepreneurship. Kirzner's formulation, whether in its earlier or later versions, was geared to he explanation of market processes, that is, to the way in which markets actually succeed in reaching a final equilibrium state. Such an analysis of market processes is perfectly compatible with a Schumpeterian theory of economic chance, but it is designed to deal with a different problem from that which motivated Schumpeter. In short, entrepreneurial activity may indeed be categorized into three major classes – arbitrage, speculation and innovation (Casson, 1995: 105–7) – but that blurs what is a distinction between a theory of market processes in any economy, whether stationary or expanding, and a theory of technical progress in a growing economy. The entrepreneur in Kirzner is someone who buys cheap and sells dear in circumstances where others are resting on their laurels. The entrepreneur in Schumpeter is almost but not quite a swashbuckling business tycoon. No wonder these two images cannot be made to jell.

A NON-AUSTRIAN CONTRIBUTION

A valuable but non-Austrian approach to the theory of entrepreneurship is offered in a study by Mark Casson (1982, 1987) who synthesizes and extends the ideas of Knight, Schumpeter, Kirzner and many others. Casson (1982: 23) defines an entrepreneur as 'someone who specialises in taking judgemental decisions about the co-ordination of scare resources', every term in this definition being carefully chosen to highlight the specific content of the entrepreneurial role. The entrepreneur is a person, not a team, committee or organization, and he/she is someone who has a comparative advantage in making decisions; moreover, he/she reaches a different decision from other people in the face of identical circumstances either because of access to better information or, more typically, because of a different interpretation of the same information.[13] The entrepreneurial function is, in principle, performed in all societies by individuals whose judgement differs from the norm, and military and political life may provide as much scope for entrepreneurship as the economic one; even under communism, entrepreneurship was exercised behind the façade of legal markets. Capitalism, then, is simply an economic system that harnesses entrepreneurship to industrial decisions. Even economic entrepreneurship under capitalism, however, may range from Kirznerian arbitrage and financial speculation to Schumpeterian non-routine decisions of salaried managers and the daring innovations of self-employed businessmen. It is perfectly true, as Schumpeter used to argue, that ownership and entrepreneurship are conceptually separate functions and that one can be an entrepreneur without being a capitalist. Nevertheless, Schumpeterian entrepreneurship in practice is likely to be packaged together with asset ownership because financial intermediaries are reluctant to lend to an entrepreneur precisely because the entrepreneur's assessment of a situation necessarily differs from everybody else's assessment, including that of the lender. In other words, personal wealth, or at least the wealth of friends and relatives, is in fact a major constraint on the scale of entrepreneurial activity, and bank credit has only a limited role to play in providing finance to entrepreneur.[14]

Casson's theory throws new light on the long-lived reluctance in classical economic thought to divorce proprietorship from entrepreneurship, thus identifying the capitalist with the entrepreneur. The industrial entrepreneur frequently was and still is a capitalist, and this association between the two roles is not accidental but stems from the very nature of entrepreneurship as consisting of an eccentric evaluation of economic events that other people are unwilling to support. Casson's theory also clears up another long-standing bone of contention in the history of entrepreneurship (see Hébert and Link, 1988: 25–6). Schumpeter always insisted paradoxically that risk-bearing is not an entrepreneurial function, and that all the risks of an enterprises are borne by the capitalist. As we have seen, Kirzner too denies that entrepreneurship involves risks and hence costs. Casson, however, argues that the profits of entrepreneurship are 'earned income' in the true sense of the term. In the short run, the entrepreneur's reward is a 'rent of ability', a temporary monopoly rent to judgement, and in the long run it is in fact a necessary compensation for the time and effort involved in identifying and making judgemental decisions and obtaining financial backing to undertake the search for information. Since it is frequently the entrepreneur's own wealth that supports this activity, the entrepreneur risks his own capital but, in addition, he always risks the opportunity cost of his time and effort and the value of his good will for future operations. It is clear that, despite Casson's wide-angled vision of entrepreneurship, his discussion stays closer to the Schumpeterian than to the Kirznerian end of the spectrum of theories about entrepreneurship.

Be that as it may, private ownership of the means of production and private entitlement to the profits of entrepreneurship do not lack economic justification. Entrepreneurship may be a universal feature of all society but capitalism provides a unique institutional setting to release the entrepreneurial spirit. The technical dynamism of capitalism, which Marx attributed to the organizational invention of the factory, the despotic control of workers by capitalists, and the restless urge of the bourgeoisie to save and invest, must instead by credited in large part to the institution of private property, which channels the entrepreneurial spirit into productive outlets where previously it remained locked into speculative and purely merchandizing activity. It provides, as Baumol (1993) puts it, the institutional structure that makes profit-seeking pay off more than rent-seeking. If we fully understood that structure of payoffs, we would at long last be near to answering the great question with which economics began: what are the causes of the wealth of nations?

NEW THEORIES OF THE FIRM

We said earlier that there is no room for entrepreneurship in the neoclassical theory of the firm. However, this theory has not stood still and seems lately to have evolved in ways that may eventually give scope to a theory of entrepreneurship. I refer to the so-called New Institutionalist theory of the firm that has grown out of Coase's pioneering article 'The nature of the firm' (1937). For Coase, firms exist to supersede the market because the transaction costs involved in multiple exchanges are more cheaply conducted by fiat within an organization called the firm than by the price co-ordinating relationships between firms. Not so, argued Alchian and Demsetz (1972) in an equally influential article published 35 years after Coase; what accounts for the existence of firms is the problem of monitoring and policing the individual members of a productive team, the residual rewards of this effort going to the 'monitor', who may of course be more than one person. They carefully avoided the use of the term 'entrepreneur' but they did insist that the notion of a residual claimant in the firm has nothing to do either with uncertainty or risk-aversion or authority: both Knight and Coase (and incidentally Marx) are simply wrong, argued Alchian and Demsetz (1972: 31–2). Barzel likewise explains the nature of the firm by the measurement and policing costs of monitoring but he views the entrepreneur's non-contractual status as playing the role of avoiding what would otherwise be a moral hazard problem: who monitor the monitor if he did not monitor himself? (see Eggertsson, 1990: 165–70). Enough has now been said to suggest that the new institutionalist theory of the firm shows every sign of taking account of entrepreneurship – although not quite yet. It is still far from clear whether this is an equilibrium theory of the firm – equilibrium subject to transaction costs – or a disequilibrium theory, since transaction costs – the costs of making deals and seeing that they are implemented – are in a constant state of flux by virtue of competitive rivalry.

WHERE DO WE GO FROM HERE?

The very fact that entrepreneurship involves imagination, vision, creative effort and the discovery of novelty has been advanced more that once as the reason that a systematic analysis of entrepreneurship is literally impossible (e.g. Baumol, 1983). Even in Keynes, investment undertaken by entrepreneurs depends, not on any 'reasonable calculation', but on 'animal spirits', a spontaneous urge to action for its own sake, and clearly spontaneity cannot be standardized and therefore described in general terms. Are all attempts at a *theory* of entrepreneurship therefore doomed?

Economists are inclined to settle all such questions by further attempts at purely analytical refinement: the notion is that deeper thought will one day resolve all difficulties surrounding the concept of entrepreneurship. But perhaps here is an occasion to try a different approach, an inductive one, more common in the other social sciences than it is in economics. What conditions encourage or discourage entrepreneurship? What sort of people become entrepreneurs and what sorts of skills make up the successful entrepreneur? Why is entrepreneurship more common in some societies than in others and more common in some historical periods than in others? There are 'stylized facts' that need explaining, such as that innovations are rarely the dramatic breakthroughs that Schumpeter may have had in mind but rather small improvements in a new process or product in which genuine novelty and imitation-with-a-difference shade imperceptibly into one another. Some tentative examples of this sort of research are already in evidence (Ronen, 1983; Casson, 1982: 384–93; Baumol, 1993: chs. 2, 3; Rosenburg, 1994; Harper, 1995). It is along these lines that I am convinced we shall make further progress in coming to grips with entrepreneurship.

NOTES

1. This is a revised and expanded version of an earlier paper in Blaug (1986: ch. 12).
2. See Hébert and Link (1988), ch. 3. Hébert and Link's history of entrepreneurship is so comprehensive that I hereby abandon all references to primary sources with a single reference to their study.

3. Pesciarelli (1989) struggles to make a case for Smith but only succeeds in finding hints of the entrepreneurial function in *The Wealth of Nations*. He also credits Bentham with the Schumpeterian idea of the innovating entrepreneur and here he seems to be nearer the mark.
4. Jean Baptiste Say is frequently hailed as the first to give entrepreneurship its due but in fact he overemphasized the role of the entrepreneur as co-ordinator of inputs and virtually equated management with entrepreneurship. Say's entrepreneur is a superintendent and administrator, a superior kind of worker and, on balance, Say did almost as much to minimize the true function of entrepreneurship as Smith and Ricardo. This is say no more than what is said by Schumpeter or by Hébert and Link. However, see Rothbart (1995: 25–7) for a much more favourable interpretation of Say's contribution, without however providing any supportive evidence for this heterodox reading.
5. But the idea that profits arise only in dynamic disequilibrium nevertheless proved inspiring, particularly to Schumpeter (see Walker, 1996: ch. 13).
6. Kirzner (1979: ch. 4; 1992a: ch. 5) has a much higher opinion of Menger's discussion of entrepreneurship.
7. Even 23 years later, when Schumpeter (1934: xi) wrote a preface to the English translation of his book, he found himself moved to exclaim that the central arguments of his old book 'might usefully be contrasted with the theory of [static] equilibrium, which explicitly or implicitly always has been and still is the centre of traditional theory'.
8. Streissler (1994) has discovered a number of proto-neoclassical German authors of the first half of the century, particularly K.H. Rau and A.F. Riedel, who were influential forerunners of Schumpeter in the treatment of innovative entrepreneurship.
9. As Baumol (1968: 51) put it: 'there is one residual and rather curious role left to the entrepreneur in the neoclassical model of the firm. He is the indivisible, non-replicable input that accounts for the U-shaped cost curve of a firm whose production function is linear and homogeneous! How the mighty have fallen!'
10. Hébert and Link (1988: 158) attribute the disappearance of entrepreneurship in modern economies solely to the growth of mathematical methods of analysis: this is part, but only part, of the story. Demsetz (1983: 273–4) attributes it entirely to the concern with the co-ordinating role of prices and a lack of interest in the problem of economic change, which distracted attention away from the co-ordinating problem; but this ignores Marshallian partial equilibrium analysis and identifies modern economics with Walrasian general equilibrium theory. Barreto (1989: ch. 4), on the other hand, attributes it entirely to a technical flaw in the received theory of the firm: a confusion between minimizing the cost of producing a given output in short-run equilibrium, and minimizing the cost of producing all possible output levels in long-run equilibrium, is said to run through the literature right up to the middle of the 1930s, in consequence of which the 'profits' of the entrepreneurs are thought to be fully eroded by competition. As a characterization of the pre-1935 theory of the firm, this is perfectly accurate but it is at best a superficial explanation of the disappearance of entrepreneurship in modern economics.
11. Schultz (1990: 54) insists that entrepreneurial earnings are amenable to marginal productivity theory, implying that entrepreneurship is a factor of production. But a factor of production is defined as both divisible and strictly homogeneous, neither of which is true of entrepreneurship (Blaug, 1985: 458, 593); see also Hébert and Link, 1988: 123–7). Entrepreneurship is not functionally related to a cost of deploying it and cannot be analysed in terms of demand or supply curves.
12. Vaughn (1994: 141–50) provides a critical but sympathetic account of Kirzner's theory as it has evolved over the last 20 years.
13. As Knight (1921: 280–281) put it: 'whether any particular person becomes an entrepreneur or not depends on his believing ... that he can produce services yield more than the price fixed upon them by what other persons think they can make them yield'.
14. This is in sharp contrast to Schumpeter's conviction that bank credit is a main source of finance for innovations, a belief that may have reflected contemporary patterns of bank credit in Germany and Austria (see Streissler, 1990).

REFERENCES

Alchian, A.A. and H. Demsetz (1972) 'Production, information costs and economic organisation', *American Economic Review*, **62**, December; reprinted in *The Legacy of Ronald Coase in Economic Analysis*, vol. 1, ed. S.G. Medema, Aldershot, Hants.: Edward Elgar, 1995, 25–43.

Barreto, H. (1989) *The Entrepreneur in Microeconomic Theory*, London: Routledge.

Baumol, W.J. (1968) 'Entrepreneurship in economic theory', *American Economic Review*, **58**(2); reprinted in M. Casson (ed.), *Entrepreneurship*, Aldershot, Hants.: Edward Elgar, 1990, 180–97.

—— (1983) 'Toward operational models of entrepreneurship', in J. Ronen (ed.), *Entrepreneurship*, Lexington, Mass.: D.C. Heath, 1983

—— (1993) *Entrepreneurship, Management and the Structure of Payoffs*, Cambridge, Mass.: MIT Press.

Blaug, M. (1985) *Economic Theory in Retrospect*, 4th edn, Cambridge: Cambridge University Press.

—— (1986) *Economic History and the History of Economics*, Brighton, Sussex: Wheatsheaf Books.

—— (1995) 'Competition as an end-state and competition as a process' in *Essays in Honour of Richard Lipsey*, ed. C.B. Eaton and R. Harris, Aldershot, Hants.: Edward Elgar.

Buchanan, J.M. (1980) 'Rent seeking and profit seeking', in J.M. Buchanan, R.D. Tollison and G. Tullock (eds), *Towards a Theory of the Rent-seeking Society*, College Station, Texas: A & M University Press; reprinted in *The Economic Analysis of Rent Seeking*, ed. R.D. Tollinson and R.D. Congleton, Aldershot, Hants.: Edward Elgar, 1995, 46–58.

Casson, M. (1982) *The Entrepreneur: An Economic Theory*, Oxford: Martin Robertson.

—— (1987) 'Entrepreneur', in *The New Palgrave: A Dictionary of Economics*, ed. J. Eatwell, M. Millgate and P. Newman, London: Macmillan, 1987, II, 150–53.

—— (ed.) (1990) *Entrepreneurship*, Aldershot, Hants.: Edward Elgar.

—— (1995) *Entrepreneurship and the Business Culture*, vol. 1, Aldershot, Hants.: Edward Elgar.

Demsetz, H. (1983) 'The neglect of the entrepreneur', in J. Ronen (ed.), *Entrepreneurship*, Lexington, Mass.: D.C. Heath, 1983, 271–80.

Eggertsson, T. (1990) *Economic Behaviour and Institutions*, Cambridge: Cambridge University Press.

Fisher, F. (1983) *Disequilibrium Foundations of Equilibrium Economics*, Cambridge: Cambridge University Press.

Haberler, G. (1951) 'Schumpeter's theory of interest, in *Schumpeter, Social Scientist*, ed. S. Harris, Cambridge, Mass.: Harvard University Press.

Harper, D.A. (1995) 'Entrepreneurship and liberty: institutional conditions for entrepreneurship', in *Liberty Fund Conference on Entrepreneurship and Liberty*, New York: Liberty Fund.

Hébert R.F. and A.N. Link (1988) *The Entrepreneur: Mainstream Views and Radical Critiques*, 2nd edn, New York: Praeger.

Kirzner, I. (1973) *Competition and Entrepreneurship*, Chicago: University of Chicago Press.

—— (1979) *Perception, Opportunity and Profit: Studies in Entrepreneurship*, Chicago: University of Chicago Press.

—— (1992a) *The Meaning of the Market Process: Essays in the Development of Modern Austrian Economics*, London: Routledge.

—— (1992b) 'Commentary on entrepreneurship, uncertainty and Austrian economics, in *Austrian Economics: Tensions and New Directions*, ed. B.J. Caldwell and S. Boehm, Boston, Mass.: Kluwer, 85–102.

—— (1994a) 'A tale of two worlds: comment on Shmanske', in *Advances in Austrian Economics*, ed. P.J. Boettke and M.J. Rizzo, Greenwich, Conn.: JAI Press, 223–6.

—— (1994b) 'Entrepreneurship', in *The Elgar Companion to Austrian Economics*, ed. P.J. Boettke, Aldershot, Hants.: Edward Elgar, 103–10.

Knight, F.H. (1921), *Risk, Uncertainty and Profit*, New York: Houghton Mifflin.

Leff, N.H. (1979) 'Entrepreneurship and development: the problem revisited', *Journal of Economic Literature*, **17**(1), 46–64.

Loasby, B.J. (1983) 'Knowledge, learning and enterprise', in *Beyond Positive Economics*, ed. J. Wiseman, London: Macmillan; reprinted in M. Casson (ed.), *Entrepreneurship*, Aldershot, Hants.: Edward Elgar, 1990, 220–37.

Pesciarelli, E. (1989) 'Smith, Bentham, and the development of contrasting ideas on entrepreneurship', *History of Political Economy*, **21**(3); reprinted in *Adam Smith (1723–1790)*, vol.1, ed. M. Blaug, Aldershot, Hants.: Edward Elgar.

—— (1992) 'The undertaker's role in Marshall's approach to economic growth', in *Alfred Marshall's Principles of Economics, 1890–1990*, ed. M. Dardi, M. Gallegati and E. Pesciarelli, Milan: n.p.

Ricketts, M. (1992) 'Kirzner's theory of entrepreneurship: a critique', in *Austrian Economics: Tensions and New Directions*, ed. B.J. Caldwell and S. Boehm, Boston, Mass.: Kluwer, 67–102.

—— (1994) *The Economics of Business Enterprise*, 2nd edn, New York: Harvester Wheatsheaf.

Ronen, J. (1983) *Entrepreneurship*, Lexington, Mass.: D.C. Heath.

Rosenberg, N. (1994) *Exploring the Black Box: Technology, Economics and History*, Cambridge: Cambridge University Press.

Rothbart, M. (1995) *Classical Economics: An Austrian Perspective on the History of Economic Thought*, Vol. II, Aldershot, Hants.: Edward Elgar.

Samuelson, P.A. (1981) 'Schumpeter as an economic theorist', in *Schumpeterian Economics*, ed. H. Frisch, New York: Praeger.

Schultz, T.W. (1990) *Restoring Economic Equilibrium*, Oxford: Blackwell.

Schumpeter, J. (1934) *The Theory of Economic Development*, Cambridge, Mass.: Harvard University Press.

—— (1954) *History of Economic Analysis*, New York: Oxford University Press.

Streissler, E. (1990) 'The influence of German economics in the work of Menger and Marshall', *History of Political Economy*, **22**, supplement: 31–68.

—— (1994) 'The influence of German and American economics on Joseph Schumpeter', in *Schumpeter in the History of Ideas*, ed. Y. Shionoya and M. Perlman, Ann Arbor, Mich.: University of Michigan Press.

Tullock, G. (1996) 'Rent-seeking and the law', in *Current Issues in Public Choice*, ed. U.C. Pardo and F. Schneider, Aldershot, Hants.: Edward Elgar, 179–88.

Vaughn, K. (1994) *Austrian Economics in America*, Cambridge: Cambridge University Press.

Walker, D.A. (1996) *Walras's Market Models*, Cambridge: Cambridge University Press, forthcoming.

Williamson, O.E. (1983) 'Organizational innovation: the transaction-cost approach' in J. Ronen (ed.), *Entrepreneurship*, Lexington, Mass.: 1983, 101–33.

9. Why is the quantity theory of money the oldest surviving theory in economics?[*]

My paper is prompted by another, David Laidler's 'The quantity theory is always and everywhere controversial – why?' (1991a), but my answer to the question posed by that title is different from his. Laidler believes that the theory has remained controversial because of the technical difficulty of sorting out the direction of causation between money and prices and, on a deeper level, because ideological issues about the functioning of markets are at stake in the controversy. My answer is that the theory manifests a common difficulty with most economic theories, namely, that they are expressed in logical time and not in real time; hence we are rarely provided with 'correspondence rules' to tell us how to distinguish the so-called short-run and long-run consequences of the theory. This opens the door to endless equivocation of what observations arc to count as confirmations or refutations of the theory.

Since this problem is not unique to the quantity theory of money, we ought to direct our attention to the limitations of current econometric techniques rather than to the quantity theory of money as such. But there are special features of the quantity theory of money that make it an ideal candidate for a discussion of the classic problem of testing economic theories. For one thing, this is one of the oldest reputable economic doctrines, going back to a remarkably complete statement of the theory by David Hume in 1752, and one which survived the marginal revolution of the 1870s without being affected in any of its essentials to emerge in modern times as 'the monetarist counterrevolution' to Keynes.[1] For another, it was one of the first economic theories to have been extensively 'tested', or at least massively confronted by economic data in Thomas Tooke's famous *History of Prices* (1838–57); since then it has been tested again and again by historical, statistical and econometric methods. If we still cannot agree whether and in what sense this theory is true or false, we might as well write off the truth-value of all economic ideas. Finally, it turns out that, despite two centuries of debate, the theory remains imprecisely expressed – this in a subject like economics that prides itself on analytical rigour! Precisely what

[*] First published in *The Quantity Theory of Money*, ed. M. Blaug *et al.*, Aldershot, Hants.: Edward Elgar Publishing, 1995, 27–49.

is meant by the quantity theory of money? Does it apply to any commodity-money regime or only to irredeemable fiat money? Is it essentially a long-run equilibrium theory about the relationship between the quantity of money and the level of prices, or is it rather a short-run theory about the transmission mechanism relating money and prices? Is money 'neutral' in the long run in the sense that any change in the money supply will eventually be transmitted entirely in prices, leaving real output unaffected! Does this imply that the demand curve for money is a rectangular hyperbola such that the demand for real cash balances is always a constant? Does money cause prices to change or can prices also cause money to change, in which case what is left of 'the quantity of money theory of the purchasing power of money'? Besides, why do we need a special theory of the value of money? Why not simply apply ordinary value theory to the case of money? Unanswered questions of this sort have haunted the quantity of money throughout its long history, persisting down to present times. In short, this oldest of received economic doctrines is also one of the most misunderstood economic doctrines. I argue that we can learn a great deal about what are called 'theories' in economics by studying the history of the quantity theory. Perhaps that is sufficient justification to go once more down this well-worn road.

DEFINING THE QUANTITY THEORY OF MONEY

There is absolutely no doubt that the quantity theory of money is, and always has been, a theory of the determination of the general price level, which treats it as the variable to be explained and the quantity of money as the key factor causing it to change (Humphrey, 1986: ch. 1).[2] Likewise, there has been, since at least Henry Thornton's 1803 treatise on *The Paper Credit of Great Britain*, broad agreement that the transmission mechanism between money and prices is made up of 'direct' and 'indirect' elements. When there is an exogenous increase in the supply of nominal money, it must flow into the pockets of at least some economic agents, who, being satisfied with their existing holdings of cash, will spend the extra money on goods and services; the resulting pressure on scarce resources will cause prices to rise. This is the 'direct' or 'real balance' effect of an increased quantity of money. In addition, the new money will typically be injected into the economy via the banking system. The banks will either receive new deposits or have their reserves enhanced; in either case they are liable to increase their lending operations. If we start with the bank lending rate equal to the real rate of return on physical capital, including a margin for the riskiness of physical investment, the new lower loan rate will encourage borrowing for productive investment (alternatively, technical progress may lift the real rate of return above an unchanged loan rate with similar results). Via this 'indirect' mechanism, prices will rise independently of more direct consumption spending. The sum of these two effects constitutes the reason that quantity theorists believe that an increase in the stock of money will cause prices to rise.

It is obvious from all this that the quantity theory really consists of three interrelated propositions: (a) the causal arrow runs from money M to prices P, and not from prices to money, which is to say that the initiating change in the supply of money must be assumed to exogenous; (b) there is a stable demand for nominal money-balances-to-hold, sometimes know as the velocity of circulation of money V, meaning that the demand for money changes slowly if at all and, in particular, that it changes independently of changes in the money supply; and (c) the volume of transactions T, or the volume of output Y (depending on whether we use a Fisherine transactions-approach or a Cambridge income-approach to the quantity theory), is determined independently of the quantity of money or the level of prices but rather by real variables such as endowments, preferences and technology. All three propositions are highly controversial and by no means truisms. Having been brought up on the idea that the equation of exchange $MV = PT$ or $M = kPY$ is an identity, we are faced with the problem of so defining the quantity theory of money that all quantity theorists would accept the definition. In fact, it is surprising how often the quantity theory is defined by some authorities as if the theory were adequately captured by the equation of exchange.[3] But whatever definition is used, the direct and indirect transmission mechanism is the very heart of the theory and there is nothing in the equation of exchange to tell us that the theory can only deal with exogenous changes in M, or that V and T are always assumed to change independently of each other.

The object of the quantity theory, from its very outset in Hume's formulation, was to demonstrate that the absolute size of the money stock was of no real significance in an economy: the price level would eventually adjust via the direct and indirect transmission mechanism to equate the real value of the nominal money stock M, that is, M/P, to the real demand for it, the fraction $1/V$ of the real volume of transitions T that the public wished to hold in the form of real cash balances. Written as $M/P = T/V$, the quantity theory stands exposed immediately as a particular species of demand-and-supply explanations of economic phenomena.

'Would eventually adjust'! This is the notorious proportionality theorem, the idea that money and absolute prices will in the long run vary proportionately, such that a doubling of M will double P, no more, no less, leaving relative prices including the rate of interest, and hence the level of real output, unaffected. This theorem came to be known in the 1930s as 'neutrality of money' (Patinkin, 1987) but it was a familiar quantity-theory proposition all through the nineteenth century long before a memorable name for it had been invented. Alongside this long-run theorem about neutral money ran the notion that money in the short run was almost certainly non-neutral; here too, the inspiration was Hume (and possibly Richard Cantillon) who had argued, not only that the *level* of output in an economy is invariant to the *level* of the money supply, but also that it can be raised by a positive *rate of change* of the money supply (Hume, 1955: lxiii–lxvi; Vickers, 1959: chs 10–11; Duke, 1979). What was called 'neutral money' in the inter-war period has come to be known more recently as the vertical long-run Phillips curve or the 'policy ineffectiveness' proposition of the New Classical Macroeconomics. Hume apparently did not believe in the neutrality of money with respect to a sustained rate of change of the money supply; in other words, he denied what is now called 'superneutrality'.[4] Had he expressed himself in a modern language, he would have repudiated Friedman's notion of a natural rate of unemployment and insisted on the existence of a trade-off between output and inflation even in the long run (see Blaug, 1985: 20–1). Be that as it may, the quantity theory of money is still relevant and discernible in modern macroeconomic arguments.

THE CLASSICAL ECONOMISTS AND THE QUANTITY THEORY

The quantity theory of money received its greatest fillip with the suspension of specie payments in 1797, which introduced an entire generation of monetary thinkers to the notion of inconvertible fiat paper money and floating exchange rates, a monetary regime in which the money supply is exogenous as it had never been before. When David Hume and Richard Cantillon were writing about the effects of an increase in the money supply in the early eighteenth century, Britain was an open economy on a fixed exchange rate gold standard, in which case the domestic price level and the domestic money supply are simultaneously and endogenously determined by the workings of the balance of payments and the international flow of specie. It is true that Hume had introduced the idea of a mental experiment involving an exogenous increase of the money supply – 'suppose that all the money of Great Britain were multiplied fivefold in a night', as he expressed it – but that was not the typical way in which classical economists thought about the effects of a change in the stock of nominal money in an economy. Believing as they did in cost-of-production theories of value, they applied their value theories as much to the money metal as to any other commodity and argued that absolute prices are determined by comparative costs in the production of gold and of goods in general. This was perhaps the reason that Adam Smith never mentioned Hume's specie-flow mechanism and more or less rejected the quantity theory, endorsing as he did the 'real bills doctrine': if banks confined their lending to self-liquidating commercial transactions – issued only real bills – bank credit would never exceed the 'needs of trade', in which case even the volume of fiat money, not to mention the volume of bank credit, would be endogenously determined (Humphrey, 1986: 80–9, 180–7; Perlman, 1986).

In any case, 1797 created a new era in which the supply of money was determined either by the Bank of England, if David Ricardo was to be believed, or by grain imports and war remittances, if Henry Thornton was to be believed: for the first time, causality ran clearly and unambiguously from money to prices and not the other way round.

However, Ricardo continued to expound the labour theory of value of the monetary metal while at the same time espousing a hard-line version of the quantity theory. He might have reconciled the two by reserving the quantity theory for short-run problems and for inconvertible paper, while maintaining the cost-of-production theory for the long run and for specie money and convertible paper only. In fact, however, he left the two doctrines standing in an unresolved relationship to each other (Blaug, 1985: 130, 198–9).[5] When convertibility of paper was restored in 1821, the members of what soon came to be known as the Currency School argued as if the quantity theory was relevant even for commodity money, while the members of the Banking School echoed the truly classical, pre-Ricardian cost-of-production theory.

The irony of the great Currency–Banking controversy that divided the early Victorians on the questions of monetary policy was that the quantity-theorists, Lord Overstone, George Norman and Robert Torrens, upheld *the* currency principle, namely, that a mixed gold–convertible-paper currency should so be regulated that it would vary in the same way as a purely metallic currency, thereby responding automatically to any inflow or outflow of gold. But if this could have been achieved, which it never was, it would have tied the currency to the movement of the foreign exchanges and thus re-established the endogeneity of the money supply that ruled in the eighteenth century. In other words, the Currency School employed the quantity theory of money to advocate a form of statutory control of the currency that would have made the quantity theory more or less irrelevant.

Be that as it may, it is evident that all the monetary controversies that led up to the Bank Charter Act of 1844 and that attended the many amendments of the Act in the 1850s and 1860s turned almost exclusively on short-run issues. The 'neutrality of money' in the long run was a convenient stick with which to beat the Birmingham paper-credit inflationists (such as Thomas Attwood) but, apart from such special uses, not much was heard of the notorious proportionality theorem and certainly little emphasis was placed on it. As for the short run, every classical economist regarded money as non-neutral in the short run, and since the label 'classical economist' is frequently misused, we may as well say that we refer to such writers as Hume, Malthus, Ricardo, Thornton, Bentham,

McCulloch, James Mill, John Stuart Mill and Torrens (O'Brien, 1975: 162–5; Humphrey, 1993, 251–63).[6]

Short-run non-neutrality was explained by a variety of phenomena: sticky prices, sticky nominal wages, sticky nominal interest rates, fixed nominal charges such as rents and taxes, fixed nominal incomes of wage earners and rentiers even under conditions of full employment ('forced saving'), fixed inventory–sales ratios, absolute price-relative price confusions *à la* Lucas, market size encouragements to specialization and, lastly, deliberate efforts on the part of organized groups to maintain real incomes (Humphrey, 1993: 252–3). It is true that Ricardo and especially James Mill only grudgingly admitted non-neutrality in the short run but admit it they did (Ahiakpor, 1958). And when they asserted long-run neutrality of money, it was of course fiat money they had in mind.

I wish these were original thoughts but in fact this has become almost a standard interpretation of classical monetary economics in recent years. 'The central message', says Humphrey (1993: 252), 'is that the notion of at least some nonneutrality is part of an endearing classical monetary tradition and that theories stressing neutrality are always a departure from that tradition.'[7] Likewise, Niehans (1987: 413) remarks that the proportionality theorem, widely regarded as the centrepiece of classical monetary theory, 'is only a secondary offshoot of somewhat suspect legitimacy ... The controversies were all about the short-term adjustments.'[8]

Having robbed the classical quantity theory of much of its punch, some commentators have taken historical revisionism one step further, going so far as to argue that classical monetary theory has been misunderstood by just about everybody. We noted earlier that the quantity theory of money applies fully only to exogenously determined fiat money and that its application to a convertible paper currency as obtained in Britain after 1821 was controversial: it depended on whether the monetary authorities had any real control of 'money' produced by the banking system. Now the Banking School denied that the Bank of England had such effective control; they used the real bills doctrine and the 'law of reflux' to argue that the money supply was demand-driven and endogenously determined by the 'needs of trade', any tendency of banks to over-issue bank notes being corrected in the process of interbank note clearing by rivalrous competitive banks and external drains via the specie flow mechanism. The recent revival of the theory of free banking has drawn attention to the classical-period literature in favour of competitive, unregulated banking driven underground by the Bank Charter Act of 1844, which complimented the arguments of the Banking School (Smith, 1936: ch. 7; White, 1984: ch. 3; Dowd, 1993: ch. 11). In any case, the new thesis is that the victorious Currency School applied the quantity theory to a monetary regime for which it was, strictly speaking, inappropriate: 'many classical theorists sometimes confused their

theories by introducing quantity-theoretic propositions into arguments in which
the quantity theory was not applicable. Such misplaced propositions have
fostered the misconception that the quantity theory was the essential classical
monetary theory' (Glasner, 1985: 226).

However, if this is a misconception, it was one widely shared by the classical
writers themselves: Glasner concedes that Hume and Ricardo and to some
extent John Stuart Mill had it wrong, with only Thornton and Nassau Senior
getting it right (ibid., 226–8, 232). Much of this reinterpretation therefore
depends for its force on the trick of confining the label 'classical monetary theory'
to those who either denied the exogeneity of the money supply, like the members
of the Banking School, or who confined their arguments essentially to
inconvertible paper-money, like Ricardo and Thornton.[9] In the final analysis,
the issue of the relevance of the quantity theory in that or any other period depends
on the exogeneity or endogeneity of the money supply, which is in every case
a matter of fact and not a question of textual exegesis. This is an issue to which
we shall return.

THE NEOCLASSICAL ECONOMISTS AND THE QUANTITY THEORY.

As mentioned earlier, so far as the quantity theory is concerned, the Marginal
Revolution of the 1870s might just as well never have happened. To be sure,
it did eventually result in a choice – theoretic analysis of the demand for
money, but not until the opening decade of the twentieth century. For a long time,
the 'circularity' bogey inhibited the application of marginal utility theory to
money.[10] Even the notion that velocity, or the demand for money, is a function
among other things of the rate of interest only appears parenthetically in the
writings of the leading quantity theorists in the 'golden age' of the quantity theory
c. 1870–1920 (Patinkin, 1965: 15, 165–6, 545, 580; 1982: ch. 6; 1990). Having
failed to give convincing accounts of the 'indirect' transmission mechanism
between money and prices, most of the leading neoclassical economists of the
period, with the singular exception of Wicksell and Fisher, even failed to
provide complete and systematic statements of the 'direct' transmission
mechanism or real balance effect (Patinkin, 1965: 164–9, 581, 604). The short-
run non-neutrality of money that characterized the classical versions of the
quantity theory also appeared in the writings of such major neoclassical quantity
theorists as Marshall, Pigou, Walras, Cassel, Fisher, Wicksell, Hawtrey and
Lavington (Patinkin, 1981: 3–24). They devoted even more attention to the short
run than had the classical authors and in some cases did not even mention the
idea that money was supposed to be neutral in the long run. Hume's ancient denial
of 'superneutrality', the assertion that real output does react to persistent

changes in the rate of growth of the money supply, reappeared in the writings of Wicksell and Fisher and provided still more reasons (forced saving, falling real rates of interest, wages lagging behind prices, and so on) for doubting the proportionality theorem (Patinkin, 1987: 640–3).[11]

It is true that Marshall, Walras, Wicksell and Pigou drew a 'demand curve' for money, distinguished from other demand curves by being a rectangular hyperbola asymptotic to the two axes, showing 1/P as the inverse of the price level and M as the quantity of money, thus suggesting that the elasticity of demand for money is always equal to unity, implying the validity of the proportionality theorem.[12] We have learned from Hegeland (1951: 135, 170–3) and Patinkin (1965: 46–50, 169–73, 187, 583–7, 605–10) that this is a simple confusion between an individual money demand curve and a market-equilibrium money demand curve; the market-equilibrium demand curve will exhibit unitary elasticity because it is a locus cutting through a family of individual demand curves for each of which the price level is adjusted to the money supply in accordance with market-clearing requirements, thus defining the precise sense in which money is said to be neutral in the long run.

By the way, it is worth noting that long-run neutrality of money depends on the precise way that new money is injected into the economy; unless the economy is already in long-run equilibrium, the new money must increase the nominal money holdings of all individuals in the same proportion; any violation of this assumption makes money non-neutral even in the very long run (Patinkin, 1957: 44–59). Not a single pre-war writer in the neoclassical tradition ever recognized this requirement and therefore it may be said that no rigorous statement of the proportionality theorem was every provided before modern times. In any case, despite frequent references in the literature to the alleged unitary elasticity of the demand curve for money and hence the proportionality theorem, the emphasis in monetary economics throughout the last quarter of the nineteenth century and first quarter of the twentieth was on the question of an appropriate monetary policy to stabilize prices in the wider interest of ironing out the fluctuations of the business cycle; in other words, the short run was just as much in the forefront for neoclassical economists as it had been for classical economists (Schumpeter, 1954: 1095–1122).[13] In consequence, the old long-run cost-of-production theory of the value of the monetary commodity was abandoned, it now being accepted that, even if it were true, the gold stock was so large relative to the annual output of gold mines that the cost of producing gold could only have a negligible effect on its exchange value (Laidler, 1991b: 83, 120–3).

Was this *The Golden Age of the Quantity Theory*, to cite the tile of a recent study by David Laidler (1991b)? No, say some, because the 'golden age' 1870–1914 was also the era *par excellence* of the international gold standard in which the nominal stock of money in small, open economies like that of Great Britain was adjusted to the level of prices via the balance of payments, so that the quantity theory was simply irrelevant. 'The mainstream of the classical and neoclassical tradition focused on commodity money', says Niehans (1987: 412), 'to which the quantity theory does not apply. The quantity theory is, so to say, the illegitimate sideline of the classical tradition, the classical theory for unclassical fiat money.' If that were all there was to it, we should be surprised, not that the long-run neutrality of money is mentioned so rarely by neoclassical monetary writers, but that it is acknowledged at all. What could monetary theorists have been thinking of when they referred to the special case of the unitary elasticity of demand for monetary gold?

REVERSE CAUSATION

We have seen that there have always been good arguments for believing that the quantity of money is endogenously determined under a fixed exchange rate gold-standard regime, in which case it might be more appropriate to speak of a 'contraquantity theory of money'. The great exponent of the contraquantity theory in the nineteenth century was Thomas Tooke (Arnon, 1990: ch. 7) and Laurence Laughlin (Girton and Roper, 1978). Although neither Tooke nor Laughlin made the best of their case, the fact remains that even convinced quantity theorists have always conceded that the money supply in a single country is almost never entirely exogenous and that, even so, reverse causation from prices to money is always possible.

Causation in economics does not necessarily imply that the cause must temporally precede the effect; agents may forecast the variable constituting the cause and act in anticipation of it. Thus, John Elliot Cairnes, writing on the Californian and Australian gold discoveries in the 1850s – an exogenous increase in the money supply if there ever was one – argued that the new gold acted on British prices even before British exporters to the colonies had been paid in gold. Similarly, according to the indirect transmission mechanism of money on prices, if the rate of profit on capital rises about the loan rate of interest, say, because of a burst of technical innovations, money creation will occur endogenously, leading to rising prices. As Irving Fisher argued, nominal interest rates are sticky and therefore real rates of interest tend to fall during periods of inflation. In consequence, there is a further rise in the demand for productive loans, which leads to still further price rises. Under these circumstances, if monetary policy is not accommodating, or if for any other reason bank loan rates are not raised, we have a situation in which the money supply is increasing because prices are rising, not because the quantity theory is false but because it is true. Finally, if cost-push factors are causing prices to rise, quantity theorists have typically argued that, whatever the monetary regime, prices would never have risen unless the cost-push had been accommodated by an increase in the money supply; nevertheless, on the face of it, such circumstances will look like a contraquantity theory scenario.

These and other examples of possible reverse causation between money and prices prompted David Laidler (1991a: 299) to comment: 'the test of the quantity theory position, at least as set out by its exponents, lay not in evidence on the timing of data, but in the outcome of a counter-factual experiment: what would happen if the time path of the money supply were different'. Summing up with particular reference to the US monetary accommodation of the oil price shock in the early 1970s, he concluded: 'it is precisely the impossibility of bringing empirical evidence directly and unambiguously to bear on questions concerning the feasibility of non-accommodating policy and, if feasible, upon its consequences for prices, which lie at the heart of continuing controversy about the quantity theory' (ibid.).

But surely we must bring to bear the whole weight of evidence of past episodes, of fiat paper and commodity money regimes, of relatively open and relatively closed regimes? And as we shall see, we have ample empirical evidence of both the direct and indirect transmission mechanism to provide us with evidence of the effects of this or that policy shock. In the meanwhile, note that even Milton Friedman and Anna Schwartz (1963: 695) in their magisterial study of the history of money in the United States do not deny that there is reverse causation of prices on money even if, on balance, the causal chain runs fundamentally from money to prices:

> While the influence running from money to economic activity has been predominant, there have also been influences running the other way ... Mutual interaction, but with money clearly the senior partner in long-run movements and in major cyclical movements, and more nearly an equal partner with money income and prices in the shorter-run and milder movements – this is the generalization suggested by our evidence.

THE EXOGENOUS–ENDOGENOUS MONEY SUPPLY ISSUE

Again and again throughout its long history, the exogeneity or endogeneity of money has been at the back of every controversy surrounding the quantity theory. We have repeatedly touched on the issue but we have not so far confronted it directly. We must now ask: how does one decide whether a change in the supply of money is exogenous? There are at least two senses in which the money supply may be said to be exogenous. The first is the one in which it is not itself explained by our economic model, which in this case is the quantity theory of money. A perfect example is fiat money, which is always 'outside' money in the language of Gurley and Shaw; that is, issued by some agency exogenous to the economic system itself for motives that are presumably political. Let us call this 'model exogeneity'. A rather different definition of exogeneity of the money supply is 'policy exogeneity': the case in which the monetary authorities can effectively control the money supply if they wish to do so. Although these two definitions of exogeneity frequently overlap, they are not identical: a government may be unable to control a monetary aggregate – policy endogeneity – but may have difficulty in modelling this failure – model exogeneity.

For the most part, it is policy exogeneity and no model exogeneity that has proved to be the bugbear of the quantity theory. The standard interpretation of the basic assumption of the quantity theory that the money supply is policy exogenous is that it is capable of being varied without any prior change in the demand for money, the demand and supply of goods and services, and hence the level of prices; in the language of the equation of exchange, M is capable of varying without any prior change in V, T or P. There are essentially two ways in which this can happen: (a) under an international gold standard, if there is a discovery of new gold mines or if there are cost-reducing innovations in gold production anywhere in the world; and (b) if the monetary authorities alter the volume of 'high-powered money' of coins and currency held by the public plus the cash reserves of banks, which they may do even under a gold standard even though it violates the gold standard 'rules of the game'. The second case is particularly troublesome because it is always a matter of degree, not a matter of kind. The question really is: even if the monetary authorities control the monetary base, how much control do they actually have over the total money supply?

Under a fully 'loaned up' fractional-reserve banking system, the monetary authorities determine the quantity of 'outside money' (such as fiat money, gold and foreign exchange reserves), the reserve–deposit ratio and possibly the currency–demand ratio, but the volume of 'inside money' and hence that of bank credit is endogenously determined; moreover, what control there is via the reserve–deposit ratio is asymmetric, that is, expansions may be controllable but contractions are uncontrollable. When the banks are not fully loaned up, there is not even total control of 'high-powered money'. It is evident, therefore, that the total money supply is almost never entirely exogenously determined even under classic gold standard conditions and in any case control of the money supply is always a matter of degree.

An analogy may be helpful. Does the government control the crime rate? Yes and no. In the short run, there is no doubt that additional policing is capable of reducing the crime rate. But in the long run, the crime rate depends on a host of sociological, psychological and economic variables from standards of law and order, moral attitudes inculcated at home and in schools, to levels of employment and living standards; in the long run, the authorities as such have virtually no control over the crime rate. Analogously, we may say that the money supply is always more exogenous in the short run than in the long run. In other words, the quantity theory is always a better explanation of the price level in the short run than in the long run. But how long is the run relevant to the determination of something like the level of prices?

Friedman and Schwartz (1991: 41–2) deny that exogeneity or endogeneity is a characteristic of the money supply as such; it all depends, they say, on the purpose of the analysis in question. In other words, they seem to subordinate policy exogeneity to model exogeneity. Thus, they argue that the monetary authorities under a gold standard do have considerable control over domestic monetary policy over short periods, but for a run of 'more than a few years' the stock of money in each country is determined by the requirement that international prices must be such as to preserve equilibrium in the balance of payments. So presumably the quantity theory was of little use in explaining secular changes in American and British absolute prices in the period before the First World War when both the purpose of the analysis and the monetary regime in question indicated that the money supply was endogenously determined. However, in accounting for the role of the Federal Reserve System in contracting the US money supply in 1929–33, in effect producing the Great Depression of the 1930s, Friedman and Schwartz (1963: ch. 7; Bordo, 1986: 353–63) clearly treat the money supply as exogenous. Much depends not just on the focus of the analysis but also on its scope. The quantity theory of money was born in the sixteenth century as a response to the global price revolution set off by the gold and silver discoveries of the New World, that is, by the attempt to explain world-wide inflation by an exogenous increase in the money supply; exogenous, that is, in a model sense of the term. Nevertheless, for one country considered in isolation the change in the money supply was endogenous because it depended on the elasticity of supply of its exports and the elasticity of demand for its imports. Similarly, the monetary approach to the balance of payments introduced in the 1970s has made us aware of how open-economy macroeconomics renders the money supply endogenous, whether or not the economy in question is small or large. However, the larger the economy, the less is the domestic price level determined by international trade flows. Thus, the size of the economy in question is a relevant consideration in assessing the exogeneity–endogeneity of money question quite apart from the degree of openness.

We may conclude that there cannot be a hard-and-fast answer to the question whether the money supply is exogenous and hence whether it is legitimate to employ the quantity theory of money. In part, the answer depends on the purpose at hand; but surely, for policy exogeneity, it depends on the prevailing monetary regime? We are safe in doubting the exogeneity of the money supply since 1971, the year in which the entire world adopted a regime of irredeemable fiat paper without any anchor in commodity money. The deregulation of financial markets in the late 1970s and the spread of offshore banking in the 1970s and 1980s further reduced the degree of control exerted by governments over their domestic money supply. Nevertheless, even under today's entirely fiduciary standard, there are profound disagreements among monetary experts over the extent to which governments can vary the monetary base and control various monetary aggregates. Thus, in *The New Palgrave Dictionary of Economics* we find Charles Goodhart (1987: 501) denying that the money supply is an exogenously determined variable, and Karl Brunner (1987: 527–9) asserting that it is. The most famous proponents of the endogenous money thesis in modern times are Nicholas Kaldor (1970) and James Tobin (1970), but that is not to say that they would insist on the endogeneity of money and hence the contraquantity theory of money for all past monetary regimes (see Humphrey, 1993: 144–54). Similarly, post-Keynesian economists (see Lavoie, 1992: ch. 4) have made the endogeneity of money one of their major themes but without necessarily coupling it to an attack on the quantity theory as such. The exogeneity–endogeneity of money issue is of course intimately connected with the famous difficulty of defining precisely what is 'money'. It is noteworthy that, with the passage of time, the set of assets referred to as 'money', whose quantity is supposed by the quantity theory to determine the price level, has systematically broadened from gold and silver coins in Hume and Cantillon, to coins and bank notes in the Currency School, to coins, notes and bank deposits, time deposits, bank reserves and the liabilities of financial intermediaries in modern monetarism (Laidler, 1991a: 295). The boundaries of a nation's money supply have become surrounded by an ever fuzzier penumbra which has further bedevilled the issue of whether money is or is not exogenous.

THE DEMAND FOR MONEY

Exogeneity of money is, as we have said, the first of three critical propositions that define the quantity theory. The second, to which we now turn, is the notion that there is a stable demand for money-to-hold. There have always been two traditions within the quantity theory: the 'motion theory of money', captured by Fisher's transactions approach and the quantity equation $MV = PT$, and the 'rest theory of money', enshrined in the Cambridge income approach and the equation $M = kPY$. Both approaches assume that people will want to hold, for transactions, precautionary and possibly speculative motives, a constant quantity of real cash balances at the economy's full-capacity level of output, and that this demand function is stable in the sense that it is not subject to erratic shifts; it varies, when it does vary, slowly and independently of both the size of the money stock and the level of prices. But the better-known transactions approach made the velocity of money a function of payment habits, the spread of banking institutions and advances in the means of transportation and communication, that is, non-price variables. The rate of interest as the opportunity cost of holding cash did not appear explicitly in the equation of exchange, and although Fisher was of course perfectly aware of the Thornton–Wicksell doctrine of the 'two rates', the fact is that the indirect transmission mechanism of money on prices almost disappeared from view in the transactions approach to the quantity theory.

It was the income approach in Marshall, Pigou and Lavington that bequeathed the idea of the interest-elasticity of the demand for money to the generation of which Keynes was a prominent member. However, what in Keynes appeared as 'motives' for liquidity preference was more than the renaming of ideas found repeatedly in the writings of Cambridge monetary economists. Nevertheless, by the time he came to write *The General Theory*, Keynes entirely rejected the notion that there was a stable demand for money, and indeed his principal criticism of the quantity theory was the assertion that V or k was unstable and unpredictable.

Somehow Keynes and Keynesians planted the idea that the old quantity theorists had believed in the virtual constancy of V or k, but nothing could be further from the truth: the doctrine of the two rates required an inverse relationship between V and the money rate of interest, not to mention V and the rate of inflation (as the result of a falling real rate of interest), and the usual list of the velocity determinants suggested that V would rise over time as a consequence of improvements in communication and monetization.[14] Such vulgarizations of the quantity theory may have been encouraged by the statistical work of Carl Snyder and Holbrook Working in the 1920s, purporting to demonstrate that pro-cyclical fluctuations in V were always neutralized by contracyclical fluctuations of T, producing a rigidly constant T/V ratio, otherwise known as the proportionality theorem or long-run neutrality of money (Humphrey, 1993: 112–43).

Notwithstanding these distortions of the evidence, stability of the money demand function remains a vital element in the quantity theory and in modern statements of monetarism. It is a principal bone of contention in Friedman and Schwartz's study of *Monetary Trends in the United States and United Kingdom* (Hendry and Ericsson, 1991: 13, 16; Friedman and Schwartz, 1991: 47; also Mayer, 1982: 1532–5) and has been the subject of a book-length survey by Laidler (1985). The question is given added piquancy because it is generally agreed that, no matter how money is defined, the income-velocity of money on both sides of the Atlantic became extremely unstable in the early 1980s, leading to the abandonment of money supply targets in the United Kingdom and a marked decline in the popular appeal of monetarism in the United States (Mayer, 1990: 70–6). Nevertheless, despite the instability of the demand-for-money function in the 1980s, the weight of the empirical evidence surveyed by Laidler (1985: 124, 135, 143) supports the idea that there is a stable negative relationship between the demand for nominal money and the rate of interest and a stable proportional relationship between the demand for nominal money and the general price level (see also Goldfeld and Sichel, 1990: 302–7, 349–50).

THE NEUTRALITY OF MONEY

The quantity theory depends, as we have said, on three propositions: (a) the exogeneity of the money supply; (b) the stability of the demand-for-money function; and (c) the real determinants of the level of output or transactions. The notion that physical output is a function only of real variables and is therefore determined independently of both M and P is of course implied by the doctrine of the long-run neutrality of money. This is often said to be a key proposition of the quantity theory, and it is now time that we ask what reasons we have for believing that prices indeed vary equiproportionately with money. Whatever these reasons, they are empirical, not analytical. Of course, we can set up a correct general equilibrium model *à la* Patinkin in which every individual's utility function includes cash balances held as a good, in which every exogenous increase in the money supply is distributed equiproportionately to the initial money endowments of individuals, and in which the 'real balance effect' will ensure that absolute prices will rise in the same proportion as the money stock, but we can hardly expect the real world perfectly to mimic this theoretical scenario. All the great economists of the past, as we have seen, had no difficulty in conjecturing reasons that money might fail to be neutral in the long run and very few laid much emphasis on the alleged long-run neutrality of money. So the question remains: what evidence is there that money and prices vary proportionately?

No one disputes the remarkably close correlation between money and nominal income over the medium and long run in most industrialized countries for which we have historical data. But nominal income is PY and the split of PY into P and Y is very much in dispute. The quantity theory consists of the assertion that any increase of M will begin by affecting PY but will eventually affect only P. Here is a distinction so often encountered in economics, between effects in the short run and effects in the long run, the actual length of the run being left unspecified. Although this is fair comment in respect of the long history of the quantity theory, it is actually belied by the pronouncements of the most recent prominent advocate of the quantity theory, Milton Friedman. Milton Friedman has always been fairly explicit about the length of the short run and long run during which the effects of an increase in the money supply work themselves out.

> For most Western countries, a change in the rate of monetary growth produces a change in the rate of growth of nominal income about six to nine months later ... The effect

on prices, like that on income and output ... comes some twelve to eighteen months later, so that the total delay between a change in monetary growth and a change in the rate of inflation averages something like two years. In the short run, which may be as long as three to ten years, monetary changes affect primarily output. Over decades, on the other hand, the rate of monetary growth affects primarily prices.   (Friedman, 1992: 478; also 1987: 16–17; 1991: 16)[16]

So money is certainly non-neutral in the short run and the 'short run' is typically two years but may actually be as long as 3–10 years; long-run neutrality will only be observed after a decade and will only amount in any case to near-proportionality between money and prices. If 'neutrality' and 'superneutrality' mean that the effect of a once-and-for-all change in the money supply or the rate of growth in the money supply on the real variables of the economic system are nil, and that is the standard definition of these terms (see Patinkin, 1987: 641–3), there is only lukewarm support for either concept in Friedman's writings. Superneutrality is the same thing as a vertical long-run expectations-augmented Phillips curve set at the so-called 'natural rate of unemployment' and, of course, this is one of Friedman's most famous contributions to modern macroeconomics. But its actual importance to Friedman's thinking about economic policy is grossly exaggerated. Certainly, an effect that can take as long as ten years to show itself is not a practical policy proposition. Nevertheless, it may take on importance as ideological ammunition against Keynesian fiscalism. In any case, it is interesting to note that the quantity theory, which began with Hume as a qualified argument in favour of creeping inflation, has come full circle in Friedman with the denial that there is any trade-off between output and inflation in the long run, where 'long run' means 'over decades'. In case this should be thought to be a statement which is uncomfortably ambiguous, let me point out that this is the only statement of its kind in the long shelf of books that constitutes the literature on the quantity theory: no quantity theory before Friedman ever stipulated the actual time span that it took for an increase in money to work its whole way through to an increase in prices.

EMPIRICAL EVIDENCE

At the end of our story, we are struck by the failure of just about every quantity theorist to provide any rigorous statement of the theory. Wicksell and Fisher are the best of them, but even they fell short of specifying the determinants of the money-demand function or of setting out the precise conditions required to validate the proportionality theorem. Moreover, even they 'dichotomised the pricing process', as Patinkin (1965: 171–86) put it; that is, divorced the determination of relative prices and the rate of interest in value theory from the determination of absolute prices in monetary theory as if commodity markets could be hived off from money markets without loss of content. Likewise the idea that the price level cannot be altered with altering relative prices, and vice versa, which appeared as early as Cantillon in the 1750s (Blaug, 1985: 21), more or less disappeared in economics until Mises and Hacek revived it in the 1930s. In short, an almost indescribable analytical sloppiness characterized some 200 years of development in monetary theory.

Money, we have learned, can affect both output and prices in the short run and it may even affect output in the long run, depending on how and at what rate the extra money is injected into the economy. Do we really need the heavy artillery of the quantity theory to tell us this? No doubt the quantity theory is a wonderful framework for thinking about monetary questions and it certainly comes into its own during every hyperinflation: when irresponsible governments seek to finance fiscal deficits in periods of civil war or social unrest by printing unbacked paper notes, we get all the conditions required to make the quantity theory operative: exogenous money, a stable or slowly changing demand for money, and output unable to respond quickly to monetary expansion.[16] I dare say that is why the quantity theory is the oldest surviving economic theory of them all. Nevertheless, in normal times the quantity theory is largely irrelevant except for the very long run and it is hopelessly indeterminate in the short run. In any monetary regime, any dramatic and unexpected increase in the quantity of money will in due course raise prices although not necessarily in the same proportion – that is all the quantity theory of money amounts to.

Nevertheless, painting with a broad brush, the quantity theory is supported by an overwhelming body of empirical evidence. This is evidence that goes back to Thomas Tooke, whose data were admittedly anecdotal, but which were greatly extended and improved by Irving Fisher. We tend to forget that a quarter of the text and one-third of the appendices of *The Purchasing Power of Money* were devoted to the 'statistical verification' of the quantity theory (see Laidler, 1991b: 79–82; Friedman, 1987: 5). The equation of exchange, as Humphrey (1993: 288–9) has said, 'was the chief single-equation macroeconomic model in use up to the 1930s'. In other words, the quantity theory of money was, prior to the Keynesian Revolution, a 'progressive' research programme in the sense of Lakatos. The recent historical studies of Friedman and Schwartz mark the next step in what has now become a major research industry (see Bordo, 1986).[17] In addition, there is a mountain of econometric evidence, partly summarized by Laidler (see also Schwartz, 1973; Blanchard, 1990). Laidler's (1991a: 303) conclusion at the close of his discussion of the quantity theory is so judiciously worded that it may serve as our own.

> The overwhelming weight of evidence is consistent with the quantity theory and inconsistent with certain extreme criticisms of it. To the extent that one comes to this

evidence with a prior belief that the quantity theory is a plausible doctrine, that belief is strengthened by it.

The point is, and perhaps this is my main point, that if we believe that the quantity theory of money is true, it is not because we find the theory underlying it so plausible and precisely expressed that we feel impelled to assent to it. It is facts and not analytical rigours that make the quantity theory good economics. I venture to assert that this is so with most if not all economic theories.

NOTES

1. As Milton Friedman (1968: 433) has said: 'The contemporary economist can still read David Hume's essay 'Of Money' (1752) with pleasure and profit and find few if any errors of commission.' Thomas Mayer (1990: ch. 3) himself noted the striking similarity of Hume's writings on the quantity theory of money to those of Friedman on monetarism: of the twelve propositions that he identified as characteristic of modern monetarism, five were explicitly in Hume's work.

2. It is worth stating this emphatically since it was explicitly denied in Milton Friedman's opening salvo in the monetarist counterrevolution: 'The quantity theory is in the first instance a theory of the *demand* for money. It is not a theory of output, or of money income, or of the price level' (Friedman, 1965: 52). Patinkin (1969) showed conclusively that this was historically inaccurate, and Friedman's reply to Patinkin touched every issue in Patinkin's critique (Friedman, 1970: 158–68) but not his characterization of the essential nature of the quantity theory.

3. For instance, Lawrence Boland (1991: 97) remarks: 'There are some statements which are of the form that economists call tautologies, yet that can also appear to be confirmed. The most obvious example is the "quantity theory of money". This "theory" is represented by the equation MV = PT. On close examination it turns out that the two sides of this equation are merely what is obtained by reversing the order of summation between i and j for the double summation $\Sigma\Sigma p_{i}q_{ij}$. Confirming a statement which cannot conceivably be false cannot really contribute anything positive to economic science.' Similarly, Joseph Schumpeter (1954: 703) defines the quantity theory to mean all of the following four propositions: (a) that M varies independently of P and T; (b) that V is an institutional datum that varies slowly and independently of P and T; (c) that T or output is unrelated to M; and that variations in M 'unless they are absorbed by variations in output in the same direction, *act mechanically on all prices*, irrespective of how an increase in the quantity of money is used and on what sectors of the economy it first impinges' (my italics). This definition does not mention either the direct or indirect transmission mechanism, although elsewhere in the book Schumpeter (ibid.: 720–4) does of course recognize them; likewise the suggestion that money according to the quantity theory is 'neutral' even in the short run is belied later in the book (ibid.: 724–5, 1115–16n). Samuel Hollander (1987: 265) quotes this definition of the quantity theory of money by Schumpeter uncritically, after which he has difficulty, or rather less difficulty, in clearing Ricardo of the charge of being a crude quantity theorist, which of course he was.

4. Failing to recognize that the quantity theory, as Locke had stated it (Walter Eltis provides a restatement in Chapter 1), presupposes a different amount of money everything else being the same, that is, a once-and-for-all change in the money supply, Hume introduced the notion of a causal relationship between money and prices as a temporal process. In the essay 'Of Money', he (Hume 1955: 37) said that 'it is only in the interval or intermediate situation, between the acquisition of money and the rise of prices, that the increasing quantity of gold and silver is favourable to industry' – the assertion of long-run neutrality of money – but in the essay 'Of the Balance of Trade', he argued (ibid.: 39–40) that 'The good policy of the magistrate

consists only in keeping it [the quantity of money], if possible, still increasing: because, by that means, he keeps alive a spirit of industry in the nation' – which denies superneutrality. Mayer (1990: ch. 3) fails to stress Hume's denial of superneutrality, a principal element in twentieth-century monetarism.

5. The tension between them was never resolved in the classical tradition, and even John Stuart Mill and Karl Marx discussed the quantity theory of money and the labour theory of value applied to money as if the two had little to do with each other (see Lavoie, 1986). Nassau Senior (1840) went so far in his *Three Lectures on the Value of Money* as to attack Mill for suggesting that relative prices are determined by costs of production, while the value of money is determined by a completely different theory, the quantity theory. On all this, see Niehans (1978:145–8).

6. Thus, when Don Patinkin published his famous 1954 paper on 'The Indeterminacy of Absolute Prices in Classical Economic Theory' (1949), he meant 'in neoclassical economic theory' because his argument was all about Walras, Pareto and general equilibrium theory. A whole series of papers then appeared on the dichotomization of pricing in neoclassical economics, the watertight separation of value theory and monetary theory, all under the heading of 'classical economic theory'. Eventually, Samuelson and Patinkin (1972b) switched labels to 'the neoclassical dichotomy'.

7. Having cited Humphreys once again, it must be said that he is to monetary economics what Jacob Viner was to international trade, the undisputed master of its history.

8. This is a point almost completely overlooked in Green (1992), who represents long-run neutrality of money as the essence of the classical theory of money.

9. Glasner (1985: 226) himself wonders whether 'I have exaggerated the difference between what I call the classical theory and the quantity theory'. He then proceeds to redefine the classical theory: 'Those that I have called the classical theorists [Smith, Thornton, Ricardo, J.S. Mill, Tooke and Fullarton] excluded the convertible money created by the banking system from the quantity of money that could be said to have an independent effect on prices. From their point of view, the quantity of money produced by the banking system behaved passively' (1989: 282). It is difficult to imagine how this statement can be made to fit Thornton, Ricardo and even J.S. Mill.

10. The 'circularity' bogey is the idea that the value of money cannot be said to be determined by its marginal utility, as the ordinary commodities, because the utility of a given nominal quantity of money depends on its real value and this cannot be known until the price level is first determined; that is, to assume that the price level depends on the marginal utility of money is to argue in a circle. This simple confusion between the demand for money and the amount demanded was not cleared up until the 1930s (Patinkin, 1965: 115–16, 573–80).

11. It is noteworthy that Keynes in *The General Theory* took exactly the same position in 1936 that Wicksell and Fisher took in 1903 and 1913, namely that long-term neutrality of money implied by what Keynes (1973: 289–91) called 'the crude quantity theory of money' was qualified 'practically' because of adverse expectations and falling real interest rates in a credit boom. Who now remembers that Fisher (1913: 71; also 56) said in Chapter 4 of *The Purchasing Power of Money* that 'Since the periods of transition are the rule and those of equilibrium the exception, the mechanism of exchange is almost always in a dynamic rather than static condition'?

12. As Patinkin (1956: 608) has observed: 'Marshall and Pigou made the phrase "unitary elasticity of the demand for money" a standard fixture of the literature on monetary theory.'

13. But perhaps Milton Friedman (1968: 433) goes too far when he denies that anyone ever held the proportionality theorem, 'although statements capable of being so interpreted have often been made in the heat of argument or for expository simplicity'.

14. Actually, V has displayed a V-shaped pattern over the past century in a large number of advanced countries, declining from about 1890 to 1945 and then rising secularly to the 1980s (Bordo, 1986: 350–2).

15. Carefully worded statements such as these have to be set next to more dramatic claims in Friedman's writings, such as 'There is perhaps no empirical regularity among economic phenomena that is based on so much evidence for so wide a range of circumstances as the connection between substantial changes in the quantity of money and in the level of prices'

(Friedman, 1987: 15), and 'For the United Kingdom ... a simple quantity theory that regards price change as determined primarily by monetary change and output by independent other factors fits the evidence for the period as a whole [1871–1985] (excluding wars)' (Friedman and Schwartz, 1982: 463).

16. The great German inflation of 1922–3 is an awful reminder of what happens when the central bank and all the leading economists of a country have been brought up on the contraquantity theory of money (Barkai, 1989). The present Russian regime seems to be duplicating the German experience.

17. That this historical method of inquiry, so much praised by Marxists, radicals and institutionalists, should have been the principal research tool of that arch-libertarian, Milton Friedman, is one of the great ironies of intellectual history.

REFERENCES

Ahiakpor, J.C.W. (1958) 'The operational significance of the non-neutrality of money in the short run', *History of Political Economy*, Spring; reprinted in David Ricardo, ed. M. Blaug, Aldershot, Hants.: Edward Elgar, 1991.

Arnon, A (1990) *Thomas Tooke: Pioneer of Monetary Theory*, Aldershot, Hants.: Edward Elgar.

Barkai, H. (1989) 'The old historical school: Roscher on money and monetary issues', *History of Political Economy*, **21**(2): 170–200.

Blanchard, O.J. (1990) 'Why does money affect output? A survey', in *Handbook of Monetary Economics*, ed. B.M. Friedman and F.H. Hahn, Amsterdam: North-Holland, 2.

Blaug, M. (1985) *Economic Theory in Retrospect*, 4th edn, Cambridge: Cambridge University Press.

Boland, L.A. (1991) 'Current views on economic positivitism', in *Companion to Economics Thought*, ed. D.A. Greenaway, M. Bleaney and I. Stewart, London: Routledge.

Bordo, M.D. (1986) 'Explorations in monetary history: a survey of the literature', *Explorations in Economic History*, **23**: 339–415.

Brunner, K. (1987) 'Money supply' in *The New Palgrave: A Dictionary of Economics*, ed. J. Eatwell, M. Millgate and P. Newman, London: Macmillan, **3**.

Dowd, K. (1993) *Laissez-faire Banking*, London: Routledge.

Duke, M.I. (1979) 'David Hume and monetary adjustment', *History of Political Economy*, Winter; reprinted in *David Hume and James Steuart*, ed. M. Blaug, Aldershot, Hants.: Edward Elgar, 1991.

Fisher, I. (1913) *The Purchasing Power of Money*, rev. edn, New York: Macmillan; reprinted New York: Augustus Kelley, 1963.

Friedman, M. (1965) 'The quantity theory of money: a restatement', *Studies in the Quantity Theory of Money*; reprinted in *The Optimum Quantity of Money*, Chicago: Aldine Publishing, 1969.

—— (1968) 'Money, quantity theory', in *International Encyclopaedia of the Social Sciences*, ed. D.L. Sills, New York: Macmillan, **10.**

—— (1970) 'Comments on the critics', in *Milton Friedman's Monetary Framework: A Debate with his Critics*, ed. R.J. Gordon, Chicago: University of Chicago Press.

—— (1987) 'Quantity theory of money', in *The New Palgrave: A Dictionary of Economics*, ed. J. Eatwell, M. Milgate and P. Newman, London: Macmillan, **4**.

—— (1991) *Monetarist Economics*, Oxford: Blackwell.

—— (1992) *Monetary Mischief: Episodes in Monetary History*, New York: Harcourt Brace Jovanovich.

—— and A.J. Schwartz (1963) *A Monetary History of the United States, 1867–1960*, Princeton, NJ: Princeton University Press.

—— (1982) *Monetary Trends in the United States and the United Kingdom: Their Relation to Income Prices and Interest Rates. 1867–1975*, Chicago: University of Chicago Press.

—— (1991) 'Alternative approaches to analyzing economic data', *American Economic Review*, **81**(1): 39–49.

Girton, L. and D.J. Roper (1978) ' J. Lawrence Laughlin and the quantity theory of money', *Journal of Political Economy*, **86**(4): 499–625.

Glasner, D. (1985) 'A reinterpretation of classical monetary theory', *Southern Economic Journal*, July; reprinted in *George Scrope, Thomas Attwood, Edwin Chadwick, John Cairnes*, ed. M. Blaug, Aldershot, Hants.: Edward Elgar, 1991.

—— (1989) 'On some classical monetary controversies', *History of Political Economy*, Summer; reprinted in ibid., 1991.

Goldfeld, S.M. and D.E. Sichel (1990) 'The demand for money', in *Handbook of Monetary Economics*, ed. B.M. Friedman and F.H. Hahn, Amsterdam, North-Holland, **2**.

Goodhart, C. (1987) 'Monetary base', in *The New Palgrave: A Dictionary of Economics*, ed. J. Eatwell, M. Milgate and P. Newman, London: Macmillan, **3**.

Green, R. (1992) *Classical Theories of Money, Output and Inflation*, London: Macmillan.

Hegeland, H. (1951) *The Quantity Theory of Money*, Göteborg; reprinted New York: Augustus Kelley, 1969.

Hendry, D.F. and N.R. Ericsson (1991) 'An econometric analysis of UK money demand in *Monetary Trends in the United States and the United Kingdom* by Milton Friedman and Anna J. Schwartz', *American Economic Review*, **81**(1): 8–38.

Hollander, S. (1987) *Classical Economics*, Oxford: Blackwell.

Hume, D. (1955) *Writings on Economics*, ed. E. Rotwein, Madison, Wis.: University of Wisconsin Press.

Humphrey, M. (1986) *Essays on Inflation*, 5th edn, Richmond, Va: Federal Reserve Bank, Richmond.

—— (1993) *Money, Banking and Inflation*, Aldershot, Hants.: Edward Elgar.

Kaldor, N. (1970) 'The new monetarism', *Lloyds Bank Review*, July 1970; reprinted in *Further Essays on Applied Economics*, London: Gerald Duckworth, 1978.

Keynes, J.M. (1973) *The General Theory of Employment, Interest and Money,* in *The Collected Writings of John Maynard Keynes*, London: Macmillan, **7**.

Laidler, D. (1985) *The Demand for Money: Theories, Evidence and Problems*, 3rd edn, New York: Harper & Row.

—— (1991a) 'The quantity theory is always and everywhere controversial – why?', *Economic Record*, **67**: 199, 289–306.

—— (1991b) *The Golden Age of the Quantity Theory*, New York: Philip Allan.

Lavoie, M. (1986) 'Marx, the quantity theory, and the theory of value', *History of Political Economy*, Spring; reprinted in *Karl Marx*, ed. M. Blaug, Aldershot, Hants.: Edward Elgar, 1991.

—— (1992) *Foundations of Post-Keynesian Economic Analysis*, Aldershot, Hants.: Edward Elgar.

Mayer, T. (1982) 'Monetary trends in the United States and the United Kingdom: a review article', *Journal of Economic Literature*, **20**(4): 1528–39.

—— (1990) *Monetarism and Macroeconomic Policy*, Aldershot, Hants.: Edward Elgar.

Niehans, J. (1978) *The Theory of Money*, Baltimore, Md: John Hopkins University Press.

—— (1987) 'Classical monetary theory, new and old', *Journal of Money, Credit and Banking*, **19**(4): 409–24.

O'Brien, D.P. (1975) *The Classical Economists*, Oxford: Clarendon Press.

Patinkin, D. (1949) 'The indeterminacy of absolute prices in classical economic theory', *Econometrica*, **17**, January; reprinted in Patinkin (1981).

—— (1956) *Money, Interest and Prices*, New York: Harper & Row.

—— (1965) *Money, Interest and Prices*, 2nd edn, New York: Harper & Row.

—— (1969) 'The Chicago tradition, the quantity theory, and Friedman', *Journal of Money, Credit and Banking*, February; reprinted with a postscript in Patinkin (1981).

—— (1972a) 'On the short-run non-neutrality of money in the quantity theory', *Banco Nazionale del Lavoro Quarterly Review*, **100**, March: 3–22.

—— (1972b) 'Reflections on the neoclassical dichotomy', *Canadian Journal of Economics*, **5**, May; reprinted in Patinkin (1981).

—— (1981) *Essays on and in the Chicago Tradition*, Durham, N.C.: Duke University Press.

—— (1982) *Anticipations of the General Theory? and Other Essays on Keynes*, Chicago: University of Chicago Press

—— (1987) 'Neutrality of money', in *The New Palgrave: A Dictionary of Economics*, ed. J. Eatwell, M. Milgate and P. Newman, London: Macmillan, **3**.

—— (1990) *Irving Fisher, the Cambridge School, and the Quantity Theory*, Seoul: Korea Development Institute.

Perlman, M. (1986) 'Adam Smith and the paternity of the real bills doctrine', *History of Political Economy*, Spring; reprinted in *Adam Smith, 2*, ed. M. Blaug, Aldershot, Hants.: Edward Elgar, 1991.

Schumpeter, J. (1954) *A History of Economic Analysis*, Oxford: Oxford University Press.

Schwartz, A.J. (1973) 'Secular price changes in historical perspective', *Journal of Money, Credit and Banking*, Part II, February; reprinted in *Monetarism*, II, ed. KA Crystal, Aldershot, Hants.: Edward Elgar, 1991.

Senior, N.W. (1840) *Three Lectures on the Value of Money*; reprinted in *Commodity Monies*, ed. A.J. Schwartz, Aldershot, Hants.: Edward Elgar, 1992.

Smith, VC (1936) *The Rationale of Central Banking and the Free Banking Alternative*, Westminster: P.S. King & Son; reprinted Indianapolis: Liberty Press, 1990.

Tobin, J. (1970) 'Money and income: *post hoc ergo propter hoc*', *Quarterly Journal of Economics*, **84**, 301–17.

Vickers, D. (1959) *Studies in the Theory of Money 1690–1776*, Philadelphia: Chilton Co.

White, L.H. (1984) *Free Banking in Britain: Theory, Experience and Debate 1800–1845*, Cambridge: Cambridge University Press.

10. Public enemy no. 1: unemployment not inflation*

On 16 May 1991, Norman Lamont, then Chancellor of the Exchequer in the United Kingdom, told the British House of Commons: 'Rising unemployment and the recession has been the price we have had to pay in order to get inflation down ... but that is a price well worth paying.' With one sentence, he revealed the rationale of 14 years of economic policy, first under Mrs Thatcher and then under John Major – and not only under Thatcher and Major but also under Kohl, Mitterand, Andreotti and to a lesser extent Ronald Reagan. Economists are perfectly familiar with this theory: it is nothing more nor less than the negatively sloped Phillips curve. But the term 'Phillips curve' is never mentioned by politicians because it implies that there is a trade-off between inflation and unemployment and of course politicians will never admit that patients may have to swallow bitter pills before they get better; in politics, all pleasures are painless and every lunch is free. No wonder then that Norman Lamont's remark in the House of Commons was widely regarded as another gaffe from a man notorious for his indiscretion.

For 14 years, British (and European) conservatives have told the electorate that the great enemy of economic progress is inflation and that the costs of inflation are much greater than the costs of unemployment; indeed, to neglect the fight against inflation is to court both inflation and unemployment whereas apparently 'a little unemployment' is a price that may be worth paying to get rid of inflation. Like all lies endlessly repeated, this lie has come to be believed and in fact so deeply believed that to question it is taken to be a sign of economic illiteracy. But on the contrary, there is absolutely no warrant in economic theory to support the contention that the costs of inflation are greater than the costs of unemployment. It is perfectly true that greater concern about inflation than about unemployment and deflation is the workaday philosophy of commercial bankers since time immemorial and that the torturous reasoning of the New Classical Macroeconomics may be employed to buttress it. The fact remains, however, that mainstream macroeconomics continues to assign greater priority to the battle against unemployment than to the battle against inflation. Keynes is as much a hero to modern macroeconomists as he was to his contemporaries.

* First published in *Economic Notes by Monte dei Paschi di Siena*, **22**(3), 1993: 387–401.

ANTICIPATED AND UNANTICIPATED INFLATION

In analysing the costs of inflation, it is essential to keep in mind the fundamental distinction between anticipated and unanticipated inflation. If inflation were fully anticipated, if every increase in the price of goods bought were matched by a rise in the price of services hired out, if all incomes were so to speak fully indexed, then inflation would be tantamount to adding zeros to all nominal prices and incomes, leaving everything as it was before in real terms. But inflation in practice is never perfectly anticipated and never can be perfectly anticipated: to make inflation perfectly anticipated, all economic transactions would have to be instantaneous in time.

Nevertheless, inflation never comes as a complete surprise; it is always anticipated to some extent, the more so the longer it goes on and the faster it proceeds. It will become apparent that it is impossible to contemplate the disadvantages of inflation without confronting the distinction between anticipated and unanticipated inflation.

THE REAL COSTS OF INFLATION

The two most famous real costs of inflation, which would obtain even if inflation were perfectly anticipated, are 'menu costs' and 'shoe leather costs'. Menu costs refer to the fact that real resources have to be used up during periods of inflation to post new prices, to revise catalogues, to amend vending machines and to renegotiate wage rates. Efforts to estimate these menu costs at various hypothetical inflation rates, however, suggest that the annual rate of inflation has to be 20 per cent before menu costs amounts to as little as one-tenth of one per cent of GDP.[1] In other words, the menu costs of moderate inflations are too small to be taken seriously. Nevertheless, it is interesting to see how firms and shops have responded to continuous moderate inflation in recent years by anticipating future menu costs: thus, books are no longer published with fixed prices printed on their dustjackets and many supermarkets have adopted price codes that can be adjusted by computer at the checkout desk.

Next, we have the shoe leather costs of even perfectly anticipated inflation. Everyone holds cash or checking deposits to finance routine transactions but since these pay no interest, people have an incentive to keep these balances to a minimum. Money placed in time deposits (deposit accounts as they are called in the UK) typically grows in line with inflation because nominal interest rates have a tendency to rise to compensate depositors for anticipated inflation. So people will usually prefer to build up their time deposits and to economize on their holdings of cash and demand deposits (current accounts), implying frequent trips to the bank to affect these transactions between different accounts. Anyone who has read a description of the great German hyperinflation of 1922–3 will have come across stories of shops closed for hours while shopkeepers hurried to place the day's receipts on deposit at a bank – these are precisely the sort of real costs of inflation envisaged in the concept of shoe leather costs.

A considerable amount of research has been devoted to quantifying the shoe leather costs of inflation, but like the menu costs, they have turned out to be relatively modest at least for standard inflation rates experienced in recent years. For example an inflation rate of 20–30 per cent would be required to cause an output loss of even as much as 0.5 per cent. Moreover, financial innovations in modern banking systems are continually reducing the shoe leather costs of inflation, the more so as inflation comes to be better anticipated. For example, many banks have introduced time deposit accounts which combine facilities for cheques, instant access to cash and the payment of interest, thus in effect combining the old demand deposit and time deposit accounts: even when the two types of account are kept separate, arrangements are made to allow instant transfer between them by phone. We can be sure that such innovations in banking techniques would be accelerated if inflation once again reached two-digit levels (as it did in the 1970s) and therefore came to be even better anticipated than it has been. Thus, future inflations ae likely to impose lower shoe leather costs than were imposed by past inflations.

Menu costs and shoe leather costs of inflation are economists' arguments, too subtle and complex for the man-in-the-street. The next argument, however, is the favourite of politicians and journalists: inflation, spreading from prices to wages, threatens the international competitiveness of industry, particularly if the country in question is a member of a fixed exchange rate mechanism. It is of course *relative* inflation that is the problem, so the argument must be that any inflation in excess of a country's trading rivals is costly in that it causes a deficit in a country's balance of trade and, unless offset by capital movements, by a deficit in a country's balance of payments.

This particular cost of inflation appeared particularly relevant to Britain in the 1980s when the UK share of world exports of manufactured goods fell disastrously, while the UK inflation rate continually exceeded those of its major industrial competitors. However, it is elementary economics that international competitiveness depends on price, yes, but almost as much on non-price variables such a design, reliability of product and after-sales service, and moreover on price after allowing for exchange rates. Now, a principal reason for UK poor trade performance in the 1980s was the rapid appreciation of sterling in the later 1970s and early 1980s, in part because of North Sea oil and in part, no doubt, because speculators regarded sterling as likely to lose value in the future.

Speculators thought so because the UK inflation rate exceeded the average of the industrial world, and it did so, so the argument goes, because UK wage rates were too high. But the argument proves too much because if high wage rates caused high prices, Germany ought to be uncompetitive *vis-à-vis* the rest of Europe. Higher productivity of labour is quite capable of producing low unit labour costs even with wages in excess of the European average. Thus, Germany combines one of the highest wage rates in Europe with relatively low unit labour costs, particularly after allowing for the strength of the Deutschmark in the ERM. In any case, the argument that the cost in international competitiveness was a major cost of inflation to a weak economy like that of Britain has been nullified by Britain's exit from the ERM. The options of offsetting a long-term upward trend in the UK prices of goods by sustained sterling depreciation is now available via a freely fluctuating exchange rate. It is going to be much more difficult in the years to come to argue that the UK should do battle with inflation because it is somehow harmful for sterling to depreciate without limit.

Next is the idea, first introduced by Milton Friedman in 1967, that inflation introduces 'noise' into the economy, interfering with the Hayekian transmission of information that changes in relative prices provide to economic agents. For example, a rise in the relative price of a product normally indicates excess demand for it, inducing a switch of resources to its production to alleviate the shortage; but when all prices are rising, this change in relative price is likely to be misunderstood as a reflection of a general inflationary upsurge. In this way, it is argued, inflation causes a misallocation of resources in all sorts of ways. Moreover, as inflation rises, it frequently becomes more volatile from month to month, accelerating and decelerating, and this adds an additional element of uncertainty to every market transaction. In short, inflation inhibits the clear reception of price signals and the more inflation there is, the greater the level of noise and the lower the efficiency of the price mechanism.

Unlike so many theories of inflation, this particular theory has a clear testable implication, namely, that inflation retards the rate of economic growth. Unfortunately, the empirical evidence shows that moderate and even severe inflation is consistent with economic growth, with economic decline, and with economic stagnation, and Milton Friedman for one is perfectly candid about admitting that the theory of inflationary noise lacks compelling empirical support. The reason is that the inflationary noise theory is itself highly dubious. Business enterprises usually have specialist knowledge of their own product markets and are not likely to confuse the general rate of inflation with a greater demand for its products, and as for consumers, they may occasionally confuse a higher price as the sign of greater scarcity for a particular product which they wish to purchase but such a mistake is likely to be short-lived. The inflationary noise theory not only lacks firm evidence in its favour but also convincing foundations in standard price theory.

THE REDISTRIBUTIVE EFFECTS OF INFLATION

All the four costs of inflation discussed so far would be incurred even if inflation were perfectly anticipated, and some of the, like the shoe leather costs, might be greater if inflation were perfectly anticipated. But as we said earlier, inflation is almost bound to be imperfectly anticipated, to surprise everyone by its pace. Because inflation is never perfectly anticipated, it is certain to alter the distribution of income and wealth in an economy, depending on the speed with which different individuals and groups of individuals react to it. These redistributive effects of inflation are in fact the effects that older economists in the nineteenth and early twentieth century would have seized on at the outset of the discussion and they would hardly have noticed what we have called the four real costs of unemployment.

Who are the main social groups affected differentially by inflation? In the standard literature on inflation stretching back to the eighteenth-century, there are four groups that always appear prominently in any discussion of the costs and benefits of inflation: (a) wage-earners versus profit-receivers; (b) debtors versus creditors; (c) fixed-income receivers versus variable-income receivers; and (d) real-asset holders versus financial-asset holders. Let us touch briefly on all these in turn.

If prices rise faster than wages, inflation will alter the distribution of national income in favour of profits. On the other hand, if wages race ahead of prices, the relative share of wages in national income rises and the share accruing to profits falls. Recalling the old distinction between demand-pull and cost-push theories of inflation, we may predict that demand-pull inflations are likely to raise the relative share of profits in national income, while cost push inflations are more likely to benefit wages at the expense of profits. That we can say this shows immediately that inflation as such may redistribute income in respect of wages and profit in either direction.

What is the empirical evidence? The question has been investigated historically and econometrically for different periods and different countries with almost every result showing up sometime and somewhere. There is a widespread belief that wages typically lag behind prices and hence that inflation is a threat to the living standards of workers. But the wage lag hypothesis is as frequently denied by the data as supported by them.

Next is what must be one of the most famous, if not the most famous, redistributive effects of inflation: the shift of income from creditors to debtors. If Mr Creditor lends Mr Debtor $100 for a year at a 10 per cent interest rate and prices rise by 20 per cent during that year, then Mr Creditor has paid a total price, including the cost of credit, of $110 for goods which, had he saved up for them and not borrowed at all, would have commanded a cash price at the end of the year of $120. This happens because the nominal rate of interest does not usually rise as fast as the general rate of inflation (as Irving Fisher never tired of pointing out), so that the real rate of interest falls in an inflation, and the reason for this is precisely that inflation is never fully anticipated by either creditors or debtors. When we recall that the biggest debts incurred by most ordinary people are mortgages, one of the effects of unanticipated inflation is to shift part of the cost of buying a house from the mortgagee to the mortgagor, who in Britain are typically building society depositors, and elsewhere maybe insurance companies and commercial banks. If the mortgagees are young and relatively better off and the mortgagors old and relatively poor, we get a regressive redistribution of income; but it can easily go the other way, depending on the way house purchases are financed in a particular country.

There may be offsets on the creditor–debtor front because the largest debtor in the economy is the government and hence it is the state that is normally the greatest winner from unanticipated inflation. The government can transfer resources from one group in society to another by an 'inflation tax': aggregate demand is increased by expansionary fiscal and/or monetary policy and the government employs the tax revenues generated by the higher nominal value of national income to provide benefits in kind, such as education and health care or cash benefits to the old and the unemployed. Because these benefits are more likely to be received by the poor than the rich, it may well be that the inflation tax is more progressive in its redistributive impact than conventional taxes. But so far, at any rate, no one has succeeded in putting any convincing numbers on these conjectures.

That brings us to the third group said to be adversely affected by inflation: those who live on fixed incomes, particularly old-age pensioners. In the nineteenth century, this was one of the principal reasons for disapproving of inflation but nowadays little is heard of this argument. In most countries, pensions are now tied either to the retail price index or to the average rate of increase of wages of public employees; pensions are not only indexed but sometimes they are over-indexed.

Lastly, we have the effects of inflation on those who hold wealth in the form of real rather than financial assets. Real assets, such as houses, works of art, antiques, Persian carpets and jewellery, which are in limited supply, tend to rise in price more rapidly than goods and services and so are suitable as 'inflation hedges'. But the importance of such inflation hedging depends on whether financial assets, the alternative store of wealth, are or are not inflation-proofed.

Clearly, if the individual holds his or her financial wealth in the form of cash, inflation will erode its value. But if, instead, the individual invests funds in time deposits, building societies, government securities or stocks and shares, they may be able to avoid most if not all of the tendency, mentioned earlier, of the real rate of interest to become negative during periods of inflation. If they combine such judicious holdings of financial assets with heavy inflation hedging via multiple house purchases, such that their overall position as a wealth-holder is that of a debtor rather than a creditor, they may actually do very well from inflation, the more so if most of society fails fully to anticipate the inflation they are experiencing.

These particular effects of inflation, involving the redistribution of wealth rather than income may be very large and may be progressive in their incidence, that is, falling more heavily on the more affluent households. For example, there is ample evidence for the United Kingdom and for the United States that the oil price shocks of the early 1970s, which brought the inflation rate in 1975 to 27 per cent in the UK and 9 per cent in the US, was attended by negative real interest rates throughout most of the decade and clearly surprised owners of financial assets who failed adequately to protect themselves against inflation. The share of UK and US wealth owned by the most affluent sections of society declined sharply during the inflationary years 1971–8. Since then, of course, it may well be that these losses suffered under unanticipated inflation were recouped during the years of the 1980s when the inflation rate slowed down.

It is time to sum up our discussion of the redistributive effects of inflation. One can say two things about these effects: firstly, they are probably very significant in magnitude and, secondly, they are haphazard in their incidence, hitting the young because they are first-time home buyers, benefitting the old because they possess appreciating real assets, but also favouring the young because they are debtors and harming the old because they are creditors. These arbitrary effects make little economic sense in that the gainers do not earn their gains and the losers do not deserve their losses. No wonder then that inflation sometimes encourages and sometimes stunts economic growth.

INFLATION AS A CUMULATIVE PROCESS

We have argued that the real costs of inflation are likely to be very small and that the redistributive effects of inflation are capricious and unpredictable in their direction. Nevertheless, we have failed to capture what it is that worries most people about inflation, namely, the fear that even moderate inflation will accelerate, will come to be more and more anticipated, and will therefore turn into hyperinflation, at which point money itself will lose its value and anything like orderly economic life will become impossible. The German and Hungarian hyperinflations in the early 1920s, the Chinese hyperinflation in the 1940s and recent hyperinflations in Latin America have left lurid stories of walls being lined with paper money because paper money was cheaper than paint as prices rose first by 1,000 per cent per month, then 1,000 per cent per week and eventually 1,000 per cent per day.

Undoubtedly, it is easy to argue that inflations are bound to cumulate because when economic agents expect prices to rise, they are likely to act in such a way as to fulfil their expectations. If consumers expect inflation, they tend to hoard goods before the price has risen, and sellers; producers becoming aware that consumers expect prices to rise, tend to charge more for the same goods; in consequence, the expectation of inflation works to bring inflation about. But this argument is too simple. If it were true, every moderate inflation would sooner or later end up in hyperinflation and that is clearly not what happens: single-digit inflation rates have sometimes continued for 30–40 years without ever accelerating into two- or three-digit inflation. The explanation for this failure of inflation to cumulate constantly is that governments frequently bring the inflationary process to a halt by various deflationary fiscal and monetary policies or by fundamental currency reform (as in Germany in 1924 and Hungary in 1926). Even when governments fail to act or to act decisively, the fact that inflation is never fully anticipated acts as a built-in deflationary stabilizer: economic agents typically suffer from 'money illusion' in the sense that they fail to realize that when prices are moving, their higher nominal wages do not reflect higher real wages, while their higher nominal interest earnings do not reflect higher real earnings. Moreover, their expectations of rising prices tend continually to lag behind the rate of inflation – in technical jargon, their elasticity of expectations is less than unity – so that they are being continually surprised by the pace of rising prices. In other words, they do hoard goods when they expect prices to rise but they always hoard less than they would later have liked to, given the benefit of hindsight. There is nothing pre-ordained about this tendency of people to underestimate the rate of inflation. It is simply that all the evidence about the way in which agents form price expectations shows there is a quite understandable tendency to expect the future path of prices to be like the past. In any case, this is one reason why inflations do not always explode and turn into runaway inflation.

Is all this what politicians mean when they claim that inflation can actually cause unemployment and that this may be the fundamental indictment of inflation? Well, yes and no. The most sophisticated version of this claim is due to Milton Friedman and consisted of the introduction of expectations into Phillips curve reasoning. The Phillips curve asserts that there is a trade-off between inflation and unemployment. So how can more inflation cause more unemployment? Quite simply by a process which starts with money illusion on the part of economic agents and ends with the realization that original expectations have not been borne out by events, resulting in the same unemployment as before but with higher inflation than we started with. All we need to do now is to add the idea of international uncompetitiveness to get a perfect recipe for the simultaneous occurrence of rising inflation and rising unemployment.

This is how Friedman's argument goes. Suppose the government tries to fight unemployment by expansionary fiscal and/or monetary policy. Higher levels of aggregate demand cause prices to rise and this induces employers to expand output and to hire more workers at the same or even somewhat higher nominal wage. Workers take up the new jobs because they believe that the higher nominal wage rate also represents a higher real wage rate – they suffer from money illusion. However, as prices continue to rise, workers come to realize that they have been fooled and quite their jobs; alternatively, they strike for higher nominal wages, and to the extent that they succeed in obtaining higher nominal wages, employers are induced to lay off workers. In either case, employment falls off and unemployment rises to its original level but, alas, at a higher rate of inflation. If the government interprets the failure of its deflationary policy as evidence that the correct medicine was applied in too small a dose, and therefore repeats the treatment, the outcome will be ever-accelerating inflation but no lasting reduction in unemployment. The rate of unemployment to which the economy constantly tends to return is what Friedman called 'the natural rate of unemployment', 'natural' in the sense that it is a product of real forces and can be altered only by supply-side and not demand-side policies. It is a vertical, long-run Phillips curve and sums up the argument that the only trade-off between unemployment and inflation is temporary.

In itself, this thesis that there is a natural rate of unemployment, a ceiling level of unemployment that cannot be exceeded without stoking inflation, does not establish the doctrine that inflation *causes* unemployment. But it does suggest that the attempt to use demand management to combat unemployment merely causes inflation, and then some argument about the real costs of inflation, like international uncompetitiveness or (for the case of floating exchange rates) the inflationary-noise theory, suffices to indicate that inflation may paradoxically bring about the unemployment that some people think it is supposed to cure. It is a messy and somewhat complicated argument and perhaps this explains why politicians never take the time to explain it to us. But do they actually understand it or have they come to believe it because they have repeated it so often?

There must be something wrong with this argument of Friedman because it implies that you can fight inflation by creating unemployment, travelling down a short-run negatively inclined Phillips curve, and as a bonus the extra unemployment will be short-lived because in no time at all we will arrive back at the old natural rate of unemployment – in two years said Hayek in 1981, in three years said Friedman in 1982. Well, the 1980s tested that prediction: as late as 1987, unemployment in the UK was still 11 per cent! The notion that inflation causes unemployment is loosely supported by the fact that inflation and unemployment drifted upward in unison in the 1970s. But in the 1980s, they travelled in opposite directions in most European countries, and in Britain (but not in the US) falling inflation rates for the last decade or so have gone hand in hand with ever higher levels of unemployment. And still John Major and Helmut Kohl and François Mitterand continue to give top priority to the goal of price stability on the grounds that the costs of inflation are much greater than the costs of unemployment.

We have seen that the gross costs of inflation are uncertain and that the net costs are small. Let us now see what are the costs of unemployment.

THE COSTS OF UNEMPLOYMENT

Compared to the costs of inflation, the costs of unemployment are easy to estimate and easy to interpret. The major cost is the loss of physical output the unemployed could have produced. This output loss is actually shared between the unemployed and employed taxpayers: the unemployed lose income, the difference between what they would have earned and the unemployment compensation payments they receive, and the employed taxpayers suffer the fiscal costs of higher taxes to finance unemployment benefits and to make up for the lost taxes that the unemployed would have paid if they had been working. The fact remains, however, that the only real loss incurred through unemployment is the potential output of the unemployed. To add to that the financial loss to the unemployed and the fiscal costs to the employed, as is so often done by journalists, is to engage in double counting. What we do need to add to the real costs of unemployment – the potential output lost – is the lasting and real effects of unemployment on the mental and physical health of the unemployed, not to mention the consequences of the possibly criminal behaviour of the unemployed on other members of society. Unfortunately, some of these costs are psychic and not pecuniary and we do not know how to add psychic to pecuniary costs. But the fact that we may not be able to add them arithmetically should not imply that we ignore them.

There is no consensus among economists about the best way of estimating the output loss associated with unemployment. Perhaps the simplest method is the 'average product' method, which assumes that everyone out of work would, if employed, produce as much as the average person already in employment. But this method is bound to exaggerate the output loss of unemployment because some of the unemployed are frictionally unemployed while they are searching for a new job. Moreover, unemployment is likely to be concentrated among young, unskilled workers so that the unemployed will on average have a lower productivity than the employed labour force.

A better method is to extrapolate the trend rate of output growth under full employment, using a base period in the 1960s or early 1970s when something like full employment conditions did obtain. The difference between potential output estimated in this way and actual output is known as 'the output gap' and forms the basis for a measure of the output loss associated with unemployment in the 1980s. However, 'the output gap' is greater than that indicated by a simple trend because, as unemployment rises, the participation rate and hence the size of the labour force decreases; people become discouraged and some give up looking for work; part-time work and overtime declines and hidden or on-the-job unemployment increases. As this is recognized in the late Arthur Okun's 'law' according to which a 1 per cent rise in unemployment rate is normally accompanied by a 3 per cent fall in national output. Okun's original estimate of 3:1 for the output elasticity of unemployment in the US has been revised downwards in recent years to 1:1, and an equivalent estimate for Britain in the 1980s is 1.5:1. Be that as it may, estimating the output loss of Okun's law is the most reliable method of measuring the output costs of unemployment.

All the three mentioned methods, the average product method, the trend method and the Okun law method, have been used to measure the costs of unemployment in West Germany, France, Italy and the UK in 1980–3. To convey the flavour of these estimates, consider the figures for the UK in one year, 1983, expressing the output loss of UK unemployment as a percentage of GDP. By the average product method, the figures vary from a low estimate of 8.5 per cent to a high estimate of 10 per cent. The trend method yields a single figure of 10.8 per cent, while the Okun results vary from 13.7 to 17.2 per cent. Averaging across all these methods produces a range of 11–13 per cent, which is perhaps as near as we can get to an acceptable estimate of the output loss of unemployment. In 1983, the UK unemployment rate was almost 11 per cent; it entailed a loss of at least 11 and perhaps as much as 13 per cent of potential GDP. To convey a sense of the magnitude of such a loss, we need only point out that at that rate the equivalent of a whole year's GNP would be lost in less than a decade.

THE MONETARY COSTS OF UNEMPLOYMENT

There are two monetary costs of unemployment, the private costs to the unemployed and the fiscal costs to the exchequer because a rise in unemployment increases unemployment benefit claims, while the associated fall in employment reduces revenue from income tax and social security taxes (or national insurance contributions as they are called in Britain). We will say nothing about the complicated subject of the extent to which unemployment compensation makes up the wage lost by the unemployed, depending on marital status and family size, except to repeat the previous point that it represents, not an additional real cost of unemployment, but a redistribution of the output or income loss from the employed to the unemployed. Similarly, the fiscal costs of UK unemployment in 1983 has been estimated to amount to 5.5 per cent of GNP but it would be a fallacy to add this 5.5 per cent to the 11–13 per cent of output loss of unemployment; it expresses the incidence and not the size of the output loss of unemployment, which falls partly on the unemployed as loss of income and partly on taxpayers whose disposable incomes are less than they otherwise would have been.

INDIRECT COSTS OF UNEMPLOYMENT

There are many statistical studies purporting to show that unemployment leads to a deterioration in physical and mental health, culminating in a higher than normal mortality and suicide rate. There is also evidence linking unemployment and crime, and unemployment-induced crime imposes both pecuniary and non-pecuniary costs on people who are not themselves unemployed but who live in areas of high unemployment; furthermore, it imposes pecuniary costs on the police in combatting such crime. In principle, these are all indirect costs of unemployment that ought to be added to the direct costs of unemployment. But they are all extremely controversial and there is little agreement among investigators as to their significance and their magnitude. Moreover, because they involve psychic elements, it is not easy to see how to add them up together. For that reason, we will pass them by without further comment. In any case, I would not want my conclusions to depend on figures assigned to this hazy area.

Nevertheless, there is one further indirect cost of unemployment that we really must mention, namely, the permanent lifelong loss of skill and working habits of the long-term unemployed, those out of work for more than a year. One of the most alarming features of the rise of unemployment throughout Western Europe in the 1980s is the rise in the proportion of long-term unemployment in total unemployment. Employers, rightly or wrongly, judge someone unemployed for 9–12–15 months to be permanently crippled by their idleness and consistently prefer to hire those who have only been unemployed for shorter periods. In consequence, long bouts of running the labour market at low levels of employment leaves an ever-growing pool of people who are not only unemployed but unemployable. In Britain, for example, the unemployment rate throughout the decade of the 1980s remained consistently above 7 per cent of the labour force, rising to as much as 12 and 13 per cent in 1982, with the result that by now the number of long-term unemployed workers amounts to almost one million people (4 per cent of the labour force) who will probably never work again as long as they live. Of course, the output we lose from their idleness has already been counted in our estimate of the direct costs of unemployment. What I am drawing attention to is the human costs of having living among us one million people who simply do not expect ever to work again. And what is true of Britain is true of just about every country in Europe.

CONCLUSION

It is a dogma of Mrs Thatcher, of John Major, of central banks everywhere, that inflation is the root of all economic evil and that price stability is the key to growth and full employment. This dogma is grounded on the endlessly repeated assertion that the costs of inflation are greater than the costs of unemployment, enforced by the claim that inflation actually causes unemployment so that the costs of the latter are the second-round costs of the former.

We have argued that adding menu costs to the shoe leather costs of single-digit inflation of a country like the UK amounts to about one-tenth of 1 per cent of GDP, and the corresponding figure for the UK has been estimated at 0.2 per cent of GNP. We rejected the international competitiveness and inflationary noise arguments on theoretical grounds and note that no one had yet succeeded in demonstrating that these were necessarily significant. In short, the costs of moderate inflation are small and there is absolutely no reason to think that moderate inflations inevitably accelerate to hyperinflation.

On the other hand, the direct costs of unemployment, not to mention the indirect costs are very large. For the UK, an unemployment rate of 11 per cent in 1983 was associated with an output loss of 11–13 per cent of GDP, while for the US in the same year 9 per cent unemployment was accompanied by an output loss of 7 per cent. In short, every 1 percentage point of the unemployment rate cuts national output by approximately 1 percentage point, perhaps a little less in the US. Remembering that UK unemployment now once again exceeds 10 per cent, the reader may draw his or her own conclusion. We would have to have an inflation rate of 50–60 per cent to experience an output loss equivalent to what we are now suffering from unemployment.

We have been grossly and consistently misled by the conservative governments and right-of-centre economists. There is no basis in economic theory and no warrant in empirical evidence for the belief that inflation is Public Enemy No. 1.

The president of the American Economic Association, William Vickrey, addressing the annual meeting of the association in Anaheim, California, in January 1993, concluded his speech on 'Today's Task for Economists' with the words:

> There is no reason inherent in the real resources available to us why we cannot move rapidly within the next two or three years to a state of genuinely full employment and then continue indefinitely at that level. We would then enjoy a major reduction in the ills of poverty, homelessness, sickness and crime that this would entail. We might also

see less resistance to reductions in military expenditure, to liberalization of trade and migration policy, and to conservation and environmental protection programs.

When did we last hear such words from a European statesman or, even a European 'socialist'?

A FINAL QUESTION

If I am right, we are left with a puzzle. If the costs of unemployment vastly exceed the costs of inflation, why have so many governments over the last decade made low inflation the prime target of economic policy, reflecting what is perhaps a generally held belief of the electorate that inflation is a more serious economic problem than unemployment? Has everyone been wrong? Have governments simply brain-washed people?

But the electorate is not actually in one mind about the trade-off between inflation and unemployment. Numerous studies in the US and virtually every European country show that across social classes and occupational categories, blue-collar workers tend to be more concerned about unemployment than about inflation, while white-collar workers, particularly professional and managerial workers, tend to be more worried about inflation than about unemployment. Well, of course and for obvious reasons. For the same reasons, parties of the left, drawing their political support from lower-income groups, tend to give priority to high employment, while parties on the right, leaning on support from the middle classes and white-collar managerial groups, are more concerned with low inflation. All this lends ideological overtones to what otherwise would be a straightforward private-interests question. The fact that inflation rates have dropped in recent years, while unemployment continues to be extremely high by historical standards, suggests that a new era in political sensitivity to unemployment and inflation is just around the corner. In a few years, we may all wonder how anyone in 1993 could have possibly imagined that inflation and not unemployment was the great bogey of economic policy.

NOTE

1. These and other figures quoted below are documented in a recent study of *Inflation and Unemployment: Causes, Consequences and Cures* by Graham Dawson (Aldershot, Hants.: Edward Elgar, 1992). I am so deeply indebted to this book for both data and arguments that the author is almost a co-author of the present essay.

PART TWO

Methodology of Economics

11. Why I am not a constructivist: confessions of an unrepentant Popperian*

They say that there are only three writers on economic methodology who espouse Popperianism, Terence Hutchison, Johannes Klant and myself. Who are *they*. Well, Bruce Caldwell has said it (1991a: 64; 1993: xix) and so has Wade Hands (1993: 23). I am not sure they are right but until others come forward, I for one declare myself to be an unrepentant Popperian. I know that Popper enjoys little esteem among professional philosophers of science. I know that there are real weaknesses and perhaps even damaging flaws in his position. But I still believe that much of the letter and certainly all of the spirit of this theory come closer to my deep-held convictions about the methodology of economics than any other philosophical thinker.

Mind you, this is a view shared by many other writers on the methodology of economics. Caldwell (1991a) is a Popperian of sorts; so are Lawrence Boland (1992), Roger Backhouse (1985: 2–6) and Hands (1993: 148–51); it is just that their reading of Popper differs from mine.[1] Still, our common philosophical sympathies are much greater than our differences. That is not true of Daniel Hausman (1989, 1992), whose hostility to Popper is unqualified, nor of Deborah Redman (1991). Alexander Rosenberg's (1983, 1992) position is more difficult to categorize but a fair description might be one that once was close to Popper but which is now far away from it. The same might be said of Neil de Marchi (1992a: 3–9). Likewise, Roy Weintraub (1988, 1991) has travelled from great sympathy with Popperianism all the way to constructivism and anti-foundationalism.

PRESCRIPTION VERSUS DESCRIPTION

The tension between the methodology of science and the history of science runs like a thread through the literature on the philosophy of science. There are those who believe like Popper that it is impossible to study the history of science without

* First published in *New Directions in Economic Methodology*, ed. Roger E. Backhouse, London: Routledge, 1994, 109–39.

some notion, however crude, of the difference between science and non-science, resting ultimately on the idea that the development of 'science' is marked by 'progress', whereas 'non-science' evolves without becoming 'better' in any sense of the term. In other words, we must start with methodological views derived from general epistemic principles and, since there is no certainty of knowledge, such views are frankly normative. Nevertheless, having derived our methodological norms, we then examine the history of science to check whether our norms are practised by at least some scientists and hopefully by most. If that expectation is refuted by historical studies, we ought to be prepared to abandon our norms just as we ought to abandon scientific theories that are repeatedly contradicted by empirical evidence.

Every critic of Popper either begins or ends up by rejecting this priority assigned to prescriptive methodology. Instead, they insist on the priority of practice, that is, on starting descriptively with the history of science in the hope of eventually inferring some general methodological principles from their historical investigations. Just as Karl Popper is the patron saint of the first view, Thomas Kuhn is the patron saint of the second: the overwhelming importance of the workaday world of the practising scientist has of course been emphasized by countless historians of science but Thomas Kuhn's *Structure of Scientific Revolutions* (1962) placed it for the first time at the centre of the philosophy of science.

To a Popperian, the Kuhnian position is simply 'the inductive fallacy' all over again. How can we study the history of science without some prior notions of what is science and indeed what is good or bad science? There is simply too much science to imagine that we can study it without some principles of selection and what are these principles if not methodology? Just as we cannot 'data' *per se* without some preconceptions, we cannot study history without some ideas of what is or is not significant in the past.

To a Kuhnian, however, the Popperian position smacks of philosophical arrogance. Why worry about methodological canons that might never have been obeyed by practising scientists and if we think they can be obeyed, surely we must have derived that conviction from historical knowledge of past developments in science?

The tension between these two views can never be decisively resolved but it can be minimized by openly confronting it. One of the attractive features of the philosophy of science of Imre Lakatos, a disciple of Popper, is the way in which he separated normative principles of methodology from positive questions about the history of science. He argued that what he called 'scientific research programmes' inevitably evolve as time passes and that their evolution is either characterized by 'progress', because amendments of the programme involve the discovery of 'novel facts', or by 'degeneration' because the amendments are merely *ad hoc*.[2] Having expounded the idea of progress in science, he then conjectured that progressive scientific research programmes succeed by gaining scientific adherents, whereas degenerating scientific research programmes steadily lose the support of fellow scientists. This is a conjecture about the history of science and he invited us to test his conjecture by what he called a 'historiographical scientific research programme'. No wonder then that the last 15 years have seen a number of case studies in the history of physics, chemistry, biology and economics to test the validity of Lakatos's conjecture.[3] In my view, 'the jury is still out on this one', at least as far as economics is concerned, but clearly if I did not believe that the jury will one day return a favourable verdict, I would not be inclined to advocate Popperianism in any form, and Lakatos is clearly Popperian. This is an issue to which we shall return.

Suffice it to say that some extreme critics of Popper deny that 'falsificationism' (which we have not yet defined) can never be applied to either natural or social science, so that in their view all talk of Popperianism in economics is simply nonsense (Redman, 1991: viii, 119). But Popper (1983: xxvi–xxx; also Caldwell, 1991a: 67) himself gave 20 examples of the use of falsificationism in the history of science 'chosen at random' and elsewhere I have furnished numerous examples from economics (Blaug, 1992: xv–xvi). None of this implies that all economists are falsificationists but it does imply that many are and that some even practice what they preach. As for those who do not, the argument so far recommends that they should try harder.

POPPERIANISM PRO AND CON

Popper begins with the logical asymmetry between 'verification' and 'falsification': nothing can ever be exhaustively verified but a single falsification suffices; in popular parlance, you cannot 'prove' anything but you can certainly 'disprove' some things. Unfortunately, the so-called Duhem–Quine thesis demonstrates that it is just as difficult conclusively to falsify a hypothesis as to verify it because every test of a hypothesis is in fact a joint test of the hypothesis in question, the quality of the data, the measuring instruments employed and a host of auxiliary hypotheses stipulating the particular circumstances of the test; in the event of a falsification, we can never assign guilt unambiguously to the central hypothesis under examination.

Popper was perfectly aware of the Duhem–Quine thesis and hence laid down a number of methodological norms or conventions to prevent endless 'immunizing stratagems' to safeguard a refuted theory. These 20 or so norms (see Blaug, 1992: 19) boil down to the idea that refuted theories may be amended to avoid future refutations but only if these amendments increase the empirical content of the theory, that is, render it more falsifiable or testable. Thus, 'science', according to Popper, involves not just propositions that are at least in principle falsifiable, but also propositions that are increasingly strengthened by being more severely tested. A falsifiable theory forbids some possible events or observations. Thus, we should ask of theories, not what observations are consonant with them, because that is a test all too easy to pass, but rather what events would never be observed if this or that theory were true. If there are no such events, the theory is either trivial or tautological.

Alas, in the course of amending our refuted theories in the effort to increase their empirical content, we never know when to stop and when to go on. There is no golden rule that will tell us when finally to abandon a frequently refuted and constantly amended theory but clearly it will depend on our past record in that area of endeavour and on the availability of alternative theories. But to infer present practice from past experience is to make use of induction as a form of gaining knowledge and Popper not only denies the validity of inductive logic but even denies the possibility of making inductions; induction for him is simply a psychological illusion.

The problem is aggravated if we face not one refuted but amended theory but two or more such theories, in which case we must compare them for their respective 'degrees of verisimilitude' as Popper calls it, that is, the extent to which each of them has so far resisted falsification. But Popper has reluctantly agreed with his critics that it is not possible to quantify the 'verisimilitude' of theories (see Hands, 1993: 126–30), so that we are thrown back in the last analysis on a qualitative judgement in comprising rival theories. Here, as elsewhere in his writings, Popper's attack on inductivism and all notions of 'supporting' evidence for theories is so extreme as to cast some doubt on the entire enterprise of falsificationism.

The point is well made by Popper's claims on behalf of 'situational analysis'. 'Situational analysis' is his label for what we in economics know as the concept of rational choice, that is, the view that economic behaviour is simply individual maximizing behaviour subject to constraints, and indeed Popper declared 'situational analysis' to be a generalization of the method of economic analysis. What is surprising is that (a) he claimed it to be the one legitimate mode of explanation in the social sciences; (b) he admitted it was false as a universal law of economic behaviour but nevertheless insisted that it should be retained as an unexamined 'metaphysical' principle; and (c) he virtually implied, without quite saying so, that it should be retained because it had shown itself to be fruitful in the past, particularly in economics. Now, (a) contradicts his 'unity of science' thesis, the doctrine that there is no difference in the structure of explanation in the natural and the social sciences and that all sciences must validate their theories in the same way. Likewise, (b) actually endorses one particular 'immunizing stratagem' in the face of refutations of rationality, namely to retain the rationality principle and to place the blame for refutation on, say, the constraints, the limited information available to agents or any other feature of the test in question. Finally, and most damningly, (c) provides an inductive argument on behalf of rational choice models of behaviour – they have worked well in the past and so might work well in the future – which flies in the face of everything that Popper has ever written on induction.

When I first encountered this argument in Hands (1985, 1993), I pooh-poohed it (Blaug, 1985) on the grounds that it appeared in *The Poverty of Historicism* (1957) which even Popper described as one of his 'stodgiest pieces of writing'. But since then it has been restated and somewhat amplified by Popper as late as 1976 (see Caldwell, 1991a: 72–81) and here is no doubt that at best it lies uneasily in the corpus of his writings and at worst it blatantly contradicts it. I think that a very good defence can be made of individual rationality as a principle of explanation in economics, particularly if we recognize that what is usually involved in economic analysis is 'means-rationality', not 'belief-rationality' or 'end-rationality', that is, consistency of actions and not necessarily perfectly informed 'reasonable' actions (Hamlin, 1986: 12–59). There is also no doubt that it has in some sense 'worked' well in microeconomics. Nevertheless, there is mounting evidence that economic behaviour frequently violates any and all senses of 'rationality' (Blaug, 1992: 232–3) and it has even been argued that economic explanations involving rational choice are a species of 'folk psychology', explaining actions in terms of beliefs and desires, variables that cannot be measured independently of the actual choices we want to predict, so that these are no genuine explanations at all (Rosenberg, 1992: ch. 5). Be that as it may, it remains true that Popper's defence of rational choice models will not wash in terms of the methodology of falsificationism.

Some lukewarm Popperians like Caldwell (1991a: 84–6), Boland (1992) and Hands (1993: 118–9, 185–8), after reviewing these and other objections to Popper's methodological views, come down in the end in favour of 'critical rationalism' as the essence of Popper. By this they mean the view that scientific theories are open to criticism in all respects and particularly with reference to the problems which the theories in question were designed to solve. In *Postscript to the Logic of Scientific Discovery* (1983), Popper makes it clear that he now subscribes to this interpretation of his views: 'the real linchpin of my thought', he writes, 'is fallibilism and the critical approach' (quoted by Caldwell, 1991a: 81; see also Hands, 1993: 160–1). By 'fallibilism' Popper means the denial that there is ever certainty of knowledge or even truth: all knowledge is conjectural and provisional in that it has not yet been shown to be false; by 'the critical approach' he means that we have just labelled 'critical rationalism'.

The principal weakness of 'critical rationalism' is that it appears to be a prescriptive methodology with very little content: 'it is a view', as Wade Hands (1993: 118) puts it, 'that may be palatable by virtue of its blandness – the epistemological analog of the ethical mandate to "live the good life"'. Of course, all theories must be criticized and all scientists ought to, and perhaps even do, tolerate criticism of all sorts, but criticism of what? Apart from pointing out internal inconsistencies we can only criticize with meta-theoretical criteria and, according to critical rationalism, the only one we are encouraged to employ is that of assessing a theory's ability to solve the problems it has set itself.[4] This is something but it is not very much and if this is what falsificationism amounts to in the end, we can say with perfect confidence 'we are all falsificationists now'. Having trimmed the lion's claw and pulled his teeth out as well, all with the aid and assistance of the lion himself, there is not much left to argue about.

CLARIFYING LAKATOS

Many surveys of recent developments in the philosophy of science have depicted the ideas of Imre Lakatos as a dilution or even a betrayal of Popper. In fact, Lakatos is 80 per cent Popper and 20 per cent Kuhn, and virtually everything that Lakatos ever said is found in Popper in some form or another. However, Lakatos's starting point, the idea that theories provide scientists with 'research programmes' which guide their daily practice, is Kuhnian. Being research programmes they consist at their centre of metaphysical beliefs, 'paradigms', *Weltanschauungen*, or Schumpeterian 'visions', and a set of pragmatic dos and don'ts for tackling the problems selected for analysis. The idea that science cannot dispense with metaphysical beliefs, but that these are kept so to speak 'out of sight', is pure Popper. Surrounding the 'hard core' of empirically irrefutable propositions ('nature is uniform in space and time'; 'everything has a cause'; there always are equilibrium solutions for every economic problem', etc.) is 'the protective belt' of scientific theories, which always have predictive implications about the slice of reality with which they are concerned. Apart from ironic language, this is again just straight Popper.

The next idea is also no more than what is found in Popper, namely that theories can only be appraised *ex post* and that such appraisals are never final because theories are in constant dynamic process of change as the appearance of anomalies leads to continuous adjustments in the theoretical framework. This is what Popper called 'assessing the degree of corroboration' of a theory, which he defined as 'an evaluating report of past performance' (quoted in Blaug, 1992: 25). As I said earlier, Popper agreed in the end that such reports were only qualitative in character and at best involved ordinal comparisons between two or more theories.

Now comes the one genuinely new element in Lakatos that is not in Popper and which has therefore attracted more controversy than any other feature of his methodology. For Popper, the evaluating report of a theory consisted of 'the state (at a certain time *t*) of the critical discussion of a theory, with respect to the way it solves its problems; its degree of testability; the severity of the tests it has undergone; and the way it has stood up to these tests' (quoted in Blaug, ibid.). All this is reduced by Lakatos to the stipulation that theories or rather 'scientific research programmes' must be altered in the face of anomalies in such a way as to continually generate 'novel facts'. Programmes that do this are dubbed 'progressive' and programmes that fail to do so, that simply produce *ad hoc* excuses whenever a refutation is encountered, are dubbed 'degenerating'. Such assessments are never final in the sense that nothing prevents a programme that has been degenerating for some time from becoming progressive again.

Even this characteristic Lakatosian idea was first formulated by Popper who, as we noted earlier, restricted the use of face-saving, refutation-avoiding theoretical adjustments to those that had 'excess empirical content', meaning 'new and testable consequences' or 'the prediction of phenomena which have not so far been observed' (quoted in Hands, 1993: 86). Lakatos at first adopted this latter definition of 'novel facts' but his followers soon weakened it to 'facts', possibly known already as isolated instances, that are logically implied by a theory; in other words, what is ruled out are known facts which are employed to construct a theory and then subsequently employed to support that theory (see Hands, 1993: 43–4). Thus, what we have in Lakatos is an even stricter empirical criterion for 'progress of knowledge' in science than we get in Popper but it is nevertheless Popperian in flavour.

But there is nothing in Popper to warrant Lakatos's idea of a 'historiographical research programme' that would attempt to falsify his own 'methodology of scientific research programmes'. That is, Lakatos conjectured that the history of science could be almost wholly written in terms of the 'rational' preference of scientists for progressive over degenerating scientific research programmes. He called a history so written 'internal history of science' and everything else 'external history', suggesting that the latter should be assigned to footnotes on the grounds that it would be swamped by the 'internal history' in the text (Blaug, 1992: 35–6). This claim is so strong that even so careful a reader as Hands (1993: 61–2; also Caldwell, 1991a: 101) simply could not credit that Lakatos had conflated historical appraisal and psychological acceptance. Of course, he did not because he did not confuse, as Hands does, the assertion that a research programme is progressive because it accurately predicts novel facts and the assertion that it is 'rational' for scientists to subscribe to that programme because it is progressive. The first is an issue in the methodology of scientific research programmes. The second is an issue in the methodology of historiographical research programmes. The twain may meet but they need not.

THEORETICAL AND EMPIRICAL PROGRESS

All this is no doubt very interesting but the question remains: is there any economics that looks at all like the practice of falsificationism? Do economists ever modify their theories so as to predict novel facts? Is there actual empirical progress in economics? These are questions we can no longer postpone addressing.

We may begin our discussion by drawing upon a list of 12 basic innovations in economics between the years 1900 and 1965, selected on the basis of the personal judgements of the editors of a study of *Advances in the Social Sciences, 1900–1980* in the light of the advice of a number of prominent economists (Deustch *et al.*, 1986: 374–84). The 12 innovations in economics are a subset of 62 basic innovations in social science over the same period, the point of the entire exercise being to demonstrate that there are such things as social science innovations and achievements that are almost as clearly defined and as operational in character as technological innovations. The innovations in economics are:

1. theory and measurement of social inequalities (Pareto, Gini);
2. role of 'innovations' in socioeconomic change (Schumpeter, Ogburn, Usher, Schmookler);
3. social welfare functions in politics and economics (Pigou, Arrow);
4. economic propensities, employment and fiscal policy (Keynes);
5. game theory (Neumann and Morgenstern);
6. economics of monopolistic competition (Chamberlin, Robinson);
7. national income accounting (Kuznets, Clark, UN Statistical Office);
8. input–output analysis (Leontief);
9. linear programming (Kantorovich, Souto, Dantzig, Dorfman);
10. theories of economic development (Rosenstein-Rodan, Prebisch, Nurkse, Lewis, Myrdal, Hirschman, Harrod, Domar, Chernery);
11. econometrics (Tinbergen, Samuelson, Malinvaud);
12. computer simulation of economic systems (Klein, Orcutt).

Apart from certain oddities (growth theory as a subset of 'economic development'? Samuelson as a econometrician?), the list nevertheless raises the interesting question: in what sense were any of these advances in economics? It seems clear that progress in economics can be usually distinguished as either theoretical progress or empirical progress or both. By 'theoretical progress' I shall mean what Lakatos termed 'heuristic progress': greater precision in the definition of terms and relationships between terms and, in general, improved conceptual clarity, frequently, accompanied by analytical innovations; in short, sharper tools for that 'box of tools' that Joan Robinson once told us is economic theory. A perfect example is the Monopolistic Competition Revolution of the 1930s to which we owe our current conceptions of different market structures and forms of non-price competition, as well as the definition of such analytical terms as 'marginal revenue' and 'the tangency solution'.

'Theoretical progress' may or may not be accompanied by 'empirical progress', which is a much more elusive idea than theoretical progress. By 'empirical progress' I mean a deeper grasp of the inner springs of economic behaviour and hence of the operations of the economic system. It is always difficult to know whether we have actually achieved such a deeper grasp and this is one reason and perhaps the major reason why economists (like most scientists) are literally obsessed with the idea of making economic predictions. Every predictive implication of our economic theories that is borne out of events strengthens our confidence that we have caught a glimpse of how the economy actually works.[5]

This is why every 'explanation' in economics must ultimately be checked by a successful prediction. Indeed, 'explanation' is simply 'prediction' written backwards which is the so-called 'symmetry thesis' of the despised logical positivists (see Blaug, 1992: 5–10). But the symmetry thesis is a much older idea and as Alfred Marshall (1961: 773) said: 'the explanation of the past and prediction of the future are not different operations, but the same worked in opposite directions, the one from effect to cause, the other from cause to effect'.

I have so far carefully avoided the use of the word 'understanding' because those who are fond of employing it do so to suggest that there is a way of gaining economic knowledge that does not involve the making of predictions. This may be accompanied by an appeal to the trappings of *Verstehen* doctrine (see Blaug, 1992: 43–4; Hutchison, 1992: 39–45) but more typically it denotes nothing more than the proposition that there is theoretical progress in economics without any empirical progress.[6]

This notion of theoretical progress, of greater understanding of economic relationships not necessarily accompanied by an improved ability to predict the economic consequences of our behaviour, is almost mystical and difficult to pin down. Nevertheless, it is that irrepressible conviction that we see further which seizes hold of us every time we read an older author. We can just *see* when we read *The Wealth of Nations* that Adam Smith could never figure out how ground rent could be price-determined in one sense and price-determining in another sense; at moments like this we have absolutely no doubt that there has been theoretical progress in economics. Nevertheless, as soon as we ask ourselves whether the scarcity of land in central London is responsible for high cinema prices in the West End, we realize that questions about theoretical progress are simplicity itself compared to questions about empirical progress. Can we actually explain the determination of ground rent in urban areas better than Adam Smith did?

I know of no economist who denies that the history of economic thought, right up to yesterday, is characterized by theoretical progress. Many economists, however, doubt that there has been significant empirical progress, at least in the intermediate run of the last half-century, although not many are willing to go as far as Rosenberg (1992: 224–7) in denying that economics is any better today at predicting the likely outcome of specific events than it was at the time of Adam Smith. In assessing the predictive power of economics, we need to distinguish between forecasting the magnitude of a change in the endogenous variables of our models in response to a change in one or more of the exogenous variables and predictions of the algebraic sign of such a change; what Rosenberg (ibid.: 69, 103–5) calls the difference between precise and 'generic' predictions or what Samuelson called the difference between the 'quantitative' and the 'quantitative calculus' (see Blaug, 1992: 88).[7] The predictive track record of economics is much better in the realm of qualitative than quantitative predictions, which explains why those who are cynical about the scientific status of economics emphasize the claims of 'real sciences', like quantum mechanics and biochemistry, to make accurate quantitative forecasts of the significant effects with which they are concerned.

Although it is tempting to deny the need for quantitative predictions in economics, so as to defend the subject against its denigrators, it is questionable whether qualitative predictability suffices for a subject like ours. Economics has always claimed to provide guidance to policy-makers and all the great economists were clearly inspired to study economics in order to 'do good'. Since the Second World War, this aspiration to be useful has been satisfied by the wholesale invasion of governments by economists; America has her presidentially appointed Council of Economic Advisers and Britain's Chancellor of the Exchequer now has his 'seven wise men'. The price that must be paid for all this glory, however, is a measure of intellectual prostitution, the tendency to oversell the subject, and a general inclination to ignore empirical evidence that is unfavourable to whatever case economists may be making at the time (see Blaug, 1992: 31–3).

Suffice it to say that the policy relevance of economics poses a little difficulty for those who are inclined to pour cold water on the predictive content of the subjects.[8] One way out of the difficulty, of course, is to pour scorn on the eagerness of economists to have practical influence and instead to uphold the importance and significance of strictly abstract economic theory. It is no accident that Joseph Schumpeter (1983: 125), a great admirer of Walrasian general equilibrium theory, decried the tendency of Keynes's *General Theory* to 'sublimate practical issues into scientific ones'. But if we accept and even welcome the inevitable policy implications of much even seemingly abstract economic theory, we cannot at the same time pour cold water on the predictably of economic theories, sometimes going so far as to suggest that the very character of economics as a social science necessarily robs the subject of any capacity to predict. The late George Shackle (1972) was not at all unwilling to go down that road but others were inclined to come half-way and then inconsistently to halt. I have shown elsewhere (Blaug, 1990: 107–18) that John Hicks managed throughout his long and influential career to uphold the view that economics is 'a discipline, not a science' because economic theories can neither be verified nor falsified, and at the same time to insist that all theory should be 'the servant of applied economics'. To hold that economic theory should be practically useful and yet to deny that there is any place for empirical testing in economics is, surely, inconsistent. I endorse the Marshallian dictum that economics is 'not a body of concrete truth, but an engine for discovery of the concrete truth', but if economics is to be practically relevant, there must be some concrete truths in which we can place confidence. In that case, economics is not just a discipline, a technique of thinking; it is a substantive subject, rich in empirical content.

To give up the policy-relevance of economics is to reduce the study of economics to the aim of satisfying 'idle curiosity' (see Rosenberg, 1992: 49–55). It is noteworthy that those who, like Frank Hahn, extol 'understanding' rather than 'explanation' as the goal of economics are not reluctant to recommend quite specific policies to governments.[9]

ADVANCES IN ECONOMICS

Let us return to the question before us: is there empirical progress in economics? Consider our list of 12 twentieth-century innovations in economics. Which fits the bill? Take the first, the theory and measurement of social inequalities, associated with the names of three Italians, Pareto, Lorenz and Gini, and in more recent years, Simon Kuznets and Anthony Atkinson. This is an area in which theoretical progress has marched hand-in-hand with empirical progress. Despite continuous controversy between statistical and economic interpretations of income distribution, certain 'stylized facts' – such as the tendency for the upper tail of incomes to follow the Pareto 'law' and the Kuznets U-curve between income inequality and the growth of GNP (see Shorrocks, 1987) – have gradually emerged from the mêlée. Similarly, that neglected stepchild of classical and neoclassical economics, technical progress, has slowly come into its own in the last half-century but it may be argued that the Schumpeterian research programme, despite a welter of empirical studies of process and product innovations, continues to be understudied and understaffed (see Freeman, 1987). There has been undoubted progress in this area but, nevertheless, few would claim that economics has yet acquired a firm background of testable knowledge about technical change. That may be due, of course, not to the limitations of economics but to the intrinsic difficulties of the subject of innovations.

The next advance is 'social welfare functions'. Needless to say, there can be no empirical progress in the area of welfare economics. Thus the 'new' welfare economics of Hicks, Kaldor and Lerner developed in the 1930s , refining and extending the concept of Pareto-optimality into that of 'potential Pareto-improvements', is a perfect example of what we have called 'theoretical progress'. Progress in this area has a peculiar significance for a subject like economics, which was virtually borne as a justification for or at least defence of the rule of competition in a regime of private property. However, once having expounded a rigorous invisible hand theorem, it is difficult to resist the temptation to argue that what is true under perfect competition is almost true in the imperfectly competitive real world. In this way theoretical progress in welfare economics easily spills over into the appraisal of empirical progress in positive economics.

That brings us to the fourth advance in economics 1900–65, namely Keynesian macroeconomics, which we may couple with no. 7 in the list, namely national income accounting. The Keynesian-cum-national-income-accounting Revolution is one of the stellar examples in twentieth-century economic thought of a scientific research programme that succeeded because it predicted 'novel facts' *à la* Lakatos, chiefly the greater-than-unity spending multiplier, and the excess of the average over the marginal propensity to consume, etc. I have elsewhere given an account of the Keynesian Revolution in these terms (Blaug, 1990: 88–106; 1992: 203–5), so will say no more about it here. However, for those who want to find evidence of empirical progress in economics, the story of the Keynesian Revolution, and that of the Monetarist Counter-revolution too, will provide ample raw material.

The same is true of the Monopolistic Competition Revolution. A textbook like Scherer and Ross (1990) is simply littered with empirical evidence in the field of industrial organization, evidence which grew naturally out of the apparatus forged by Chamberlin and Robinson.

I have passed over the fifth item in the list, namely, game theory. After a promising start in the 1940s, game theory in economics died out in the 1950s, possibly because Neumann and Morgenstern failed to carry out their research programmes much beyond that of two-person, zero-sum games, and zero-sum games have little relevance to most economic transactions. But game theory showed a remarkable recovery in the 1970s and today it constitutes virtually the dominant mathematical technique of economic theorists. As such it deserves a separate discussion, and I will return to it below.

Next we have input–output analysis. It is an avowedly empirical method for writing down the production structure of a disaggregated economy but its practical fruits are still limited (see Leontief, 1987). Oddly enough, despite its promise of immense practical usefulness, its greatest impact may well be theoretical: it has spawned and encouraged a vast outpouring of linear production models, which have figured heavily in both price theory and growth theory in the 1960s and 1970s (Burmeister, 1987).

Linear programing, no. 9 in the list, like input–output analysis was promoted as an empirical technique but, unlike input–output analysis, its aim was to develop optimal solutions to a particular class of allocation problems. As presented by Dorfman *et al.* (1958), it promised to revolutionize economics by showing that the same set of mathematical tools underlies what at first appear to be widely disparate branches of economics, such as production economics, input–output analysis, capital theory, general equilibrium economics, welfare economics and even game theory. In the fulness of time, it is probably fair to say that these expectations of a theoretical revolution around the theme of 'linearities' have faded away without leaving much trace in economics. Linear programming is still there of course but in management science rather than in economics departments. It certainly was marked by theoretical progress but it is not at all clear that much was learned from it in the way of substantive insights into the workings of the economic system.

We leave to one side 'theories of economic development'. We have certainly clarified our thinking about economic development over the last 40 years but how much we have really imbibed about the springs of economic development is a nice question. Even the famous conflict between import-competing, and export-led economic development strategies has been left up in the air; some have even questioned whether there is such a thing as 'development economics' or whether the entire field is just economics applied to the Third World. Nevertheless, there is little doubt that the literature in development economics is rich in accurate descriptions of the development problem and in that sense there has been empirical progress even in this helter-skelter branch of economics.

I say nothing about econometrics, which cannot by the nature of the case exhibit empirical progress.[10] As for 'computer simulation of economic systems', it must be said we have invested a great deal in a hammer that can still crack nothing bigger than walnuts. The present-day achievements in GNP forecasting in industrialized countries may be summed up as capable of doing just a little better than crude extrapolations for about a year or two ahead, as for predicting the precise moment of a downturn or upturn in the economy, we still go wrong as often as we go right (see Blaug, 1992: 246–7).

We may now conclude that there has been much theoretical progress in twentieth-century economics. There has also been some empirical progress which, however limited, is perhaps enough to refute the extreme pessimists. It would be salutary to set out precisely what we now know about economic behaviour that we did not know in, say, 1900 or 1920 in such fields as labour economics, development economics, industrial organization, urban and regional economics, environmental economics, international trade, public finance, financial analysis and public choice theory, but I am not equal to the task. But can anyone doubt that the list of substantive knowledge gained in these fields over the last century would be a long one?

DESCRIPTIVE ADEQUACY

But what has all this to do with Popper and Lakatos? Simply this: there is no doubt in anyone's mind that this history of economic thought is characterized by theoretical progress but, as we have seen, there is doubt in the mind of some commentators that it is also characterized by empirical progress. If that doubt were to be sustained, the irrelevance of either Popper or Lakatos to economics would be self-evident. Both rely in their philosophy of science on the notion of 'progress of knowledge' and by that they did not mean a more precise definition of terms or a greater clarification of concepts; they meant an enhanced explanatory power over the domain of the subject as manifested by more accurate or more general predictions. In short, we do need to establish the fact of empirical progress in economics if Popper and Lakatos are to be given any credence at all. Given some credence, it still remains an open question whether they are 'descriptively adequate' in respect of economics, that is, whether much or little economics conforms to their precepts.

One might have thought that the Rosenberg thesis that there has been little empirical progress in economics over the last two centuries is a minority viewpoint, but others too have implied as much. Wade Hands (1993: 44–7, 61–3), for example, scoffs at what he called the 'novel-fact fetishism' of Lakatosians; having originally denied that the Keynesian Revolution involved any 'novel facts', he now concedes that the spending multiplier qualifies but expresses amazement that anybody should bother to make the point. 'The history of great economics', he opines,

> is so much more than a list of ... novel facts. Smith's invisible hand, the Ricardian law of comparative advantage, Walrasian notions of multi-market interdependence, Marshallian welfare economics; and the basic Keynesian notion of output and employment being determined by aggregate demand: these things constitute *great* economics; such theoretical developments have given us insight and scientific *progress*, not an occasional fact.

It is clear that Hands is thinking chiefly of theoretical progress in economics and particularly so in microeconomics. It is not surprising that he couples this view with an explicit denial of the symmetry thesis:

> Neoclassical microeconomic theory is primarily an explanatory rather than a predictive theory, while Keynesian macroeconomic theory is primarily a predictive rather than an explanatory theory .... My argument is simply that the so-called symmetry thesis – the proposition that explanation and prediction are merely two sides of the same coin – does not apply in economics. What makes neoclassical microeconomics most successful is its apparent ability to provide acceptable explanations of microeconomic phenomena. On the other hand, what makes [made] Keynesian macroeconomics most successful is [was] its ability to predict the behaviour of aggregated economic variables. (Ibid.: 147)[11]

The notion that microeconomics explains without predicting, if accepted, would merely demonstrate that the explanations of microeconomics are what Hempel once called 'pseudo-explanations', that is, accounts that ascribe some unfamiliar event to a perfectly familiar generalization but which are more accurately labelled '*post hoc* rationalizations'. No doubt the term 'explanation' can be employed in a variety of meanings (Blaug, 1992: 7–12) but once we deny the symmetry thesis, statements that some branch of economics manages mysteriously to explain without predicting says little more than that the accounts in question satisfy our design for ingenuity. Everything can be 'explained' if we place no restrictions on what we mean by 'explanation'.

Even so, the thesis that modern microeconomics is 'primarily an explanatory rather than a predictive theory' is profoundly misleading. No doubt, the scope of microeconomics is wide but it is not too much to say that it all boils down to the prediction that demand curves generally, although not necessarily, slope downwards, while supply curves generally, although not necessarily, slope upwards. There has been a simply vast amount of empirical research on demand relationships going back to the 1920s, but accelerating in the 1950s and 1960s, all of which confirms the central prediction of the modern theory of consumer behaviour: demand curves are almost certain to have negative slopes and indeed no unequivocal case of a positively sloped demand curve has ever been found (Blaug, 1992: 140–7).

There has always been some question, however, about cost curves, with some studies reporting constant short-run marginal cost curves for firms, while others report L-shaped long-run average cost curves (Walters, 1963: 48–9; also Eatwell, 1987: 165–6). In any case, orthodox theory purports to deduce short-run and long-run U-shaped cost curves from the physical characteristics of production functions, coupled with axioms of profit maximization, and if cost curves are not in fact U-shaped, this is empirical progress if every one needs examples of it. There is also the mountain of evidence in the public finance literature on the effects of taxes and subsidies; finally, there are the results of quasi-controlled social experiments concerned with the effects of negative income taxes. In short, there is really no warrant for the belief that, while macroeconomics makes refutable predictions, microeconomics makes no predictions at all.

GENERAL EQUILIBRIUM THEORY

But what makes so acute an observer of the contemporary economic scene as Wade Hands arrive at this strange contrast between micro- and macroeconomics? It is simply the conviction that modern microeconomics is dominated by general equilibrium (GE) theory and GE theory, almost everyone agrees, has no empirical content (see Rosenberg, 1992: ch. 7).

In a brilliant historical study, Ingrao and Israel (1990) trace the evolution of GE theory from the pioneering efforts of Léon Walras and Vilfredo Pareto through the mathematical rebirth of the theory by Karl Schlesinger, Abraham Wald and John von Neumann in the 1920s to its emergence in the 1930s as mainstream orthodox economics in the writings of Oskar Lange, John Hicks and Paul Samuelson; this led eventually to its post-war formulation in the works of Kenneth Arrow, Gerard Debreu and Frank Hahn.

The theory was concerned from its very outset with three aspects of multi-market equilibrium: can it exist? is that existence unique? and is it both locally and globally stable? The theory has some success with respect to the first of these questions: the possible existence of general equilibrium in all markets of the economy can be demonstrated under very general assumptions, some of which, however, do not accord with any observed economic systems (such as the absence of money or any other kind of exchange intermediary, the absence of inventories or buffer stocks held by agents, and the existence of forward markets for all goods). Moreover, as far as uniqueness and global stability are concerned, the assumptions required to obtain definite results are so restrictive and patently *ad hoc* as to be unacceptable even to those deeply enamoured of GE theory. In short, after a century of more or less endless refinements of the central core of GE theory, an exercise which has absorbed some of the best brains in twentieth-century economics, the theory is unable to shed any substantive light on how multi-market equilibrium is actually attained, not just in a real-world decentralized market economy but even in the toytown economies beloved of GE theorists. Thus, GE theory has proved in the fulness of time to be a cul-de-sac: it has no empirical content and never will have empirical content; even regarded charitably as a research programme in 'social mathematics', it stands condemned as an almost total failure.

This is not to say that highly aggregated computable GE *models* (such as IS–LM) are pointless or that a GE formulation of an economic problem may not prove illuminating, but simply that Walrasian GE *theory* – the notion that the problem of multi-market equilibrium may be usefully studied as analogous to solving a set of simultaneous equations – has turned out to be an utterly sterile innovation.

Mirowski (1989) has described the whole of neoclassical economics ever since the marginal revolution of the 1870s as suffering from physics-envy, going so far as to claim that it was deliberately modelled on the energy concept of mid-nineteenth-century physics. But Walras's heroes were Newton and Laplace, not Clausius, Joule and Helmholtz, and despite some superficial references to 'energetics' in the writings of such second-generation marginalists as Pareto and Irving Fisher,[12] what constantly inspired the advocates of GE theory down to modern times was not 'scientism' but the goal of complete mathematization. GE theorists suffered from mathematics-envy rather than physics-envy: physicists faced with GE theorizing would never have dreamed of spending a whole generation on purely mathematical proofs of existence, uniqueness and stability of a virtual economic system (McCloskey, 1991).

Roy Weintraub (1988) once provided a convenient defence of the empirical emptiness of GE theory by claiming that it constituted the Lakatosian 'hard core' of neoclassical economics and 'hard cores' are non-empirical by definition. In other words, the empirical implications of GE theory are to be found in 'the protective belt' comprising the neoclassical theory of consumer behaviour, the neoclassical theory of the firm, human capital theory, search theory, etc. But apart from the curious suggestion that Marshallian partial equilibrium theory is not neoclassical economics (see Salanti, 1991), this interpretation of the meaning of the GE theory simply endorses the half-century spent ironing out every mathematical wrinkle of Walras's research programme. More recently, Weintraub (1991) has conceded that the stability component of GE theory has run into the sand, a conclusion which he shrugged off by a hermeneutical interpretation of the concept of stability: 'stability is a feature of our models, not of the world'. It is hardly surprising that this account is accompanied by a bold statement of the constructivist credo – 'Knowledge is constructed, not found' (Weintraub, 1991: 3, 109). Let us just say that this stance is extraordinarily convenient to those, like Weintraub, who are convinced of the utility of GE theory despite its unsolved puzzles.

Weintraub (1989) naturally has no use for prescriptive methodology and insists on the priority of intellectual history over all methodological preoccupations. Nevertheless, his account of GE theory never views the evolution of that theory in its historical context. Ingrao and Israel (1990) document the hostility which greeted GE theory in the years before the First World War and its virtual demise by the 1920s; as late as 1923 it was only the bowlerdized version of Walras laid down in Cassel's *Theory of Social Economy* (1918) that conveyed the essence of GE theory to English-speaking economists. By 1930, I doubt that Walras was read by more than a handful of economists in the world. It was Hicks, Hotelling, Lange and Samuelson who were responsible in the golden decade of the 1930s in bringing about the revival of GE theory. We all know Hicks's *Value and Capital* (1939) but Lange's *On the Economic Theory of Socialism* (1936–7) was probably more influential in teaching a whole generation the meaning of GE theory. Lange of course treated GE theory, as Walras did; namely, as a realistic although abstract description of price-setting in any market economy, whether capitalist or socialist (Blaug, 1992: 164). It is noteworthy that by the time we get to Debreu's *Theory of Value* (1959) or Arrow and Hahn's *General Competitive Analysis* (1971), GE theory is explicitly defended as a purely formal presentation of the determination of economic equilibrium in a decentralized competitive economy, having no practical value except as a benchmark with which to evaluate other hypothetical models of the economy

(Blaug, 1992: 162–8).[13] All this is a remarkable paradigm-switch in the interpretation of GE theory over a period lasting only 25 years.

DESCRIPTIVELY ADEQUATE

Enough has now been said to suggest that Popperian philosophy of science is not capable of describing all 'progress of knowledge' in modern economics but it does describe some of it. It is not patently inadequate as a description of what passed for economics in the twentieth-century. It is perfectly possible to tell the story of macroeconomics since Keynes as driven by empirical evidence. Not everyone would agree (see Blaug, 1992: 205) but why should they? As Caldwell (1991a: 68) remarks, testing a methodology against the history of a discipline is almost as problematic as testing a theory against the empirical evidence for it. Nevertheless, the anti-Popperians have been much too eager to assert the descriptive inadequacy of falsificationism in economics. They have retreated in respect of macroeconomics but they still delight in depicting the history of microeconomics as propelled forward by the sheer desire for theoretical refinements. And to be sure, it is not easy to pinpoint striking examples of falsificationist practice in twentieth-century microeconomics. It is easy, however, to provide examples where the steady accumulation of empirical evidence about microeconomic phenomena has gradually, albeit not dramatically, altered our theoretical conceptions and even entire analytical structures. It seemed only yesterday that constancy of the capital–output ratio and constancy of the relative share of wages in national income were regarded as 'stylized facts' of the history of industrialized economics over the last century that any adequate theory of economic growth would have to account for; today we are inclined to deny that these are facts at all (Blaug, 1990: 194–5). Similarly all the great economists of the past, including Keynes, were convinced that the rate of profit on capital showed a downward tendency over the very long run despite technical progress and yet we now think that long-run rate of profits is trendless (ibid.). Likewise, the Keynesian concept of sticky wages and prices, 'fix-price' rather than 'flex-price' markets to use Hicks's language, has trickled down to labour economics: in less than a generation, the notions of implicit contracts between employers and employees, 'efficiency wages' and 'insider–outsider models' of wage determination have so undermined orthodox marginal productivity theory that it hardly survives any more except in name (Blaug, 1992: 175–7).

Finally, the quantity theory of money, in the sense of a causative influence of substantial changes in high-powered money on the level of prices, is one of the best corroborated empirical propositions in economics but the strong version of that venerable theory – the 'neutrality' of money in long-run equilibrium because absolute prices vary proportionately with the money supply – is overwhelmingly refuted by all the available evidence (see Blaug, 1993).

Nevertheless, there is no dearth of theory-driven developments in modern economics that seem to resist all the adverse empirical evidence piled up against them. A notorious case in point is that of experimental evidence of 'preference reversals' or intransitivity of choices which have cast doubt on the expected utility model (Schoemaker, 1982: 418–22).[14] Hausman (1992: ch. 13) has documented the endless attempts on the part of economists to explain away the phenomenon of preference reversals and in particular to avoid any appeal to psychological explanations of the phenomenon. The history of job-search theory (Blinder, 1989: ch. 10; Kim, 1992) is another example of a process of inquiry that emphasized technical refinements in the formulation of ideas than the search for novel facts or corroborated predictions.

We have already referred to the story of general equilibrium theory over the last 40 years, which points in the same direction, but yet another example of theory-driven development is modern game theory, or what would be better called 'interactive decision theory', which is undoubtedly the flavour of the month in economics.[15] Now, despite the need to explore the meaning of rational behaviour in situations of strategic interactions among economic agents, which game theory has provided, game theory to date has performed poorly on both descriptive and prescriptive grounds (Blaug, 1992: 240–1). Game theory is most powerful in dealing with one-shot co-operative games in which outcomes can be expressed in money or any other one-dimensional variable. Unfortunately, much economic behaviour is basically a repeated non-co-operative game with a complex informational structure in which outcomes may not be realistically measurable in one-dimensional terms. It is well known that repeated games typically exhibit an infinity of equilibria and game theory itself gives no reasons why the players will prefer one equilibrium rather than another (Bianchi and Moulin, 1991: 183–4). In consequence, game theory does not provide definite predictions of behaviour in repeated-game situations, which is to say the sort of situations with which economists have traditionally been concerned; for example, buying and selling in highly contestable competitive markets.

Many practising game theorists will be outraged by this conclusion (but see Fisher, 1989; Kreps, 1990: 6–7, 30–1, 36; O'Brien, 1992: 267–8, 278; and Radner, 1992: 1408–9) because they minimize the enormous gulf that exists between theoretical and empirical progress. Thus, Frank Hahn's (1992a) claims that: 'Game theoretic approaches have turned old Industrial Organisational writings into stone age theory.' Backhouse (1992b: 4) contrasts this view with Franklin Fisher's sceptical assessment of these developments, denying that game theory has added any testable hypotheses to what Hahn calls 'stone age theory', that is the structure–conduct–performance approach to industrial organization. Hahn (1992b: 5) in reply expresses consternation at Backhouse's endorsement of Fisher: 'Surely Backhouse doesn't believe Fisher? All one needs to do is to read the old literature on entry prevention and contrast it with the new.' To a formalist like Hahn, progress *is* theoretical progress: pouring old wine into new bottles is what better economics is all about.[16]

Much if not most game theory is normative, concerned with prescribing how rational players *should* make decisions and very little has been done to develop a descriptive theory of how people actually make decisions under a variety of conditions.[17] Like traditional economic theory, game theory has been exclusively concerned with what Herbert Simon calls 'substantive' rationality and rarely with 'procedural' rationality, that is, what players do at the neglect of the question of how they decide what to do. And just as GE theory has solved the stability-of-equilibrium problem by eliminating disequilibrium trading, game theory has likewise adopted a static approach to equilibrium convergence by simply ignoring the adjustment process through which equilibrium is achieved (Binmore, 1987: 180–3; 1988: 10).[18] If anything, game theory in recent years has witnessed endless conceptual proliferation which has driven it even further away from a positive description of interactive decisions. Indeed, for all its strengths, game theory feeds the economists's addiction to formalistic modelling whatever its practical relevance. As Fisher (1989: 123) has remarked: what is wrong with modern game theory applied to industrial organization is that 'There is a strong tendency for even the best practitioners to concentrate on the analytically interesting questions rather than on the ones that really matter for the study of real-life industries.'

The main contribution of game theory has been to teach us the infinite subtleties of rational behaviour, reminding us that the standard economist's account of rationality is woefully inadequate in spelling out the implicit informational structure and learning process on which equilibrium outcomes do in fact depend (Bianchi and Moulin, 1991: 194). This is theoretical progress, but as to empirical progress, game theory has not so far produced a single 'novel fact'.

In the light of these manifestations of 'formalism' in economics – economic theory for the sake of economic theory – one can sympathize with even the most adamant anti-Popperian when they say:

> Economists are so little involved with testing because, first, many are involved with non-empirical conceptual work. ... Second, even those who are interested in empirical theory are also relatively uninvolved with testing (in comparison with biologists or chemists) because, given the subject matter they deal with, they do not know enough to formulate good tests or to interpret the results of tests. To test a theory requires not merely that one derives a testable prediction from the theory and a set of further statements. One must also have good reasons to regard these further statements as unproblematic in the context ... Testing requires knowledge and simple phenomena, so that few auxiliary theories are needed to derive predictions. Facing a complex subject matter and lacking such knowledge, economists cannot effectively test their theories.

If there is a cure, it can only come as a result of acquiring better experimental techniques and more detailed knowledge. This requires methodological reform ... but not better standards of theory assessment. (Hausman, 1992: 190)

Advising economists to try harder, to practise falsificationism rather than just to preach it, will only do harm, Hausman insists, because it disguises the real problem, which is to face up to the inexactness of the science of economics and to learn to live with it.

This is the depressing advice of those who would rather defend economics, such as it is, than to criticize endlessly from the sidelines. Hands (1993: 33–4) once asked why writers like myself insisted on what he disarmingly called 'the philosophic oldspeak of falsificationism' in economics. It was, he thought, to keep economics from succumbing to 'anything goes'. The problem, he went on to say, was analogous to the old dilemma in statistical inference:

If one wishes to avoid a type-II error (accepting a false hypothesis) at any cost, the obvious solution is simply to accept nothing. The problem is that this leaves the probability of type-I error (rejecting a true hypothesis) quite high. Strict falsificationist rules certainly keep the riffraff out of science, but they also keep most science out of science.

Maybe, but Hands and company would open the door to any and all economics: in refusing to prescribe they end up with economics just as it is. 'Economics is what economists do', Jacob Viner once said. This ironic definition of the science of economics could well serve as the rallying cry of the anti-Popperians. 'Recovering practice' is what they call it[20] but it is not much more than accepting economics as it is for better or for worse.

THE SCOURGE OF CONSTRUCTIVISM

Encouraging this drift towards the uncritical acceptance of the whole of modern economics, warts and all, is the new anti-modernism, anti-foundationalism, post-structuralism, hermeneutical deconstructivism, discourse analysis, radical relativism, end-of-philosophy critique, call it what you will. Leading the pack, at least in economics, is McCloskey's 'rhetoric' which comes in at least two versions, a 'thick rhetoric' in which 'Methodology' with a capital M is assailed but 'methodology' with a lower-case m is tolerated, and a 'thin' rhetoric in which methodology of any sort whatever is anathematized and everything is persuasion pure and simple (see McCloskey, 1988; Rothbard, 1989; Blaug, 1992: xvii–xx; Rosenberg, 1992: 30–44; Hands, 1993; 165–6). In this way, McCloskey has his cake and eats it too, and while this might be regarded as inconsistent, no doubt

McCloskey would regard this demand for internal consistency as another one of those hobgoblins of Popperians with their prescriptive Methodology.

Although there are endless variations in this genre, the basic theme is always that science and literature are one and the same enterprise, that all the techniques developed for analysing literary texts can be equally applied to scientific texts, that scientific ideas are just as much social constructions as are poems and novels, and in short, that the world is nothing more than a representation of words. While there is much to be said for the rhetorical analysis of the writings of economists, the upshot of all this is to undercut the empirical aspirations of economists, to pour cold water on predictive success as a central aim of economics and, in general, to supplant the goal of causal 'explanation' by that of interpretative 'understanding' (Backhouse, 1992b).[21]

Not everyone in this camp is willing to go as far as Weintraub (1991: 107–8, 109–12, 126–7) does in claiming that 'equilibrium' is a term in a Wittgensteinian language game of economists, that it is 'a feature of our models, not the world', and that 'we do not justify our theories, our research programs, on the basis of the truth of those theories, the degree to which they correspond to "the reality of the economy" as it were'. Now of course, equilibrium, its existence, its stability, are features of economic models but if we did not entertain the belief that there are definite 'correspondence rules' that relate our models to the real world, we would hardly take much interest in these models, given how crude and over-simplified they are; their logical and mathematical properties are, surely, too sophomoric to hold our attention. But we can well understand how a historian of modern GE theory, whose two books on the subject contain not so much as a single critical sentence on the Walrasian tradition, would ridicule this obsession of some economists with the empirical truthfulness of economic theory (see Weintraub, 1992; Hutchison, 1992: 119–22).

What is wrong with Walrasian general equilibrium theory is what is wrong with most game theory, namely, 'formalism'.[22] Now 'formalism' is not the same thing as 'formalization' or 'mathematization' because it is possible to express a theory mathematically and even axiomatically without necessarily degenerating into 'formalism', which simply means giving top priority to the formal structure of modelling irrespective of its content; it is to prefer rigour and precision to relevance, and elegance and logical coherence of analysis to practical implications; it is to make a fetish of theory and to deride a vulgar appeal to the real world. The form it takes in economics amounts to a sort of 'social mathematics': words like 'price', 'markets', 'households', 'firms', etc., suggest reference to an actual economy, but when the analysis is complete we are left with a blackboard 'model' in which 'prices' are not set by economic agents, and 'households' and 'firms' are merely fictional loci for 'preferences' and 'techniques'. It is not just that the assumptions are descriptively unrealistic but that any correspondence to the real world is sacrificed for the sake of analytical tractability. The final aim is to provide the aesthetic pleasure of a beautiful theorem, to solve academic exercises that we have constructed because they are soluble by existing analytical techniques, and not to provide substantive insights into observable behaviour.

CONCLUSIONS

I have made much of Popper and Lakatos and methodology in general but the fundamental bone of contention is not about philosophy of science as applied to economics but simply the kind of economics we are going to have. Thomas Mayer (1993) Has recently published a study of *Truth versus Precision in Economics*. He eschews all discussion of formal methodology but he also denies that an invisible hand always impels economists to develop the best kind of economics; in general, he argues for an empirically oriented economics against a formalistic one. As far as I am concerned, he is on the side of the angels and his book is full of illuminating illustrations of how many modern economists have sacrificed relevance for rigour, technique for substance. While familiar with the writings of philosophers of science, Mayer derives his view of best-practice economics, not from Popper or Lakatos or Kuhn, but from a lifetime of writing about monetary economics, an eminently practical branch of economics. I feel the need, on the other hand, to support my faith in an empirical science of economics by some meta-theoretical philosophical arguments. Hence, my appeal to Popper-and-all-that. if those who dislike Popperianism will take their stand with Mayer instead, I have no quarrel with them.

NOTES

1. Hutchison (1992) of course reads Popper exactly as I do.
2. I have given a more detailed account of Lakatos in Blaug (1992: 27–37).
3. For a list of English-language case studies in economics employing the Lakatosian schema, see de Marchi in de Marchi and Blaug (1991: 29–30).
4. In fact, Popper's (1983: 24–8, 64) somewhat vague discussion of the meaning of criteral rationalism includes assessing the verisimilitude of theories by examining their empirical track record.
5. See Popper's (1983: 116–17) perceptive remarks on the role of predictions in science.
6. Thus, Frank Hahn (1992a), the M. Jourdain of economics, who preaches methodology even as he professes to despise it, reflects: 'Of course Popperians, and American Popperians in particular, ask for predictions. My own view is that they will for a very long time yet be beyond us except in very special cases. Of course, all theories contain predictions, but testing these has not yet been a conspicuous success. I do not find that depressing. If I were not confined to one page I would go on to sing the praises of "understanding".'
7. Friedrich Hayek (1992: 103) seems to have aimed at a similar distinction when he limited economics to predictions of 'trends' or 'patterns but he never clarified his exact meaning. See Hutchison (1981: 203–32) and Caldwell (1992).
8. This is the general theme of Terence Hutchison's (1992) recent Hennipman Lectures.

9. Frank Hahn was one of the initiators of the famous letter of 364 British economists in March 1981, criticizing the Tory government for its tight budgetary policy at a time when the economy was still in severe recession. It is difficult to see how this 'Keynesian' recommendation could emanate from a mere theoretical and entirely non-predictive 'understanding' of macroeconomic relationships.

10. However, there is the encouraging appearance in the works of David Hendry and Graham Mizon of 'encompassing' in the evaluation of dynamic econometric models (Mizon, 1991), which is entirely in the spirit of Popper and Lakatos.

11. Caldwell (1991a: 68–9) has made observations similar in character to those of Hands but somewhat less specific.

12. It is worth noting that Mirowski's astonishing and provocative book is in some sense totally ahistorical in that little attention is paid to the date of pronouncements; even less attention is paid to precisely what is being said, and key figures like Menger, Marshall and Wicksell are simply exempted from the central argument. This is the more curious in that the author proclaims the superiority of intellectual history over methodological concerns (see Walker, 1991; Hoover, 1991; and de Marchi, 1992b, all of whom make this point).

13. How the fairytale portrait of economic life that is modern GE theory could ever serve as a benchmark to evaluate other economic models is of course difficult to say: even markets and trade at actual prices are excluded by definition in GE theory (see the brilliant, scathing analysis by Clower and Howitt, 1993).

14. This, by the way, reveals the fundamental flaw in Ludwig von Mises's 'praxeology': the notion that purposive choice as a Kantian '*a priori* synthetic proposition' is more than sufficient to account for negatively inclined demand curves. This ignores the fact that a number of *a posteriori* auxiliary propositions are also required, such as transitivity or consistency of choices (Blaug, 1992: 77–8). To this day, this failure to recognize the limited power of *a priori* synthetic propositions to generate substantive implications for economic behaviour characterizes neo-Austrian writings in defence of von Mises (Huppe, 1989: 202–5).

15. As Rubenstein (1990: xi) has said 'Many economists describe the fifties as the era of *general equilibrium*, the sixties as the era of *growth* and the seventies as the era of *economics of information*. The eighties are the years in which economics has been revolutionized by *game theory*.'

16. Tony Lawson (1992: 2) completely misconstrues Hahn's position when be ascribes his view too the influence of what he calls 'positivism'! 'Positivism, whatever else this much abused term implies, denotes a basic concern with the empirical predictability of scientific statements, and empirical predictability is the last thing that a general equilibrium theorist like Hahn would welcome.' As Hutchison (1992: 54–5, 119–50) has quite rightly observed, the term 'positivism' has become 'a kind of dustbin into which anything considered objectionable is summarily swept'.

17. However, some experimental work has been carried out, particularly in respect of the Prisoners' Dilemma game (see Rapoport, 1987; see also Smith *et al.*, 1991: 201–4, 212, 223—4).

18. This is of course only one of the many similarities and points of contact between GE theory and game theory. The existence of a general equilibrium was claimed by Arrow and Debreu in 1954 to be an *n*-person generalization of the von Neumann–Morgenstern solution to a two-person, zero-sum non-co-operative game. In 1963, Debreu and Scarf proved the existence and convergence of the Edgeworthian 'core' containing competitive equilibria by means of co-operative game theory.

19. It is interesting to note that Howard Raiffa, co-author of the pioneering text *Games and Decisions* (1957), is troubled to this day about the perspective–descriptive ambivalence of game-theoretic equilibria (Raiffa, 1992: 174–5; see also 209–10).

20. This is the subtitle of Neil de Marchi's recent book, *Post-Popperian Methodology of Economics* (1992a).

21. Even Marxists have succumbed to this new craze. In Resnick and Wolff (1987) everything is 'over-determined' and self-reflective; they even argue that Marx himself believed that 'anything goes'.

22. Although I have much sympathy with Woo's (1986) attack on formalization in economics, I am not convinced by his 'growth of knowledge' model of the development of formalization in science and he seems to me to overemphasize the role of mathematics in the formalization process.

REFERENCES

Backhouse, R. (1985) *A History of Modern Economic Analysis*, Oxford: Blackwell.

—— (1992a) 'Should we ignore methodology?', *Royal Economic Society Newsletter*, **78**: 4–5.

—— (1992b) 'Why methodology matters: A reply to Weintraub', *Methodus*, **4**(2): 53–7.

Bianchi, M. and H. Moulin (1991) 'Strategic interactions in economics: the game theoretic alternative', in de Marchi and Blaug (1991: 179–96).

Binmore, K. (1987) 'Modelling rational players, part I', *Economics and Philosophy*, **3**(2): 179–214.

—— (1988) 'Modelling rational players, part II', *Economics and Philosophy*, **4**(1): 9—55.

Blaug, M. (1985) 'Comment on D. Wade Hands, Karl Popper and economic methodology: a new look', *Economics and Philosophy*, **1**(2): 286–8. Also in Caldwell (1993) **3**: 29–31.

—— (1990) *Economic Theories, True or False? Essays in the History and Methodology of Economics*, Aldershot, Hants.: Edward Elgar.

—— (1992) *The Methodology of Economics*, 2nd edn, Cambridge: Cambridge University Press.

—— (1993) 'Is the quantity theory of money true?, in K.D. Hoover and S.M. Sheffrin (eds), *Monetarism and the Methodology of Economics*, Aldershot, Hants.: Edward Elgar.

Blinder, A.S. (1989) *Macroeconomics Under Debate,* New York: Harvester Wheatsheaf.

Boland, L.A. (1992) 'Understanding the Popperian legacy in economics: a review essay', in W.J. Samuels, (ed.) *Research in the History of Economic Thought and Methodology*, vol. 9, Greenwich, Conn.: JAI Press.

Burmeister, E. (1987) 'Linear models', in J. Eatwell, M. Milgate and P. Newman (eds), in *The New Palgrave Dictionary of Economics*, London: Macmillan, **3**: 202–3.

Caldwell, B.J. (1991a) 'Clarifying Popper', *Journal of Economic Literature*, **29**: 1–33. Also in Caldwell (1993) **3**: 60–92.

—— (1991b) 'The methodology of scientific research programmes in economics: criticisms and conjectures', in G.K. Shaw (ed.), *Economics, Culture and Education*, Aldershot, Hants.: Edward Elgar, pp. 95–107. Also in Caldwell (1993) **3**: 199–211.

—— (1992) 'Hayek the falsificationist? A refutation', in W.J. Samuels (ed.), *Research in the History of Economic Thought and Methodology*, vol. 10, Greenwich, Conn.: JAI Press.

—— (1993) 'Introduction', in B.J. Caldwell (ed.), *The Philosophy and Methodology of Economics*, 3 vols, Aldershot, Hants.: Edward Elgar.

Clower, R.W. and P. Howitt (1993) 'Foundation of economics', *Collected Essays of Robert W. Clower*, Aldershot, Hants.: Edward Elgar.

De Marchi, N. (ed.) 1992a) *Post-Popperian Methodology of Economics, Recovering Practice*, Boston, Mass.: Kluwer.

—— (1992b) 'Review of *More Heat Than Light*, Philip Mirowski', *Economics and Philosophy*, **8**(1): 163–71.

—— and Blaug M. (eds) (1991) *Appraising Economic Theories: Studies in the Methodology of Research Programmes*, Aldershot, Hants.: Edward Elgar.

Deutsch, K.W., A.S. Markovits and J. Platt (eds) (1986) *Advances in the Social Sciences 1900–1980: Who, What, Where, How?*, Cambridge, Mass.: University Press of America.

Dorfman, R., P.A. Samuelson and R. Solow (1958) *Linear Programming and Economic Analysis*, New York: McGraw-Hill.

Eatwell, J. (1987) 'Returns to scale' in J. Eatwell, M. Milgate and P. Newman (eds), *The New Palgrave Dictionary of Economics*, London: Macmillan, **4**: 165–6.

Fisher, F. (1989) 'Games economists play: a noncooperative view', *Rand Journal of Economics*, **20**(1): 113–24.

Freeman, C. (1987) 'Innovations', in J. Eatwell, M. Milgate and P. Newman (eds), *The New Palgrave Dictionary of Economics*, London: Macmillan, **2**: 858–6.

Hahn, F. (1992a) 'Should we ignore methodology?', *Royal Economic Society Newsletter*, **77**: 5.

—— (1992b) 'Answer to Backhouse: Yes', *Royal Economic Society Newsletter*, **78**: 3–5.

Hamlin, A.P. (1986) *Ethics, Economics and the State*, Brighton, Sussex: Wheatsheaf.

Hands, D. Wade (1985) 'Karl Popper and economic methodology: a new look', *Economics and Philosophy*, **1**(1): 83–99. Also in Caldwell (1993) **3**: 12–28.

—— (1993) *Testing, Rationality and Progress: Essays on the Popperian Tradition in Economic Methodology*, Lanham, Md.: Rowman & Littlefield.

Hausman, D. (1989) 'Economic methodology in a nutshell', *Journal of Economic Perspectives*, **3**(2): 115–27. Also in Caldwell (1993) **1**: 275–90.

—— (1992) *The Inexact and Separate Science of Economics*, Cambridge: Cambridge University Press.

Hayek, F.A. (1992) *The Collected Works.* IV: *The Fortunes of Liberalism: Essays on Austrian Economics and the Ideals of Freedom*, ed. P.G. Klein, Chicago: University of Chicago Press.

Hoover, K.D. (1991) 'Mirowski's screed', *Methodus*, **3**(1): 139–45.

Huppe, H.H. (1989) 'In defence of extreme rationalism: thoughts on Donald McCloskey, *The Rhetoric of Economics*', in *Review of Austrian Economics*, ed. M.N. Rothbard and W. Block, Lexington, Mass.: Lexington Books, **3**: 179–214.

Hutchison, T.W. (1981) *The Politics and Philosophy of Economics*, Oxford: Blackwell.

—— (1992) *Charming Aims in Economics*, Oxford: Blackwell.

Ingrao, B. and G. Israel (1990) *The Invisible Hand: Economic Equilibrium in the History of Science*, Cambridge, Mass.: MIT Press.

Kim, J. (1992) 'Testing in modern economics: the case of job search theory', in de Marchi and Blaug (1991: 105–31).

Kreps, D.M. (1990) *Game Theory and Economic Modelling*, Oxford: Oxford University Press.

Lawson, T. (1992) 'Methodology: non-optional and consequential', *Royal Economic Society Newsletter*, **79** (October): 2.

Leontief, W. (1987) 'Input–output analysis: in J. Eatwell, M. Milgate and P. Newman (eds), *The New Palgrave Dictionary of Economics*, London: Macmillan, **2**: 861–4.

Marshall, A. (1961) *Principles of Economics*, ed. C.W. Guillebaud, London: Macmillan.

Mayer, T. (1993) *Truth versus Precision in Economics*, Aldershot, Hants.: Edward Elgar.

McCloskey, D.N. (1988) 'Thick and thin methodologies in the history of economic thought', in N. de Marchi (1992a: 245–57).

—— (1991) 'Economic science: a search through the hyperspace of assumptions?', *Methodus*, **3**(1): 6–16.

Mirowski, P. (1989) *More Heat Than Light: Economics as Social Physics, Physics as Nature's Economics*, Cambridge: Cambridge University Press.

Mizon, G. (1991) 'The role of measurement and testing in economics', in D. Greenaway, M. Bleaney and I. Stewart (eds), *Companion to Contemporary Economic Though*, London: Routledge, 574–92.

O'Brien, D.P. (1992) 'Economists and data', *British Journal of Industrial Relations*, **30**(2): 253–85.

Popper, K.R. (1983) *Realism and the Aim of Science: From the Postscript to the Logic of Scientific Discovery*, ed. W.W. Bartley III, London: Hutchinson.

Radner, R. (1992) 'Hierarchy: the economics of managing', *Journal of Economic Literature*, **30**(3): 1382–415.

Raiffa, H. (1992) 'Game theory at the University of Michigan, 1948–1952', in E.R. Weintraub (ed.), *Toward a History of Game Theory, Annual Supplement to History of Political Economy*, **24**, Durham, N.C.: Duke University Press, 165–76.

Rapoport, A. (1987) 'Prisoner's dilemma' in J. Eatwell, M. Milgate and P. Newman (eds), *The New Palgrave Dictionary of Economics*, London: Macmillan, **3**: 973–6.

Redman, D. (1991) *Economics and the Philosophy of Science*, Oxford: Oxford University Press.

Resnick, S.A. and R.D. Wolff (1987) *Knowledge and Class: A Marxian Critique of Political Economy*, Chicago: University of Chicago Press.

Rosenberg, A. (1983) 'If economics isn't science, what is it?', *Philosophical Forum*, **14**(3–4): 296–314. Also in Caldwell (1993) **3**: 426–44.

—— (1992) *Economics, Mathematical Politics or Science of Diminishing Returns?*, Chicago: University of Chicago Press.

Rothbard, M.N. (1989) 'The hermeneutical invasion of philosophy and economics', in M.N. Rothbard and W. Block (eds), *The Review of Austrian Economics*, Lexington, Mass.: Lexington Books, 45–60.

Rubinstein, A. (1990) 'Introduction', in A. Rubenstein (ed.), *Game Theory in Economics*, Aldershot, Hants.: Edward Elgar.

Salanti, A. (1991) 'Roy Weintraub's *Studies in Appraisal*: Lakatosian consolations or something else?, *Economics and Philosophy*, **7**(4): 221–34.

Scherer, F.M. and D. Ross (1990) *Industrial Market Structure and Economic Performance*, 3rd edn, Boston, Mass.: Houghton Mifflin.

Shoemaker, P.J.H. (1982) 'The expected utility model: its variants, purposes, evidence and limitations', *Journal of Economic Literature*, **20**: 529–63. Also in Caldwell (1993) **2**: 395– 429.

Schumpeter, J. (1983) 'Review of *The General Theory of Employment, Interest and Money*', *Journal of the American Statistical Association*, December 1936; reprinted in J.C. Wood (ed.), *John Maynard Keynes: Critical Assessments*, London: Croom Helm, **2**: 124–8.

Shackle, G.L.S. (1972) *Epistemics and Economics: A Critique of Economic Doctrines*, Cambridge: Cambridge University Press.

Shorrocks, A.F. (1987) 'Inequality between persons', in J. Eatwell, M. Milgate and P. Newman (eds), *The New Palgrave Dictionary of Economics*, London: Macmillan, **2**: 821–4.

Smith, V.L., K.A. McCabe and S.J. Rassenti (1991) 'Lakatos and experimental economics', in de Marchi and Blaug (1991: 197–226).

Walker, D.A. (1991) 'Review article: economics as social physics', *Economic Journal*, **101**: 615–31.

Walters, A.A. (1963) 'Production and cost functions: an econometric survey', *Econometrica*, **31**(1–2): 1–66.

Weintraub, E.R. (1988) 'The neo-Walrasian programme is empirically progressive', in de Marchi (1992a: 213–27). Also in Caldwell (1993, **3**: 165–79).

—— (1989) 'Methodology doesn't matter but the history of thought might', in *The State of Macroeconomics*, ed. S. Honkapohja, Oxford: Blackwell.

—— (1991) *Stabilizing Dynamics, Constructing Economic Knowledge*, Cambridge: Cambridge University Press.

—— (1992) 'Roger Backhouse's straw herring', *Methodus*, **4**(2) 58–62.

Woo, H.K. (1986) *What's Wrong with Formalization in Economics? An Epistemological Critique*, Newark, Cal.: Victoria Press.

12. Afterword*

Neil de Marchi and I have been interested and to some extent even fascinated by Imre Lakatos's philosophy of science since before we attended the Nafplion Colloquium on Research Programs in Physics and Economics in 1974. At that colloquium he produced a most illuminating early case study in the application of Lakatos's methodology of scientific research programmes (MSRP) (de Marchi, 1976) and I followed on shortly thereafter with a somewhat jejune exposition of the differences between Popper, Kuhn and Lakatos (Blaug, 1976a). Over the years, many others contributed Lakatosian appraisals of particular research programmes in economics and in 1985, during conversations at a methodological symposium in Amsterdam (de Marchi, 1988), we decided that it might be time to hold a second Lakatos conference to see where we stood in regard to the applicability of MSRP to economics. We put together a list of like-minded economists and approached Spiro Latsis, himself responsible for the very first exploration of how Lakatos can shed light on what economists do (Latsis, 1972), for financial support. Thanks to the generosity of the Latsis Foundation under the chairmanship of Spiro Latsis, we were able to convene the conference in Capri in October 1989.

I say that 'we put together a list of like-minded economists', but that conjures up a closed shop of committed Lakatosians. However, right from the outset, we were determined to kill three birds with one stone: (a) to promote the writing of further case studies in the application of Lakatos's MSRP, particularly to such apparently intractable fields as game theory, and Sraffian economics; (b) to re-examine the coherence of Lakatos's MSRP both in purely philosophical terms and in terms of its cogency for a subject like economics; and (c) to follow the spirit of the Nafplion conference by adding to a meeting of economists a sprinkling of physicists, philosophers and sociologists of science. Hence we invited some whom we knew to be deeply sympathetic to the Popper–Lakatos tradition but also some who had long declared their antipathy to all that; by letter and by word of mouth we encouraged an open-minded attitude both to MSRP and its relevance to economics – the last thing we wanted was the sort of veneration of Lakatos that Popper has received in some circles (though thankfully not in economic circles). At most we suggested that there were potentially positive

---

* First published in *Appraising Economic Theories*, ed. Neil de Marchi and Mark Blaug, Aldershot, Hants.: Edward Elgar Publishing, 1991, 499–512.

elements in Lakatos's approach that had not yet been fully exploited and, therefore, that all participants should make an earnest effort to take Lakatos seriously.

No one could possibly have predicted how the mixture of people collected at Capri would react to our instructions but I was personally taken aback by what can only be described as a generally dismissive, if not hostile, reaction to Lakatos's MSRP. Of the 37 participants, I estimate that only 12 were willing to give Lakatos a further run for his money and of the 17 papers delivered at the conference not more than five were unambiguously positive about the value of the MSRP. The objections to Lakatos ran along many lines but there were two notes that were struck repeatedly. The first was the recognition that there is no way of writing down once and for all the precise content of the hard core of any SRP in economics that would command the universal assent of all the protagonists of that programme. The relative arbitrariness of any such specification was somehow regarded as a serious shortcoming of Lakatos's methodology. Misgivings on that score were often associated with a sense of irritation that Lakatos nowhere provides any criteria for attributing a particular theory to a particularly SRP; in short, Lakatos is too vague about how to get started with a Lakatosian appraisal of an economic theory. But all such objections were only preludes to a deeper one, namely that of measuring scientific 'progress' by an empirical yardstick. Lakatos's insistence on the importance of 'novel facts' in the appraisal of rival SRPs struck most participants as inappropriate to a social science like economics. Speaker after speaker railed against what Wade Hands called 'novel-fact fetishism' and complained that Lakatos's methodology lacked a way of capturing gains in understanding that do not directly issue in testable predictions about hitherto unsuspected or previously regarded as irrelevant and even forbidden 'novel facts'.

The first of these objections to MSRP is not, I think, a serious one, but the second is deeply troubling as symptomatic of a general attitude not just to methodology but also to economics as a whole. Let me explain.

The distinction between the 'hard core' and the 'protective belt' of a research programme is at bottom a purely logical one. Once we have accepted the notion that individual scientific theories are necessarily linked together in a network of ideas called an SRP and that, being a programme of promising work to be carried out in the future rather than a perfectly finished product, such an SRP must change and evolve in time, it follows that there is some core in the SRP that changes much less than the rest of it. If this were not the case, how would we know that we were talking about the same SRP? Similarly, to the extent that the SRP is a *programme*, it must provide its protagonists with some list of dos and don'ts in research practices. Consequently it must be possible in principle to specify the hard core, the positive and negative heuristics and the protective belt of theories in any SRP. But that is not to say that such a specification is set in concrete for all time, nor that everyone will agree to the precise outlines of that specification. I have been a classic 'liberal' all my life (well, ever since the age of 21) but I am not the liberal today that I was 40 years ago and there are certain notions which I have held on to all these years even thought I am not sure that I could write down precisely what they are and even thought I know that my list would probably not agree with those of Friedrich Hayek or Milton Friedman or George Stigler. But, surely, that is not an argument against the proposition that 'liberalism' is a well-defined *programme* for thinking about the nature of power and the role of the state? Likewise, we economists do not agree on the 'essence' of Keynesian economics and we are not absolutely sure that we can set down in so many words the characteristic ideas of a Keynesian economist and yet we have no difficulty in labelling Paul Samuelson and James Tobin and Paul Davidson and James Meade as Keynesians, even though volumes could be written on what separates each from the other in their interpretation of Keynes.

The task of delineating the structure of an SRP in terms of its hard core and protective belt is, I do believe, immensely clarifying in attempting to assess its value but the notion that this is simple and unambiguous exercise is, surely, naive.

That brings us to 'novel-fact fetishism', the Lakatosian thesis that progress of knowledge is ultimately to be judged in terms of the 'excess empirical content' of successive amendments of a programme. This, as I said earlier, is the great bugbear of the anti-Lakatos camp. Wade Hands (1990: 78) expressed the point in these words:

> Why would we want to accept the position that the sole necessary condition for scientific progress is predicting novel facts not used in the construction of the theory? Surely humankind's greatest scientific accomplishments have amounted to more than this. We in economics and those in every other branch of science choose theories because they are deeper, simpler, more general, more operational, explain known facts better, are more corroborated, are more consistent with what we consider to be deeper theories: and for many other reasons. Even if we can find a few novel facts here and there in the history of economics, and even if those novel facts seem to provide an occasional 'clincher', the history of great economics is so much more than a list of these novel facts. Smith's invisible hand, the Ricardian Law of comparative advantage, Walrasian notions of multimarket interdependency, Marshallian welfare economics and the basic Keynesian notion of output and employment being determined by aggregate demand: these things constitute *great* economics; such theoretical developments have given us an insight and *progress*, not an occasional novel fact.

This is an argument that deserves careful dissection. There is a subtle distinction in Lakatos between MSRP, the methodology of scientific research programmes, and MHRP, the methodology of historiographical research programmes, that is, between the notion of an SRP, made up of a hard core and a protective belt, plus the proposition that the evolution of an SRP *should* be appraised in terms of excess empirical content, and the quite distinct historical thesis that scientists in fact adopt and reject SRPs in accordance with that appraisal criterion. MSRP is defended in the first instance *à la* Popper on purely normative grounds: 'scientific progress' is progress in achieving 'objective knowledge' of a world that exists independently of our wishes and the only way we can be sure that we have achieved objective knowledge of reality is to commit ourself to the prediction of novel facts.[1] Of course, even then we cannot be *sure* that we have achieved objective knowledge. The case for placing so much emphasis on the importance of making accurate predictions is basically what Hands calls the 'no miracles argument': a theory that successfully predicts out-of-sample data from sample data is likely to have captured some aspect of objective reality because otherwise its record of predictive success is simply miraculous. Theories may also be simple, elegant, general and fruitful but none of these desirable properties in any way guarantees verisimilitude, that is, nearness to truth about an objective world.

It is perfectly true that Popper failed to provide any quantitative measure of the verisimilitude of a theory: when faced with competing theories A and B, we can never say unambiguously that theory A is better than theory B because it is nearer to the truth. Indeed, the quest for a numerical measure of verisimilitude stands condemned on a priori grounds. When we consider the complexity of scientific theories and the fact that their domains rarely overlap perfectly, the notion of being able to compare them in terms of a single metric seems almost absurd. But that does not imply that we are left without any epistemological basis for appraising competing theories. We may continue to rank theories in terms of their predictive success, indeed we must do so if we care about verisimilitude, but we cannot defend our rankings as anything but qualitative and necessarily questionable judgements.

All this is familiar Popperian territory in which we lay down methodological standards by drawing solely on logical and epistemological considerations. But Lakatos went beyond Popper in arguing that MSRP may also be defensible on positive grounds in terms of the history of science. In other words, it is one thing to define an SRP as 'progressive' because it accurately predicts novel facts and quite another to assert that scientists actually subscribe to the progressive SRPs that can be found in the history of a science. Lakatos conjectured that both propositions hold but he invited us to study the history of science to bear him out, holding out the possibility of course that this fundamental conjecture might be refuted. There is, therefore, no inherent connection between MSRP and MHRP and it may well be that the former is true and the latter is false. Thus, in my *Methodology of Economics* (1980), I argued that modern economists preach the methodology of falsificationism but rarely practise it: they are 'innocuous falsificationists'.[2] This thesis may be expressed by saying that in economics MHRP is largely false; however that in no way denies the force of MSRP: the normative case for falsificationism might stand up even if the positive one fell to the ground.

To give one more example of the separability of MSRP and MHRP, I argue in Blaug (1991a) that Keynesian economics was a 'progressive' RP in the 1930s and 1940s because it successfully predicted a number of novel facts, in particular that the numerical value of the expenditure multiplier is greater than unity, lying somewhere between 1.5 and 3. This fact was not novel in the sense of being totally unknown before the publication of *The General Theory* because Richard Kahn and Jens Warming had both hit on the idea apparently independently. However, the multiplier remained a more or less isolated idea in both these expositions and, in so far as it was embedded in a wider theoretical structure, it was that of Keynes's *Treatise on Money* rather than *The General Theory*. What made the multiplier argument so telling in *The General Theory* was that it was derived from a more fundamental idea about economic behaviour, namely, the consumption function, and that the particular form which Keynes adopted for the consumption function turned out to imply other novel facts about saving behaviour and the relationship between saving and investment, which in turn were corroborated by empirical studies almost as soon as they were announced. In addition, Keynes developed a monetary theory of interest to complement his theory of effective demand, according to which variations in output and not variations in the rate of interest bring saving and investment into equilibrium. In short, Keynes's multiplier 'explained' the fact of the more than proportionate impact of investment on income whereas Kahn's multiplier merely calculated its value (in terms of employment).

This is a different argument from the standard account of the Keynesian Revolution according to which the merit of Keynes was that he 'explained' the existence of protracted unemployment which the orthodox theory of the day ruled out as impossible. But I contend that pre-Keynesian orthodox economists had no difficulty whatsoever in 'explaining' mass unemployment. To 'explain'' anything is to relate the unfamiliar to the familiar and there was nothing more familiar to orthodox economics than the idea that imperfections of competition, such as trade unions, the growth of monopoly and the constant interference of governments in the setting of prices and wages, not to mention erroneous monetary policies, might cause a breakdown in the natural recuperative powers of the capitalist system. In other words, Keynesian economics was unnecessary if all that was wanted was an explanation of mass unemployment.

Now this may or may not be a valid contention, but the point is that it does not by itself begin to account for the Keynesian Revolution, that is, the unprecedented speed with which Keynes conquered the minds of his fellow economists. That is a question in MHRP rather than MSRP and it is possible to argue that Keynesian economics was a progressive SRP in its day and age because it predicted the novel fact of the positive multiplier; but economists joined the camp of Keynesian economics for other reasons, say, because they wanted to believe in a kind of economics – any kind of economics – that made it easy to recommend active policies to combat the depression.

So, if we are going to attack 'novel-fact fetishism', we ought to make it clear whether we are attacking it on normative or positive grounds: the methodology of science is not reducible to the history of science; neither is the history of science reducible to the methodology of science.

I would insist that Lakatos was quite right to highlight the prediction of novel facts. Nevertheless, there is no warrant for the apparently common belief that Lakatos never recognized anything like 'theoretical progress' or the pure refinement of ideas and techniques as an end in itself. Here again we are threatened by a Babel of tongues: Lakatos called the process of predicting novel facts 'theoretical progress' and the corroboration of these predictions 'empirical progress'. What is usually called 'theoretical progress', Lakatos labelled 'heuristic progress', and Lakatos certainly did *not* lose sight of the role of advances in problem-solving techniques; he was perfectly willing to recognize model improvement as a sign of progress and only regarded excess empirical content as *desirable* in each model improvement. As a historian of mathematics, it is hardly likely that he would have failed to notice that some proofs are better than others, that an increase in analytical rigour is not to be despised, and that a simpler, more elegant demonstration of a proposition is a matter for genuine congratulation. However, neither he nor anyone else has ever succeeded in quantifying this notion of what we shall now continue to call 'theoretical progress', meaning Lakatosian heuristic progress. This is a point worth remembering for those who make much of Popper's failure to solve the problem of verisimilitude. Never mind! There is such a thing as theoretical progress even though we can do little to compel a sceptic to agree that it has taken place.

Although we can make much or little of Lakatos's observations on the role of the problem-solving abilities of scientific theories – and I do think that de Marchi makes too much of it – there is every reason in a subject like economics to insist again and again on the ultimate litmus-paper test of excess empirical content: Lakatosian methodologists may suffer from 'novel-fact fetishism' but modern economists suffer from 'novel-fact deprivation'.

The self-image of economists is extraordinarily close to the idea portrayed in MSRP: they see themselves to a considerable extent as Lakatosian methodology would imply. However, when pressed, they consistently minimize the importance of empirical progress as against theoretical progress. John Hicks had doubts all his life about the need to submit economic theory to an empirical test and had little use for Lakatos and all that; nevertheless, he also believed that economic theory must serve as a handmaiden of economic policy, a position which clearly contradicts his apparent rejection of verisimilitude as a criterion for better or worse economics (Blaug, 1988). Similarly, Kenneth Arrow, when asked by George Feiwel: 'What criteria would you use to evaluate the soundness of an alternative theory?', replied:

> Persuasiveness. Does it correspond to our understanding of the economic world? I think it is foolish to say that we rely on hard empirical evidence completely. A very important part of it is just *our* perception of the economic world. If you find a new concept, the question is, does it illuminate your perception? Do you feel you understand what is going on in everyday life? Of course, whether it fits empirical and other tests is also important.   (Feiwel, 1987: 242)

Both Hicks and Arrow shared the Nobel Prize for their contributions to the development of general equilibrium (GE) theory and it does not require more than a nodding acquaintance with GE theory to realize that its advocates are very likely to play down the role of testing and empirical evidence. GE theory simply has no empirical content whatsoever. But what about input–output analysis or computable GE models or IS–LM, which was, after all, the first operational, albeit highly simplified, GE model of the entire economy (Patinkin, 1990)? Alas, here once again we must distinguish between radically different theoretical conceptions travelling under the same label.[3] We can speak of GE theory in at least two senses. The first is the Walrasian notion of the problem of multi-mark equilibrium – does it exist? is it unique? is it stable? Let us agree from now on to call this the Walras–Arrow–Debreu GE theory or Walras GE theory for short. The second is the more general notion of an economic model expressed as a set of simultaneous equations in which two or more but typically a large number of endogenous variables are simultaneously solved in terms of one or more exogenous variables. Let us agree to call this the GE *model* as distinct from the Walrasian GE *theory*.

Now, clearly, the GE model is rich in empirical content. Indeed, its only *raison d'être* is to demonstrate the difference it makes to assume that everything else remains constant in a partial equilibrium treatment of an economic problem. At the same time we need constantly to remind ourselves that there is nothing obvious or commonplace about a GE view of a problem: all-round multi-market equilibrium is a feature of certain *models* of the economy and not necessarily a reflection of how that economy is constituted. Thus we assume too readily after studying GE theory that prices are actually determined simultaneously in the real world, but a sequential process of determination – first the price of coal, then the price of steel, and then the price of automobiles – is perhaps a more plausible representation of how prices come to be set in the course of real-world competitive rivalry. In any case, the superiority of general over partial equilibrium models is fundamentally an empirical question: taking account of all interdependencies is obviously better than ignoring them, but it is also much harder work and the pay-off in predictability may not warrant the extra effort.

The Walrasian GE *theory*, on the other hand, rests on totally different foundations. Walras's masterstroke was not just to seize on multi-market equilibriums as *the* central economic problem – a thought that had not truly occurred to any economist before him – but to pose its solution as *analogous* to the algebraic problem of solving a set of simulations equations. Walras's procedure, as we all know, was to write down a set of abstract demand and supply equations and then to 'prove' the existence of a solution for this set of simultaneous equations by counting the number of equations and unknowns. This strictly static picture of the determination of multi-market equilibria was then followed up by a quasi-realistic explanation of how the competitive mechanism might establish such an equilibrium in practice, namely by automatic price adjustments in response to the appearance of excess demand and supply. He struggled to provide a realistic account of this process of *tâtonnement* in successive editions of his *Elements of Pure Economics* but in the end virtually admitted it himself to be a failure.

Walrasian GE theory went into a decline almost as soon as Walras had formulated it and for over 60 years remained the prerogative of a small number of mathematically inclined economists here and there in Europe and the United States. Then, in the 1930s, largely as a result of the writings of Hicks, Samuelson and Lange, Walrasian GE theory began its long climb from relative obscurity to the very forefront of economic theorizing in the famous Arrow–Debreu articles of the 1950s. It is a story brilliantly told by Weintraub (1985) in a style recalling Lakatos's own in *Proofs and Refutations*. In the course of that telling Weintraub fails to notice that attitudes to Walrasian GE theory have gone through a 180-degree revolution since Walras's own times. Walras himself seems to have conceived of his model as an admittedly abstract but not misleading representation of the manner in which competition drives prices to their equilibrium values in a capitalist regime. Similarly, in the 1930s it was common to regard it as a reasonable approximation to the description of an actual capitalist economy. Thus, in the great Socialist Calculation Debate, Oskar Lange argued that socialism could employ a procedure for equilibriating prices that would mimic the one ostensibly employed under capitalism, namely a Walrasian *tâtonnement* (Kowalik, 1987; Lavoie, 1985: ch. 4). However, nowadays the Walrasian schema is defended as a purely formal statement of the concept of general equilibrium, telling us what we *mean* by a logically consistent equilibrium model; not even the most enthusiastic advocates of GE theory pretend for one moment that it provides any kind of description of, or prescription for, a capitalist economy, preferring indeed to speak of GE as a 'framework' or a 'paradigm' rather than a 'theory' (Hahn, 1984: 45–6).[4]

Roy Weintraub has argued that GE theory must be construed as the hard core of the neoclassical SRP and his account of the long upward struggle of GE theory from the 1920s to the 1950s is presented as a critical case study in the 'hardening' of that hard core. But there was neoclassical economics before the revival of GE theory; surely we are not denying that Marshallian economics is neoclassical economics and yet Marshall relegated GE to a brief appendix to his *Principles*. Similarly, modern economics is full of partial equilibrium theories that draw little even on GE models and certainly nothing at all on Walrasian GE theory. In short, there is something wrong with Weintraub's story. What seems to have happened historically is that GE theory invaded neoclassical economics and in the process transformed it into an increasingly technical, highly formal apparatus for talking about an economy as if that talk corresponds to a real economy. We can establish the existence, stability and determinacy of general equilibirum with a rigour that would have amazed Walras but we cannot even begin to describe how competition actually operates in real markets. As Frank Fisher (1987) has said: 'the very power and elegance of [general] equilibrium analysis often obscures the fact that it rests on very uncertain foundations. We have no similarly elegant theory of what happens *out* of equilibrium, of how agents behave when their plans are frustrated. As a result we have no rigorous basis for believing that equilibrium can be achieved or maintained if disturbed.'

Modern Austrian economists go so far as to suggest that the Walrasian approach to the problem of multi-market equilibrium is a cul de sac: if we want to understand the *process* of competition, rather than the equilibrium *end-state* achieved by competition, we must begin by discarding such static reasoning as is implied by Walrasian GE theory. I have come slowly and extremely reluctantly to the view that they are right and that we have all been wrong. To imagine, as do Arrow and Hahn (1971: vi–vii) that Walrasian GE theory makes precise an economic tradition that is as old as Adam Smith is to commit a category mistake: Adam Smith's 'invisible hand' referred to the dynamic process of competition and not to the static, end-state conception of perfect competition that came into economics with Cournot (see Backhouse, 1990). The fact is that modern economics comes equipped with an elegant analysis of the nature of equilibrium as the final outcome of the workings of the competitive mechanism and yet is virtually silent on the precise means by which buyers and sellers resolve their differences on the way to final equilibrium. This lacuna in modern microeconomics is deeply embarrassing because most of the acclaimed virtues of competition in the public utterances of economists derive from the dynamic characteristics of competition in fostering technical dynamism and cost-cutting innovations. But these are the disequilibrium features of the process of competition that have disappeared by the time we come to consider the final equilibrium outcome. In short, whatever the analytical virtues of GE theory, it is of little help and is perhaps a positive hindrance in explaining the true merits of competition.

But so what? We are not all doing GE theory, so why decry the work of Arrow, Debreu, McKenzie, Hurwicz, Sonnenschein, *et al.*? It is only one kind of economics after all. On the contrary: it is the most prestigious economics of all and it has absorbed an entire generation of some of the finest minds in modern economics. And yet despite the enormous intellectual resources that have been invested in the endless elaboration of GE theory – with and without money, with and without increasing returns, and the rest – it is extremely questionable, to say the least, whether these efforts have thrown any light at all on the way economic systems function in practice.

Worse still, it has fostered an attitude to economics as a purely intellectual game in which we model economic processes that bear a vague resemblance to real-world processes and then comfort ourselves that their constant technical improvement will one day bear surprising fruit in generating substantive hypotheses about economic behaviour. When I read in Ian Steedman's paper to the Capri conference that Sraffian economists, having established the logical possibility of re-switching and capital-reversing, have no obligation to demonstrate its empirical importance, I could almost weep. What he seems to be saying, as did Joan Robinson who invented this stance (Blaug, 1980: 206–7), is that Sraffians care more about economic theory than about the economy: they would rather score a nice logical point against neoclassical economics than advance our understanding of how the economy actually works. But they have learned this attitude to economic theory as a purely intellectual game from their orthodox colleagues working on GE theory.

Can Sraffian economics be criticized for not yet have produced interesting testable propositions, Steedman asks? No, he replies, because Sraffians are few in number and 30 years is too soon and, anyway, is empirical progress really the norm in economics? There we have it! His defence might carry some conviction if lack of empirical thrust in Sraffian economics, its total preoccupation with what Steedman rightly calls 'negative logic', were regarded as a worrying problem by Sraffians. But an exhaustive survey of the Sraffian literature reveals not a single discussion of the empirical emptiness of Sraffian economics before that of Steedman. Some Sraffians see their efforts as rehabilitating classical political economy, but, as Zamagni points out in his commentary on Steedman, the Sraffian model is a curiously misplaced starting-point for a revival of the economics of Smith, Ricardo and Marx. Theirs was fundamentally a dynamic economics, whereas Sraffa is essentially a particular species of the Walrasian genus and hence condemned as a static, end-state theory. Note too that Steedman appraises Sraffa implicitly on grounds of mathematical consistency, while rejecting Lakatos's MSRP. However, he fails utterly to justify *his* methodology, which seems to be that of a theory improvement as an end in itself: economists can safely do economics in an arm-chair.[5]

After this diatribe against the 'noxious influence' of Walras on modern economics, I return to the fundamental role of novel facts and empirical progress in appraising the evolution of a SRP. I have tried to make a normative case for 'novel-fact fetishism' in terms of the philosophy of Realism but, despite all that I have said about Walrasian GE theory, there is also a positive case to be made for it. After all if economists *never* paid attention to empirical evidence and *never* rejected a theory that had been repeatedly refuted by the evidence, I would be prepared to abandon both MHRP and MSRP. But there is much Chicago-style neoclassical microeconomics that is deeply imbued with the spirit of empirical testing and there is little doubt that the pursuit of empirical validation has driven the old Monetarism as well as the New Classical Macroeconomics. Kurt Klappholz in discussions at Capri asked how many examples there are in economics of even low-level regularities being decisively refuted, and he cited the Phillips curve as the only example that came to mind. But in fact there are many more examples: Marshall's conjecture that there are Giffen goods and hence positively sloped demand curves; Bowley's 'law' of constant relative shares; Smith–Ricardo–Marx–Keynes's 'law' of the downward trend in the profit rate; Keynes–Hansen's thesis of secular stagnation; the permanent-income hypothesis; and even the quantity theory of money as a proposition about the stability of velocity and the 'neutrality' of money. Of course, much depends on what is meant by a *decisive* refutation of an economic generalization and, needless to say, I agree that economists generally lack 'universal laws' in the natural-science sense ofo the term. Sttill I find it difficult to imagine how one can account for the rise and decline of Keynesian economics, the rise a decline of monetarism (in the Friedman sense of fighting inflation by means of money supply targets) and the rise and virtual decline of the New Classical Macroeconomics in entirely theoretical terms. These research programmes began to fail either because they contradicted some patently observable facts about the world – stagflation in the case of Keynesian economics; the failure to control inflation by controlling the money supply alone in the case of monetarism – or because they implied predicted relationships that were not borne out by the evidence collected expressly to support the programme – as in the case of Lucas and company (see Blaug, 1985: 678–92). In other words, economists may be 'innocuous falsificationists' but they *are* falsificationists and Lakatos's MHRP is far from refuted.

Despite the jaundiced reaction to Lakatos of many of the Capri participants, I remain convinced that Lakatos is still capable of inspiring fruitful work in methodology. Vernon Smith *et al.*, Roger Backhouse and particularly Neil di Marchi summarize what is valuable in Lakatos and I do not need therefore to labour the point. In retrospect, I wish that we had succeeded in obtaining

Lakatosian appraisals of such SRPs as behavioural economics, post-Keynesian economics and both the old and new Institutionalism, each of which might have taught us lessons of their own. But perhaps that is an agenda for a third Lakatos conference in another five or ten years.

NOTES

1. Economics is not poetry or music or art and in economics we do have to ask whether the theories we espouse 'correspond' to a world that we may wish to change – this is why, McCloskey, Mirowski and Weintraub notwithstanding, we do better to model a methodology of economics on the philosophy of science than on literary criticism.
2. It is not always clear what is meant by the label of 'falsificationism'. I defend it as 'a methodological standpoint that regards theories and hypotheses as scientific if and only if their predictions are, at least in principle, empirically falsifiable'. Bruce Caldwell (1982), in attacking my argument, introduced the distinction between 'confirmationism' and 'falsificationism'. He noted that modern economists believe 'that theories should be testable; that a useful means of testing is to compare the predictions of a theory with reality; that predictive accuracy is often the most important characteristic a theory can possess; and that the relative ordering of theories should be determined by the strength of confirmation, or corroboration, of those being compared' (Caldwell, 1982: 124). These four principles, he declared, define the methodology of 'confirmationism'. 'Falsificationism', he alleged, is a tougher doctrine. In its simplest form it implies that 'scientists should not only empirically test their hypotheses, they should construct hypotheses which make bold predictions, and they should try to refute these hypotheses in their tests. Equally important, scientists should tentatively accept only confirmed hypotheses, and reject those which have been disconfirmed. Testing, then, should make a difference' (Caldwell, ibid.: 125). Clearly, the difference between confirmationism and falsificationism is a difference of degree; my notion of 'innocuous falsificationism' is virtually identical to Caldwell's confirmationism, in which case it is difficult to see in what sense he is really objecting to my argument (see Blaug, 1984).
3. The following pages draw heavily on my pamphlet (Blaug, 1988).
4. See also Arrow's highly ambiguous defence of GE theory in interviews with George Feiwel (1987: 196ff), during which he continually conflates the GE model and the Walrasian GE theory.
5. Zamagni shows that even Sraffa himself sometimes appealed to facts to justify some of his very abstract assumptions. But once we begin to appeal to facts, where do we stop? These are methodological questions which Sraffians have not even begun to ask.

REFERENCES

Arrow, K.J. and F.H. Hahn (1971) *General Competitive Analysis*, Edinburgh: Oliver & Boyd.

Backhouse, R. (1990) 'Competition', in J. Creedy (ed.), *Foundations of Economic Thought*, Oxford: Blackwell.

Blaug, M. (1980) *The Methodology of Economics*, Cambridge: Cambridge University Press.

—— (1984) 'Comment 2', in P. Wiles and G. Routh (eds), *Economics in Disarray*, Oxford: Blackwell.

—— (1985) *Economic Theory in Retrospect*, 4th edn, Cambridge: Cambridge University Press.

—— (1988) *Economics Through the Looking Glass*, London: Institute of Economic Affairs.

Caldwell, B. (1982) *Beyond Positivism: Economic Methodology in the Twentieth Century*, London: Allen & Unwin.

Eatwell, J., Milgate, M. and P. Newman (eds) (1987) *The New Palgrave: A Dictionary of Economics*, London: Macmillian, 4 vols.

Feiwel, G.R. (1987) *Arrow and the Ascent of Modern Economic Theory*, London: Macmillan.

Fisher, F. (1987) 'Adjustment processes and stability', in Eatwell, Milgate and Newman (eds), *The New Palgrave*, **1**.

Hahn, F. (1984) *Equilibrium and Macroeconomics*, Oxford: Blackwell.

Kowalik, T. (1987) 'Lange–Lerner Mechanism', in Eatwell, Milgate and Newman (eds), *The New Palgrave*, **3**.

Lavoie, D. (1985) *Rivalry and Central Planning: The Socialist Calculation Debate Reconsidered*, Cambridge: Cambridge University Press.

Marchi, N. de (ed.) (1988) *The Popperian Legacy in Economics*, Cambridge: Cambridge University Press.

Patinkin, D. (1990) 'In defense of IS–LM', *Banco Nazionale del Lavoro Quarterly Review*, no. 172: 119–34.

13. Methodology of scientific research programmes

In Imre Lakatos's methodology of scientific research programmes (MSRP), the subject under consideration is not an individual scientific theory but an entire network of interconnected theories dubbed a 'research programme' (Lakatos, 1978). An SRP is defined, according to Lakatos, by a 'hard core' surrounded by a 'protective belt'. The 'hard core' consists of a set of metaphysical assumptions accepted by anyone working within the programme plus a set of rules governing research within the programme; these rules are in turn divided into 'negative heuristics', directing researchers not to question the hard core of the programme, and 'positive heuristics' laying down guidelines for conducting research. The theories that constitute the bread and butter of the research programme make up the protective belt. A research programme, therefore, includes a well-defined procedure for applying hard-core assumptions to the solution of selected problems with the aid of a theoretical structure as well as a strategy for dealing with anomalies so as to ensure the survival of the programme.

Some writers on the philosophy of science depict Lakatos's thinking as a dilution or even a betrayal of the ideas of Karl Popper. But others would argue that Lakatos is lots of Popper with a dash of Kuhn and that virtually everything that Lakatos ever said is found in Popper in some form or other. However, Lakatos's starting point, the idea that theories provide scientists with 'research programmes' that guide their daily practice, is Kuhnian. Being research *programmes*, scientific theories consist at their centre of metaphysical beliefs, 'paradigms', *Weltanchauungen*, or Schumpeterian 'visions'. The idea that science cannot dispense with metaphysical beliefs, but that these are kept, so to speak, 'out of sight' is pure Popper. Surrounding the 'hard core' of empirically irrefutable propositions, Lakatos opines, is the 'protective belt' of scientific theories which always have predictive implications for the slice of reality with which they are concerned; apart from ironic language, this formulation is again just straight Popper.

The next idea is also no more than what is found in Popper, namely that scientific theories can only be appraised *ex post* and that such appraisals are never final because theories are in a constant dynamic process of change as the appearance of anomalies – unexplained phenomena – leads to continuous adjustments in the theoretical framework. These retrospective appraisals involve what Popper describes as 'assessing the degree of corroboration' of a theory, defined in turn as 'evaluating reports of past performance' (quoted in Blaug, 1992: 25). In the end, Popper argued that such reports were only qualitative in character and at best involved ordinal comparisons between two or more theories.

Now comes the genuinely new elements in Lakatos that is not in Popper and which has attracted more controversy than any other features of this methodology. For Popper, the 'evaluating report' of a theory consists of an assessment of its degree of testability, the severity of the tests it has undergone, and the way it has stood up to these tests. All this is reduced by Lakatos to the stipulation that SRPs must be appraised in term of their response to the appearance of anomalies. Programmes that are altered in the face of anomalies in such a way as to general 'novel facts' are dubbed 'progressive' and programmes that fail to do this, that simply produce *ad hoc* excuses whenever a refutation is encountered, are dubbed 'degenerating'. Such appraisals are always provisional in the sense that nothing prevents a programme that has been degenerating for some time from becoming progressive again.

Even this characteristic Lakatosian idea was first formulated by Popper who restricted the use of face-saving, refutation-avoiding theoretical adjustments to ones that have 'excess empirical content', meaning new testable consequences. Lakatos at first adopted this definition of 'novel facts' but his followers soon weakened it to 'facts', possibly known beforehand as isolated instances, that are logically implied by a theory; in other words, what is ruled out are known facts which are first employed to construct a theory and then subsequently employed to support it (Hands, 1993: 43–44). Thus, what we have in Lakatos is a somewhat less-strict empirical criterion for 'progress of knowledge' in science that we get in Popper but it is nevertheless Popperian in flavour.

But there is absolutely nothing in Popper to warrant Lakatos's notion of a 'historiographical research programme' (HRP), a research programme for testing his own methodology. Lakatos conjectured that the history of science could be almost wholly written in terms of the 'rational' preference of scientists for progressive over degenerating SRPs. He called history so written 'internal history of science' and everything else 'external history', suggesting that the latter could be assigned to footnotes on the grounds that it would be swamped by the 'internal history' in the text (Blaug, 1992: 35–6). This claim is so strong that some have accused Lakatos of conflating historical appraisal and psychological acceptance (Hands, 1993: 61–2). But Lakatos always distinguished between the assertion that an SRP is progressive because it accurately predicts novel facts and the assertion that it is 'rational' for scientists to subscribe to that programme because it is progressive. The first is an issue in MSRP. The second is an issue in MHRP, the methodology of historiographical research programmes. The twain may meet, but they need not.

Lakatos's MSRP has been criticized by economists at a number of levels. First, there is the criticism that the central concept of a research programme in Lakatos is both too narrow and too imprecise. Secondly, there is the objection that Lakatos's appraisal criterion, the successful prediction of novel facts, is too restrictive and would rule out much good economics. Finally, there is the rejection of Lakatos's MHRP as the rewriting of history so as to make it conform to Lakatosian strictures. Let us take these in turn.

We begin by noting that economists find it all to easy to recognize the Lakatosian concept of a SRP. The perfect example that immediately comes to mind is orthodox so-called 'neoclassical economics'. Its 'hard core' is clearly made up of rational economic agents maximizing utility subject to technical and institutional constraints plus the notion that all significant economic behaviour is summed up in the equilibrium solution of demand and supply equations. Its 'negative heuristics' include such prohibitions as 'do not construct theories in which agents act irrationally' and its 'positive heuristic' includes such directives as 'classify all the relevant variables into the forces of demand and supply', 'assume identical agents possessing perfect information', etcetera. The 'protective belt' is made up of such separate individual theories as the theory of consumer behaviour, the theory of the firm, the theory of international trade, and so on, but they are all held together by a common hard core and a common set of heuristics. Moreover, these theories in the protective belt will be judged by most economists in the light of their predictive record and while commitment to neoclassical economics is no doubt influenced by a whole host of ideological and even sociological elements, ultimately it is the fact that neoclassical economics has proved to be both theoretically and empirically 'progressive' that has secured its professional dominance over rival SRPs. In short, neoclassical economics is a perfect example of Lakatos's SRP.

That notwithstanding, can we really view neoclassical economics as one SRP, ranged against Marxian economics, institutional economics, post-Keynesian economics and so on, or should we define human capital theory, Hecksher–Ohlin trade theory, the Chicago economics of the family, and so on, not just as sub-programmes of a larger SRP but as SRPs in their own right (Remenyi, 1979)? Similarly, is there a single neo-Walrasian SRP, including neo-Keynesian and New Classical Macroeconomics as one SRP, because they both adhere to methodological individualism as a research strategy, or should we classify them as separate SRPs because the former assumes fix-price and the second flex-price market clearing? And again, is monetarism Mark I *à la* Friedman really the same SRP as monetarism Mark II *à la* Lucas–Sargent since the former concedes that there is a short-run negatively inclined Phillips curve while the latter denies it (Backhouse, 1992; Hoover, 1991)? The point is not that we fail to find answers to these questions in Lakatos, but that the Lakatosian apparatus is so loosely described that we can fit it to any answer we care to find. Research programmes, at least in economics, frequently overlap, the implications of one programme feeding into another programme as a crucial input. Whether this is a serious criticism of Lakatos depends on one's point of view. Why should the role of overarching research programmes in one discipline perfectly match that of another?

Likewise, Lakatos's concept of SRPs has been criticized on the grounds that it may be difficult unambiguously to characterize the hard core of a programme. For example, is the hard core of neoclassical economics really that of individual optimizing behaviour, or is it that of rigorous mathematical modelling, or is it that of Pareto-efficient equilibrium outcomes? The arbitrariness of the answer suggests once more that SRPs in economics are not self-contained entities but also that the Lakatosian concept of an SRP is hopelessly imprecise. Against that it must be said that the Lakatosian separation of a 'hard core' from a 'protective belt' is partly a logical distinction. Once we agree that SRPs evolve, they must contain a flexible and an inflexible part if we are going to identify a changing research strategy as nevertheless the same essential strategy; the part that does not change may be labelled 'inflexible', 'unchanging' or 'hard core'. Perhaps that is all there is to Lakatos's categories.

That brings us to the second and more serious criticism of Lakatos, namely, what Wade Hands (1993: 44–7) calls 'novel-fact fetishism' as the criterion of 'progress of knowledge'. Lakatos's methodology of SRP enjoyed some esteem among economists in the late 1970s and 1980s as according with their view that sound economic theories are capable of accounting for out-of-sample data, thus demonstrating connections between events that had previously been thought unconnected. But a recent conference on economic methodology organized precisely to reassess that status of Lakatos's ideas in economics revealed a surprising wide-ranging hostility to it (de Marchi and Blaug, 1991: 500). Most of that hostility centred in fact on Lakatos's appraisal criterion, the dominant argument being that while the history of economics frequently reveals 'analytical progress', it rarely demonstrates 'empirical progress'. By 'analytical progress' (or what Lakatos, 1978: 179, called 'heuristic progress') we mean the refinement of ideas and techniques, the clarification of terms, the honing of concepts and so forth. By 'empirical progress', we mean corroborated 'theoretical progress' *à la* Lakatos, that is, an improved grasp of the workings of the economic system as exemplified by more accurate predictions of the effects of changes in exogenous variables on the values of endogenous variables. There is no question that economics constantly exhibits analytical or heuristic progress but there is great doubt that it exhibits empirical progress, except intermittently. If so, the fear is that a Lakatosian appraisal of modern economics would leave little of it standing as a 'progressive' SRP. This may or may not be a fatal criticism, and it may be as much a criticism of modern economics as of Lakatos (de Marchi and Blaug, 1991: 504–10; Blaug, 1994), but the fact remains that the emphasis on novel facts as a criterion of appraisal remains one of the least-developed aspects of MSRP.

That brings us to the third objection directed specifically against Lakatos's meta-methodology for appraising methodologies. Lakatos proposed that historians of science should set down a 'rational reconstruction' of that history in the light of the methodology they are trying to appraise; they should then compare that reconstruction with the actual history because an acceptable methodology must be capable of endorsing the decisions made by practising scientists. In other words, a rational reconstruction must show that successful SRPs were 'progressive'; otherwise, the methodology that motivated that reconstruction is to be rejected as not capturing the 'rationality' of scientists.

Unfortunately, testing a methodology against the history of a discipline is almost as problematic as testing a theory against the empirical evidence for it. Moreover, the structure of incentives facing a scientist, the 'sociology' of the scientific profession, may be such as to distort the actual practice of scientists. There is no guarantee, therefore, that the history of a discipline will mirror an empirically-orientated methodology. Be that as it may, the attraction of Lakatos's scheme is to separate clearly a positive and normative methodology, a study of what economists actually do as revealed by the history of economics, and the attempt to evaluate what economists do as enshrined in methodological precepts. No one in the philosophy of science has come closer than Lakatos to resolving the perennial tension that exists between these two separate but highly related activities.

Lakatos (1978) first defined his approach in 1970 in a paper entitled 'Falsification and the Methodology of Scientific Research Programmes' and further developed his ideas in 'History of Science and Its Rational Reconstruction', published in 1971. The first application of MSRP to economics came in 1972 and since then here have been some 25 case studies of Lakatos's methodology in economics (for a list, see de Marchi and Blaug, 1991: 29–30). In the final analysis, the utility of MSRP proves itself in these applications and the perusal of a few of them is more telling than all the general descriptions of MSRP or accounts of 'what Lakatos really meant'.

REFERENCES

Backhouse, R. (1992) 'Lakatos and economics', in *Perspectives on the History of Economic Thought*, vol. VIII, ed. S. Todd Lowry, Aldershot, Hants.: Edward Elgar.
Blaug, M. (1992) *The Methodology of Economics*, 2nd edn, Cambridge: Cambridge University Press.
—— (1994) 'Why I am not a constructivist, or confessions of an unrepentant Popperian', in *New Directions in Economic Methodology*, ed. R. Backhouse, London: Routledge.

De Marchi, N. and M. Blaug (1991) *Appraising Economic Theories: Studies in the Methodology of Research Programmes*, Aldershot, Hants.: Edward Elgar

Hands, D. Wade (1993) *Testing Rationality and Progress: Essays on the Popperian Tradition in Economic Methodology*, Lanham, Md: Rowman & Littlefield.

Hoover, K. (1991) 'Scientific research programme or tribe? A joint appraisal of Lakatos and the New Classical Macroeconomics', in de Marchi and Blaug (1991).

Lakatos, I. (1978) 'The methodology of scientific research programmes', in *Philosophical Papers*, ed. J. Worrall and G. Currie, vol. 1, Cambridge: Cambridge University Press.

Remenyi, J.V. (1979) 'Core demi-core interaction: toward a general theory of disciplinary and sub-disciplinary growth', *History of Political Economy*, **11**(1), Spring.

14. The positive–normative distinction

In Book III, part 1, section 1 of *A Treatise of Human Nature* (1739), David Hume claimed that all previous writers on ethics passed imperceptibly from observations about human affairs expressed with 'the usual copulation of propositions, *is* and *is not*' to conclusions 'connected with an *ought*, or an *ought not*': but, he argued, no one had ever given any good reasons for believing that 'this new relation can be a deduction from others, which are entirely different from it'. This passage is not unambiguous in meaning but it has traditionally been interpreted to assert that it is illegitimate to deduce an 'ought' from an 'is', implying that there is a class of statement of facts which are logically distinct from a class of statements of value, and hence that the former cannot by themselves entail the latter. Max Black has aptly called this assertion 'Hume's Guillotine' (Hudson, 1969: 100) because it seems to cut off descriptive from prescriptive statements. To believe otherwise, to allege that ought-propositions are not essentially different from is-propositions, has ever since G.E. Moore's *Principia Ethica* (1903) been dubbed the 'naturalistic fallacy'.

Hume wrote in 1739. By 1836, the date of John Stuart Mill's (1967) pioneering essay 'On the Definition of Political Economy; and on the Method of Philosophical Investigation in that Science', followed in the same year by a discussion of the 'Limits of the Science' in Nassau Senior's *Outline of the Science of Political Economy*, the Humean distinction between is/ought propositions has been transmuted into the science/art distinction by steps which no one has ever traced in detail (but see Hutchison, 1964: ch. 1). The distinction was reiterated by John Elliot Cairnes, Henry Sidgwick, John Neville Keynes and Vilfredo Pareto later in the nineteenth century and by Max Weber in a series of influential papers written between 1903 and 1917; it seems to have been Neville Keynes who first employed the positive/normative in place of the science/arts distinction and by the time of Weber's essays this language had become commonplace. Nevertheless, it was Lionel Robbins's *Essay on the Nature and Significance of Economic Science* (1932) that finally made a dogma of the positive/normative distinction, a virtual hallmark of what it means to talk like an economist. Ironically enough, John Neville Keynes really proposed a triple distinction between a 'positive science' of economics that would establish uniformities, a 'normative science' of economics that would determine ideals, and an 'art' of political economy that would formulate precepts (Hutchison, 1964: 36–7), but this tripartite classification never caught on.

Having distinguished positive from normative economics, mainstream economists without fail go on to insist that the distinction can be and should be clearly maintained in all economic discourse and particularly in applied economics. This has become, and still is, what might be called the fundamental tenet of 'orthodox' economic methodology: there is a well-defined area of 'positive economics' that is, at least in principle, value-free. While some well-known philosophers are critical of the standard is/ought distinction (see Hudson, 1969), it is the case that the positive/normative distinction is endorsed by most modern moral philosophers (MacIntyre, 1967: ch. 18). Nevertheless, the distinction between positive and normative economics has been frequently denied by radical economists and institutionalists, most conspicuously by Gunnar Myrdal, a Nobel laureate (Hutchison, 1964: 44–50; Wilber and Hoksbergen, 1984; Roy, 1989: chs. 2–4; Blaug, 1992: 118–21; Proctor, 1991: ch. 13.).

In considering that denial, it will be helpful to underline the various shades of meaning that have been assigned to the dichotomy between positive and normative economics. The following list is suggestive, not exhaustive (Machlup, 1978: 428–9):

Hume's Guillotine

is	ought
science	art
positive	normative
facts	values
description	prescription
explanation	recommendation
true/false	good/bad
empirical	ethical
laws	rules
objective	subjective
testable	non-testable
theory	policy
pure	applied

The simplest way to throw doubt on the doctrine of value-free positive economics is to note that all theoretical analysis must begin with the recognition of a significant problem that requires solution and 'significance' is not itself a fact but rather a value judgement; moreover, the mode of analysis that is undertaken and even the type of data that are gathered to support that analysis involves a further series of value judgements; finally, if the conclusions depend in any way on statistical inference, the level of statistical significance at which the so-called 'null hypothesis' is accepted or rejected is purely conventional and in this sense is again a value judgement. Thus positive economics begins and ends with norms and hence is not really different from normative economics.

So runs a leading argument against value-free economics. To assert the logical distinction between positive and normative economics therefore requires a further distinction between two types of value judgements; namely, what Ernst Nagel calls 'characterising value judgements' and 'appraising value judgements' or what I prefer to call 'methodological value judgements' and 'normative value judgements' (Blaug, 1992: 114). The former involves the choice of subject matter to be investigated, the mode of investigation to be followed and the criteria for judging the validity of the findings, which are part and parcel of any inquiry whether in the social or in the natural science; the latter refers to evaluative assertions about states of the world, including the desirability of certain kinds of human behaviour and the social outcomes produced by that behaviour which can, at least in principle, be kept separate from existential assertions of facts. Such, at any rate, must be the contention of those who assert the *possibility* of value-free positive economics.

Having denied that positive economics is just a certain kind of normative economics, we must now consider whether normative economics is not after all very much the same as positive economics. Just as positive economics seems to involve two different types of value judgements, so normative economics also invokes two very different sorts of value judgements; namely, what Amartya Sen has called 'basic' or 'non-basic' value judgements (Blaug, 1992: 115–16). Basic or pure value judgements are those that apply under all conceivable circumstances and which are thus impervious to any factual beliefs; non-basic or impure value judgements, on the other hand, are held subject to definite factual beliefs about social causation or the relations between the relevant variables of the subject matter in question. It is doubtful that anyone is ever wholly committed to basic value judgements – 'all wars are wrong'; 'life is always sacred'; 'I value this for its own sake' – but there is certainly nothing in logic to preclude such value judgements. In any case, if most value judgements are non-basic or impure, it follows that virtually all propositions in normative economics rely on propositions in positive economics and, to that extent, Hume's Guillotine fails to cut cleanly. Nevertheless, this is a practical and not a principled argument against value-free economics and indeed might be employed to emphasize the importance of trying to separate positive from normative economics.

Enough has now been said to suggest that the positive–normative distinction has been bedevilled by the indiscriminate use of the term 'value judgements' to cover not just qualitative evaluative appraisals but also subjective assertions of facts and indeed any and all untestable metaphysical propositions that colour the pre-analytic vision of an economist. Thus, interpersonal comparisons of utility are frequently dismissed as 'value judgements' when they are actually untestable statements of facts: they are true or false but to this day we know of no method of finding out which is the case (Blaug, 1992: 199). Likewise, the modern doctrine of Pareto optimality rests, among other things, on the fundamental postulate of consumer sovereignty – only self-chosen preferences count as yardsticks of welfare or, in popular parlance, an individual is the best judge of his or her welfare – and it has long been argued that consumer sovereignty is a value judgement *par excellence*, implying that Paretian welfare economics is fundamentally normative. However, Chris Archibald and Peter Hennipman have argued instead that the theorems of Paretian welfare economics are theorems in positive economics; on this view the assumption of consumer sovereignty is not a value judgement but simply the assertion of the axiom that individual preferences are to be taken as given for purposes of assessing a potential Pareto improvement, without endorsing or approving of these preferences (Blaug, 1992: 124–6). Be that as it may, it demonstrates the difficulty of deciding just what is a value judgement and what precise role postulates that look like value judgements play in economic analysis. A final confusion in the definition of value judgements is the widespread belief that non-controversial, unanimously held value judgements, such as consumer sovereignty or the Paretian definition of an improvement in social welfare, are by virtue of that unanimity converted from value judgements into empirical judgements. This is simply a logical error but it is nevertheless productive of much misunderstanding about value-free economics.

To sum up: the doctrine of value-free positive economics asserts, first of all, that the logical status of factual, descriptive is-statements is different in kind from that of normative, prescriptive ought-statements, and, second, that the methodological judgements that are involved in reaching agreement on is-statements differ in important ways from those used to reach a consensus on normative value judgements, at least if these are basic value judgements; on the other hand, if normative value judgements are typically non-basic or impure, securing agreement on them involves a process identical to that involved in reaching agreement on positive questions of fact (see Taylor, 1961: chs. 3, 9). The claim that economics can be value-free in this sense does not deny that ideological bias creeps into the very selection of the questions that economists investigate, that the inferences that are drawn from factual evidence are sometimes influenced by value-laden concepts and categories (rational choice, maximizing individuals, free competition and so forth) nor even that the practical advice that economists offer is frequently loaded with concealed value judgements, the better to persuade rather than merely to advise. It is precisely for this reason that we must insist on the *possibility* of value-free positive economics, on clearly maintaining the positive–normative distinction as far as it can be maintained. If there are not at least some descriptive, factual assertions about economic uniformities that are value-free, it seems difficult to escape the conclusion that we have a license in economics to assert just about anything we please.

REFERENCES

Blaug, M. (1992) *The Methodology in Economics*, 2nd edn, Cambridge: Cambridge University Press.

Hudson, W.D. (ed.) (1969) *The Is–Ought Question: A Collection of Papers on the Central Problem in Moral Philosophy*, London: Macmillan.

Hutchison, T.W. (1964) *'Positive' Economics and Policy Objectives*, London: George Allen & Unwin.

Machlup, F. (1978) *Methodology of Economics and Other Social Sciences*, New York: Academic Press.

MacIntyre, A. (1967) *A Short History of Ethics: A History of Moral Philosophy from the Homeric Age to the Twentieth Century*, London: Routledge.

Mill, J.S. (1967) *Essays on Economics and Society, 1824–1845: Collected Works of John Stuart Mill*, vol. IV, ed. J.M. Robson, Toronto: University of Toronto Press.

Proctor, R.N. (1991) *Value-free Science? Purity and Power in Modern Knowledge*, Cambridge, Mass.: Harvard University Press.

Roy, S. (1989) *Philosophy of Economics: On the Scope of Reason in Economic Inquiry*, London: Routledge.

Taylor, P.W. (1961) *Normative Discourse*, Englewood Cliffs, N.J.: Prentice-Hall.

Wilber, C.K. and R. Hoksbergen (1984) 'Current thinking on the role of value judgements in economic science: a survey', in *Research in the History of Economic Thought and Methodology*, vol. II, ed. W.J. Samuels, Greenwich, Conn.: JAI Press, 179–94.

PART THREE

Economics of Education

15. The economic value of higher education

INTRODUCTION

We all know that higher education throughout Europe is heavily subsidized by the state: tuition costs are almost wholly paid for by direct grants to institutions and the maintenance expenses of students are in greater or smaller part covered by grants or loans to individuals; in addition, there are subsidized meals, subsidized accommodation and tax relief to parents in varying amounts in different countries. It is widely believed that such subsidies are generally endorsed by economists and sanctioned by economic theory. Higher education is supposed to be an example of 'market failure', the type of good that never could be adequately provided by a market mechanism. Moreover, it is also widely believed that economic theory furnishes arguments for still higher levels of public spending on higher education. Higher education contributes to economic growth and economic growth nowadays is increasingly knowledge-based and dependent on the computerization of both white-collar and blue-collar jobs. It follows according to this argument that future economic growth will require ever increasing numbers of higher-educated people who will only be forthcoming if we expand higher education. QED.

Is it really true that economics provides firm ground for recommending public subsidies to higher education and indeed reasons for believing that present subsidy levels are too low? I am afraid not. The economic justification for public subsidies to higher education is based on its so-called 'external effects', that is, on the benefits of higher education which do not accrue to individual graduates. For example, higher education may make a person more prone to participate in political and civic functions, less inclined to commit crime and to fall back on social security, and all these are benefits external to the graduates themselves which they are unable to appropriate. But the problem is that none of these externalities has so far been quantified and there is some doubt that they ever can be, in which case they seem to provide no guide to public spending on higher education except to increase it without limit. Of course, all that supposes that they are actually positive in magnitude. However, there are also negative externalities of higher education. For example, higher education raises the job expectations of graduates and when these are not matched by job opportunities the result is personal frustration and disillusionment, which occasionally leads to rioting in the streets. In short, in the absence of measurement we cannot be sure that the sum of positive and negative externalities of higher education are in fact positive. Hence the economic case for subsidizing higher education is at best weak and at worst non-existent.

Similarly, higher education no doubt contributes to economic growth – we shall see in a moment how – but so does medical care and public transport and infrastructure of all kinds, so it is not of much practical use to be told simply that higher education contributes to economic growth. What we want to know is: how much does it contribute? This is a question to which economists have devoted a great deal of effort in the last quarter-century or so. The 1960s witnessed what has been called 'the human investment revolution in economic thought': the old view that education is a type of consumption undertaken by people for the sake of present enjoyment gave way to the new doctrine that education is a type of investment undertaken for the sake of future returns in the form of bigger earnings from employment. Ever since, economists have been busy measuring the 'rate of return' to education as a form of investment both for individuals and for society as a whole. In addition, an almost endless series of studies correlated every conceivable measure of educational attainment with every possible indicator of economic performance in the effort to demonstrate that the observed association between education and economic growth around the world is causal and not just casual, and causal in the right direction, that is from education to growth and not the other way round (see Blaug, 1972: ch. 3).

In retrospect, it is extraordinary to realize how little was achieved by all this research on the part of an entire generation of economists of education. We economists cannot demonstrate that education, however measured, is a necessary condition for economic growth; we cannot even show that it is a sufficient condition and hence that any poor country, not to mention the rich industrialized countries of the EEC, is well advised to spend as much as possible on providing additional schooling for its people. It is all too easy to spend too much on education from the standpoint of maximizing the rate of economic growth, judging by the history of such developing countries as Jordan, Egypt, Libya and Zambia, countries that have long spent a larger than average proportion of their gross national product on education and yet have lower than average records of economic growth. What is true of education in general is doubly true of higher education: it is all too easy to spend too much on one level of education as against another without any justification in better economic performance. Just as there are many countries that have overspent on education without generating any discernible economic benefits, so there are also many countries that have had remarkable achievements in economic growth without conspicuous attention to education. Thus, the NICs or newly industrialized countries of East Asia were not great spenders on education in the 1950s and 1960s when they were laying the foundations for their subsequent high-growth performance (in the First World, the same remark applies to the Federal Republic of Germany). Since then they have indeed emerged as relatively high spenders on education. However, that is only to say that rich countries spend more on education than poor ones; which proves, not that education produces economic growth, but that fast growth produces more education.

At one time, chiefly in the 1960s, it was fondly believed that it was possible more or less precisely to specify the manpower requirements of certain chosen targets of economic growth. Thus, once a country had decided that it wanted to grow at a certain rate, the implications of that growth rate for upper secondary and tertiary education could be quantified, furnishing a definite foundation for technical and higher education planning (see Blaug, 1972: ch. 5). This belief in the art of manpower forecasting died away in the 1970s as experience showed that long-term and even medium-term manpower forecasts were notoriously unreliable and not much better than pure guesswork (see Ahamad and Blaug, 1973; Youdi and Hinchliffe, 1985). In short, whatever education contributes to economic growth, it is not true that growth is impossible unless a country has the prerequisite of a certain stock of highly qualified manpower.

All this amounts to virtual nihilism in respect of the economic impact of education. Is there absolutely nothing economists can say about educational policy? I believe there is, but what we can say is qualitative and subject to many ifs and buts. We can pronounce on matters of tactics even if we must perforce remain silent on questions of strategy.

RATES OF RETURN

I said earlier that economists of education have a long record of calculating rates of return to investment in education. I also implied that these calculations do not add up to a solid case for spending public funds on higher education. I must now take a moment to explain both what is meant by rates of return to education and why I think that they do not serve to establish the social profitability of higher education.

Rates of return to education are a special case of general technique of investment appraisal, namely, cost-benefit analysis. What we do is to measure or estimate the benefits of an investment project over its lifetime and then to express it as an annual percentage rate of return to the cost of constructing that project. In the case of education, the *costs* of the 'project' are straightforward but the *benefits* are somewhat peculiar, or at any rate, somewhat special.

For the individual student, the costs of, say, an additional year's post-compulsory education is the sum of out-of-pocket expenses (tuition fees if any, books, stationery, travel expenses, and so on) and earnings forgone in consequence of studying instead of working. The benefits of the extra year's schooling, on the other hand, are the extra earnings after tax that he or she can expect to receive as a result of more education, suitably adjusted to take account of all the other differences between individuals, such as natural abilities and social class origins. The private rate of return in that case is a measure of the extent to which an individual can expect to add to annual earnings for the rest of his or her other working life by incurring the cost of remaining in the educational system for another year. If the private costs of that extra year of schooling is say, $1,000, and the rate of return is 10 per cent, then that individual will earn $100 more in the first years of working, $110 more in the second year, $121 more in the third year and so on, compared to another identical individual who did not have the benefit of that additional year of education. This private rate of return to education can be compared to what that individual could have earned by investing the equivalent sum of money in the market or the stock exchange.

The calculation of the *social* rate of return involves exactly the same data, but both the costs and the benefits have a different meaning from that which they had for the individual. The costs to society as a whole of the extra year of education is the sum of the associated outlays on teachers, buildings and equipment; these usually exceed the corresponding private costs for the simple reason that the tuition fees paid by students rarely cover more than a small part of the costs of educating them. In addition to these direct social costs, there are the indirect costs of output lost as a result of individuals staying on in school for an extra year; these are, for practical purposes, approximated by the earnings forgone by students. As for the social *benefits* of the extra year, these are, like the private benefits, measured by the earnings differentials attributable to the additional year of schooling, now taken inclusive of the taxes individuals will pay on their earnings so as to capture the 'externalities' generated by education. Once again, the social rate of return is actually calculated as the annual rate at which the costs of another year of education multiply into the extra earnings of better-educated citizens.

Rate-of-return calculations for all levels of education have now been carried out for almost 60 countries in the world and in a half-dozen countries such calculations have been made at different points in time. Virtually all these calculations, with only one or two exceptions, show a remarkable similarity in pattern (Blaug, 1987: 113–15). First, private rates of return invariably exceed social rates of return. Secondly, private rates are always close to, and in many cases just above, market rates of interest in the countries concerned. Thirdly, both private and social rates of return decline, not invariably but frequently, with additional years of education. Fourthly, and most significant of all, the rates are almost always higher in poor than in rich countries. It is evident that these figures mean something because their systematic character could never have been produced country after country by the action of pure chance.

Nevertheless, there is a world of difference in these figures between the private and the social rates of return. The private rate of return is helpful in interpreting the private demand for education and is presumably of interest to individuals in guiding their choice between earning and learning. But why should the social rate influence the decisions of government to spend more or less on this or that stage of education? For one thing, it is not clear what special discount rate should be invoked for purposes of comparison with social rates of return to educational investment: governments do not usually operate with one single cut-off rate to apply to all forms of social investment and most governments even lack a minimum rate of return that must be satisfied by, say, road transport projects of electricity-generating programmes. For another thing, the inclusion of taxes in gross earnings to express the externalities generated by education may well be grossly misleading.

There is no doubt that an educated individual *may* contribute something to the output and earnings of less-educated individuals with whom he or she works: to that extent education raises not just the productivity of educatees but also the productivity of non-educated individuals. However, as we noted earlier, economists have so far failed to quantify the 'external' effects of education and hence cannot even guarantee that it is positive (Blaug, 1987: 229–30). It is perfectly possible, therefore, that all the reported social rates of return are wild overestimates. But equally, we cannot preclude the possibility that they are wild underestimates. We may conclude, therefore, that evidence about the social rate of return to education cannot be taken seriously as indicating anything about the appropriate size of the higher education system in a country.

SCREENING HYPOTHESIS

It will be evident from everything we have said so far that the positive correlation between years of formal education and personal earnings forms the bedrock of the doctrine of education as human capital formation.

The fact that education and personal earnings are highly correlated does not itself *prove* that the cause of higher earnings is extra schooling but, nevertheless, the simplest explanation for the observation that employers offer higher pay to more highly educated workers is that education imparts vocationally useful skills that are in scarce supply. This simple explanation has been questioned in recent years by the so-called 'screening hypothesis', which argues that while education may be associated with increased earnings and perhaps even with increased productivity, it does not necessarily cause them. Employers seek high-ability workers but are unable at the point of hiring to distinguish them from those with low ability. Faced with a lack of reliable information about the personal attributes of job applicants, employers are forced to make use of 'screens' that separate high-ability from low-ability workers, such as evidence of previous work experience, personal references, membership of distinct social groups (such as ethnic minorities) and, of course, educational qualifications. Moreover, knowing that employers are making use of screens for hiring purposes, job applicants have an incentive to make themselves distinct by some sort of 'signal'. According to the screening hypothesis, education beyond a basic level fills exactly this function. By and large, it is high-ability individuals who perform well in the educational system. Educational achievement is therefore associated with higher productivity but does not cause it, and hence is no more than a screening or signalling device to prospective employers which it is in the individual's interest to acquire, although acquiring it serves no useful social purpose. Just as an individual's good health may be due more to a naturally strong constitution than to medical care, so according to this view is superior productivity the result of natural ability than post-compulsory education.

The screening hypothesis, in its strongest version, argues that secondary and higher education do nothing to increase individual productivity and have no economic value at all. There are at least three counter-arguments to this devastating refutation of human capital theory. The educational system may select students according to their natural aptitudes but in the process it may also improve these aptitudes; thus, the educational system is perhaps more than just a screening device. Secondly, the screening hypothesis may explain the association between education and earnings at the point of hiring workers; but surely, once at work, employers will soon be able to sort out the more from the less able without resorting to paper qualifications. In other words, employers no doubt use educational qualifications as a hiring screen but experience is constantly testing the accuracy of that screen. Thirdly, a deep information problem is inherent in the very process of hiring workers and if we somehow eliminated the use of educational qualifications as proxies of ability in hiring, it is not at all obvious that we could replace it by some superior social selection mechanism, as for example, a national aptitude testing centre; in short, the educational system may well be the most efficient social screen we can devise. Of course, we shall never know the answers to this question until some country performs the appropriate social experiment. Since the experiment involves nothing less than Illitch's 'deschooling society', I doubt whether it will ever be performed.

In any case, the validity of the screening hypothesis is an empirical matter. Despite a good deal of research, the verdict is undecided and, given the almost intractable problem of testing the hypothesis, is likely to remain so (see Blaug, 1987: 119–22). 'Credentialism', or the use of educational qualifications as proxy measures of ability, so contaminates all aspects of labour markets around the world that it would require a long-sustained taboo on the issue of diplomas and certificates to discover the precise impact of education on individual productivity. The screening hypothesis in its strongest version cannot be entirely true but it is not yet possible to show whether it is partially or wholly false. Nevertheless, to the extent that it is a half-truth or even a quarter-truth, it throws even more doubt on the use of social rates of return as criteria for public investment in education.

The suspicion that the screening hypothesis is at least half true also casts a new light on the economic value of education.

THE ECONOMIC VALUE OF EDUCATION

I can best make my point by summarizing Benjamin Bloom's *Taxonomy of Educational Objectives* (1956), a book that is still the veritable bible of curriculum reformers. Bloom made the extraordinary claim that the objectives of all curricula in any subject at any stage of education can be exhaustively classified into three categories, namely (a) 'cognitive knowledge'; (b) 'psychomotor skills'; and (c) 'effective behavioural traits'. By cognitive knowledge, Bloom meant the sum of memorized facts and concepts that are crammed into the heads of students; by psychomotor skills, he meant the manual dexterity and muscular co-ordination that a student is supposed to acquire; and by effective behavioural traits, he meant the values and attitudes shaping behaviour, which a student is supposed to take away with him or her at the completion of a course. The same idea has been expressed much earlier in much simpler language by a famous nineteenth-century philosopher of education, Johann Heinrich Pestalozzi. Pestalozzi said that all education touches either the 'head', the 'hand' or the 'heart' of the child and these three Hs correspond exactly to Bloom's more forbidding terminology.

Now, when we say that education is economically valuable, that it makes people more productive, most of us think immediately of the first H, cognitive knowledge. We assert, in other words, that it is the educated worker's knowledge of certain facts and concepts that makes him valuable to employers. We might call this 'the pilot fallacy': in order to fly a plane, you need a pilot, and flying a plane requires cognitive knowledge (and some psychomotor skills) which can only be learned by a formal training course. But what employers really value in most workers is, not what they know, but how they behave. What matters is the third H, Bloom's 'effective behavioural traits', such as punctuality, attentiveness, responsibility, achievement drive, co-operativeness, compliance, and so on. The cognitive skills required to carry out most jobs in industry and agriculture are learned by doing, by what is call on-the-job-training. What formal education does, therefore, is not so much to train workers as to make them trainable. As for university graduates, what employers demand is, once again, not cognitive knowledge, but rather a set of personality traits, such as self-esteem, self-reliance, versatility and the capacity to assume leadership roles. In a nutshell, we may say that elementary and secondary education breeds foot-soldiers, while higher education trains the lieutenants and captains of the labour force.

Now, it is a curious fact that these crucial behavioural traits which largely account for the economic value of education cannot be efficiently conveyed directly but only as a byproduct, as a 'hidden agenda', of an educational process directed at cognitive knowledge. Imagine a class in punctuality: it could be possible but it would also be immensely tedious and probably ineffective; but punctuality is powerfully fostered by an educational process rigidly tied to a timetable throughout every moment of the school day. One of the greatest problems in running a factory in a newly industrialized country is that of getting workers to arrive on time and to notify the plant manager when they are going to be absent; the lack of punctuality in the work-force can raise labour costs in a developing country by as much as 50 per cent over those of a developed country.

This is a simple but telling example of a general phenomenon: the economic value of education resides much more in the realm of behaviour than in the realm of cognitive knowledge. This is why an almost endless series of studies have shown that in all countries there is little if any relationship between the subject graduates have studied at university and the jobs they eventually take up. To be sure, the fields of study offered by universities run the entire gamut from engineering, maths, computing, physics and chemistry at one end, to humanities, history, sociology and psychology at the other. In the first group, there is a fairly close match between occupation and education, the job making direct use of the subject-specific knowledge acquired in the classrooms. However, in the second group there is virtually no relationship between curriculum studied and occupation entered subsequently, and this group in fact comprises a much larger proportion of graduates that the first group. But even in the first group, more general competencies, such as the ability to digest information and to communicate it, matters as much as the subject-specific knowledge.

BACK TO MANPOWER FORECASTING

We can now see that the basic error of the manpower forecasting approach is what we have labelled 'the pilot fallacy'. If only all jobs in an economy were like those of the pilot, there might be some merit in forecasting manpower requirements, although there would still be a problem of the gross inaccuracy of these forecasts. But pilots, brain surgeons, mechanical engineers, physicists, computer scientists, and so forth, are an extremely small portion of the labour force even in rich countries and are a poor basis for fundamental thinking about the economic role of education.

It is sometimes said that America, Japan, and Western Europe have entered the tertiary stage of industrialization in which the service sector will afford employment to an ever-larger fraction of the labour force; moreover, these tertiary-stage service industries are increasingly based on the processing of computerized information, hence requiring highly educated men and women to staff the computer terminals. Here then is an entirely new 'manpower-forecasting' argument for the expansion of higher education in the industrialized countries.

Unfortunately, this argument is dubious for all the reasons given above referring to the economic value of higher education. In addition, the argument ignores the dynamics of personnel development, namely the phenomenon of 'deskilling'. Technical progress is constantly raising the skill requirements of industrial processes and, in the absence of countervailing forces, this would result in ever-rising labour costs per unit of output. But these cost pressures motivate industrial engineers to break down and simplify the ever more demanding cognitive requirements of new techniques. Thus, in the 1950s in the early stages of the microchip revolution, the shortage of computer programmers was so acute as to lead to an explosive demand for numerate university graduates willing to retrain as computer programmers. Within a decade, however, a high school diploma was regarded as adequate for potential programmers and today even 16-year-old school-leavers are taught to write software programmes in a two or three week training course. In short, computer programming has been 'deskilled', and this is in fact a constant feature of the adaptation of new techniques and products to the existing labour force.

In a careful analysis of the match between the educational composition of the labour force and levels of economic development in more than 50 countries around the world, the OECD (1970) concluded that the actually observed educational levels of workers in manufacturing and services are more the result of supply than of demand, more the result of what they called 'push' rather than 'pull' factors. Workers in, say, the USA are better educated than those in India, not because American industry is so advanced as to require highly educated workers but because hiring standards for jobs in the USA have been upgraded to employ the vast hordes of American graduates.

JUSTIFYING PUBLIC SUBSIDIES

I hope that I have now said enough to demonstrate the proposition that the economic value of higher education is widely misunderstood. That still leaves open the question, however, whether higher education should receive further public subsidies or whether it should be increasingly privatized and left to the market place.

The economic case for public subsidies to higher education is, as we have said, extremely weak because it rests on an alleged tendency of higher education to generate external benefits which no one has ever succeeded in quantifying. However, it is not the alleged external effects of higher education that are responsible for the present universal system of public support for higher education. In almost every case, it was electoral support for policies deemed to be fair and just in creating equality in educational opportunities that accounted for the particular mix of subsidies that one actually observes in different countries. No wonder, then, that we find an incredible variety in the pattern of higher education subsidies in different countries as well as wide variations in the total level of subsidy from the most generous end of the spectrum in Britain to the most niggardly in Japan (see Blaug, 1987: 166–96; Johnstone, 1986). The question is: what principles could possibly govern this mix of elements in the subsidy package?

We may neatly divide these principles into two kinds, having to do with efficiency on the one hand and equity on the other. Economists have traditionally concentrated on questions of efficiency, leaving matters of equity to political scientists. By efficiency, an economist always means the application of scarce means to achieve given ends. But when the ends of an activity are multiple rather than single, as in the case of higher education, it is never easy to say what is meant by efficiency, or inefficiency. Universities are designed to achieve at least four objectives: (a) the dissemination of knowledge, that is, the teaching function; (b) the creation of knowledge, that is, the research function; (c) the certification of students for purposes of employment, that is, the selection function; and (d) the active participation of academics in political and social life via such things as journalism, public speaking, advice to governments, that is, the so-called 'civilizing' function. Properly to appraise subsidies to higher education from the standpoint of efficiency is to weigh up the consequences of every subsidy in terms of all the four multiple functions of universities. Neither space nor time permits us to develop this theme with the care it deserves, so let us jump in the deep end.

If we are going to subsidize higher education at all, the easiest way of doing so is to subsidize tuition fees, and the most efficient way of doing that is to subsidize students, not institutions, via a system of education vouchers. If we subsidize students, institutions will be forced to become consumer-oriented in the competition for students. Since manpower forecasting is inaccurate and since students have a personal incentive to be well-informed about employment opportunities, we are much more likely to avoid manpower shortages and surpluses by allowing students to choose both the subjects they wish to study and the institutions at which to study them. In addition, by forcing institutions to compete for students, we also encourage them to become cost-conscious and hence to minimize the cost of producing a graduate of given quality. Finally, by subsidizing students rather than institutions, we remind students of the social costs of their eduction, which in turn induces them to maximize the educational benefits of four to six years of higher education. On the other hand, to subsidize institutions instead of students, as we now do, encourages the maintenance of courses for which there is no longer any demand, promotes the inefficient use of academic resources or at least does nothing to discourage it, and disguises the true costs of higher education to the community. In other words, we have managed everywhere to subsidize higher education in the most inefficient possible manner. From that point of view, I welcome the recent decision in Britain to introduce differential tuition fees by subject groups to reflect the very different costs of educating students in, say, medicine rather than literature.

Similarly, the living expenses of students should be subsidized, if they are to be subsidized at all, by means of loans, not grants. There is a clear economic case for student loans to finance both tuition fees and living expenses. One of the single distinctions between physical capital and human capital is that one can borrow in the capital market to finance investment in physical capital but one cannot typically borrow in the capital market to finance investment in human capital. Banks are perfectly happy to lend to anyone on the strength of collateral, but in a non-slave economy we cannot place a lien on our future earnings; hence, we can offer no collateral to a bank to secure a loan on our own education. In consequence, commercial banks are unwilling to finance the personal cost of higher education even at exorbitant rates of interest. Thus, the finance of education in a non-slave capitalist economy represents a genuine case of 'market failure', that is, an inability of the market mechanism to produce optimal results under any and all circumstances. There is, therefore, a clear argument either for a government-sponsored loans scheme or for a scheme operated by private banks with the loans secured by the government against default.

The ideal student loans scheme is one in which the repayment of the loan is income-related, that is, graduates pay a surtax throughout their working lives or 2–3 per cent of income earned. Thus, some very successful graduates end up paying back more than the costs of their own higher education, thereby financing the education of graduates who fail to take up employment after graduation. The advantages of such an ideal scheme is that repayment is automatic, lowering collection costs and minimizing the default rate, and female graduates do not enter marriage with a 'negative dowry'. Characteristically, however, this is not the sort of loans scheme that most countries have adopted. Income-related loans schemes are confined to some private American universities, and most governments around the world insist instead the student loans should be treated like a personal loan that is repayable in five or ten years after graduation. The result is that default rates run at 10–20 per cent of loans made, the costs of collecting repayments is fairly high, female graduates do carry a 'negative dowry', and a good deal of resentment is built up against the scheme on the part of its beneficiaries. It is not easy to account for the failure to implement income-related student loans in any terms other than political ones, reflecting a puritanical attitude to educational loans of any kind on the part of legislators and government officials. My own government, the British government, after years of resisting any student loan scheme whatsoever, is now about to introduce the wrong kind of scheme in which loans are repayable in a limited number of years, against the advice of absolutely every British economist who has ever written on the subject (Barnes and Barr, 1988; Barr, 1989).

Virtually all countries in the world combine some sort of loans scheme with one or another variety of maintenance grants to assist students in financing their living expenses. Since the argument for grants is one of equity, grants ought to be strictly means-tested. But in fact they almost never are, thus sustaining the doctrine that students are entitled not only to free higher education but also to partly free maintenance while studying. Even if one were to swallow this particular doctrine of 'natural rights', the effects of outright grants on the efficiency with which students pursue higher education is almost always unfortunate. Anything available for nothing is little valued, and higher education, available at the expense of taxpayers who are less well off than the student eventually will be, is apt to be squandered. In other words, the only merit of grants is to enable poor students to take up higher education; hence grants ought always to be stringently means-tested, such that they become available only to the poorest of students.

Summing up, we may conclude that the ideal system of public subsidies to higher education would consist of: (a) a level of tuition fees that would cover at least some of the real costs of educating students; (b) the remainder of tuition costs to be financed with the aid of vouchers issued to students, which could be cashed at any university of their choice (adding to the value of the voucher in countries that have private universities); (c) a system of maintenance grants, which are stringently means-tested in relation to parental income; and (d) a system of income-contingent student loans to finance tuition fees and living expenses repayable via a 'graduate tax'. I can think of no country in the world that even begins to approximate this ideal package, although many countries practice at least one or two elements in the total package.

RESEARCH

I want to close by taking up an issue near and dear to the heart of every academic: the funding of higher education research. In the United States, Canada and most of Europe the real resources devoted to research in both the natural and social sciences are bound up in fixed proportions with the instructional costs of higher education, such that in expansion of student numbers and the addition of academic staff to teach them inevitably represents an equiproportionate increase in the resources devoted to research, and vice versa for a contraction of student numbers. This follows from the fact that universities are subsidized so as to permit academic staff to devote something like half of their time to research; this 1:1 ratio between instruction and research time is somehow regarded as optimal for each and every member of staff. In addition to this channel of support, there is a second channel of research councils or centres, that is, official or semi-official bodies which provide earmarked finance for both pure and applied research carried on in colleges and universities. It is worth noting that the funds flowing through this secondary channel do not vary systematically across countries in proportion to the size of the higher education systems; moreover, there appears to be no systemic internal patterns in the allocation of these funds among specific disciplines (Blaug, 1987: 238).

What economic principles should govern the total level of specific grants for higher education research? This is a radically different issue from that of public funding for the teaching element in higher education. Research contributes to the total stock of human knowledge and the creation of knowledge, unlike the dissemination of knowledge, is what economists call a 'public good'. It is impossible to confine the consumption of a public good to those that pay for it: if it is consumable by anyone, it is consumable by everyone. Hence, no individual consumer has any incentive to pay for it; in short, it is impossible to price a public good because no consumer will reveal their true preference for it. The classic example of a public good is national defence, but the creation of knowledge is perhaps an even better example.

Since research cannot be efficiently privatized (although it sometimes is), the case for public support for research activities is indubitable. But how much public support? Spending on research is by its very nature spending on an activity whose consequences are subject to an unusually high level of uncertainty. In other words, the social benefits of academic research are painfully difficult to assess and with all the post-mortems in the world the outcome of research will remain impossible to predict with any degree of accuracy. In the light of these considerations, any level of research support other than zero is purely arbitrary and that is just about all one can say on rational grounds about the total size of outside finance for research in higher education institutions.

We can say something much more definite, however, about the other side of the research picture, namely the research activities of teachers that form part of their standard terms of contract. How do we induce teachers to maximize the quantity and quality of research contributions? Let me start by planting a subversive thought. I believe, as you probably all do, that teaching and research are generally complements – that we do one thing better if we also do the other thing – therefore we reject the Soviet model of financing academic research in specialized research institutes, leaving universities to devote themselves exclusively to teaching. Yet I also believe that academics are not all equally endowed with identical abilities in both teaching and research. This suggests that there might well be advantages in subsidizing higher education institutions as if they were largely teaching factories; individual teachers who wished to specialize in research would then have to apply to research councils for funds, not just to purchase equipment and to hire research assistants, but also to replace a fraction of their own research time. Rejecting the assumption that teaching and research must always be combined in fixed proportions, we would thus maximize the benefits of the age-old principle of comparative advantage in different activities. If economics suggests anything about the way we conduct higher education, it creates the strong assumption that the research funding principle just outlined would result in a more efficient university system. Needless to say, I know of no country that has ever seriously considered this proposal.

There is little doubt that across the range of most subjects, the best and certainly the largest quantity of research is being conducted in the USA. That is not to say that American academics are cleverer than European academics but simply that there are more of them. America is a large country and it is the only country in the world that has achieved mass higher education, enrolling a little over half of all 18–22-year-old youngsters in one or more years of higher education; in consequence, there are over 4 million American university students and every year America produces 3,000 completed PhDs in the social sciences alone. Ultimately, therefore, it is a game of numbers: produce enough post-graduates and you will produce some geniuses.

But this is not the whole story of America's outstanding publication record in subject after subject. The American higher education system – some 3,000 institutions of higher learning ranging all the way from small, private, second-rate finishing schools to large public, first-rate state universities to equally large private institutions that rank among the best universities in the world – is probably the most perfect system man could have devised for providing academics with a personal incentive to publish. There are no national salary scales as in Europe and hence a professor at Harvard might well earn six to seven times the salary of the instructor at a small state community college. Tenure, which in many European countries is automatic after being hired, is enjoyed by only half of American academics and is generally awarded only to those who have established a firm publication record. Finally, American higher education sometimes strikes a European observer as a game of musical chairs: every year, every second member of staff in any department moves to another university to improve their rank and of course their salary. No wonder then that American academics publish more than European and, because they publish more, they also publish more items of outstanding quality than we do.

Most European countries, on the other hand, have devised higher education systems which provide few, if any, financial incentives to publish. The mystery is that nevertheless European research is as good and plentiful as it is at least in some subjects in some countries. However; despite our national salary scales, our low academic mobility and our system of automatic tenure, it is possible to imagine a number of ways in which European academics might be encouraged by financial incentives to increase the quantity and quality of their research publications. For example, the UK has recently asked university departments to submit pages published by their staff in books and refereed journals in the previous academic years, which is then combined with a submission of research funds received by members of the department into a composite index of quality; in the future, universities will be encouraged to allocate their public grants among departments in accordance with that index; in time, the governments may even aggregate the index by departments into an index by universities, at which point it will allocate more money to universities with superior track records in pages published and research contracts received. This is the market mechanism with a vengeance and will undoubtedly spur individual academics to publish more, if only as a result of peer pressure within each university.

In Taiwan, I recently learned of a more direct method of inducing academics to publish. Any Taiwanese academic who publishes five or more papers per year in a list of refereed journals may submit these papers to a national committee of recognized authorities in their subject in order to qualify for a stipend of $5,000; articles published in foreign journals receive double weight on the grounds that these compete with a global community of scholars instead of a local Asian community. On average, about half of all applicants for the stipend persuade their subject committee to approve their publications. The successful applicants are ranked in order of excellence and the top 5 per cent receive an annual stipend of $10,000; similarly, the top 1 per cent qualify for a stipend of $25,000 and their names are published in leading Taiwanese newspapers. Strangely enough, ever since this system was introduced in the early 1970s the numbers and attested quality of Taiwanese publications in natural and social science has constantly accelerated.

I say 'strangely enough', although of course economists do not find it strange at all. On the contrary, it confirms their fondest belief that the supply curve of academics, as of plumbers and carpenters, is positively inclined; pay more and more labour will be forthcoming.

CONCLUSIONS

It is time to draw this discussion to a close. I hope I have demonstrated that economists are the last people to consult on the great question whether there is too much or too little higher education in the industrialized world when what is wanted is guidance on the total volume of public spending on higher education. On the other hand, economists are the first people to consult on questions of how to spend the public funds that are in fact devoted to higher education. There is hardly a country in the world that would not be well advised radically to overhaul its system of higher education finance so as to make it conform more closely to what are after all rather elementary economic principles of equity and efficiency. Higher education is inordinately expensive and hence every mode of subsidizing higher education ought to be designed to make both students and institutions cost-conscious, while at the same time ensuring that public support is targeted on poor students and not, as at the present, dispensed to largely middle-class students on the hypocritical argument that everyone is entitled to 'free' higher education.

REFERENCES

Ahamad, B and M. Blaug (1973) *The Practice of Manpower Forecasting*, Amsterdam: Elsevier.
Barnes, J. and N. Barr (1988) *Strategies for Higher Education*, Aberdeen: Aberdeen University Press.
Barr, N. (1989) *Student Loans: The Next Steps*, Aberdeen: Aberdeen University Press.
Blaug, M. (1972) *An Introduction to the Economics of Education*, London: Penguin Books.
—— (1987) *The Economics of Education and the Education of an Economist*, Aldershot, Hants.: Edward Elgar.
Johnstone, D.B. (1986) *Sharing the Costs of Higher Education*, New York: College Board.
OECD (1970) *Occupational and Educational Structures of the Labour Force and Levels of Economic Development*, Paris: OECD.
Youdi, R.J. and K. Hinchliffe (1985) *Forecasting Skilled Manpower Needs*, Paris: UNESCO-IIEP.

16. The current state of the British economics profession[*]

INTRODUCTION

This was a study of the UK labour market for professional economists. As we started to analyse the demand and supply of economists in the United Kingdom, we soon discovered that published data were inadequate for the purpose. We therefore decided to mount a survey of staff and students in all departments/schools/faculties/divisions of economics in universities, polytechnics, colleges of higher education and Scottish Central Institutions to obtain information about the supply of economists. On the demand side, we used published and unpublished data on the 'First Destinations' of economics graduates and we also conducted structured interviews with a non-random sample of leading employers of economists and careers officers. From both the survey and the interviews we gained indications of salaries; in addition, we looked at what little work has been done by others on the earnings of economists. It was on the basis of this evidence that we reached our conclusions.

This is a summary of a report commissioned by the Royal Economic Society in 1987 and published by RES in 1988. Page references in the text refer to the published report. The opinions expressed in it are ours and not those of the RES.

DEFINING AN ECONOMIST

There is no precise way to define the economics profession. Lawyers, doctors, dentists, engineers, accountants, architects and town planners become licensed members of their respective professions by passing examinations monitored by the relevant professional association. Defining membership of such professions is therefore fairly straightforward, although even here the edges are blurred. The economics profession, however, is unlicensed and hence there is no natural way of defining an 'economist'. But of course this is also true of many other professions, such as philosophers, historians, biologists, mathematicians, to name

[*] First published in the *Economic Journal*, **100** (March 1990): 227–36 (written with Ruth Towse).

a few. In all such cases, we may define membership in a profession by education, by occupation, or by self-identification as a member of a definable group.

On balance, and particularly if we are interested in the workings of the labour market, the occupational definition is the best way of defining the economics profession. Unfortunately, such a definition cannot be strictly applied in Britain. Although the job title 'economist' appears in the decennial Census of Population, it is not accompanied by a careful specification of the tasks economists are required to carry out. This type of 'job analysis' – an examination of the actual work content of occupations – applied to economists would have to be carried out over a wide spectrum of thousands of jobs, since we literally do not know the population from which we are sampling. Such an exercise would be extremely costly and that perhaps explains why it has never been carried out in Britain for any professional group, much less for economists.

In America, the National Register of Scientific and Technical Personnel makes it possible to define an economist by self-identification, a method which establishes a population of people claiming professional competence in economics whose jobs can then be sampled to implement the definition by occupation. This option is not available in Britain. The simple-minded way to define an 'economist' is by education but this is also unsatisfactory because economics graduates are distributed, as we show later, across a broad spectrum of occupations. Anyway, it is the occupational definition that we are after if we are concerned with the labour market of economists. When we looked at the supply of economics graduates, we were clearly employing the educational definition in terms of paper qualifications, but when we interviewed employers hiring economists, we were naturally impelled to make use of something like a definition of occupation.

Nevertheless, all our findings drove us to the conclusion that the labour market defines a professional economist as someone with at least a second degree in economics. Employers treat a first degree in economics as virtually the same as any other first degree, having a slight edge in earnings and ease of gaining employment over, say, English, history, classics and sociology, but not much more than a slight edge. Besides, First Destinations data (p. 16) reveal that only 6 per cent of first degree economics graduates from universities entered the UK labour market in 1987 and only 1 per cent from polytechnics went into jobs classified as 'economist' (tables 6, 9). It is true of course that even higher degree economics graduates do not all become economists: 31 per cent went into work in 1987 with the job title 'economist', a figure which rises to 51 per cent if we assume that the 20 per cent who went into 'teaching' were teaching economics. In other words, whatever definition of 'economist' we accept, it would be absurd to treat the output of economics graduates as being the same thing as the supply of professional economists. On the other hand, the output of post-graduates does more nearly equate to the supply of professional economists.

Professional economists in Britain are to be found in higher education, government and in the private sector; by far and away the largest group is to be found in universities. Though not all university economics teachers have higher degrees (17 per cent do not, compared to 10 per cent in polytechnics – table 36), they nevertheless fit the occupational definition of an economist; new recruits will almost certainly be required to have a second or even a third degree. The Government Economic Service (GES) and heads of economics divisions we interviewed in the City and industry all specified a second degree in economics as a minimum entry requirement for recruitment. Thus there is a strong correlation between the educational definition of an economist based on the possession of a higher degree and the occupation one based on job title.

FIRST DEGREE GRADUATES

For all practical purposes, then, a study of the economics profession in the United Kingdom is a study of higher degree graduates of economics; this is not a definition which we impose on the data but the result of our examination of the evidence, consisting of patterns of employment, employers' opinions, information from the careers services and evidence about earnings differentials. Economics departments in higher education institutions, however, are largely concerned with undergraduate teaching, which is to say that they are not fundamentally engaged in supplying professional economists except for 8 per cent of undergraduates who go on to obtain a masters degree or PhD in economics. Nevertheless, this fact has never been allowed to undermine the perception of most academic teachers of economics that all of their undergraduate students must be trained as if they were going to be professional economists.

Are we saying that this widespread perception is misguided? Indeed we are. We said earlier that the labour market treats a bachelor's degree in economics as virtually indistinguishable from any other first degree. This is, however, something of an exaggeration and it is worth spending a moment to express the idea more precisely. Among the many functions of higher education is the provision of skills, consisting of both subject-specific knowledge and more general work-related competencies such as the analysis of information and the ability to communicate. Now, the persistent differences in the employment patterns of graduates with different subject qualifications, as revealed by First Destinations data, leave no doubt that certain subjects impart specific skills demanded by employers. Engineering, maths, computing, physics and chemistry are clear examples of this end of the labour market, exemplified by specific subject requirements laid down in advertised vacancies, a close match between occupation and education, the job making more or less direct use of the cognitive knowledge acquired in classrooms, and hence a short period of search before gaining employment. However, at the other end of the labour market are subjects with few advertised vacancies specifying that subject, little relationship between curriculum studied and occupation entered subsequently and hence relatively long waiting periods before gaining employment (however, even they gain employment within a year – graduate unemployment is insignificant 12 months after graduation). Examples of such subjects with general and highly transferable skills are English, humanities, history and sociology.

From all indicators, economics lies somewhere in the middle of this spectrum but tending definitely more to the general than to the specific end of the range. Some 65 per cent of economics graduates enter the labour market on obtaining a first degree and, as we have said above, at most 6 per cent take up jobs that make some use of what they have learned in their undergraduate economics course; they enter jobs with the title 'economist' but even so they work alongside others with the same job title who have never studied economics (tables 6, 9, p. 16). It is too much to say that no first degree economics graduate ever becomes a real economist but it is true to say that most will not. The vast majority of first degree economics graduates enter a general labour market in which employers express no particular preference for economics degrees except in so far as they signal a willingness and ability to deal with figures, that is, an economics qualification denotes numeracy plus an interest in the business world. The most important occupational destination of economics graduates is accountancy (38 per cent of all economics graduates entering UK employment) and the second is banking.

The growth of joint degrees in recent years is no doubt a tacit recognition of the general nature of a first degree in economics. Indeed, so great has been the growth of joint degrees that students graduating from them now exceed those taking a single honours degree (pp. 9–10). In addition, as our figures on service teaching show (p. 83), many students now take courses in economics as part of other degrees. The service elements can be so dominant that there are actually universities, polytechnics and colleges without departments of economics but with identifiable groups of economists engaged entirely in this type of teaching; this is almost always in connection with business studies and management courses. (It is worth noting, by the way, that published data about economics graduates refer exclusively to single rather than joint degrees and so give a grossly misleading picture of both the output of economics students and the workload of economics departments.)

To say that undergraduate economics is a general rather than a subject-specific degree, more academic than vocational education, is not to denigrate it. On the contrary: the growth of joint degrees that include economics is surely a testimony to the perceived value of economics as an intellectual discipline. Nevertheless, to pretend that it must be taught as an intellectual discipline regardless of the occupational destination of the average student seems peculiarly myopic. The fact of the matter is that most economics teachers blithely instruct their undergraduate students as if they were going to be professional economists, and indeed economists teaching economics in higher education institutions, despite the fact that on average this is true for only one out of every twelve students sitting in a class. We do not pretend to tell our fellow economists *what* they ought to be teaching – curriculum was not part of our terms of reference – but we do insist that what is taught ought to take some account of the actual pattern of employment of economics graduates. *How* to take account of this is a difficult question but we do urge that the question itself ought to be more widely debated among economists than it is.

Furthermore, we were told by virtually every employer of professional economists that new recruits lack familiarity with economic data and that many seem never to have been taught national income accounting. Indeed, the complaint that economics degrees are too theoretical, too impractical and too unrelated to the possible uses of economics in business and government was a constant note in just about all the interviews we conducted (pp. 45–7). Admittedly, some of these complaints are due more to a crisis of confidence about economics as a discipline in the world at large than to the way economics is taught. Nevertheless, we teaching economics need to recognize that the image of our profession in the outside world is poor – and perhaps justifiably so.

BACK OF THE ENVELOPE MANPOWER FORECASTING

Our guesstimate of the stock of professional economists in the United Kingdom is 3,500 individuals, of whom about 2,500 are employed in higher education institutions, 400 or so in the GES and about 600 in private industry and commerce (pp. 5–7). These figures are based on the responses to the questionnaire (which was in effect a census of economists working in higher education), data supplied by the GES and membership figures of the Society of Business Economists. It is only the numbers in the private sector that are possibly inaccurate and hence controversial. But even if the figure of 600 business economists wildly underestimates the true number, one would still conclude that the total stock of professional economists in the United Kingdom is unlikely to be more than 4,000.

The evidence suggests that the annual flow demand for economists is declining, while supply has remained more or less constant over the last four years (pp. 9–12, 17–18). We are therefore driven to the conclusion that there is, if anything, an oversupply rather than a shortage of professional economists, an opinion which is borne out by the fact that at most 50 per cent of economics postgraduates become professional economists (see above).

Moreover, all the qualitative indications we picked up show that demand will fall rather than rise in the foreseeable future. Industry no longer wants economists and many economics divisions closed in the late 1970s. Banks are shedding economists and the feeling is that more will go. While the demand for economists in the GES is currently buoyant, this is because its staff are regularly poached by the private sector (a few years with the GES is regarded as a necessary complement to a master's degree); as private sector demand falls off, so will future demand in government. As for universities and polytechnics, demand is greater now than it was two or three years ago but the lasting effect of the 1981 cuts has been an overall drop in the number of posts in both universities and polytechnics. The loss of demand will exacerbate any disequilibrium that already exists.

We do not wish to see this prognosis taken too seriously. One of us has spent a professional life-time attacking the art of manpower forecasting (Blaug, 1970: ch. 5) and we are not likely therefore to place much credence in the sort of numerology that characterized our previous paragraphs. What is striking about the figures, such as they are, is not that supply exceeds demand but how small are the relevant magnitudes. This is a market subject to exaggerated reports of 'dire shortages' and 'wasteful gluts' whenever annual demand or supply temporarily rises by 20 or 30 individuals. Thus, the slight current surplus of professional economists is no more a matter of alarm than was the slight shortage of the late 1960s, particularly when it is realized that senior professional economists in the private sector move readily into management positions, thus making room at the bottom for young blood.

SALARIES

The notion of an oversupply, however small, of professional economists sits uneasily next to stories of high salaries earned nowadays by economists working in the City. However, salaries on the order of £150–250,000 a year, while earned by some, are entirely atypical of the general pattern of earnings for professional economists in commercial banking and industry. We had hoped to present a thorough analysis of the earnings of economists but that proved to be more difficult than we had ever imagined.

We encountered two problems: one is that there are no reliable data on earnings which relate to professional economists defined by job title, and the other, far more damaging to the economist's *modus vivendi*, is that the majority of economists are working for organizations which do not distinguish pay by individual specialists.

All economists in higher education and in government are paid on salary scales which do not specifically relate to them as economists. Since this covers almost

3,000 professional economists, this presents a major problem for drawing any conclusions from earnings data. Nevertheless, we were able to make one or two observations about the supply of economists willing to work on these pay scales. The GES clearly has problems in retaining economists though not in recruiting them (pp. 32–5). There is an acute shortage of school teachers offering economics, though pay may not be the only issue (p. 79). In the universities the average salary of £15,600 paid to economists in 1986–7 was practically the same as the average of £15,800 for all teachers and researchers, according to data provided by the Universities' Statistical Register. Only 4 per cent of university teachers of economics left the sector in 1987 (p. 13), suggesting no great dissatisfaction. Evidence from the questionnaire showed that in 1988 economics departments were not generally experiencing difficulties with recruiting economists, nor were they dissatisfied with recruits (pp. 68, 69). We concluded that there is no shortage of academic economists at current pay scales. In the City and industry, where earnings are much higher than in academia or government, the question of recruitment hardly arises, since the demand for economists is declining; where recruitment had taken place, there were plenty of candidates to choose from. As we said before, the supply of professional economists appears to be sufficient, therefore, though demand is falling.

What is the value of an economics degree outside the economics profession? Since only a small proportion of economics graduates become professional economists, earnings reflect the pay of those occupations they enter. Accounting is a case in point; successful accountants could expect (in 1988) to earn £18,000 after three years at work and double that after five. This must push up the average earnings of economics graduates since so many of them go into accountancy. But we were also told that there is no preference for economics graduates over any others. The same was true of general banking, the first destination of the second largest group. Therefore, the relatively high earnings of economics graduates may simply reflect the fact that a larger proportion of them go into a high-paying profession; what is being measured is the earnings of accountants, not the relative merits of an economics degree.

What we need to measure the value of the economics profession are data on job-titled economists. The National Survey of 1980 Graduates and Diplomates by the Employment Research Unit of the Department of Employment, the database for the studies by Taylor (1989) and Dolton and Makepeace (1989), turned up too few to be worthwhile. But this is hardly surprising – their numbers were small because the economics profession is. Academic and government economists are on occupational pay scales, unrelated to their being economists. The Society of Business Economists conducts its own annual earnings survey but the results are not reliable because the response rate is extremely low. For a variety of reasons, therefore, we have to say that little can be concluded about the value of the economics profession or of an economics degree by looking at existing earnings data.

THE QUESTIONNAIRE RESULTS

We mounted the questionnaire survey of economics departments because published data were inadequate for our purpose. We had expected that a survey was necessary to find out about promotions, workloads, reasons for staff leaving, etc. We had not realised in advance how few data there are even about university staff broken down by subject. The questionnaire therefore yielded valuable information about a range of aspects of the economics profession that were previously unquantified. At present, we can only offer a snapshot profile with very little possibility of making comparisons either over time or with other subjects. If the questionnaire is repeated, as we believe it should be, then trends can be identified.

Economists in higher education are not all to be found in economics departments; indeed, in quite a few institutions there is no economics department either because of the way teaching is organized or because economists service other courses and departments. Thus there is no necessary correlation between staff and student numbers. This is most clearly seen in the case of polytechnics, where large numbers of economists exist, producing a relatively small output of students (see tables 16, 17, 18, 30 and 31). In addition, the definition of academic economists, including economic statisticians, economic historians, econometricians and agricultural economists, appears to be considerably broader than that adopted by the Universities' Statistical Register: hence our count of economists in universities is much higher than theirs (see pp. 5, 6). We estimate that there are just over 2,500 academic and research economists in the UK, of whom three-quarters work in universities. Of these only 10 per cent of academic staff are women; 20 teaching departments have no women members of staff and there are only seven women in senior academic posts (p. 54). Just over half university teachers of economics of all ranks are lecturers. In the polytechnic sector, where transfer from lecturer to senior lecturer is automatic, two-thirds of academic staff are senior lecturers.

Perhaps the most striking finding from the questionnaire was that the number of students graduating with joint degrees which include economics exceeds those with a single honours degree in economics. This finding has quite far-reaching implications, since published data on most features of graduates – place of study, first destinations, class of degree, etc. – are for single honours graduates only. What this means is that these data give only a partial picture of the contribution of economics as a discipline and economists as an academic group. A good example is First Destinations data; a great deal of emphasis is placed on them, yet because they only show employment patterns of economics graduates of single honours degrees, they fail to tell us about the majority.

The prevalence of joint honours degrees also blurs the relation between student and staff numbers. We estimate that for every student graduating in economics, five more are on other years and other courses (p. 73). The effect on workloads is measured by student:staff ratios which rose from a common average of 13.25 in 1982–3 to 14.17 in universities and 15.62 in polytechnics, reflecting the different effects of the 1981 cuts in funds to higher education; the university sector protected the 'unit of resource' by holding back student intake while the polytechnics absorbed increasing numbers of students without a corresponding increase in staffing or other resources (p. 82). So the number of university graduates in economics, which had been rising, fell by 6 per cent after 1982, while there was a 47 per cent increase in polytechnics (pp. 8, 9). Despite this huge percentage increase, however, the majority of economics graduates continue to be produced by universities, with single honours degrees being offered in 44 universities as compared to 17 polytechnics (tables 30 and 31). There is, by the way, a noticeable tendency for student numbers to be more concentrated in polytechnics (though as these figures are for single honours, joint degrees could balance things out). However, there are clearly some fairly small teaching departments in universities; and this shows up also in small concentrations of postgraduate numbers (p. 74). Overall, the output of postgraduate economists was the same in 1987 as in 1981, with a steady 40 per cent over the period being home students despite a dramatic fall from 168 to 69 of ESRC postgraduate studentships going to economists (pp. 11, 12). Total student numbers in universities then, appear to be stable. Some departments seem to be too small to be efficient.

The growth of student numbers in polytechnics did not prevent cuts in staffing taking place, though absolute losses were lower than in universities. Between 1981 and 1987 polytechnics had a net loss of 11 posts in economics, compared with 44 in universities, and 8 more expected by 1990. In both sectors the loss was of higher-ranking posts, while gains were made at the bottom end; a quarter of the posts lost in universities were professorships. Loss of posts was often brought about by staff retirement, either early retirement or at the normal retirement age: a quarter of university staff and one-third of polytechnic staff left for these reasons, with a quarter moving to another university or polytechnic and a further quarter (15 persons) went to a university abroad or left academic life (pp. 62–3).

The chief reason given by heads of department for staff leaving was poor promotion prospects, and this is borne our by the fact that many staff, particularly lecturers, are stuck at the top of their pay scale. Low salaries were cited as the reason for 21 per cent of university staff leaving and 30 per cent of polytechnic staff (polytechnic staff appear to earn less than their counterparts in universities). Low salaries were cited as causing problems in hiring staff, though few department heads expressed dissatisfaction with the quality of applicants and there were signs of excess supply (pp. 60–70).

We tried to measure changes in the quality of life of academics in the five years following the 1981 cuts and succeeded in collecting a lot of detailed information about research, sabbaticals and the like from the questionnaires. But the problem was that there was nothing with which to make a comparison; for example, no one was able to take leave of any sort in 1987–8 from 18 university and 7 polytechnic departments (p. 93): though this seems a poor show, we do not know what earlier norms were and hence if this is attributable to the cuts or not. What does seem to have been a direct result of the cuts is the relative loss of senior academic posts and the switch to more junior posts. This has been accompanied by the effective loss of tenure and a growth of temporary lectureships (p. 58). An associated feature is the extensive use of part-time teachers, but here is another case where comparisons are not possible.

The picture we gained of the current state of the economics profession in higher education is that demand has probably fallen slightly. Academic posts have been lost, but the number of research posts has increased which, however, are often short-term and dependent upon current levels of research funding. With the weakening of tenure, the uncertainty of a career in universities must have increased; as job security was an important non-pecuniary benefit in an occupation which already had relatively low salaries; in the long run supply must be affected. At the time of the survey, though, there were no signs of a shortage of economists entering higher education. We were largely unable to measure changes in the quality of academic life; one identifiable trend was that student ratios in universities have risen slightly, and those in polytechnics quite a bit more.

What of the future? In the immediate future, the demand for academic economists will fall slightly with a future small loss of posts expected, but that could be reversed if student numbers were allowed to rise. However, as the current stock of economists ages we would expect there to be a rise in the demand for economists in 10–12 years' time.

The Robbins era of the 1960s accompanied by the explosion of GES in the days of Wilson virtually doubled the stock of economists employed in academia and government in less than a decade. So rapid a growth of employment in a brief period of time typically produces an echo effect 40 years later as an entire cohort hired in their twenties reach retirement in their sixties. In the case in question, the year 2000 or thereabouts will therefore see some extraordinary growth in the demand for economists to replace those retiring in universities, polytechnics and the Civil Service. Until then, however, there may well be no net positive demand for professional economists in the economy as a whole.

REFERENCES

Blaug, M. (1970) *An Introduction to the Economics of Education*, London: Penguin Books.

Dolton, P. and G. Makepeace (1989) 'The earnings of economics graduates', University of Hull Labour Economics Research Unit, Discussion Paper 89/3.

Royal Economic Society (1988) 'The current state of the British economics profession', Imperial College, London: RES.

Taylor, J. (1989) 'Economics graduates in the UK labour market', Department of Employment (unpublished).

17. The University of Buckingham after ten years: a tentative evaluation[*]

BUCKINGHAM IN 1986

We begin with a brief description of the University of Buckingham as it appears today. Its most distinctive features are its small size in relation to the conventional British university – it has a student body in the region of 600 and an academic staff of 56 – and its two-year honours degree in contrast with the standard three-year degree programme in England and Wales and the four-year degree programme in Scotland. The two-year degree is made possible by the adoption of four intensive ten-week terms per year, so that students complete 80 weeks over a two-year period compared to 72–80 weeks of normal contact typified by the three-year programme of other universities.

Buckingham opened its doors in 1976 as the University College of Buckingham, issuing licences rather than degrees. It was granted a Royal Charter in 1983 and since then has issued degrees in law; accounting and financial management; economics; business studies; history, politics and English literature; politics, economics and law; biology and society; computer science (with four distinct optional programmes); and European studies (involving five distinct options) (see Table 17.1). Graduates of Buckingham in law and accountancy enjoy the same exemptions from the examinations of the relevant professional bodies as do graduates from other universities.

The Buckingham degree course is not only shorter than in other universities but is also more broadly based: students are required to pursue courses outside their area of specialization and, in addition, are required to pursue a two-term foreign language course. The university also awards postgraduate degrees from the BPhil to the PhD. There are student exchange programmes with private universities abroad, such as Koblenz School of Corporate Management in Western Germany, Claremont College in California and Lehigh University in Pennsylvania.

Almost 40 per cent of students at Buckingham are British, many of whom receive mandatory grants from their local authorities, including some £1,500 towards the annual tuition fee of over £5,000. About a third of the students are

[*] First published in *Higher Education Quarterly*, **42**(1) 1988: 72–89, (written with G.K. Shaw).

female and likewise, about one-third are aged 25 years or more (see Table 17.1). Some 10 per cent of the students are either in receipt of bursary rewards of about £2,000 per year or have borrowed various sums repayable over five years at favourable rates of interest (see Table 17.2).

Table 17.1   Summary of student population, winter term 1985

Total student registrations: 582	(Undergraduates	571)
	(Postgraduates	4)
	(Occasionals	7)

Distribution of undergraduates between schools and degree programmes (figures in brackets give new entry, January 1985):

Accounting, Business and Economics

Accounting and Financial Management	51	(23)
Business Studies	91	(54)
Economics	28	(8)
	170	(85)

Humanities

European Studies	19	(10)
History, Politics and English Literature	25	(13)
Politics, Economics and Law	35	(20)
	79	(43)

Law	307	(121)

Sciences

Biology and Society	15	(8)

Postgraduates:

MSC Fisheries Management	3
PhD Economics	1

Of the total student population: 392 (67%) are male
180 (31%) are aged over 25 years

Principal nationalities

British	225	(38%)
Malaysian	106	(18%)
Nigerian	79	(13%)

Table 17.2   Student numbers and types of student support, 1976–85

	Student numbers	Gross cost bursary awards (£)	No. of students receiving bursary awards	Average value of bursary awards (£)	No. of students receiving LEA awards	No. of students on loans
1976	65	10,461	16	654	1	8
1977	161	15,983	23	695	5	10
1978	231	17,060	23	742	6	5
1979	267	14,217	16	889	5	6
1980	367	29,396	22	1,336	7	2
1981	416	42,571	31	1,373	66	3
1982	447	57,294	38	1,508	94	7
1983	479	82,780	52	1,592	139	21
1984	518	69,430	42	1,653	151	22
1985	582	74,087	38	1,950	149	12

Note: Loans-students have only been included during the year(s) in which they used a loan to finance their course.

BEGINNINGS

Having described the distinguishing characteristics of Buckingham University, we are now ready to evaluate its relative success. But precisely what do we mean by success in this case? Buckingham has been successful in that it has survived in the face of heavily subsidized competition; to have founded the first private university and raised some £6 million in a country like Britain with no tradition of private donations to universities, or of alumni organizations dedicated to supporting their *alma mater*, is a remarkable achievement. Nevertheless, even this commonsense definition of success raises the question of purpose: why would anybody want to create a private university in Britain? what could be the object of such a difficult exercise? Such questions suggest a more precise meaning of success in the assessment of a new institution, namely, congruence between original intentions and ultimate outcomes; in other words, does the institution turn out to be, after the passage of x years, exactly what was intended by its founders?

In this more precise sense, Buckingham cannot be declared an unqualified success. Its distinguishing characteristics ten years after its foundation bear little relationship to the objectives of those who founded it, being instead the result of a series of *ad hoc* decisions, none of which was foreseen in the 1970s and some of which were not even apparent as late as 1976 when the first cohort of students was admitted. To substantiate these assertions, we need to consider the history of the idea of an independent, private university in Britain.

In May 1967, *The Times* published a letter from Dr J.W. Paulley advocating the foundation of an independent university. The publication coincided with niggling doubts among some academics about the pace of the Robbins expansion of higher education and the weakened autonomy of the British university system that was implied by the growing reliance on state finance.

Apart from those worries, there were critics of the increasing tendency towards single-subject specialization in British higher education as expressed in the general complaint of industry that science graduates were largely illiterate while arts graduates were largely innumerate. Such critics looked with favour on the concept of an independent university as a means of permitting a broader style of education than that currently in vogue in the state-financed institutions and they saw eye to eye with those who viewed the concept of an independent university as a safeguard for the maintenance of academic excellence in the face of a general decline in academic standards.

The idea of an independent university, therefore, possessed a certain appeal to a wide variety of opinion who were by no means united in one political philosophy or educational standpoint. Indeed, there was no obvious political bias in the initial consensus in favour of an independent university. The basic concept was compatible with a non-residential urban campus, with a heavy reliance on part-time degree courses, and the intention to meet a substantial portion of tuition fees by scholarship aid, bursaries and the provision of fully costed student loans. In short, the eventual polarization on opinion about the independent university between right-wing (Tory) supporters and left-wing (Labour) opponents was not inevitable but instead derived to a considerable extent from the policy decisions of the early planning board. Again, it is perhaps worth noting that these initial discussions were not always harmonious; there were often substantial disagreements, which in some cases led to original supporters of the project resigning from the planning committee. Today the University of Buckingham and the Open University are widely regarded as standing at opposite ends of the ideological spectrum. Yet one of the earliest proposals discussed by the planning board (and rejected) contemplated the transfer of Open University students at the end of their foundation-year course to an accelerated degree programme at the independent university.

Nevertheless, Dr Paulley's letter was only taken up by the market-oriented Institute of Economic Affairs (IEA), which soon published a pamphlet on the subject by Professor H.S. Ferns of the University of Birmingham, entitled *Towards an Independent University* (Ferns, 1969). This pamphlet was followed up by a conference in January 1969, which issued a declaration of *The Urgency of an Independent University*, establishing the provisional planning board under the chairmanship of Sir Sydney Caine, then Director of the London School of Economics.

The planning board operated through the years 1969–73 after which time its activities were handed over to the College Council. By this time sufficient funds had been raised to make the launching of an independent university a distinct if distant possibility. During the four years of its existence, the planning board met frequently to debate various issues and to decide on matters of academic policy. Always, however, its deliberations were tactical rather than strategic, being dictated by the forces of events, in particular the possibilities of various locations and the insufficiency of finance that defeated many of the available options. Repeatedly, the planning board went into debt and several times its continued existence was made possible only by generous loans and guarantees from the IEA. Not surprisingly, no clear philosophy about the new university emerged from the protracted discussions of the planning board. There was a general commitment to the principle of independence, by which was meant both freedom from government interference and independence of government finance; but the bulk of the discussions were devoted to a number of highly specific but interlocked issues that had to be settled if the new university was ever to be launched.

THE ISSUES

In what follows we attempt to list the more relevant issues whose resolution, wisely or otherwise, have served to dictate the character of the university.

Teaching versus Research

An appealing feature of an independent university to many of its advocates was the belief that self-financed students were better motivated than students financed by taxpayers. The corollary of this proposition was the notion that the greater commitment of students to learning demanded greater emphasis in staffing on good teaching rather than research. Thus the independent university would strive to excel in teaching and research would take a second place in initial appointments and subsequent promotions. These two tenets – that independent university students would be better motivated and that independent university staff would be more dedicated towards teaching, were frequently advocated and widely endorsed amongst the early proponents of the independent university.

In the event, it is probably true that teaching loads at Buckingham were and are somewhat lighter than in the state sector.[1] It is also the case that Buckingham promotes close personal contacts between staff and students, making for a good deal of informal tuition not normally included in the assessment of teaching loads in other universities. Amongst the criteria for promotion, in addition to research, teaching and administrative ability is a sense of commitment to the college, and a willingness to be involved in its promotion in the form of marketing activities, school visits and so forth. In this respect, Buckingham tends to resemble the small private American liberal arts college rather than the large private research-oriented American university.

Political Stance

One of the earliest questions to be addressed was the need for support and the creation of a distinguished panel of patrons. Should the latter make a conscious attempt to reflect all shades of political opinion and thus attempt to remove the issue of independence from the political arena? There were many people who felt that this was indeed the ideal and others who argued that too close an alliance with the forces of the right would be counterproductive, especially in relation to fund-raising efforts. It was argued that Labour's traditional hostility to private education at the secondary school level need not logically extend to the higher education sector.

In the event Buckingham University became closely identified with the political right. A number of forces contributed to this outcome. First of all, the eventual decision to become a residential university pursuing full-time degree courses produced the inevitable outcome that Buckingham's clientele are largely drawn from the ranks of the wealthy. Secondly, the fact that Max (now Lord) Beloff was appointed the first principal of the college played a large part in shaping its political character because Beloff saw the issue of independence essentially in political terms and strongly resisted the attempt to straddle the political parties in seeking support. Thirdly, the fact that the admittedly right-wing IEA was closely involved in the early planning stages and viewed the issue of university independence as one of free markets versus collectivism certainly played its part. The final outcome has seen Mrs Thatcher and Sir Keith Joseph numbered amongst the University's patrons, Lord Hailsham as the University's Chancellor and open hostility from the Labour Party, in particular from Neil Kinnock. The Denning Law Library, the Patrick Hutber Cottages and Hailsham House all bear testimony to a strong Conservative presence and support. One unfortunate consequence of this outward manifestation is a tendency to create the impression that the University must be equally partisan in its teaching, particularly within the fields of politics and economics, which is certainly not the case. The IEA has continued to provide generous financial support to the Department of Economics by funding its research activities, its visiting speakers seminar programme and its economics discussion papers series but without any attempt to attach any conditions to the manner in which the money is used. Nonetheless, the impression sometimes remains that economics teaching at Buckingham must necessarily consist of right-wing monetarist and free market doctrines.[2]

Location

Nothing could illustrate better the *ad hoc* evolution of the independent university than the decision to locate at Buckingham. The initial preference had been for an urban site, preferably close to London. Apart from the desire to attract potential part-time students on a non-residential basis (rather like the evening courses taught at Birkbeck College), it was also believe that London would be attractive to American students taking a summer school abroad. In the event, the barriers to a London site became insurmountable. The Greater London Council was opposed to another university being located in the London area. Croydon, which had been the early preferred site, indicated planning objections and there was opposition from the Labour MP for Croydon South to the siting of an independent university in his constituency. While the difficulties over a London site were emerging, the University Hall at Buckland, which prepared students for London external degrees, came on to the market at a reasonable price of £30,000. Buckland became a distinct possibility and initial negotiations were entered into, despite the fact that it implied a fundamental departure from the original conception towards a small-scale, elitist Oxford-type college. Yet within a month the Buckland site had been superseded by an unexpected suggestion from the Buckinghamshire planning authority, attracted by the prospect of including a university in the North Bucks development plan. The Buckinghamshire planning authority were prepared to offer a substantial site and to allow the purchase of existing buildings on reasonably advantageous terms. There was the additional attraction that Buckingham was near to both the University of Oxford and the Open University, both of which might be able to provide the part-time teaching staff that would be required in the initial years.

Student Numbers

One of the most difficult questions facing the creation of the independent university turned upon the size of the market it could reasonably expect to appeal to and the student numbers that would be required to make the university a viable commercial proposition. All the evidence indicates that the planning board's initial forecasts were wildly overoptimistic: they envisaged a much larger university being created in a comparatively short period of time. That might have been a realistic assumption in 1967 but not in 1976. In 1967 when the idea of an independent university was first broached, it was generally held that the situation was one of excess demand, that there were many students who were highly qualified but who were unable to gain a university place.

In the event the expansion of the 'new' universities under the Robbins proposals together with the growth of first degree courses in polytechnics pre-empted the market. Accordingly, the growth of the independent university has been much slower than was initially envisaged and, as a consequence, its entry requirements have been substantially below the average maintained by the state sector (see below). The initial planning estimates refer to a target figure of 3,000 students and a capital sum of £15 million being attained by 1977 (assuming the college was to open in 1973).[3] This was the global figure assumed in general discussion. It also appears to be the figure which influenced the Buckingham planning authorities and which lay behind their belief that the university would lead to a creation of some 1,500 jobs.

As time went by, and as funds failed to materialize in any substantial amounts, the proposed opening date of the new university was progressively pushed back and the target numbers substantially curtailed. As more modest targets were announced, the original estimates were quietly forgotten. Thus, for example, at the ninth meeting of the new council on 27 February 1974, it was affirmed that the initial objective remained, namely to establish by 1979–80 a university college of 500–600 students for which a royal charter could be granted. Even this more modest figure, however, was looked upon even at this comparatively late date as forming but 'a nucleus of a full university'. It seems clear that the founding fathers envisaged a number larger university than that which eventually materialized and were wildly overoptimistic concerning the amount of funding that would be forthcoming.

As the shortage of funds dictated a drastic downward revision in the potential numbers of students, and as it became increasingly recognized that a fully fledged university on conventional lines was an extremely remote possibility, more consideration began to be given to the claim that 'small is beautiful'. The metamorphosis was dramatic and suddenly the ideal became closely identified with the typical small-scale Oxbridge college, emphasizing the benefits of an intimate relationship between staff and students. Once again, what evolved due to the sheer force of events and financial constraints became rapidly assimilated into the philosophy of the independent university. To quote directly from Dr Watson, the Assistant Dean of Admissions, writing within months of the college's opening:

> It is an important feature of our educational philosophy that the tutorial system is advantageous – and not only academically; it also enables a genuine personal relationship to develop between students and teachers ... Connected with this belief

is the College's commitment to a maximum target of 500–600 student places.
(Watson, private memo, 1976)

If the University of Buckingham has had a much smaller impact upon the
higher education scene than formerly envisaged by those who proposed its
establishment, it is doubtless partly because it is minuscule in size in relation
to the competing state institutions.

The Buckingham Degree

No other issue generated such diversity of comment and such controversy
among the founders of the independent university as did the question of the nature
of the Buckingham degree. Fundamentally there was the duration of the course
and the degree of generality and broadness involved. From the beginning, a broad-
based degree was always considered part of the underlying philosophy; indeed,
it was the charge of excessive specialization within the state system which was
said to render the concept of a new independent university attractive to potential
industrial benefactors. Beyond this general principle, however, there were very
few firm ideas governing the nature of the degree programmes to be adopted.
Indeed, to a very large extent this was inevitable since detailed course programmes
could not be devised until key staff had been appointed; but key staff of
adequate standing and reputation could not be appointed until sufficient funds
had been established to guarantee their salaries. Thus, in the absence of adequate
funding, detailed prospectuses could not be prepared and, moreover, no
meaningful negotiations with bodies such as the Council for National Academic
Awards could be entered into. In this climate of uncertainty, the nature of the
Buckingham degree was still to be determined.

   The two-year honours degree has emerged as the truly radical and innovative
feature of the Buckingham experiment. By abolishing the long 'summer
vacation', a historical relic which has no academic justification, and replacing
the three-term academic year by four terms, each of ten weeks' duration, it
permitted the Buckingham student to cover more or less the same ground as he
or she would normally encounter in the more conventional three-year programme.
Moreover, the four-term student year was combined with a three-term teaching
year for academic staff (each staff member having one study term per year free
of teaching or administrative duties); without such a provision it is doubtful that
Buckingham would have been able to attract staff of sufficiently high calibre
and research potential to justify its eventual university status.

   The two-year programme soon came to be regarded as 'central to the College's
original experimental purpose' (University College at Buckingham, 1976).
This, however, appears to be a classic case of wisdom with hindsight. As with
most other issues, the practice evolved more from *ad hoc* considerations than

from any clearly defined grand design or underlying philosophy, although the idea of a two-year degree had been mooted by G.H. Rawcliffe in 1971 (Rawcliffe, 1971).

In any case, it appears that the early suggestion of a two-year programme had reference to a broad general degree of two years' duration upon which later specialization could build, leading to an honours qualification by an additional year of study. In the early discussions of the planning board and later meetings of council, a two-year *honours* degree was never envisaged. In the first ever *Newsletter*, issued by the College in September 1973, the basic principles of the curriculum are laid down:

(i) The academic year will consist of four terms of 10–11 weeks with intakes in July and perhaps January.
(ii) Degree standard will normally be reached in two years (eight terms). A further course of two or three terms will enable the standard of a specialist honours degree in a particular field to be reached.

Thus, initially at least, the honours degree programme was scheduled to take the best part of three years, comparable with standard practice in other English universities. What then was the purpose of the more intensive four-term year? The answer, it seems clear, lay in producing the well-rounded student rather than the narrow specialist. Again, quoting from the first *Newsletter*:

The programme of studies of each student will be of a semi-specialised nature. About five-eighths of his effort will be devoted to work in one of a limited number of fields – initially, it is expected, Law, Economics, Life Sciences and Mathematical Sciences – and three-eighths to broadening and supporting courses in these and related fields ... All students will also be expected to attain a good reading knowledge of two modern languages (other than English) and a basic knowledge of Mathematics ...

Clearly, the programme envisaged a much broader and more general form of education than is currently in vogue in the United Kingdom, and the two-year foundation course was not intended to produce students with honours degree qualifications.

However, as time progressed, the distinction between a general honours degree became less well defined. For example, by November 1973, *Newsletter* No. 3 was to claim that 'On present expectations the first 100–150 degree students would be admitted in April 1975 or April 1976 and will complete their course in two intensive years.'

While reference was made to further courses permitting further specialization, the reference to an honours degree gained in this way was discreetly dropped. How is this transformation to be explained?

Looking back it now seems clear that the members of the early planning board and the succeeding council fell into two distinct groups, although the groups undoubtedly overlapped on certain issues. Upon the one hand, there were those who for want of a better name we might term the 'Idealists'. This group at one extreme had the utopian view that excellence in education would attract the gifted student regardless of the nature of the qualification to be obtained (if any!). In contrast, there were those whom we may term the 'Practicalists', who recognized that fee-paying students would only be forthcoming in any numbers if they could expect a paper qualification which would enhance their future income and earning potential. In the very early days of the planning board, much emphasis was given to a golden age view of the 'Leonardo Man', educated in all fields and ignorant in none, and little attention was paid to the time and cost involved in attaining this end. However, as time progressed those people charged with preparing the prospectus and with recruiting potential students adopted a more prosaic approach. Two factors undoubtedly influenced them. First, a growing awareness that a three-year honours degree course would impose heavy costs upon potential students and, secondly, that industrial sponsors would be less willing to finance degree courses which produced only general degrees. The conflict between utopian ideals and the practical steps necessary to produce a saleable product was inevitably resolved in favour of the latter.

The same type of practical considerations also conditioned the ultimate choice of disciplines to be offered by the college. As early as 1972 Dr Gillian Peele, newly recruited to the planning board, argued the necessity of launching the independent university forthwith and suggested that legal studies would be a suitable first school of study. More specifically, she proposed a detailed two-year course leading to a formal qualification (diploma) which might qualify for exemption from Part I of the Bar examinations. Thus, although the general philosophy of the founding fathers has talked in lofty terms of a host of wide-ranging faculties, including the physical sciences, in practice it was the provision of vocational training which rendered the university a practical possibility. It is not surprising that Buckingham's two-year law degree has been by far the most successful in attracting student numbers and this has been followed by accounting and financial management, where again exemption from the examinations of professional bodies has been secured, and more recently by the new business studies degree.

The Student Intake

Of all the assumptions made concerning the initial years of the independent university, none was more optimistic or misplaced than that concerning the entry qualifications of the student body. In a situation believed to correspondence to excess demand for university places, the commitment to independence combined with an excellence in teaching and the general philosophy embracing a broad-based educational training was expected to appeal to students of above-average calibre.

Table 17.3 *Degrees (licenses) conferred by the University of Buckingham (University College of Buckingham) by class awarded, 1977–85*

Year	1st	2.1	2.2	3	P	Total
1977	1	8	12	9	13	43
1978	4	14	12	21	16	67
1979	–	12	29	15	9	65
1980	2	11	41	23	23	100
1981	1	23	56	28	31	139
1982	4	33	66	22	28	153
1983	3	30	86	24	25	168
1984	4	30	87	41	29	191
1985	3	52	106	35	31	228[a]
Total	22	213	495	218	205	1154[a]
Percentages	1.9	18.5	42.9	18.9	17.8	100

Note: [a] Includes Aegrotat degree.

Table 17.4 *'A' level qualifications of registering January 1985 students and prospective 1986 entry students*

Degree programme	Registering students January 1985			Prospective 1986 Entry		
	Points	No.	Average	Points	No.	Average
Accounting and Financial Management	58	10	5.8	86	12	7.2
Business Studies	122	18	6.8	167	26	6.4
Economics	26	6	4.3	31	7	4.4
History, Politics and English Literature	51	9	5.7	32	5	6.4
Politics, Economics and Law	40	9	4.4	61	9	6.8
European Studies	44	7	6.3	76	15	5.1
Biology and Society	25	7	3.6	10	2	5.0
Computer Science	–	–	–	35	6	5.8
Law	276	41	6.7	193	127	7.1
Total	604	107	5.6	691	109	6.3

Note: This table has been compiled by using the Universities Central Council on Admissions points system, A grade = 5, B grade = 4, C grade = 3. For a comparison of these entry qualifications by course studies across all universities and polytechnics, see Heap (1986).

In the event, Buckingham's students, while often highly motivated, have not possessed outstanding admission qualifications and it would be fair to conclude that they fall somewhat below those obtaining in the state sector (see Tables 17.3 and 17.4). In conceding this point, two important caveats should be noted. First, Buckingham has appealed to many mature students who, having left school without 'A' levels, find their subsequent advancement hindered by the lack of formal academic qualifications. These students, often highly intelligent and certainly strongly motivated, look upon the intensive two-year Buckingham programme as a means of overcoming a career cul de sac; they do, however, adversely impinge on the average entry qualification aggregated across the board. Secondly, Buckingham's two-year degree programme has been especially appealing to overseas students, since it offers a cheaper alternative to paying three years' full-cost tuition fees at state-subsidized British universities. Overseas students in many cases are less qualified in terms of 'A' level grades than their English counterparts, partly because of certain language difficulties but also because many of them are financially constrained to take 'A' levels after one year of intensive study in tutorial colleges specializing in such programmes. The large proportion of overseas students at Buckingham are thus bound to pull down Buckingham's overall entry standards. Finally, and encouragingly, the admissions standards are gradually rising, despite the expansion in student numbers at the rate of approximately 30 per year, and this improvement is reflected in the ratio of applications to admissions. As of 31 December 1986, for example, the number of applications to acceptances for the forthcoming entry was 1,482 to 288, a ratio slightly in excess of five to one.

Table 17.5   Number of staff publications by subject area, 1976–85

	1976	1977	1978	1979	1980	1981	1982	1983	1984	1985	Total
Accounting and Financial Management		0	0	1	0	2	2	1	1	0	7
Economics	2	0	14	10	18	22	23	18	17	27	151
Politics	2	0	0	0	0	0	2	4	8	6	22
Law		2	1	1	7	9	3	8	8	10	49
History		1	1	2	2	0	1	3	3	1	14
English Language, Literature	1	3	1	1	2	2	4	4	2	2	22
Maths/Stats	2	0	6	5	2	8	7	5	4	9	48
Life Sciences		0	0	0	3	8	6	7	8	6	38
Business Studies							0	0	0	0	0
Other	4	2	2	3	3	4	1	4	2	0	25
Total	11	8	25	23	37	55	49	54	53	61	376

Table 17.6   Publications by schools of study

Year	1983	1984	1985	Total	Staff[a]	Annual Ratio[b]
ABE	19	18	27	64	12	1.77
Humanities	13	14	9	36	19	0.63
Law	8	8	10	26	15	0.57
Science	12	12	15	39	8	1.63
U/B				165	54	1.02

Notes
[a]   This figure should be treated as an average figure since staff numbers have ben subject to persistent change in line with the University's expansion.
[b]   Publications–staff ratio divided by three.

CONCLUSION

Bernard Crick, reviewing MacCallum Scott's book on *University Independence* in the *THES* on 15 October 1971 argued that the fact 'that there is no blueprint of the independent university by now, no clear agreement as to objectives and method, is reprehensible and incredible. The only agreement is that £15 million is needed from private sources – but for what?' This assertion was a little unfair because some of the contributors to the book did mention certain objectives for an independent university, such as the greater possibility of experimenting with new teaching methods, of attracting more mature students, and of forging international links (MacCallum Scott, 1971). Still, it is true that by 1971 most of the founders of the independent university had no very precise idea of what was to be accomplished by a private university that could not be achieved by a state-financed university. We have shown that the same thing was true as late as 1975, the year before the new university was opened. All the essential distinguishing features of Buckingham have emerged, not as a consequence of clearly defined objectives originally laid down, but as a result of events, such as the approval of the newly elected Thatcher government, or of concrete circumstances, such as the difficulty of raising money. Thus, Buckingham is a success in spite of itself, in spite of the fact that almost none of the specific outcomes of 1986 were envisaged in 1967, 1971, or 1976. However, Buckingham was created in part to have an effect on the higher education system as a whole. Judged in terms of that objective, the experiment of creating a private university must be judged as yet a failure: Buckingham has not so far had the least influence on the rest of British higher education. In the bitter words of R. Geiger (1985): 'The Buckingham founders have proved to the world that they could succeed in founding a private university, but they have not yet demonstrated why they should have bothered.'

What of Buckingham's future? The independent university has been successful in demonstrating its ability to survive against heavily subsidized competition and in a harsh economic climate which has rendered fund-raising extremely difficult. Its continued existence has confounded expectations. It has now reached a size where it has attained an operating surplus and has been able to reduce substantially its accumulated deficit (which peaked in 1982–3) at approximately £1.3 million). All the short-term indicators are favourable, especially given the recent cutbacks in the state sector of higher education. Yet none the less, its long-term future remains clouded by uncertainty. Punitive measures by an incoming Labour administration, such as the ending of charitable status or the abolition of mandatory grants, might jeopardize the survival of Buckingham.[4]

Even ignoring the attitude of a future Labour government, there remain other clouds upon the horizon. All the projected demographic trends point to a substantial drop in the home demand for university places – by almost 30 per cent or more – over the forthcoming decade. In consequence, the competition between the universities and polytechnics for students will become more intense and here the conventional universities have an advantage over Buckingham when it comes to sustained marketing activities. Moreover, as the demand by British students for university places continues to fall, Buckingham will face increased competition in overseas markets for foreign students. Nor is it feasible, given the existing standards of admission, to broaden substantially the base from which Buckingham draws its students. Any real attempt to follow this course of action would so reduce standards as to question the very reason for Buckingham's existence. In the long term, therefore, Buckingham's continued existence must remain uncertain.

NOTES

1. The norm for full-time members of staff is 243 contact hours per year and, unlike in universities, there is no such thing as the sabbatical term's leave every seven terms.
2. Griggs concludes a slam bang attack on Buckingham University with the words: 'one would not be surprised ... that the traditional conservative interpretation of society was promoted in the lecture theatre' (Griggs, 1985). Actually, one would be very surprised. In any case Griggs did not cite a single publication in economics and politics of members of staff of Buckingham to support his allegation (see Table 17.5).
3. H.S. Ferns (1969) had noted that most British universities were too small to reap the advantages of economies of scale and therefore concluded that 'enrolment in each year in a viable private university will have to be at least 3,500'.
4. Buckingham's status as a charity, entitling it to certain tax concessions and rate relief from local authorities, has been criticized by some (e.g. Griggs, 1985). But the alternative was to

incorporate as a profit-maximizing enterprise, which would surely have been criticized still more. Similarly, Buckingham's decision to petition for the award of mandatory grants to its students has been condemned by some as having one's cake and eating it too. But as Professor Alan Peacock, the former Vice-Chancellor or Buckingham, has remarked: 'If Buckingham had refused to negotiate for mandatory grants for its students, it would then have been accused of catering only for the rich' (Peacock, 1986).

REFERENCES

Ferns, H.S. (1969) *Towards an Independent University*, London: Institute of Economic Affairs; reprinted in J. and J. Pemberton, *The University College at Buckingham: A First Account of its Conception, Foundation and Early Years*, Buckingham: Buckingham Press, 1979.

Geiger, R. (1985) 'The private alternative in higher education', *European Journal of Education*, **20**(4).

Griggs, C. (1985) *Private Education in Britain*, London, Falmer Press.

Heap, B. (1986) *Degree Course Offers for Entry to British Universities and Colleges*, London: Career Consultants.

MacCallum Scott, J.H. (1971) *University Independence: The Main Questions*, London, Rex Collings.

Peacock, Alan (1986) 'Buckingham's fight for independence' *Journal of Economic Affairs*.

Rawcliffe, G.H. (1971) 'University science teaching', in J.H. MacCallum Scott, *University Independence: The Main Question*, London: Rex Collings.

University College at Buckingham (1976), *The University at Buckingham 1973–76*, Buckingham: University College at Buckingham.

18. Can independent education be suppressed?*

Private Schools, a Labour Party National Executive Committee Discussion Document, sets out the divisive social and educational effects of private schools and spells out a feasible solution of integrating them into the state system of education with a view to abolishing private schooling altogether, not today or tomorrow, but certainly the day after tomorrow. The recommendations of *Private Schools* were redrafted, with one or two alterations, in *A Plan for Private Schools*, published jointly by the TUC and the Labour Party in July 1981, with the aim of terminating all public support to private schools within one year of the election of a Labour government, and of abolishing fee-paying in private schools within a period of no more than ten years. These are hard-hitting documents: the case against private schools is pungently stated and the analysis of available policy options is informed by practical realism. Nevertheless, I am struck not so much by what is put into the argument but by what is left out, and in particular by the failure seriously to address the central philosophical question at issue in all debates about private schooling: should individuals in a democratic society in which incomes are not equally distributed be allowed to employ their incomes to purchase privileges for themselves (or members of their families), such as yachts, Rolls Royces, large houses, private medical care, private pensions and private education?

Let me declare my sentiments at the outset. This is a subject on which it is almost impossible to 'keep one's cool'. I feel as passionately about private schooling as the authors of the documents. It happens that I dislike 'public' schools, not because they are private, but because they are typically boarding schools and typically single-sex boarding schools in secluded rural areas. I believe that the hot-house, boarding atmosphere of the average public school has a lasting, disastrous psychological effect on children and I find this much more alarming than what I take to be the no less disastrous social effects of these schools. Having spent large parts of my youth in the Netherlands and the United States, I am amazed by the apparent eagerness of British middle-class parents to send their children away at the earliest possible age. Other countries have private schools: all over Asia and Africa there are more private than public secondary schools

* First published in *Economic Affairs*, October 1981: 30–7.

and even in America, where in the past private schools were few and far between, recent years have seen a steady growth in private schooling even at the elementary level.

But outside Britain, the debate about private schools is a debate about private day schools, and most foreigners are amazed to learn that many British parents think nothing of sending their 13-, 11- and even 7-year-old children away to a boarding school for nine months of the year. On the other hand, the boarding phenomenon is simply taken for granted in Britain and many of the enemies of public schools, like the authors of these documents, seem almost unaware of the vast difference between buying *private* education and buying private *boarding* education.

Having declared my prejudices against public schools, I nevertheless resist any notion of legislating private schools out of existence. I am a libertarian, and since we all believe in freedom when it comes to behaviour or activity we approve of, the litmuss-paper test of a libertarian is whether he will tolerate behaviour or activities he disapproves of. There is an alarming paragraph in *Private Schools* which illustrates the point in question: 'Freedom necessarily involves rights which can be exercised by *all*. Private education is not a freedom but a privilege confined to a tiny elite ... Labour believes that the only real freedom are those available to all citizens.' If we pursue the logic of this proposition, it follows that we must put an end to private medical care, private medical insurance and private pensions. This might not worry the members of the Labour Party's National Executive Council. But why should wealthy parents be allowed to purchase large houses, thus providing their children with the undoubted advantage of private study space, or houses near good state schools, which again confers an unequal advantage? Thus, private housing privilege must also be abolished, or at least severely circumscribed. Furthermore, wealthier parents must also be prevented from buying private tutoring for their children, or from taking them on continental holidays, because these too confer special advantages in the educational 'rat race'. Where indeed we do draw the line in ensuring that freedoms are available in equal amounts to all citizens?

CHOICE AND STATE EDUCATION

The authors of *Private Schools* mock the language of 'free choice' invoked by the advocates of private schooling. What is wrong with a state monopoly of education, they ask? All parents make use of maintained primary schools without worrying about 'freedom of choice' and why should a state monopoly of *secondary* education be considered any more threatening than a state monopoly of *primary* education? As a matter of fact, many parents opt out of the state system well before the age of secondary education, as witnessed by the large numbers of private preparatory schools admitting children after the age of seven. But apart from this debating point, it seems odd that the authors have forgotten about the entire history of 'progressive' primary education under largely private auspices. If British primary education is now something to be proud of, it is in part due to the influence of many educational iconoclasts who opened private schools to promote new ways of teaching young children. Similarly, 'alternative medicine' would have been doomed from the start if it had had to rely entirely on the National Health Service.

PAYING TWICE

So much then for the fundamental philosophical question. If we value freedom more than equality, we must tolerate private schools whether we like them or not. Yet I can see no reason to use public money to *subsidize* private schools as we do through such things as tax and rate relief, boarding allowances for military and diplomatic personnel, and local authorities paying private school fees for bright pupils. Parents who purchase private education pay for education twice over: once for maintained education by their contribution to general tax revenues, and once for private education by the fees paid to private schools. There is a sense in which such parents are relieving the rest of the community of the expense of educating their children for which they may in justice demand a *quid pro quo*. This is an argument which (the reader will not be surprised to learn) is never mentioned in either document before us. It is an argument which must be taken seriously and yet I find it unconvincing, particularly as the subsidies in question are little understood by the general public and are deliberately played down by spokesmen for the public schools. By all means let us fight for a genuine alternative to state education but let us have the courage of our convictions by insisting that it be a choice between subsidized state education and unsubsidized private education.

I hope I have now said enough to reveal my own biases. Let us return to the content of *Private Schools*. It begins with some factual background and then proceeds to make the case against private schools. Taking all private schools together, including the remaining direct grant grammar schools, private enrolments amount to only 6 per cent of the total school population but their share of pupils rises to 7 per cent for children over the age of 13 and to 10 per cent for sixth-formers over the age of 16. Almost 40 per cent of the students at the 150 most prestigious independent schools are boarders; in the remaining 220 independent schools most students are day-students. The authors rehearse the familiar facts about the middle-class composition of students in these schools, emphasizing the extent to which the private school system is hereditary, the bulk of demand coming from parents who themselves attended private schools, whose parents in turn attended private schools. The ethos of independent schools, which derives principally from those which have boarders, claims to develop unique qualities of self-confidence and leadership in students – which claims seem to be largely justified by their results. As we all know, there are a disproportionate number of former public school pupils in positions of power and influence in the civil service, the judiciary, the armed forces, the Church of England, the banking community, and, of course, Parliament (60 per cent of Conservative MPs and 8 per cent of Labour MPs attended public schools, and as many as 21 members of Mrs Thatcher's Cabinet are products of public schools). The authors might have added, but do not, that the products of public schools earn more than the products of maintained schools even when we hold constant the total years of schooling received, the level of qualifications attained, and their fathers' occupations. Evidence such as this is profoundly paradoxical. On the one hand, it can be used to show that public schools should be eliminated because they serve to create a tiny power elite. On the other hand, it can be employed to show that parents are perfectly rational in thinking that private education confers a real advantage on their children which is worth the cost of a £2,000–3,000 fee; surely, if we could show that the demand for private schooling is simply pure snobbery, having no real return in enhanced occupational income for their children, the case for public schools would long ago have collapsed under its own weight?

The authors struggle to disprove the widely held view that independent schools are more efficient in producing O-level and A-level results than maintained schools, or, to express it in popular language, that public schools are of superior 'academic quality'. They do not deny that private schools have smaller classes and superior teaching resources, but they argue that most of the superiority in examination results is due to the rigid selection of students in independent schools at the point of entry and to a tendency to hold on to students until the age of 18 or 19. In short, they argue that the available figures on the comparative educational attainments of private and maintained schools do not compare like with like, particularly as so many of the existing comprehensive schools are comprehensive in name only because neighbouring private schools cream off all the local pupils with high academic attainments.

BETTER RESULTS IN PRIVATE SCHOOLS?

The evidence on this question is extremely mixed: it is perfectly true that we cannot say that students with similar IQs and similar family backgrounds have a better chance of ending up with higher educational achievements if they attend a private school rather than a comprehensive school. On the other hand, we also cannot assert the opposite with perfect confidence. *Private Schools* cites some irrelevant evidence from a longitudinal study by the National Children's

Bureau, which reported that bright children do as well in comprehensive schools as in selective maintained schools, which is interesting news but neither here nor there as far as the question at issue is concerned. Other evidence suggests that private schools are more efficient examination factories than maintained schools for pupils of identical characteristics (for example, G. Kalton, *The Public Schools: A Factual Survey*, London: Longmans, 1966). There is also little doubt that private schools corner the market for higher education places in general and Oxbridge places in particular – the maintained school applicant has only a one-in-three chance of getting an Oxbridge place as against an even chance for his or her private-school counterpart – and this has less to do with their intrinsic academic excellence than with the single-mindedness with which they pursue the task of sitting examinations. We may deplore this mania for A-level results, which distorts the whole of the upper secondary education and produces earlier specialization in Britain than anywhere else in the world, and we may lay much of the blame for the situation at the doors of the public schools. The fact remains, however, that this is what British parents want and are willing to pay for – if they can afford it. Either we must persuade them to want something else, or we must remind them how much more it would really cost if the rest of us refused to subsidize them.

In the meanwhile, and here I fully endorse the arguments of the Discussion Document, the more the government encourages local authorities to buy places in private schools for children selected on grounds of their attainment, the more difficult it is for comprehensive schools ever to match the achievement records of private schools, which then justifies parents in the belief that schools ought to be judged exclusively in terms of paper qualifications, and that private schools are superior in this respect to state schools. The government's Assisted Places Scheme, small as is its effect in total numbers of places in private schools, is nevertheless well designed to encourage some of the worst tendencies in British education; the scheme is means-tested to help 'pupils of high academic ability from less well-off families' but the stipulation that students must be able to pass the common entrance examination of private schools at age 11 or 13 severely limits its potential for helping the disadvantaged.

INDIRECT SUBSIDIES

The heart of the problem is the large number of indirect subsidies going to private schools. As a result of their charitable status they are exempt from income tax, corporation tax and capital gains tax, and they are entitled to reclaim income tax at source from dividends received on investments held by charitable trusts acting on their behalf, from interested received by parents on educational annuity insurance policies, and from payments received under deeds of covenant for, say, a school appeal. They are also entitled to a 50 per cent reduction in rates on property occupied. The tax loss from the charity status of independent schools has been officially estimated at £25 million in 1977 and the rate of loss at something like £1 million. In addition, the remaining direct grant schools continue to receive a direct per-pupil grant, which was estimated at £15 million in 1977. More important than all of these are the boarding school allowances paid by the government to military and diplomatic personnel irrespective of whether they are stationed overseas or not. Over 20,000 private school places are thereby paid for wholly or in large part out of public funds, to the tune of £37 million in 1978, three-quarters of which, by the way, goes to government personnel stationed in Britain. Next, there are a variety of schemes whereby parents receive tax relief on capital used to pay their children's school fees either now or in the future through trusts set up by specialist brokers or insurance companies; the costs to the Exchequer of these forms of tax avoidance have never been officially estimated but I would venture to say that they must amount to £1–2 million. All these figures are dwarfed by the £80 million paid by local education authorities for some 56,000 public places in private schools; even if we deduct from this the £44 million paid in 1978 for handicapped pupils to independent special schools, we are still left with £36 million paid by LEAs to the independent sector. Finally, there is the Assisted Places Scheme which will add £3 million to the annual income of private schools in 1981–2, rising to as much as £55 million in 1987–8 when the scheme is fully implemented.

Adding all these public subsidies together, we arrive, as *Private Schools* observes, at a *minimum* sum of £121 million in 1977–8 or £178 million in 1980–1 prices. And all this says nothing about the peculiar and perhaps controversial subsidy: most of the 40,000 teachers in private schools have been trained at taxpayers' expense at a cost of £8,000–10,000 per teacher. It might be argued that this is no subsidy because the state should accept as much responsibility for teachers in independent as in maintained schools. Yet neither the private school nor the trained teacher ever compensates taxpayers for a training received at public expense. If the parents of students in private schools are to be subsidized because they pay twice over for education, they ought likewise to be taxed for imposing on the rest of the community a higher teacher-training bill than would otherwise be required. On the other hand, it would be an innovation to charge all charities the real cost of any publicly produced resources they may happen to employ (roads, ports, the National Health Service, etc.). On the whole, one is inclined to shrug off the notion of counting the training costs of teachers in private schools as one of the indirect public subsidies to private education.

Still, there is the figure of £178 million for total current public subsidiaries to private schools, the withdrawal of which could only be offset by a rise of fees of 35–40 per cent from current levels of £2,500 for public boarding schools to about £3,500. At this point, however, hard-heeled realism finally breaks into the Discussion Document:

> It would be a mistake to think that a Labour Government could made net savings by ending all public support to private schools and at the same time embark on a policy of integrating all private pupils within the maintained sector. The net recurrent institutional cost of educating the half million private school pupils within the maintained sector would be almost £300 million per year (at 1980 prices). The capital cost of providing places (including boarding places) in the maintained sector would have to be added to that cost.

It is not clear how this figure is arrived at but presumably it allows for the taking-over of buildings and equipment with financial compensation to the owners of schools, the loss of a certain proportion of teachers in private schools who would rather leave the profession than teach in maintained schools, and the cost of adapting specialized buildings to new uses. A more practical course of action, the Document goes on to say, would be to deprive independent schools of the fiscal privilege of £178 million while incurring the expense of shifting the 56,000 hitherto publicly supported students in private schools to the maintained sector at a cost of £33 million, thus saving the Exchequer at least £146 million. This is not a new policy recommendation: it echoes Labour's manifesto pledges of 1974 and 1979.

The closing pages of the Discussion Document canvass a range of policy options, repeated with minor alterations in *A Plan for Private Schools*, for implementing the long-run aim of eliminating private schools:

1. prohibiting attendance at private schools: this is rejected in principle and condemned as being unenforceable in practice;
2. prohibiting the continuance or establishment of private schools: this, too, is rejected on the same grounds of both principle and practice;
3. prohibiting private schools charging fees: the door is not closed to legislation along these lines in the future but it is granted that some wealthy public schools might nevertheless survive entirely on endowment income;
4. public ownership: unless the schools were confiscated, nationalization would have to be accompanied by legislation prohibiting the owners from using their compensation payments to establish new private schools; the costs of re-allocating students and converting existing schools to new uses would be considerable, as noted above, and the main aim of ensuring that private schools are used to serve community purposes would not necessarily require public ownership;
5. withdrawal of public support: 'the most immediately practical option for a Labour Government to adopt is to withdraw all public support from private schools and thus isolate them'; this would not cause more than a certain

fraction of private schools to 'wither away' but it would mark a first step and present few practical difficulties; the law on charity and the Finance Act would have to be amended but there is ample legal precedence for such amendments; private schools could be charged VAT on their fees in line with other private institutions charging fees; they could also be charged for being inspected by Her Majesty's Inspectorate, currently a free service rendered by the state; and, finally, they might be charged a surcharge for employing publicly trained teachers;

6.   withdrawal of higher education grants for students educated in private schools: rejected in principle.

Withdrawal of public support is taken to be a first step towards the eventual integration of private schools into the maintained sector. The next step would be to persuade private schools to cater for children with special psychological or social needs for residential education, as well as for community needs in non-boarding education (sixth-form colleges, retraining schemes for younger workers, etc.), and to do so without charging fees. Legislation to prohibit the charging of private fees after a given date and to enable the Secretary of State to take over particularly recalcitrant schools could be employed to give teeth to the use of persuasion. Private schools and LEAs could prepare development plans for the use of such schools for community purposes, leaving them in private ownership and retaining their charitable status, provided they charged no private fees, co-operated with the maintained comprehensive schools in the area, and abandoned selection on grounds of attainment or social background. They would thus enter the state system on more or less the same basis as voluntary schools in 1944. For all practical purposes that would be the end of private education.

I subscribe to the withdrawal of all forms of public finance for private schooling but I reject all the subsequent steps in the total operation. The 1980 Discussion Document and *A Plan for Private Schools* both underrate the importance of breaking the chain that runs from private schools to Oxbridge to the civil service. It is the special entrance examinations of Oxbridge that favour the products of public schools. Oxbridge is dependent on public money for 90 per cent of its income (only a little less than the 95 per cent ruling for other universities) and the public insistence that it should bring its admission policies into line with other universities would break the chain at its weakest link. The continued preponderance of Oxbridge graduates in civil service recruitments under both Labour and Tory governments is another link in the chain which could so easily be broken. Breaking the chain would significantly weaken demand for independent schools and a fee of £3,500 would make parents think again about the value of private schooling. It is the state that stimulates both the public demand for and the supply of public school places. If it withdrew its stimulus, there would be little need for the draconian measures proposed in either *Private Schools* or the later document.

19. The 'pros' and 'cons' of education vouchers*

The idea of education vouchers – coupons of prescribed purchasing power that can be cashed at any school whatever and that can be topped up like book tokens or luncheon vouchers – was invented by Milton Friedman in 1955 (although earlier versions of the idea go back to the eighteenth century) and developed further by a number of British and American economists in the 1960s. It caught on in America in the early 1970s, particularly among radicals and Black activist groups, so much so that a five-year voucher experiment was launched in one school district in California – the so-called Alum Rock Experiment. In addition, six voucher feasibility studies were conducted in various American cities. In Britain, on the other hand, the notion of education vouchers, while vigorously promoted by the publications of the libertarian Institute of Economic Affairs, remained a taboo subject among both educators and politicians all through the 1960s and 1970s.

The election of Mrs Thatcher in 1979 changed all that: the new Tory Secretary of State for Education, Keith Joseph, was known to be sympathetic to vouchers and, besides, the concept fitted remarkably well into the Tory programme of 'privatization' of the social services. Nevertheless, seven years later we are no nearer to implementing any practical scheme of education vouchers, even on an experimental basis, and this despite a voucher feasibility study in the Ashford area of Kent County, completed in 1978, which showed that education vouchers are perfectly practical in British circumstances.

It is interesting to ask why the present Tory government has found it so difficult to translate the idea of education vouchers into policy. It is easy to see why most civil servants and local education officers are opposed to it: it would substantially reduce their authority and power. It is also easy to see why most of the teacher unions are opposed to it: it would make teachers directly accountable to individual parents and threaten their job security. But it is not easy to see why most politicians are opposed to it, which is merely to say why most members of the electorate, including parents, are opposed to it, or more precisely expressed, are uninterested in it; in short, the idea of education vouchers in Britain has lacked political appeal. One reason may be that the concept itself is difficult

* First published in *Economic Review*, 4(5), May 1987: 16–21.

to grasp, particularly as both the advocates and critics of education vouchers employ the term 'vouchers' to mean quite different things. Therefore, before considering the merits and demerits of education vouchers, we must begin by setting out the various possible types of voucher schemes.

AN OMNIBUS OF VOUCHERS

Imagine a country (like Britain) with ten years of compulsory education and a mixed system of state and private schools; state education is financed out of general tax receipts, so that there is no connection between the taxes families pay and the education their children receive, but parents may opt out of the state system by sending their children to private schools, thus paying 'twice', so to speak, for education. We now introduce a system of education vouchers, which is we issue to every parent with children of school-going age a 'coupon' whose value is just sufficient on average to 'buy' a place in any state primary or secondary school (for Britain in 1986, roughly £900 for a primary place, £1,200 for a lower secondary place and £1,800 for an upper secondary place). If we have done our sums correctly, the tax bill for education will be exactly the same as before because all we have really done is to 'de-zone' state schools, that is we have eliminated the legal provision that gives parents a right to send their children to state schools but only in the catchment area in which they reside. We shall call this rather uninteresting kind of voucher a 'limited' voucher and, in effect, the Education Act of 1980 achieved the aims of such a limited voucher.

Suppose, however, that education vouchers were made 'unlimited' by permitting parents to cash them at any school whatever, including private schools. Most private schools, and particularly residential private schools, charge fees that exceed the average current-plus-capital costs per place in a state school. It would be necessary, therefore, to allow parents who opted for private education to supplement the value of a voucher out of their own pockets. I shall call such vouchers 'supplementable' vouchers in contrast to 'fixed-value' vouchers and it is obvious that any system of 'unlimited' vouchers would also entail 'supplementable' vouchers.

So far, I have gone along with the common belief that all state schools at a given level of education cost the same. This is clearly not the case. State schools differ in the age of their buildings, in the size of their plant, in the mix of their teachers and hence their teaching bill per student. In short, there are cheap and expensive state primary and state secondary schools. Suppose we now allow state schools to charge cost-covering rather than uniform fees. The value of the voucher is sufficient to buy a place in a cheap state school but parents can top up the voucher and thus choose expensive state schools as well as private

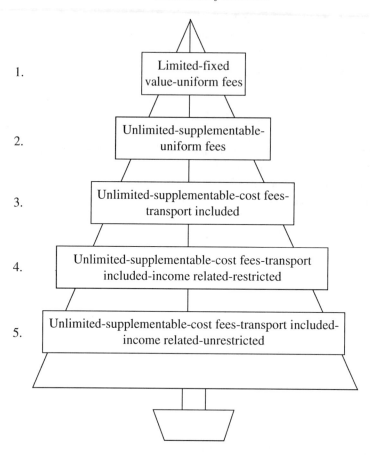

Figure 19.1   The voucher tree

schools. I label such a system one of 'cost-fees' vouchers, taking it for granted that such vouchers are also unlimited and supplementable.

We may be inclined to think that such a system would maximize the scope of parental school choices but we have forgotten the major constraint on such choices, which is distance and the implied cost of transportation. To underwrite a system of unlimited, supplementable and cost-fees vouchers, we need to include transport costs (up to some limit) in the value of the voucher. I label such vouchers 'transport-included' vouchers.

Nothing said so far has expressed itself to the issue of equality in educational choices: rich parents can normally afford to buy more expensive education for their children than poor parents and a system of unlimited, supplementable, cost-fees and transport-included vouchers would merely increase their superior position in the education market. However, it is easy to deal with this problem under a voucher scheme: we simply make the value of the voucher a declining function of parental income (like student grants in higher education). The obvious way to do this is to make the voucher part of taxable income to the full extent of its value; the progressive income tax will then guarantee that the voucher will be worth less to rich than to poor parents. If this fails to reduce the nominal value of vouchers sufficiently to better-off parents, we can stipulate that it be taxed at twice or three times its value. In other words, we can scale down the value of 'income-related' vouchers to any extent we like.

All advocates of vouchers from Friedman onwards have assumed that, whatever system is adopted, the government sets minimum educational standards that must be reached by all private and state schools. Some voucher enthusiasts have gone further and argued that no school in receipt of vouchers ought to be permitted to deny access to pupils on racial, religious or ethnic grounds – no white-only schools, but also no Jewish, Catholic or Muslim schools. And to go still further, some have argued that private schools in receipt of vouchers must be required to practise the present open-door policy of state schools by having to admit all students who apply, regardless of their previous school performance – no Common Entrance Examination or its equivalent. I shall label vouchers that deny schools the right to bar admission to some students on any ground whatsoever as 'restricted' vouchers and vouchers that leave schools free to exclude some potential students as 'unrestricted' vouchers.

To sum up, I have constructed a tree of possible voucher types, running from the most modest to the most ambitious version of the concept (see Figure 19.1).

PUTTING THE VOUCHER TREE TO USE

The voucher model that Friedman originally proposed was in my language an unlimited, supplementable, cost-frees, unrestricted voucher whose value did not vary with income, that is level 3 of the voucher tree plus the notion of unrestricted vouchers (Friedman argued vehemently in favour of letting Whites and Blacks in the USA open their own schools if they wanted to). On the other hand, the Alum Rock Experiment used a limited, fixed-value, uniform fees, transport-included, restricted voucher with an income-related feature in the form of a bonus voucher issued to low-income families, that is level 1 of the voucher tree plus an element of income-scaling. The most prominent British advocates of education vouchers, namely Alan Peacock, Jack Wiseman and Edward West, have generally endorsed the most ambitious voucher model, that is level 5, an unlimited, supplementable, cost-fees, transport-included, income-related, unrestricted voucher.

Finally, the voucher scheme that the Department of Education and Science was said to be considering in 1982 for primary and lower secondary schools (and which it rejected in 1983) falls roughly halfway between the most modest and the most ambitious voucher model. Parents were to be given means-tested vouchers worth the annual cost of an average place in a maintained school which, however, could also be cashed at an independent school, provided they were used only to buy day places. Maintained schools would continue to charge uniform fees but would adopt an open enrolment policy, popular schools being assisted with loans to expand and unpopular schools encouraged to contract and eventually close. Maintained schools would have to admit all students applying to them, exactly as under the present system, and independent schools would be allowed to refuse students as they do now. It is not clear whether transport costs to distant maintained schools were to be paid for out of public funds (as is now the case in large cities), but at any rate nothing was said about financing transport to private day schools. So, in my terminology, the DES scheme was one of unlimited, supplementable, uniform fees, partly transport-included, income-related, partly restricted vouchers.

THE EFFECTS OF VOUCHERS

There is little point in discussing the effects of a limited, fixed-value voucher since it amounts in effect to the dezoning of schools, which has been achieved in Britain without the introduction of vouchers. The moment a voucher is made unlimited, however, the total fiscal costs of the scheme must exceed those of the present educational system by virtue of the vouchers issued to families with children in private schools (is it this that took the steam out of the voucher movement in Britain?) Such families are better off under an unlimited voucher scheme than they are now, despite the fact that they will share the higher tax burdens of the voucher schemes with all other families. The long-term effect of an unlimited voucher on total education expenditure is difficult to predict. A number of families might switch out of the state into the private sector, thus increasing private expenditure on education. Since the level of taxation would vary directly with the face value of the unlimited voucher, there might well be broader electoral support for more public spending on education under a voucher scheme than exists at present – better-off parents with children in private schools have little reason under the present system to press for more public expenditure on education because they share the burden of increased taxation but receive none of its benefits.

Once we allow state schools to charge fees in accordance with their different cost structures – level 3 of the voucher tree – we begin to get the efficiency effects invoked by advocates of education vouchers: vouchers would be the principal source of income for schools which would therefore have to compete for customers, in the course of which outright waste and slack would be eliminated. Moreover, competition between schools would generate a much greater diversity of educational services because, like it or not, parents have radically different tastes for schooling: some schools would specialize in expensive, academic-type education; others would only provide cheap, vocational-type education; some schools would offer a narrow, carefully chosen curriculum; others would offer a broad, comprehensive curriculum; some schools would invest heavily in buildings and other physical facilities; others would instead devote their funds disproportionately to teachers and paraprofessional assistants; some schools would innovate in teaching methods with or without the panoply of modern educational technology; but others would stick to the traditional teacher-plus-students model. But whatever the choice, each school would be forced to provide the best possible service for its particular clientele at the lowest possible resource cost.

Such are the claims of voucher enthusiasts: vouchers would establish consumer sovereignty, raise standards, increase efficiency, reduce costs and encourage technical dynamism in education. The critics of vouchers, however, point to the danger that rivalry among schools would force schools to advertise themselves. In the effort to differentiate their product much of the advertising might be misleading: schools would appeal to their opulent buildings, fancy equipment and examination results (even if these were only obtained by a highly selective admission policy). Education being a difficult process to evaluate, parents might be forgiven if they judged quality by price. Thus, high-fee schools would attract the wealthier parents, the higher fees at the same time allowing such schools to hire better teachers and to purchase up-to-date equipment. Poorer parents would be driven to choose low-fee state schools, which would then become educational 'ghettos' for children with deprived backgrounds. The division into high-fee and low-fee schools would soon become a self-perpetuating vicious circle, thus exacerbating the segregation that already exists under the present system between those who pay and those who do not pay for education. In short, vouchers would be socially divisive.

Although such criticisms raise serious objections to a voucher scheme, they seem to be based on a number of implicit assumptions derived from the existing state system of education. Even the friends of vouchers agree that the quantity and quality of information in the education market is critical to the operation of any voucher scheme. The great merit of educational vouchers is that they would generate a demand for information that is irrelevant to parents under the present system of education finance. Because education vouchers will force parents to choose between schools, they will create a market for advisory services that will assist parents to interpret the information provided by schools. Moreover, the state might regulate school advertising to ensure that information is provided in a common format so as to facilitate comparisons between schools. Besides, the very existence of vouchers would constitute, as it were, an education in making educational choices and these choices would naturally improve with practice. Finally, vouchers and the pressure to advertise would force schools to become more aware of their own objectives and more eager to determine the degree to which they succeed in achieving these objectives. In consequence, vouchers would almost certainly make schools more cost-effective and anxious to be seen to be cost-effective.

The notion that vouchers would create a dual system of education, condemning the children of the poor to attend slum schools, presupposes that poor parents are indifferent about education and that only middle-class parents are willing to make financial sacrifices to send their little children to better, more expensive schools. There is little reason to think that parental attitudes to education are so nearly linked to family income even under present circumstances and, under the greater diversification of schooling promoted by a voucher scheme, parental attitudes would likewise become more diverse. In other words, vouchers *may* promote the polarization of schools into 'good' and 'bad' schools, but there is no necessity for them to have this effect.

In any case, any such tendency towards educational 'apartheid' can be offset by making vouchers income-related. Indeed, an extreme version of the income-related voucher would reduce the after-tax value of the voucher to zero at a median family income level; in that case, only 'poor' families would receive effective vouchers, giving them an advantage over 'rich' families that they totally lack under the present system of financing education (the Assisted Places Scheme of 1980 comes close to achieving this in miniature for some 21,000 students from low-income families). It is difficult to imagine a better demonstration of the extraordinary flexibility of the voucher mechanism than this: education vouchers can be adjusted to achieve almost any objective that is deemed desirable. However, perhaps this apparent strength of vouchers is actually its principal weakness: any government wishing to enact a voucher scheme would be faced with almost endless controversy about the specific features of the scheme.

Of all these specific features, the most troublesome are those pertaining to the admission criteria of schools eligible for vouchers. The American comprehensive high school and the British comprehensive secondary school are both predicated on the melting-pot theory that schools mixing children of different home backgrounds would work to break down racial and class barriers. The concept of the melting-pot has always been applied in the state sector to admission standards: state schools have to accept all children, regardless of their educatability. There is an argument, therefore, for extending the same restriction to private schools that enter the voucher scheme. Why should public money be used to subsidize schools that claim the right to select children on any grounds other than financial ones?

However, such restricted vouchers would have a very different social effect from unrestricted vouchers and, moreover, they would also have different economic effects. It is one thing to talk about cost-effectiveness in a high-fee school that selects its pupils to be of outstanding quality and quite another to talk about it in a high-fee school with children of mixed abilities. A completely unrestricted voucher, allowing any group of parents to set up any kind of school provided it met minimum educational standards, takes us into a hitherto untried area without historical precedence. No wonder, then, that it consequences invite almost unlimited speculation.

PRACTICAL EXPERIENCE WITH VOUCHERS

All this seems very inconclusive. Is there nothing to be learned from the Alum Rock experiment and the various feasibility studies in both America and Britain? Yes, something, but not enough to clinch the argument. The Alum Rock experiment was, as we said earlier, a peculiar mixture of a level 1 voucher with an element of means-testing and thus throws little light on the more ambitious types of levels 4–5 vouchers. The six American feasibility studies do illuminate the nature of the demand for education in the USA, but so country-specific are the educational circumstances of these studies that almost none of the results carry over to Britain. The only British feasibility study in Ashford, Kent, demonstrated that there is a definite demand among parents for unlimited, supplementable vouchers, that nevertheless only some 10 per cent of parents would change schools under a voucher scheme, and that the costs of implementing such transfers would add 7–8 per cent to public expenditure on education in the county.

This sort of evidence cannot support or refute the claims made for education vouchers. There has never been a practical trial of unlimited, supplementable, cost-fees, income-related, unrestricted vouchers, and yet many of the arguments in the voucher debate are precisely about their effects on the size of the private sector, the fate of different state schools with different cost structures, the demand for schooling when poor parents are given an inherent advantage in the education market, and the proliferation of schools segregated by race, religion, ethnic origins and educational qualifications. On all these controversial questions one gains little insight from Alum Rock and the existing feasibility studies.

Can we not, instead, learn from the experiences of private schools, both here and abroad? Also, no, because few private schools are operated as profit-maximizing firms; most rely on endowment income to escape the penalties of the market place. And yet all the classic arguments in favour of education vouchers rely ultimately on the idea that a really ambitious voucher scheme would force all schools to operate like profit-maximizing firms. There are in fact few profit-maximizing schools that could serve us as laboratories to study the possible effects of vouchers.

CONCLUSIONS

Education vouchers have been assessed in terms of six criteria: parental freedom of choice, cost-effectiveness, innovation, diversity, the level of educational spending, and equality of educational opportunities. On all these criteria, the debate has failed to come down decisively on one side or the other. But that is in the nature of the case. For one thing, the participants in the debate do not agree on what is meant by freedom of choice, efficiency, diversity, equity, etc. For another, some friends of vouchers defend the idea by employing the familiar, wholly static arguments of the orthodox theory of the firm, while some of the enemies of vouchers indict the idea by employing much less rigorous dynamic arguments about the process of competition in an industry like education that has never known it. Employing different standards, the arguments are never fairly joined.

In one sense, however, the debate has hardly started, at least in Britain. The present state monopoly of education – subordinating parents to educational professionals, disguising the true cost of education, repressing the diversity of tastes for educational services – has had such a powerful hold on our minds that even the friends of vouchers, and certainly its critics, have been unable to think through the radical implications of an unlimited, supplementable, cost-fees, income-related, and possibly unrestricted voucher. It would totally alter the locus of power in the educational system, shifting it from educational administrators, headmasters, principals and teachers to parents. In the final analysis, parent power is what the entire debate is about.

In the meantime, it is worth keeping in mind that the sort of voucher plan that was under discussion in Britain in 1982 – unlimited, supplementable, uniform fees, partly transport-included, income-related, partly restricted vouchers – is a far cry from the ambitious cost-fees vouchers that Friedman, Peacock, Wiseman and West originally had in mind. It would do nothing to spur competition between maintained schools and it amounts quite simply to an additional subsidy for independent schools. Independent schools already enjoy subsidies of about £200 million per annum as a result of various tax exemptions, as well as school places purchased out of public funds. These subsidies are usually regarded as a *quid pro quo* for the double taxation imposed on parents who have opted out of the state system. But most of the 40,000 teachers in private schools have been trained for a year at taxpayers' expense, which somewhat dilutes the force of the argument of double taxation. At any rate, even if one favoured more competition between maintained and independent schools on grounds of efficiency, one might have doubts about increased subsidies to independent schools on grounds of equity. Besides, it is a little perverse to argue for 'privatization' in education by means of more subsidies to private schools while leaving maintained schools as they are. So long as the fiction persists that the costs of education are the same in all maintained schools, many if not most of the acclaimed virtues of education vouchers fall to the ground.

FURTHER READING

Blaug, M. (1984) 'Education vouchers – it all depends on what you mean', in J. Le Grand and R. Robinson (eds), *Privatisation and the Welfare State*, George Allen & Unwin.

Friedman, M. (1982) *Capitalism and Freedom*, University of Chicago Press, Ch. 6.

Peacock, A.T. and J. Wiseman (1964) *Education for Democrats*, Institution of Economic Affairs.

Seldon, A. (1986) *The Riddle of the Vouchers*, Institute of Economic Affairs.

West, E.G. (1968) *Economics, Education and the Politician*, Institute of Economic Affairs.

20. Education and the employment contract

INTRODUCTION

All wage labour under capitalism is hired in accordance with an explicit or implicit employment contract. This contract is typically 'incomplete' in the sense of specifying the duration of work and the rate of pay but not the intensity and quality of effort. The incompleteness of the hiring contract is not an accidental feature of the relationship between employer and employee; it is a necessary feature which can be mitigated but which can never be wholly eliminated.

It is impossible to complete the employment contract for the simple reason that workers, unlike machines, must be given an incentive to work effectively. Labour is the only human input in the productive process and the hire of labour at the time-rate implies a conscious willingness to work at a minimum level of intensity, a willingness which cannot be adequately written down in a contractual agreement. If that were not bad enough, there is the further difficulty that much of output in modern production systems is carried out by teams, in which case output cannot be unambiguously traced to individual workers. The American labour movement used to fight for higher wages and better working conditions under the slogan 'a fair day's work for a fair day's pay'. Even if we waive the question of what constitutes 'a fair day's pay', the incompleteness of the employment contract in an industrial society can be neatly expressed by saying that there is no natural way of determining the meaning of 'a fair day's work'. In short, labour power under capitalism is not, as Marx claimed, a commodity like any other; if it were it would be bought and sold subject to a contract that would fully specify all the characteristics of the commodity being traded; alas, that is impossible in the case of labour.

SOME IMPLICATIONS

The standard manner in which employers attempt to complete the employment contract is by the combination of carrot and stick: the carrot is the promise of continuing employment and eventual promotion to higher rates of pay; the stick

* First published in *Education Economics*, **1** (1), 1993, 21–33.

is the threat of instant dismissal. Both the carrot and stick imply full knowledge of the worker's efforts throughout the working day. Clearly, that is out of the question, but intermittent first-hand monitoring by foremen and supervisors, accompanied by quality checks at nodal points in the production process, serves to evaluate individual workers where possible or the average performance of a team of workers in the case of batch production. Since most plants even in the same industry are to some extent unique, these performance ratings of workers rarely involve cardinal comparisons; at best, they rank workers ordinally as in a tournament. It follows that if workers act in concert, say, by slowing down in unison, even constant monitoring may not be effective in preventing shirking and malingering.

The management of a labour force, therefore, necessarily involves a strategy of 'divide and rule', particularly if the presence of trade unions impels collective rather than individual wage bargaining. The most effective way of preventing workers from synchronizing their work efforts is to promote sexual, racial and ethnic stratification of the labour force, which in any case merely reproduces sexual, racial and ethnic discrimination in the outside world. This is not to say that sexism and racism are inherent in capitalist society but simply that where there is sexism and racism, it proves to be most convenient for the requirements of efficient management.

MARXIST TREATMENT

It is a curious fact that the incompleteness of the employment contract under capitalism as well as its significance for industrial relations is part and parcel of Marxian economics, radical economics and, in recent years, mainstream economics. The origin of the idea is undoubtedly Marx's analysis of 'the valorization of the labour process' in Chapter 7 of the first volume of *Capital*. The employment contract, Marx argued, is an entirely voluntary exchange of labour power for wages and, being voluntary, should benefit both parties to the transaction. However, in the course of the process by which labour is combined with raw materials and capital goods to produce a saleable product, profit emerges as the difference between the value of labour power and the net value of the final product; this difference is surplus-value, said by Marx to be due entirely to the 'exploitation' of labour. This surplus-value does not emerge naturally but only if workers are coerced to produce enough to exceed their own subsistence requirements as expressed in the wage payment. It is this extraction of surplus-value from workers that Marx labels the 'valorization' of the labour process. The apparently free employment contract under capitalism in effect masks 'the despotism of the workplace', an authoritarian control of production by capitalists, which for Marx is both the key to the nature of profits and the key to the technical dynamism of capitalism.

In essence, although expressed in rhetorical language, this is the heart of the thesis of the incomplete employment contract. Marx's discussion of the labour process was long neglected by his followers; however, in recent years, particularly since the publication of Harry Braverman's *Labour and Monopoly Capital* (1974), the variety of ways by which management controls the labour force has been a subject of vigorous study by Marxists (Littler, 1990).

RADICAL TREATMENT

However, it is American radical economists who have built an entire paradigm on the need of capitalists to secure labour discipline on the factory floor. 'What do bosses do?', asked Steve Marglin (1974) in a famous paper; they exercise coercive social power over the production process, he replied, and that is just about all they do. Indeed, he traced the origin of the division of labour in the eighteenth-century factory, not to the superior efficiency of occupational specialization or the technical advantages of a hierarchical organization of production, but simply to the desire of capitalists to 'divide and rule' the workforce. From the point of view of economic growth, he implied, labour-managed enterprises would have proved just as effective as the typical factory of the Industrial Revolution.

Similarly, because there is a fundamental conflict of interest between workers and capitalists in maintaining the employment relationship, capitalists actively promote sexual and racial discrimination in the labour market. For radical economists, therefore, the problem is not to explain why there is discrimination against women and blacks under capitalism but how anyone could imagine that sexism and racism could ever be eliminated in a capitalist society (Reich, 1981).

Analysis of sexism and racism as inherent features of capitalism is intimately associated with the concept of segmented labour markets (SLM), which is perhaps the most important contribution that radical economists have made to economics. The theory of SLM is not itself radical in origin and was first broached by American labour economists of the Institutionalist School in the 1920s, culminating in the famous distinction by Doeringer and Piore (1971) between 'internal' and 'external' labour markets. Normally we think of hiring labour as a process of recruiting workers on a labour market that is external to the firm. However, a great many jobs in firms are filled internally by promotion. If we picture the occupational structure of a typical business enterprise as a pyramid with a lower stratum of shop-floor workers, succeeded by a thinner stratum of foremen, and supervisors and a still thinner stratum of managers, new workers are recruited at only two or three 'ports of entry', i.e. at the base and at the zenith of the pyramid; all other vacancies are filled from within the company by drawing on the 'internal labour market'. Apart from misleading language – an administrative process of filling vacancies by internal promotion has none of the characteristics of a market process – this notion of an 'internal labour market' captures an important and, perhaps increasingly important, feature of job placements in a modern industrial society.

The idea of SLM builds on, but is distinct from, the concept of internal labour markets. The institutionalists' version of SLM refers to a contrast between two sectors of the economy, the so-called 'primary' labour markets of large corporations (with trade unions, job security and steady career prospects) and the 'secondary' labour markets of small business (with no unions, dead-end casual jobs and high turnover rates); such a dichotomization of labour markets is said to be due to certain structural changes in the twentieth-century American economy. In radical theories of SLM, however, a segmentation, apart from involving three rather than two strata, is not so much a matter of contrasting sectors of economic activities but rather of contrasting categories of workers within each and every firm in every sector. In other words, segmentation runs to some degree through all capitalist enterprises (Edward, 1979) and this is precisely why sexism and racism is judged to be endemic to capitalism.

ORTHODOX TREATMENT

All this might be shrugged off as so much radical chic were it not for the fact that all these Marxist and radical ideas are echoed in the 'new' orthodox labour economics of the 1970s. In standard neoclassical economics, labour and capital are treated as perfectly symmetrical inputs purchased on spot markets, which are somehow combined in a 'black box' called the firm. Ronald Coase argued years ago that firms are non-market institutions in which authoritarian allocation replaces the price system; firms are 'command economies' in miniature. More recently, the rise of human capital theory fundamentally altered the way in which economists view the recruitment of labour. The simple investment concept – that individuals, like firms, spend now through schooling and on-the-job training to reap rewards later, thereby producing an upward tilt to age–earnings profiles – directed attention to life-time considerations in methods of payments to labour. The fact that the process of recruiting labour and assigning them to different tasks in the enterprise involved considerable transaction costs, which accounted for many well-attested characteristics of labour markets, generated a wholly new style of labour economics in the 1970s (e.g. Alchian and Demsetz, 1972). Nevertheless, it was developments in macroeconomics rather than microeconomics that really gave the theme of the incomplete employment contract a central place in the agenda of neoclassical economics.

Keynes had demonstrated that macroeconomic equilibrium might well be an unemployment equilibrium, in which case the economic system lacked a stabilizing mechanism that would automatically generate full employment. However, why did the labour market fail to clear in the presence of involuntary unemployment? To say that both money and real wages were rigid downwards for institutional reasons and hence that Keynesian equilibria are quantity- rather than price-constrained equilibria, seemed arbitrary and *ad hoc*. In short, Keynesian macroeconomics lacked a microeconomic foundation in standard rational choice theory. Thus arose the idea of formulating a Keynesian unemployment equilibrium that would meet all the analytical requirements of Pareto-optimal Walrasian general equilibrium theory.

INVISIBLE HANDSHAKE

The formal development of the notion of an 'implicit contract' mutually agreed upon by workers and employers, and capable of demonstrating that all unemployment is fundamentally voluntary, appeared independently but more or less simultaneously in the mid-1970s in three papers by Bailey, Gordon and Azariadis (Azariadis, 1987). The first problem was to show that lay-offs are preferred to work-sharing in times of depression, even by workers, not to mention managers. Why else is a fall of aggregate demand always associated with lay-offs and never with work-sharing? The answer is that workers are risk-averse and are unwilling to contemplate a future income profile that fluctuates with aggregate demand. Hence risk-neutral firms relieve their employees of the market risk of unemployment when aggregate demand declines in return for the right of management to make allocative decisions about the use of labour, including discretion about the volume of employment. Another way of expressing the same idea is to note that the employment contract is in part an insurance contract that protects workers from fluctuations in their marginal product and hence wages as a consequence of output fluctuations. As a result the employment contract takes on the character of a personal agreement over a long period of time between a worker and a firm rather than the impersonal instantaneous spot exchange characteristic of old-style labour economics.

This game-theoretic formulation of the conundrum of involuntary unemployment is not entirely convincing because some workers will be laid off when demand slackens and they will presumably be worse off even if there is a dole. However, just as deferred compensation or less-pay-now for more-pay-later and fringe benefits that improve with length of service are management tools for discouraging shirking on the part of workers, so the promise of continuing employment or security of job tenure becomes yet another incentive to individual workers (Lazear, 1987). In other words, every worker expects to be one of the 'insiders' who will be kept on when demand slackens and in that sense it is perfectly rational for utility-maximizing workers to accept unemployment for some as a preferable alternative to sharing whatever work is available, implying a drop in earnings in a recession or depression.

There are many ways of skinning a cat, and the 1970s and 1980s saw a number of other ways of explaining the persistence of involuntary cyclical unemployment within the constraints of the Walrasian paradigm. Let me mention only one of these, the so-called efficiency wage hypothesis, which appeared in simply dozens of papers around 1980. The efficiency wage hypothesis is a corollary of the 'principal–agent problem' applied to the labour-hiring process. A principal–agent problem arises whenever someone, the principal, wants a task carried out and hires someone else, the agent, to do it but cannot continuously observe or perfectly infer the agent's action and cannot assume that the self-interest of the agent is identical to his or her own (Stiglitz, 1987). In the case before us, the principals are the firm's managers or owners and the agents are the workers. Since their interests are not necessarily the same, the problem is to provide workers with an incentive to work efficiently in accordance with managerial instructions. The stick for achieving that result is, as we said earlier, the threat of being fired. However, firing a worker imposes the cost of recruiting, placing and evaluating a new worker, and hence it may be profitable for firms to pay existing workers a wage which on average exceeds the wage that could be earned elsewhere. The penalty for workers who are caught shirking is now not just unemployment but also the loss of the wage premium paid by the firm. Thus, the total wage payment is an 'efficiency wage' in the sense that firms are better off paying it and workers are better off receiving it, and yet it is a non-market-clearing wage in excess of the competitive wage that on average would be necessary to get them to supply their labour.

There is a striking overlap between these orthodox explanations of unemployment equilibrium and typical radical explanations of chronic unemployment under capitalism (see Reich and Devine, 1981; Stiglitz and Shapiro, 1986). However, orthodox economists pay little attention to, and sometimes even deny, the likelihood of a conflict of interest between workers and capitalists in maintaining the employment relationship, whereas radical economists of course emphasize the 'contested terrain' of industrial relations (Edward, 1979). There is little doubt that if workers controlled production, they would choose more job enrichment and more frequent job rotation, i.e. a lower division of labour than capitalists now do. In general, there is no reason to believe that the worker's goal of maximizing the pecuniary and non-pecuniary rewards of labour always gives the same results as the capitalist's goal of maximizing profits. Moreover, workers prefer collective rather than individual labour contracts and in this sense too the interests of workers and capitalists are bound to clash.

We have seen that personnel managers have long devised a variety of 'incentive contracts' to induce workers to co-operate in the maximization of the joint welfare of all members of the firm. Nevertheless, in the words of Okun (1981: 86), 'the basic problem of the need for trust [in the employment relation] and the inherent reasons for distrust is not soluble. Distrust is a pervasive fact of ... the career labor market.' In the end, the employment relation boils down entirely to a sense of attachment between employer and employees. In Okun's (1981: 89) memorable phrase, employers must rely on 'an invisible handshake' to take the place of 'the invisible hand' that fails to operate in labor markets.

SUMMARY

Let us sum up the achievement. When a firm hires a worker it hopes to obtain a reliable, achievement-motivated and committed employee: the worker, however, hopes that the first seriously intends to furnish him or her not just with a casual job, but with a long-term career. Both sides to the bargain will try to create reliable expectations about their own intentions, which simply cannot be spelled out explicitly in a written contract. It is in this sense that we have spoken of the *incomplete* employment contract.

The incompleteness of employment contracts has enormous significance for the idiosyncratic character of labour markets, which has struck endless observers as far back as Adam Smith. The fact that it is necessary to rely on an implicit rather than on an explicit contract is certainly not confined to labour markets: it arises, for example, in insurance markets, in capital markets, in tenant–landlord relationships and, indeed, in every transaction in which the quality of an output is a major element of output. Nevertheless, no implicit contract is as pervasive or as central to the fortunes of an economy as the implicit employment contract. Economists have been discussing the sources of economic growth and the reasons for the unequal rates of growth of different countries for over 200 years: natural resources, capital investment, the growth of the labour force, technical progress, management styles, all have been canvassed as keys to economic growth. However, the quality of the labour force, its attitude to work and leisure, its willingness to submit to discipline, are rarely mentioned as factors in a country's economic performance. It does figure in radical writings on the causes of the so-called 'productivity slow-down' in the American economy (e.g. Sherman, 1976; Gordon, 1981); however, I have in mind a more far-reaching analysis of differential rates of growth of, say, the UK and Germany or Italy and Japan. Why does the German economy grow faster than the UK economy? Possibly for no other reason than that German workers have a sense of loyalty to German firms that UK workers lack to UK firms. Why are the economies of Eastern Europe at a standstill? A major reason is that workers in these economies, long accustomed to perfect job security, have virtually stopped working. Marx was quite correct to argue that unemployment is vital to the survival of capitalism; what he did not realize is that it is equally vital to the survival of socialism! The secret of economic growth lies not in the questions traditionally studied in economics. It lies in industrial relations.

SCREENING AND SIGNALLING

What has all this to do with education? Simply this: the process of hiring workers poses a problem of 'asymmetric information', i.e. information not equally available on both sides of a market. For example, employers possess superior information about their demand for labour but workers possess superior information about their willingness to supply labour. Concentrating on employers for a moment, employers face the problem of predicting the future performance of job applicants in the absence of any accurate measure of the worker's past performance. Of course, the employer can require a certain number of years of work experience but it will be experience in a different firm under different circumstances and, in the case of young recruits, there may well be no prior experience. In the event, the employers will find it advantageous to use certain 'filters' in selecting workers. The first is age as a proxy for work experience. The second is sex as a proxy for labour force commitment. The third is marital status, again as a proxy for commitment and perhaps eagerness for continued employment. Finally, the fourth is educational qualifications as a proxy, well, for what?

Let us say, somewhat crudely, that so long as production is hierarchically organized in large enterprises, what is required at the bottom of the job pyramid is the ability to take orders, while at the top of the pyramid what is required is the ability to give orders. Employers have learned from past experience that there is a general concordance between the attributes required at various levels of the occupational pyramid and educational attainments. In that sense, educational credentials act as surrogates for qualities which employers regard as important, predicting a certain level of job performance without, however, making any direct contribution to it. This is the so-called 'screening hypothesis' according to which education acts merely as a filter to identify workers with desirable work habits. Screening by employers in terms of educational qualifications then creates an incentive on the part of employees to produce the 'signal' that maximizes the probability of being selected, i.e. the possession of an educational qualification. In short, 'signalling' is the other side of the coin of 'screening'.

This screening–signalling hypothesis gains cogency once we recognize that employers value education not so much for what educated workers know than for how educated workers behave. The economic value of education is not what it is usually supposed to be. I can best make my point by summarizing Benjamin Bloom's *Taxonomy of Educational Objectives* (1956), a book that still is the veritable bible of curriculum reformers the world over. Bloom made the

Economics of education

extraordinary claim that the objectives of all curricula in any subject at any stage of education can be exhaustively classified into three categories, i.e. (a) 'cognitive knowledge'; (b) 'psychomotor skills'; and (c) 'affective behavioural traits'. By cognitive knowledge, Bloom meant the sum of memorized facts and concepts that are supposed to be crammed into the student's head; by psychomotor skills, he meant the manual dexterity and muscular co-ordination that a student is supposed to acquire; and by affective behavioural traits, he meant the values and attitudes shaping behaviour, which a student is supposed to take away with him or her at the completion of a course. The same idea had been expressed much earlier in much simpler language by a famous philosopher of education, Johann Heinrich Pestalozzi. Pestalozzi said that all education touches either the 'head', the 'hand' or the 'heart' of the pupil and these three 'h's' correspond exactly to Bloom's more forbidding terminology.

When one says that education is economically valuable, that it makes people more productive, most of us think immediately of the first 'h', cognitive knowledge. We assert, in other words, that it is the educated worker's knowledge of certain facts and concepts that makes him or her valuable to employers. We might call this 'the pilot fallacy': in order to fly a plane you need a pilot and flying a plane requires cognitive knowledge (and some psychomotor skills) which can only be learned by formal training. However, what employers really value in most workers is 'affective behavioural traits', such as punctuality, persistence, attentiveness, responsibility, achievement-drive, co-operativeness, compliance, etc. The cognitive skills required to carry out most jobs in industry and agriculture are learned by doing on-the-job. What formal education does, therefore, is not so much to train workers as to make them trainable.

Now, it is a curious fact that these crucial behavioural traits largely accounting for the economic value of education cannot be efficiently conveyed directly but only as a by-product, as a 'hidden agenda', of an educational process directed at cognitive knowledge. Imagine a class in punctuality; it would be possible but it would also be immensely tedious and probably ineffective. However, punctuality is powerfully fostered by an educational process rigidly tied to a timetable throughout every moment of the school day. One of the greatest problems in running a factory in a newly industrialized country is that of getting workers to arrive on time and to notify the plant manager when they are going to be absent; the lack of punctuality in the work-force can raise labour costs in a developing country by as much as 50 per cent over a developed country. This is a simple but telling example of the phenomenon in question: the economic value of education resides much more in the realm of behaviour than in the realm of cognitive knowledge.

The notion that most jobs in a modern economy require high levels of literacy and numeracy, and increasingly so as industry becomes more computerized, is simply erroneous. It lies behind the frequent tendency to 'vocationalize' secondary education in the fond belief that this will increase the employability of school leavers; this despite the fact that vocational school graduates almost always experience higher unemployment rates than academic school graduates. The very distinction between 'academic' and 'vocational' education, in which only the latter is supposed to be geared to the needs of the labour market, plants the suggestion that much, if not most, education is economically irrelevant. However, the 'hidden curriculum' of teacher–pupil relations in academic-style education has as much to do with the world of work as the explicit curriculum of mental and manipulative skills in vocational education. The frequently repeated research finding that few workers ever make specific use of the cognitive knowledge acquired in schools thus indicates, not some sort of monstrous mismatch between education and work, but the pivotal role of effective behavioural traits in job performance. The truth of the matter is that most jobs in a modern economy require about as much cognitive knowledge and psychomotor skills as are necessary to drive an automobile.

SOME IMPLICATIONS OF SCREENING AND SIGNALLING

The screening hypothesis neatly accounts for the fact that earnings rise with additional education; it even explains why so many educational qualifications appear to be unrelated to the type of work that students eventually take up; and it certainly helps to explain why the educational explosion of the last 40 years has had so little effect on equalizing the distribution of income.

If education acts merely as a filter to separate the wheat from the chaff, the steady expansion of, say, higher education dilutes the significance of a degree and induces employers to upgrade the hiring standards of jobs previously filled by university and college graduates; graduates will then be worse off in absolute terms. However, if secondary schooling is expanding at the same time, so that secondary school leavers are likewise being squeezed into lower-level jobs, earning differentials between the two cohorts may nevertheless remain more or less the same. What is true of these two categories of labour is true of every category – the expansion of post-compulsory education is simply passed down the line and ends up in a chronic core of unemployed school leavers without, however, much visible effect on the distribution of earned income from employment.

The screening hypothesis clearly has dramatic implications for educational policy. The difficulty with the hypothesis is that it comes in two versions, a strong version and a weak one. In its strong version, it is virtually untenable, whereas in its weak version, it is difficult to pin down with any precision. The strong version of the screening hypothesis assets that education merely identifies students with particular attributes, acquired either at birth or by virtue of family background, but does not itself produce or improve those attributes. It is difficult to conceive how this strong version of the hypothesis could possibly be true. After all, colleges screen twice, once when they select students for admission and a second time when they pass or fail students at the end of an educational cycle. If there is screening in the strong sense, only the first screen serves any useful economic function, the second being a piece of window-dressing designed purely to create employment for teachers. However, as every teacher knows, the correlation for any individual student between predicted and actual education success is by no means perfect: selection for admission to courses is wrong almost as often as it is right. In other words, 'good' students have to be discovered and it takes a protracted sequence of hurdlers, such as any educational cycle provides, to identify the traits and attributes that lead to success. The notion that they are present, only waiting to be sifted out by some ingenious filter and that any filter will do, schooling being simply one, is a naive psychological fallacy.

Moreover, the strong version of the screening hypothesis implies that there is little reward to an uncompleted degree or certificate, or at any rate that the extra rewards of, say, two years university education are much less than two-thirds of the rewards of a completed university degree. In other words, educational credentials act like a 'sheepskin' that disguises the true difference between drop-outs and graduates. Similarly, strong screening implies that, whatever differences in starting salaries between university graduates and secondary school-leavers, the gap in two salary streams gradually disappears with additional years of work experience: employers may use educational qualifications as a screen at the time of hiring when they are ignorant of the true abilities of potential workers but, as time passes, they can actually observe their job performance and reward them in accordance with their personal abilities. Finally, strong screening makes it difficult to understand why employers have not sought to replace the educational system by a cheaper screening mechanism. Surely, it is cheaper to incur the costs of testing the abilities of individual workers, say, by a battery of psychological aptitude tests, than to pay all university graduates more simply because they are university graduates.

Thus, the strong version of the screening hypothesis carried with it at least three definite empirical implications (Blaug, 1987: 118–22). All of these three implications, however, are firmly refuted by the evidence. First, the private rate of return to education for university drop-outs sometimes actually exceeds the yield of a completed university degree. Secondly, the effect of years of education on personal earnings generally rises rather than falls with additional years of work experience. Business firms and government departments do sometimes test individual workers at the point of recruitment; nevertheless, in no country in the world have such independent testing services effectively replaced the role of educational credentials in screening out job applicants. Thirdly, education ought to have no effect on personal earnings when it comes to the self-employed since there is little point in self-screening. As a matter of fact, however, the impact of years of education on earnings is as great for self-employed accountants, doctors and lawyers as it is for wage and salary earners. Of course, that may be due to screening by the customers of self-employed professionals, which in turn leads professional associations of accountants, doctors and lawyers to press for increased educational qualifications under state occupational licensing laws. Nevertheless, the evidence on the association between education and earnings for the self-employed does cast some doubt on screening in its stronger versions.

All these refutations, however, fall to the ground if we give the screening hypothesis a weaker interpretation. Let us recall that employees face information costs in recruiting suitable workers and assigning them appropriately to different tasks. Every new worker takes days or weeks to reach an adequate level of performance and thus mistakes in hiring are costly in terms of output forgone, not to mention the administrative costs of posting vacancies, sorting applicants and inducting successful recruits. No wonder then that employers resort to stereotypes like age, sex, colour, ethnic background, marital status, work experience and educational credentials to predict job performance. For crucial jobs like those of supervisors, junior managers and executives, it may pay to engage in expensive search procedures, including the use of aptitude tests, to select a particular candidate from among a group of job applicants with similar characteristics. However, for most jobs, it is cheaper to rely on group characteristics and to run the risk of occasional error. Thus, the use of educational qualifications as a hiring screen is a species of a larger genus of 'statistical discrimination' in the hiring of labour: the costs of truly identifying the talents of potential workers forces employers to discriminate against typical members of social groups. The fact that educational qualifications stand out among all the other stereotypes as being legally permitted and generally approved – most people regard educational meritocracy as being perfectly fair and legitimate – only encourages screening by education on the part of the employers.

So interpreted, the 'screening hypothesis' is a label for a classic information problem in a labour market. So far, however, we have only dealt with hiring at the point of recruitment, and we have said nothing to explain the association between education and earnings right through the entire working life of individuals. Granted that employers will pay more to better-educated workers when they know nothing about their individual aptitudes, why should they almost invariably continue to do so when they have had ample opportunity to monitor their performance over long periods of time?

One explanation may be the existence of 'internal labour markets' in many business firms and government departments. Workers tend to be recruited in such enterprises not to a job but to a career path and this means that any advantages at the point of recruitment tend to be converted into persistent advantages throughout a working life with the company. In this way, the use of educational qualifications as a screen at the point of hiring becomes an effective screen throughout the period of association with a particular enterprise. Even if he or she leaves the company to work elsewhere, the next employer is likely to give credit both for previous experience and for previous earnings, which perpetuates the earlier link between schooling and earnings. To sum up: the notion of 'statistical discrimination' in hiring and the presence of 'internal labour markets' taken together are perfectly capable of explaining why highly educated people *on average* earn more than less-educated people even though they may not be inherently more productive.

I say 'on average' advisedly. Clearly, employers do make mistakes in hiring and do discover in due course that, say, some university graduates are worse than others; these they will not promote or will only promote more slowly; alternatively, they may rotate them to a different job from which they were recruited; contrariwise, the jobs of 'high flyers' may be enriched as time passes or combined with other jobs into a new job title. Therefore, when we study the structure of personal earnings by education and occupation in any modern economy, we observe: (a) a strong positive association between earnings and education when expressed in terms of averages; (b) considerable variance in the association between education and earnings, such that the worst-paid university graduates actually earn less than the best-paid secondary school leavers, and so on for all other educational cohorts; and (c) a considerable variance for every occupational category, however finely defined, in the years of schooling of incumbents of that occupation. Such evidence is accountable by an element of 'statistical discrimination' at the hiring stage and the presence of 'internal labour markets' of various degrees of strength in many private companies and government departments.

SUMMING UP

If we add together the concepts of the incomplete employment contract, the phenomenon of internal labour markets, the notion of labour market segmentation, and the fundamental socialization function of schools in inculcating definite values and attitudes, we arrive at a picture of the economic value of schooling that is simply miles removed from the simplistic belief that education makes workers more productive and that employers pay them more because they are productive. It may be that schooling increases the productivity of individuals by making them more effective members of a production team or better able to handle machines and materials but it would matter little if it were not so, provided everyone thought so – which of course they do. What is important is that every worker accepts the principles on which some are paid more and some are paid less. Even if these payments are in reverse order of the true spot marginal products of individual workers, assuming that these could ever be identified, the maximization of the output and minimization of the costs of the firm depend critically, not on the scale of individual rewards, but on the mutual consent of all workers in the enterprise. In short, screening by educational qualifications is economically efficient not because 'good' students are always 'good' workers but because educational credentialism avoids the inherent conflict of interests between workers and employers.

It is no wonder then that labour markets tend to react to changes in effective demand by adjusting quantities rather than prices, numbers employed rather than wages: lay-offs in a slump threaten the morale of the work-force less than an across-the-board cut in wages, particularly if the lay-offs are concentrated among certain 'inferior' groups, like youngsters, women, blacks, etc.; likewise, fresh hiring in a boom generates the expectation of promotion among older workers, which is even more effective in raising morale than an actual promotion. Thus, labour markets are inherently capable of continually absorbing workers with ever higher levels of education simply by adjusting the customary educational hiring standards for jobs. However, such adjustments, precisely because they must be seen to win general approval, take time. A rapid flooding of a labour market with, say, university graduates may well produce graduate unemployment, whereas the same numbers could have been absorbed if they had been forthcoming at a slower rate. Similarly, a sudden glut of university graduates produces graduate unemployment because employers have misgivings about hiring overqualified applicants who tend to feel underutilized, making them ineffective workers. However, declining job opportunities for university graduates forces degree holders to adjust their job aspirations downwards. In time, therefore, BAs will cease to feel themselves to be overqualified for, say, a secretarial post, and in that sense the original objection to hiring them for such jobs will lose its force. Once again, it is not an absolute oversupply of university graduates but a rapid increase in that supply that causes graduate unemployment.

On the other hand, there is no real sense in which a given level of education in the economically active population of a country can be said to be technically 'required' to permit the achieved level of economic growth of that country. That sort of argument grossly exaggerates the contribution of manipulative and cognitive skills in the performance of economic functions, ignores the fact that such skills are largely acquired by on-the-job training, and utterly neglects the vital role of suitable personality traits in securing the 'invisible handshake' on which production critically depends. In short, educational policies may be fitted to literally any level or rate of economic growth and cannot be justified in terms of those patterns of growth. Education does make a contribution to economic growth, not as an indispensable input into the growth process, but simply as a framework which willy-nilly accommodates the growth process.

REFERENCES

Alchian, A.A. and H. Demsetz (1972) 'Production, information costs, and economic organization', *American Economic Review*, **62**: 777–95.

Azariadis, S. (1987) 'Implicit contracts', in J. Eatwell, M. Milgate and P. Newman (eds), *The New Palgrave: A Dictionary of Economics*, London: Macmillan, **2**: 733–6.

Blaug, M. (1987) *The Economics of Education and the Education of an Economist*, Aldershot, Hants.: Edward Elgar.

Doeringer, P. and M. Piore (1971) *Internal Labor Markets and Manpower Analysis*, Lexington, Mass.: D.C. Heath.

Edward, E.C. (1979) *Contested Terrain: The Transformation of the Workplace in the Twentieth Century*, New York: Basic Books.

Gordon, D.M. (1981) 'Capital–labor conflict and the productivity slowdown', *American Economic Review*, **71**(2): 30–5.

Lazear, E.P. (1987) 'Incentive contracts', in J. Eatwell, M. Milgate and P. Newman (eds), *The New Palgrave: A Dictionary of Economics*, London: Macmillan, **2**: 744–8.

Littler, C.R. (1990) 'The labor process debate: a theoretical review', in D. Nights and H. Willmot (eds), *Labor Process Theory*, London: Macmillan.

Marglin, S. (1974) 'What do bosses do? The origins and functions of hierarchy in capitalist production' *Review of Radical Political Economics*, **6**(2): 60–112; reprinted in A. Gortz (ed.), *The Division of Labor*, Hassocks, Harvester Press, 13–54.

Okun, A.M. (1981) *Prices and Quantities: A Macroeconomics Analysis*, Oxford: Blackwell.

Reich, M. (1981) *Racial Inequality: A Political – Economic Analysis*, Princeton, N.J.: Princeton University Press.

—— and J. Devine (1981) 'The microeconomics of conflict and hierarchy in capitalist production', *Review of Radical Political Economics*, **12**(4): 27–45.

Sherman, H.J. (1976) *Stagflation: A Radical Theory of Unemployment and Inflation*, New York: Harper & Row.

Stiglitz, J.E. (1987) 'Principal and agent', in J. Eatwell, M. Milgate and P. Newman (eds), *The New Palgrave: A Dictionary of Economics*, London: Macmillan, **3**: 967–71.

—— and C. Shapiro (1986) 'Equilibrium unemployment as a worker discipline device', in: G.A. Akerlof and K.L. Yellen (eds), *Efficiency Wage Models of the Labour Market*, Cambridge, Cambridge University Press, 45–56.

PART FOUR

Cultural Economics

21. Does the Arts Council know what it is doing?*

The arts are subsidized in Britain to the tune of about £35 million a year, the actual figure depending to some extent on how much of radio and television we include in our definition of the arts. £35 million is a small sum compared to public subsidies of over £2,000 million to health and to education. But small as the sum is, it raises with a vengeance the problem of evaluating government expenditure. It may be difficult to say just why we spend money in the way we do on schools and hospitals, but it is even more difficult to say why we support the arts in one way or another, and in particular why we support it as little as we do compared to other countries. It is clearly impossible to evaluate government expenditure in a particular direction without knowing the aims of government, particularly as there will usually be many different aims. Even if we succeeded in drawing up a list of aims – objectives, goals, ends, the reasons why – we still face the task of somehow measuring the effectiveness of various spending patterns in achieving these aims. Since the answers – one for each objective – are quite likely to go in opposite directions, we need a scale of priorities between objectives to arrive at a comprehensive evaluation. We label this evaluation technique 'cost-effectiveness analysis' and in principle it is as applicable to the arts as it is to any other area of government activity, although in practice it may be particularly difficult to apply to the arts.

Be this as it may, we must clearly begin with a statement of objectives. Unless we get this right, evaluation is impossible on anybody's theory of evaluation. In this article we examine the objectives of the Arts Council in subsidizing the arts and we shall, therefore, confine ourselves to those aspects of the arts supported by them. Although the Council is only responsible for about one-third of all public expenditure on the arts (the remainder being largely devoted to museums and galleries), it exerts a more significant influence on the arts than other public bodies, such as local authorities. Its subsidies cover all major art forms including opera, ballet, orchestras, theatre, cinema and, to a lesser degree, art galleries and the experimental arts.

Our evidence derives mainly from the Annual Reports of the Arts Council. These reports concentrate on the financial aspects of the Council's activities but

* First published in *Encounter*, September 1973: 6–16 (written with K. King).

they always contain a brief section on policy issues. The space allocated to balance sheets reflects the Council's consistently maintained view of public accountability.

> Money, rough-hew it how we may, is the subject of all our Annual Reports. Indeed, the view gains currency in St James's Square that everything in them outside the Accounts is properly called 'extraneous matter'.   (1965–6)[1]

Nevertheless, the Council has always acknowledged the right of outsiders to ask the reasons why.

> There is a need to satisfy our readers who pay taxes but may not like reading balance-sheets, that we have not wasted their money and intend to spend it to even better advantage in the future. (1965–6)

The central problem to which we address ourselves is simply: what is a 'waste' of money in the field of arts, and how would one recognize waste if one saw it?

THE ROLE OF THE ARTS COUNCIL

In his introductory speech, heralding the creation of the Arts Council in 1946, Lord Keynes asserted that:

> The purpose of the Arts Council of Great Britain is to create an environment, to breed a spirit, to cultivate an opinion, to offer a stimulus to such purpose that the artist and the public can each sustain and live on the other in that union which has occasionally existed in the past at the great ages of a communal civilised life.   (1945)

A more explicit statement did not appear until four years later, when Sir Ernest Pooley, acting as Chairman, referred to the Council as: 'a very important experiment – state support for the arts without State control. We prefer not to control, though sometimes we must; we want to support, encourage and advise' (1948–9).

Clearly, the Council saw itself playing a prominent and active role, a nucleus around which artistic activity would revolve. However, the nuclear concept was not expressed until many years later: 'the Arts Council's essential function was not to act as the universal provider but as the centre focus of activities which might otherwise remain for ever unrealised hopes' (1967–8). The position of acting simply as a cashier dispensing funds was vigorously rejected from the beginning and the Council described its role as 'not merely the pay-master of the arts, but in some sense the national trustee for the arts' (1951–2). The term 'trustee' could imply a mere 'watchdog' role, or it might be stretched to include the idea of promoting new trends. Apparently it is the latter which the Council had in mind, since subsequent reports repeatedly stress the need for a forward-looking, active approach:

> There is another function which the Arts Council is seeking to develop: that of encouraging the production of new work in music, drama, poetry and painting. Just as scholarship depends upon experiment and search so do the arts need replenishment by contemporary innovation.   (1955–6).

Despite the stress laid on innovation, however, the Council has never openly assumed the dynamic role of catalyst in the arts. Repeated references in the Annual Reports suggest that the conflicts between a hands-off policy and one of 'effective leadership' has never been decisively resolved. The problem is that of avoiding the Scylla of *laissez-faire* while likewise avoiding the Charybdis of artistic paternalism.

Unhappy with a near-monopoly position as public patron of the arts, the Council soon advocated a diversification of sources of subsidy, in order to tap local initiative and enthusiasm. It is clear from the Council's detailed proposals for new Civic Arts Trusts that considerable thought has been give to the matter of how best to promote local efforts in the arts.

> What might be the functions of a civic Arts Trust? The first might be to consider what annual provision in the various arts the city enjoys or lacks at present. Another might be to examine the reasons why some of that provision is deficient; is it, for instance, through the inadequacy of theatres and concert halls? Or through bad staff work among the managements of provincial towns? Or through the city's neglect to guarantee or underwrite the visit of some notable company? There are, again, some puzzling equations to be solved. Why was such and such a visit to the town a roaring success when another, of equal merit, proved a dismal failure? What are the seasonal, the social, and the economic factors in these contradictions? Much of what we hear about these matters at present is gossip and speculation and one of the basic activities of a civic Arts Trust would be to discover the reasons why a city is so inadequately or sporadically provided with some or all of the arts. Map-making of this kind is one of the initial functions of such a trust. Another preliminary exercise is that of costing the arts: finding out what the city must provide in entrance money and subsidy to secure the various companies it wishes to see.   (1953–4)

In the light of the evidently strong belief in local action, it is surprising that five years were to elapse before any initiative was taken, namely, the creation of the first Regional Arts Association (RAA) in 1958. Although 'more than two thirds of the Council's grant is spent outside London' (1970–1), the English RAAs together receive only about 5 per cent of the Council's budget; the rest is provided directly to individual artistic organizations. A statement by Lord Eccles, in a House of Lords debate on the RAAs, referred to the need for more locally based and locally financed activities, since the regions still depended on 'direct subsidies from the Arts Council plus events produced, packaged and subsidised in or from London and then sent round the provinces' (*Hansard*, **329**(55), 22 March 1972). This observation is borne out in the latest report: 'The Council ... is in the main regionally – not London – orientated, and this is sufficiently understood. Of the total number of grants made, 90% go outside London' (1971–2).

The Arts Council is, of course, well aware of the administrative problems created by the artistic dominance of London, combined with its own financial dominance over total public expenditure on the performing and creative arts:

> There would be little 'mutual benefit' if the Arts Council channelled all its assistance through the Regional Associations to named recipients without giving the association any say in the disposal of these funds. On the other hand, it is *intra vires*, the Regional Association, and [it is] quite right and proper, for them to allocate funds in support of local enterprises which had little or no claim to Arts Council support within the terms of our Charter ... It is perhaps easier to see than to define the principles to be followed in this case; the presence of an Arts Council representative as an assessor in the councils of the associations is the most effective safeguard. Another potential difficulty arises over the presence of an recognised client of the Arts Council (orchestra, repertory company, touring organization) within the boundaries of a Regional Association which we also support. Who is to provide the subsidy? The Arts Council alone? But then where is the 'mutual benefit'? The Association? But we have direct obligation to our client, of which we cannot divest ourselves. This is a fine field for the elaboration of case-law; the extremes to be avoided are, first, treating the Regional Associations as mere post-offices, and secondly, allowing them the sort of autonomy that constitutionally belongs to the Scottish and Welsh Committees of Council (this is something we are not entitled to devolve upon anyone in England). (1964–5)

In their statement welcoming the formation of the RAAs, the Council expressed the hope that 'such bodies will prove a rod for the Arts Council's back'. It would be interesting to know how much truth there is in this assertion. Unfortunately, the Annual Reports confine themselves to the purely positive aspects of the relationship between the Council and these local bodies. However, with the immediate prospect of a 40 per cent increase in grants to the regional associations, it has become more important than ever for the Council to define clearly its role in the total system of public patronage to the arts. We need merely note that this is *still* an unresolved aspect of the role of the Arts Council.

It is in the realm of advice that the Council has perhaps contributed most to the arts. Certainly the Annual Reports have been more articulate on this aspect of their work than on any other.

> The wording of the Charter is no doubt judicious: advice and co-operation come before holding and dealing with money. We can sometimes enjoy ourselves in the role of *sugar-daddy* to the arts, but we are at present more often, better and more

characteristically employed as match-makers, midwives and nannies ... It is by the fruit of much patient and inconspicuous discussion and correspondence, field work, expert counsel and personal liaison that we must justify our existence. (1962–3).

Moreover, these functions were not limited merely to large and influential institutions but were extended to cover small and relatively unimportant concerns:

> While respecting the rights of self-government of all the bodies it supports, the Council devotes much time and attention to the policy of these bodies. It gives guidance at one end of the scale in advising an obscure *music society* on a programme of work suitable for its means and its membership. And at the other end of the scale, it conducts a patient and independent scrutiny of the artistic and economic conditions of Grand Opera. (1951–2).

Of all the original aims of the Arts Council – 'to encourage, support and advise' – the third is undoubtedly the most consistent of its functions. But it still remains to be seen in what sense 'encouragement' has been given; it still remains to analyse the value of the achievements of the Council and to ask how far this has been a fulfilment of Keynes's original ideal. The Arts Council itself has never pretended to pass ultimate judgement on its own contribution, or even to settle once and for all the proper scope of its activities.

> The major problem is to define our scope. We remain and always will remain on auxiliary body. Artistic activity would, happily, continue without us, and the contribution we can make to promoting artistic output will always be arguable. On this score we take a modest view. We have no evidence that poets, authors, painters or composers – or any creative workers – are the more fertile because we exist and give them our support. It would be complacent to entertain such belief. (1966–7)

But a year later they claimed a little more:

> That Britain is no longer 'the country without music' (or any of the other arts for that matter) is largely due to the patient work of the Arts Council over the past twenty years or so in supporting and encouraging performing, and to a lesser extent, creative artists. (1968–9)

A recent Annual Report sums up the contribution of the Council over 26 years existence:

> Despite all the things we have not done and all the things we have done but ought not to have done, and all the things that still need to be done, the Arts Council is a good and worthy institution in a wicked world. It has provided a stimulus and a sense of purpose to a great many people and a great many projects. Much that is good would have been lost without it. Much that is hopeful would never have seen the light of day and some things that are purposeless and pointless and positively nasty would have continued to maintain unproved pretensions. (1970–1).

It seems ironic that as far back as 1952–3, the Arts Council was asserting that: 'Public patronage, whatever form it takes, must select its roles and objectives with precision, and that is one of the lessons the Arts Council is beginning to learn.' It is difficult, however, to find any evidence in subsequent reports that the lesson has actually been learned. If it had, our critique would have been redundant.

THE CASE FOR SUBSIDIES

The Annual Reports have devoted considerable space to the rationale for the existence of an organization like the Arts Council. There is clearly no difficulty in finding economic arguments for subsidizing the arts. The standard reasons in economic theory for involving government intervention apply at least in part to the arts and, in addition, there are special grounds for subsidizing artistic activity.

The standard reasons have to do with causes of '*market failure*' (either economies of large scale production, or external costs and benefits, or consumer ignorance, or any combination of these, inhibit the operation of the market mechanism) and with the case of '*public goods*' (certain goods cannot be priced at all by a market because as soon as they are produced for one person, others cannot be excluded from consuming them). It is not clear whether these arguments actually apply to the arts but, in any case, demand and supply of the arts are highly interdependent. Tastes, and hence demand, tend to be stimulated by the mere provision of artistic facilities. For these reasons, the market mechanism may be an inefficient instrument for allocating resources to the arts.

Moreover, there is the thesis (associated with the name of Baumol) which asserts that the real costs of producing artistic activity are bound to rise in the course of economic growth. There is little scope for cost-reducing technical progress in the arts, but the wages and salaries of artistic personnel tend to rise in step with wages and salaries in general. The result is a constant cost-push in the arts and hence public patronage is required to ensure a continual supply.[2]

Lastly, traditional welfare economics is silent about the question of income distribution. The market tends to equate effective demand with available supply, and effective demand clearly depends on the existing distribution of purchasing power among individuals. But many members of the electorate object fundamentally to the idea of distributing artistic goods and services on the basis of current purchasing power; in short, they have definite preferences about an equitable distribution of the arts. This, too, might constitute a reason for government support of the arts.[3]

None of these arguments appears in the Annual Reports. It is interesting, however, that the Arts Council, while dismissing almost all its critics as 'backwoodsmen', nevertheless expends much effort in defending itself against a vaguely specified attack on the very idea of public patronage of the arts. Their defence rests essentially on what we might call 'the vacuum theory': the establishment of the welfare state with its principle of redistributive taxation destroyed private patronage of the arts and consequently created a vacuum which only government can fill. This theme is repeated time and again. The survival of the arts now depends on government subsidies, and if these were withdrawn the end of artistic life would immediately follow:

> If the arts are to survive somebody must pay for them, and if the burden of subsidy, purchase or guarantee has become too heavy for the private patron it must be shouldered by the public ... The health, the education, the social welfare, the national defence of the people have all become the collective responsibility of the people, and no taxpayer or ratepayer can contract out of the obligation to contribute to the upkeep of the necessities and amenities of the Welfare State. The preservation of the fine arts is another of these collective responsibilities. (1952–3)[4]

The twenty-second Report returns to the 'vacuum theory', combining it with notions of a 'civilised' optimum amount of the arts:

> There are few thinking people to whom the need for artistic subsidy would have to be justified today. It is not a matter of choice. In some ways it might be preferable to live in a society where the measure of private support for our activities obviated the need for State assistance. But such a society has totally ceased to exist. The fiscal policies of every government in our memory have contributed to a situation where private bounty or investment is now totally inadequate to sustain a civilised ration of music and theatre, of poetry and picture. Nor need we be remotely apologetic in asking for the modest sums we need for our purposes from the public purse. The Government has garnered in much, if not most, of the wealth that cultured patricians and public-spirited industrialists could formerly bestow. It holds a portion of its treasury charged with a trust to use it for our purposes – and in fairness, the growth of the Arts Council in scope and importance demonstrates governmental recognition of this principle. (1966–7).

In short, the Arts Council exists to give back what the Inland Revenue has taken away! If so, might not a change in the tax laws be a better way of subsidizing the arts. Would it not, at any rate, be a good question to think about?

Another Council argument is based on the idea that education systematically fosters an appreciation of the arts. Since education is largely financed from the Exchequer, it follows that the arts have equal claim to be publicly supported: 'we should allocate more money than we do to ensure them [school children] an adequate provision in later life of those arts for which they are given some appetite in school' (1955–6). However, if the enjoyment of the arts merely extends the educative process, the question of *who actually attends* subsidized performances becomes paramount. A study by Baumol and Bowen, based on both American and British audiences, found that the average theatre- and concert-goer was a university graduate, earning nearly twice the median income of the population.[5] In other words, if education fosters an appreciation of the arts, it is not to school-leavers that we must look for evidence of the proposition. Moreover, believing as it does, the Council appears to have done very little to promote an interest in the arts in schools; at least the Annual Reports make no mention of any co-operative ventures with the Department of Education and Science.

Besides, it is difficult to square this faith in schooling as a great promoter of lifelong interest in the arts with the Council's defensive attitude about the low popularity rating of so many of the activities which it supports. These subsidies are, typically, defended by the argument that the tastes of the *discriminating few* are of *more* consequence because they are seeking 'enlightenment' and not just 'entertainment': 'there are abundant precedents to justify the public patronage of the arts for the benefit of the considerable minority who have cultivated a taste for serious pleasures' (1951–2).

This is precisely the supercilious attitude which Sir Ernest Pooley, one-time chairman of the Council, warned against:

> And do let us be gay; let us have entertainment. I never quite know what 'highbrow' exactly means, but in so far as it is a term of reproach, let us not be highbrow. You can have high standards of performance without being highbrow. The arts can provide for those who appreciate them a fuller life and greater happiness. But don't submit to that depressing sense of superiority and that 'preciousness', too often affected by arts clubs and arts circles. Don't let us be afraid of being amused.   (1948–9).

However, subsequent reports have ignored this entreaty and have proceeded to justify particular expenditure on grounds tantamount to 'preciousness'.[6]

Nearly all the Annual Reports have stressed the gross inadequacy of present grants to the arts. The arts, they say, find themselves permanently on the edge of insolvency, and this tends to affect their standard of performance:

> The need for public money arises not because our theatres and opera houses, our concerts and our art exhibitions are inefficiently run, or failing to draw a public. Rather the reverse. In part it arises because of their success. Subsidy is needed if the public appetite, which is now so clearly demonstrated, is to be satisfied by performances and works of the highest standard.   (1968–9)

This implies that a subsidy is needed merely to maintain standards of production, irrespective of the level of demand. Yet two years earlier they stated: 'If we could reach the point where public support was so effectively stimulated as to make subsidies unnecessary this would be a supreme justification of our work' (1966–7).

In view of the fact that Covent Garden played to 91 per cent capacity in 1968–9, while Stratford reached 97 per cent capacity in the 1970–1 season, and both receive support from the Arts Council, it is difficult to evaluate this contention. The statement clearly implies that increasing attendance would dispense with the need for subsidies – in which case what are we to make of the figures for attendance rates just cited?

That *some* subsidy is necessary may be readily agreed upon; but the amount required is still open to argument. This must obviously depend upon the potential revenue from the arts. It would be interesting to discover on what grounds the Council bases its ticket pricing policy. Its approach to the question of ticket prices, however, has been ambiguous and contradictory. The ninth Annual Report states that: 'In many establishments there have, indeed, been marginal increases in theatre and concert prices, but it would be idle to pretend that there is any hope of coaxing the public to pay much more for its arts than it does at present' (1953–4). A year later, however, they altered their previous stand: 'A rapid jolt in prices no doubt would put audiences off; a steady acceleration of prices over the years would not' (1954–5). Two years later they stated:

> Whether admission charges are being raised enough to keep pace with rising costs is a matter for argument; yet where they are being increased consumer-resistance is not fulfilling the woeful predictions of the more timorous theatre and concert promoters. ... Everything must continue to be done by the promoters of opera and music and drama to match admission prices as closely as possible to rising costs.   (1956–7)

Ten years later the Director of the Royal Festival Hall pointed out to the Estimates Committee:[8]

> I would say in general that prices of seats are increasing all the time. All promoters are trying to get that extra bit out of the box office. They are increasing some of the prices. They could keep the price range exactly as it is by having the same number of seats at each price but by having more of the middle and higher priced seats they can get a higher capacity from the house.

If it is in fact possible to charge higher admission prices as time passes and costs rise, it is not clear why subsidies are necessary. *To maintain standards? to enlarge audiences? to cultivate new audiences?* The questions are obvious, but no answers are to be found in the Annual Reports.

POLICY DILEMMA: THE CONFLICT OF GOALS

The most clearly defined statement of aims which the Arts Council has so far offered appeared in the eleventh Annual Report. These were '(a) the improvement of professional standards of performance; (b) selective diffusion [of the arts]; (c) local responsibility [for the arts]; and (d) the provision of buildings [for the arts]' (1955–6). A limited budget has given prominence to the first and second goals: artistic standards and selective diffusion have become the Council's overriding preoccupation.

Even here, however, there has been constant soul-searching. Should expenditure be concentrated on maintaining a few selected strongholds of high artistic achievement? Or would it be preferable to disperse the available funds over a wider geographical area?

> The Charter of the Arts Council enunciates a double purpose – (a) that the Council should seek to elevate standards of performance and (b) that it should endeavour to spread the appreciation of the arts. The Council has sought to observe both these injunctions. But the size of the budget in a period of rising costs may require it to re-examine how far both these objectives may be simultaneously secured. Is it wiser in such times as these to consolidate standards, rather than pursue a policy of wider dispersal?   (1950–1).

They argue that since 'high standards can only be built on a limited scale', the emphasis must fall on standards.

> The primary responsibility imposed by its Royal Charter is to preserve and improve standards of performance in the various arts. The Arts Council interprets this injunction, in relation to its income, as implying the support of a limited number of institutions where exemplary standards may be developed.   (1955–6)

These statements clearly reveal the emphasis which the Council has always placed on 'excellence'. This emphasis is sometimes rationalized (as in the previous statement) by appealing to the constraints of a limited budget. At times, however, it is advocated on deeper grounds as the right policy in and of itself.

> But even if that income were double what it is, the duty of the Arts Council would still be to nourish good standards of production and performance, rather than attempt a premature and ambitious scale of diffusion. Public patronage of the arts is a long term obligation: it must grow like the mustard-seed, not like the beanstalk.   (1959–60)

The Arts Council has firmly held to this position, at least until recently. That they have been successful in achieving the goal of raising artistic standards is almost obvious from the esteem in which British drama, music, ballet and opera is held throughout the world.

However, the goal of selective 'diffusion' is more difficult to appraise. The term 'diffusion' as employed by the Arts Council has connotations over and above that of mere dispersal. Sometimes it refers to the conflict raised by concentrating on London rather than the regions; sometimes it refers to a contrast between regional concentration and widespread diffusion throughout Britain in small towns and rural areas; and on occasion it refers to diffusion to a larger, less-homogeneous audience. As these are not consciously viewed as different aspects of the problem, the result has been to confuse the entire issue of wider dissemination of the arts.

Let us take, first of all, the question of London versus the regional cities. The Council pleads that it is not responsible for amenities in London as opposed to the relative deprivation of provincial cities:

> The capital city is also the metropolis of the nation's art: the home, for example, of its National Gallery and its British Museum. It is both proper and inevitable that its National Opera House should be located there as well. Secondly, it was not the Arts Council which decided to establish these three institutions [i.e. Covent Garden, Sadler's Wells and the Old Vic]. The Arts Council did not decide to give half its money to London; it decided to act as patron to certain institutions already established, and of these the most meritorious and representative were situated in London. If any provincial city had assumed the responsibility for creating and maintaining, say, Sadler's Wells, the Arts Council would gladly have become its patron. It is highly improbable, in fact, that any large city in the Provinces could provide a continuous home for opera and ballet; they have insufficient catchment areas (or visitors) to supply the large audience and income an operation of such magnitude requires. (1955–6)

But, of course, this says nothing about the question of touring the provinces, which is sometimes employed as a reason for subsidizing London-based companies:

> One very large fraction of its [the Council's] revenue goes to subsidizing such National Institutions as Covent Garden, Sadler's Wells and the Old Vic, which, although located in London, are as much a national inheritance as the British Museum, the National Gallery and the Victoria and Albert Museum. They even manage, in spite of innumerable difficulties, to tour many provincial centres; and the proportion of our budget which they absorb may reasonably be debited to the country as a whole, rather than to London. (1950–1)

None the less, the Arts Council admits to weaknesses in its standards for distributing funds, on one occasion going so far as to say that 'The diffusion of the arts on their higher levels is at present sporadic, unplanned and unequal' (1953–4):

> If a moratorium could be declared in the arts the present design of subsidy might indeed be radically altered. If it were possible – or ever had been possible at a given moment – to lay down a plan of subsidy based on ideal requirements in terms of music, drama, opera and ballet the structure of subsidy would doubtless be better balanced than it is. (1957–8)

This is the view that many critics of the Arts Council would no doubt endorse, although what form an 'ideal' subsidy pattern would take is unclear, especially as regional inhabitants would presumably hold different concepts of what constitutes a 'perfect' subsidy pattern. Indeed, they might dispute the following statement referring to 'arts trusts' as being little short of a gross misrepresentation of the facts: 'The Arts Council recognises is obligations to these bodies and by its continued and increasing support of them will ensure the Provinces an abundant share of the available arts' (1955–6).

The second facet of diffusion is that of regionalism on the broadest possible scale to embrace the 'cultural deserts' outside the regional cities. The Annual Report of 1951 asked the question: 'Is it good policy to encourage small, ill-equipped expeditions to set out into the wilderness and present meagre productions in village fit-ups?' (1950–1). The intended answer is obviously: *No*. But in trying to justify this attitude they rely exclusively on the costliness of living up to the doctrine of 'fair shares':

> How far, then, should diffusion go? This notion of diffusion is liable, in a democracy like ours, to get mixed up with the political axiom of 'fair shares'. When this happens it leads to the argument that, since the tax payers in Caithness or Cardigan contribute to the funds voted to the Arts Council, they should have their 'share' of the cornucopia of provision. But the economic consequences of this supposition are daunting and conclusive. (1952–3)

The dilemma that results from this conflict of aims has proved difficult to resolve, and the Annual Reports have time and time again attempted to pour oil on troubled waters:

> We are of course already providing art-below-cost. The crux of this policy is 'How much below cost?' At what point in the arithmetic progression of subsidy are we to stop? The bearing of this problem upon the accepted scale of diffusion of the arts is evident. As the figure of subsidy rises, how soon will it become expended, in the main, upon the kind of diffusion which can only be a dilution? Or when will it cease to operate, whatever its size, because there develops a dearth of the product it exists to diffuse? There is, evidently, a limit to the 'potential' of the arts. (1952–3).

A meaningful answer to these questions depends on some quantitative estimate of the price-elasticity of demand for the arts in different places and among different audiences. Are consumers more responsive to ticket prices in cities than in rural areas? If so, the distribution of subsidies can be altered so as to take such differences into account. If, for example, the demand in rural areas is relatively inelastic, prices can be raised and subsidies redirected to the cities. This is a separate issue from that of the principle of diffusion. What is not clear in the Council's statement is whether they wish to satisfy an existing demand (in which case demand may be taken to be comparatively inelastic) or whether to encourage new demand (which would undoubtedly require lower-priced tickets to attract those who now stay away).

This difficulty is largely confined to music and drama since the cost of 'diffusing' paintings and sculpture is comparatively low. The Arts Council itself, therefore, directly finances 'travelling art exhibitions' throughout Britain. The problem of rural isolation is, to some extent, mitigated by the provision of travelling grants to enable to the less-accessible areas to organize low-cost trips to the theatre: 'the Arts Council should be diligent in developing better facilities for the public to see the arts at their best and one such facility is the provision of coach parties to concerts and plays' (1955–6).

This was the most obvious and logical solution to the situation, and its widespread use would ensure a more equitable, albeit far from 'perfect' distribution of the arts. However, in spite of some success with such policies, their analysis of the problem is puzzling: 'The achievement and preservation of standards in the arts is, primarily, then, the role of the professional just as the task of diffusing the arts outside the cities is largely the business of the amateur' (1955–6). In the same report, moreover, they contradict themselves by asking:

> A matter highly relevant to this problem of how far the Arts Council should carry diffusion is the transformation wrought by radio ... With astonishing rapidity broadcasting is assuming the role of Universal Diffusor; and to that extent making it more vital than ever to preserve strongholds of standard in a limited number of places. (1955–6)

The residents outside the cities were, therefore, expected to be content with the 'mass media' plus participation in amateur activities. However, in recent years the emphasis has moved much more in favour of the regions. The twenty-third Annual Report stated:

> London presents a special problem: it is foolish to regard it as sufficiently served by artistic and cultural amenities to a point where it can now be neglected in favour of other areas, but simple justice compels us to call a relative halt to expansion in many London plans and institutions until at least something comparable to the London 'density' of culture is available in other parts of the country. (1967–8)

The previous year had stressed 'the view now firmly held in this country – that metropolitan culture, however rich and varied, cannot be a total substitute for local and regional institutions' (1968–9). Nevertheless, there is no evidence that the Arts Council has seriously attempted to achieve the goal of regional diffusion. Although public funds spent on the arts in the regions has increased in absolute terms, the *proportion* has in fact remained constant since 1965.[9]

The third aspect of diffusion is concerned with the cultivation of *new audiences*, either for the arts as traditionally conceived or for hitherto ignored and despised varieties, such as jazz, pop, folk music, etc. The Report of 1966 emphasized 'the major purpose for which we must use our money ... is to cultivate new audiences for the arts', and this goal has been reiterated in subsequent Reports.

However, there is no indication that the policy of cultivating new audiences has been given priority in the Council's objectives. To be sure, audiences for the arts have grown over the years but so has the demand for privately produced and privately financed entertainment. Without launching a single survey of audience participation in the arts, the Council nevertheless draws inspiration from what it takes to be a trend towards mass audiences: 'Within our society there is now a widespread feeling that the provision of drama and music and painting and all culture in its broadest sense is no longer to be regarded as a privilege for a few but is the democratic right of the whole community' (1968–9). How is this 'widespread feeling' to be made manifest? Is it by increasing Council grants to the RAAs so that local bodies are able to respond more fully to their particular needs, or by increasing aid to experimental projects which at present, together with the Arts Associations, arts festivals, literature and experimental projects, comprise only 11 per cent of the Council's budget?

The present distribution of subsidies shows that, although 90 per cent of the total *number* of grants are given to the regions, spending still remains disproportionately in favour of London. At present Covent Garden, Sadler's Wells, the National Theatre, and the Royal Shakespeare Company together receive 39 per cent of the total budget for England; 17 per cent is spent on music (including other grants to opera and ballet companies, e.g. the Festival Ballet). The fifty-odd repertory theatres throughout England together receive 6 per cent, while expenditure on art (including regional exhibitions, films on tour, the Hayward and Serpentine Galleries) amounts to 5 per cent. Literature (including grants for writers and poets and work in schools) receive less than 1 per cent, as to do the experimental projects and art centres. Regional arts associations receive 5 per cent and the remainder is spent on new buildings for the arts and education in the arts.

Some critics feel that Covent Garden is excessively subsidized. Whether true or not, the question in the present context is whether the amount spent on Covent Garden can be justified on the grounds of audience appeal? If not, what becomes of the goal of gaining new audiences? 'We have tried very hard', the Council says, 'to use our resources as sensibly and as equitably as possible. We have tried to supply the growing needs of a society increasingly conscious of the value of the arts to civilised life' (1970–1). But what are the Council's criteria for deciding that funds are spent 'as sensibly and equitably as possible'? The twenty-second Annual Report stated: 'We shall try to make our judgements more scientific and less rule-of-thumb, but to a large extent they must remain inspirational – others might find a less flattering word' (1966–7). Yes, indeed.

CRITERIA FOR SUBSIDY: A PATTERN FOR PATRONAGE?

The vague, imprecise nature of the statements concerning the aims of the Arts Council, as embodied in the Charters of 1945 and 1967 – 'that of developing a greater knowledge, practice and understanding to the people throughout the realm and to improve standards of execution' – has enabled the Arts Council to evade the problem of defining precise criteria in their selection procedures.

In discussing the issue, the Council has always emphasized the 'efficiency' of the recipient bodies in the sense of exemplary accountancy practices (1952–3). Efficiency in administrative practices appears to be the *only* justification which the Council has ever offered for selecting one artistic organization rather than another, despite their own admission that 'the thrift and probity of financial administration, necessary as they are, do not vindicate the ultimate use of money' (1968–9).

The Estimates Committee to examine the Arts Council and its subsidized organizations found that: 'not one single instance was brought to their notice, or suggested, of extravagance or wastage by Arts Council customers. And there was not a vestige of a suggestion of anything but the most proper and scrupulous use of the funds which we so widely disbursed into so many quarters'. Consequently, they concluded that: 'what the Arts Council was doing was needed to be done and, what is more, that the sums of money it was administering were inadequate and should be augmented'.

Budgetary efficiency is surely an inadequate justification for the activities of the Arts Council. Its effectiveness can only be judged in terms of 'what ... was needed to be done'. This, unfortunately, remains undefined.

The issue is not only that of evolving criteria to evaluate *competing claims* for subsidy, but also one of deciding just *what areas* the Council should be subsidizing. Take, for example, the question of whether to support jazz or not. This turns on the vexed question of what is 'art' and what is 'entertainment'. The Annual Reports used to contain statements such as: 'The Arts Council's concern is with the fine arts exclusively which ae only part of entertainment, however strongly we may hold that they are the best and most important part' (1963–4); the function of the Council is to 'nurture the arts, not provide popular amenities in that field' (1959–60).

This conservative bias was consistently maintained throughout all Annual Reports until 1969 – and then a new view made its abrupt appearance. In the twenty-fourth Annual Report the emphasis is on 'throwing a bridge across to the young', thereby manifesting a sudden consciousness of whole sectors of peripheral artistic activities hitherto ignored. The metamorphoses has produced so much controversy and heated debate that it has become more imperative than ever for the Arts Council to establish some basic principles rather than to continue its policy of allowing the respective expert panels to decide what, or what not, to subsidize.

How, for example, do they justify the recent decision to subsidize the Theatre Investment Fund? The twenty-second Report discussed the possibility of giving direct aid to commercial theatres in order 'to co-operate with its best elements'. The purpose of this Fund, however, is to encourage provincial touring of successful London productions of musicals, comedies, etc.[10] As these cannot possibly be defended in terms of the Council's usual standard of 'the best in the arts', the decision implies either that their standards of 'good drama' have now changed to encompass 'entertainment' or they have come to feel that it is their function to provide what the 'public' want to see, regardless of whether or not it can be considered 'art'.

The Arts Council is proud of its policy of total freedom of expression for its recipient bodies and individuals. Since it lays down no principles – at least in print – it is difficult to see how competing requests for aid are in fact compared. 'More for one means less for another' is a truism which contributes little understanding to the problem. Neither do vague statements like:

> The test for eligibility for support is easier to sense than to define but in broad terms the beneficiary must have merit or promise of merit, appeal or prospect of appeal and must satisfy a discriminating need.   (1969–70).

This statement is particularly interesting in view of the evidence given the previous year to the Estimates Committee:

> It would be complacent to suggest that we have not evolved any scientific principles because we are dealing, to a very large extent, with a historic backwash. We have started to introduce principles.[11]

If, indeed, there are underlying principles of guidelines to decisions, the Arts Council has appeared remarkably reluctant to give an account of them. There has been no attempt to clarify the situation in subsequent reports (and, surprisingly enough, the Estimates Committee did not ask for an explanation of the above statement).

THE CONFUSION OF 'SUBJECTIVITY'

There is a constant tendency in the Annual Reports to take refuge in the inherent subjectivity of all artistic judgements: 'We endeavour to discharge our duties with a very real consciousness of our own fallibility and the rooted imperfection of all artistic judgement' (1966–7).

Of course, in the final analysis artistic judgements are subjective, and so are the objectives that underlie all expenditures on the arts. What is *not* subjective, however, is the degree to which spending on one activity rather than another achieves a particular objective. For example, if our goal is to promote opera in the regions, we may have difficulty in deciding whether to spend given sum on Verdi or on Michael Tippett; but the question is, at least in principle, capable of being answered objectively. Or, alternatively, if our goal is to find new audiences for the arts, it is not a question of deciding whether John Cage is better than Richard Rodgers but whether a Cage recital will attract as large an audience as a Rodgers concert. Thus, it is perfectly possible to lay down selection criteria even though artistic judgements are subjective.

One way out of the dilemma of subjectivity might be to rely on audience response. The Arts Council, however, seems to be less clear about its responsibilities to the consumers than to the producers of the arts. They define their function for the latter as striving 'to improve the working conditions of artists and to preserve and enlarge their public', while asserting (1952–3) that 'it is not the business of the State, working through the Arts Council, to furnish a matrix of artistic performances for a receptive and captive audience'! What role, then, *do* they envisage for the audience?

> The importance of an audience response is a variable factor. If it is a commodity which depends for its survival on the response of an audience – such as a theatre or a concert hall – it is nonsense to subsidise an activity that produces no such reaction. But it is equally wrong to measure its value solely in audience terms. Hence if a repertory theatre performs a range of relatively popular plays but fails to draw an adequate audience, it is plain it should be re-sited or change its policy, or even, as the final decision, be closed. But if the subsidy is for a poet, his recognition by a single perceptive mind can amply justify support to maintain an activity which can rarely find an adequate public.   (1969–70)

The contrast between a single person's appreciation (on the one hand) and a mass audience (on the other) covers the entire spectrum of reactions. It neatly evades the question of what in fact is an 'adequate' audience size. The problem is whether the Arts Council should attempt to educate public taste in esoteric art forms, or whether it should merely confine itself to catering to established tastes. The Council, of course, has it both ways:

> We ought not to waste our resources on enterprises which prove in practice to be quite unacceptable to the public. There is a level of persistent failure, in this sense, that must be regarded as definitive. Between these two extremes the Council must find the best compromise, encouraging promise wherever it is found, but not losing touch with reality. ... Within these general conditions, the Council acknowledges a duty to foster potentially interesting experiments.   (1996–7)

Basically, this is a 'trade-off' problem. If the Council's basic objective is to gain *new* audiences for the arts, it would surely be irrational to spend a large percentage of available funds on unpopular forms of art. On the other hand, if support of new artists is an overriding objective, then some of the money should be allocated to esoterica. In either case, is it not necessary to confront this issue just a little more explicitly than the Council has done in the past?

The Council is understandably sensitive to accusations of prejudice in favour of one or another form of art. It attempts to counteract these by relying exclusively on the expert opinions of the specialist panels. As Lord Goodman put it:

> We can marshal to our aid the informed judgement of expert panels, uncoerced by rules and regulations of an academic and artificial character. If the administration of subsidy is left to the tender mercies of full-time bureaucrats, my experience compels the harsh judgement that we would be better to dispense with the system altogether. (1970–1)

Perhaps true, but there would seem to be a wide spectrum of selection techniques between the existing structure of the Arts Council and the bureaucracy of a government department. To encourage more diversity is no solution, although diversity is continually emphasized as a great virtue:

> One criticism of State patronage is that it puts too much power into two few hands and thus discourages the variety and competition of styles which patrons used to foster.... It is not by its network of Committees and panels that the Arts Council is restrained from acting like a cultural oligarchy. The fundamental check is the Council's own conscious determination not to dictate policies or impose fashions in the arts it tries to assist. So far as it enjoys a monopoly of State patronage it is, no doubt, theoretically capable of restrictive practices in the arts. But it steadfastly avoids such practices. (1952–3)

However, by avoiding the basic issue of selection criteria, the Council does in effect maintain 'restrictive practices' in the arts; and the arbitrary judgement of many people is not necessarily less restrictive than the rational judgement of a few. Actually the Council's only defence of its procedures is that government departments do no better:

> If our methods are really slipshod, brash or doctrinaire, this is not because we are an independent chartered corporation ... government departments also fall into the same failings ... Some people consider that a certain informality in our procedures is unbecoming seeing that the Council is entrusted with substantial sums of public money; they fear that our freedom from Parliamentary inquisition or official control in matters of policy makes us autocratic, and arbitrary in our choice of candidates for support – irresponsible in the plain as well as in the technical sense.   (1962–3).

Nevertheless, while acknowledging the criticism, Lord Goodman defends the need for something like the Arts Council on the grounds that sensible decisions about the arts are unlikely to emerge from government offices – the Council, being composed of 'a body of people who breathe the fresh air of ordinary life in their normal day to day activities can – whatever mistakes we make – adjudicate our problems with commonsense and appreciation of the needs of ordinary human beings' (1971–2).

The eleventh Annual Report, however, admitted this: 'The Council is not, in the limited sense, a representative body. ... They are chosen primarily as persons with a particular knowledge of, or concern for, one or more of the fine arts' (1955–6). A study by Harris on the composition of the Arts Council would seem to question Lord Goodman's assertion.[12] Harris found that the average age at appointment to the Council was 56.7, and that Council members came in most instances from upper income and better educated families.

It remains a matter for conjecture how far these facts may have influenced recent attempts to rebalance the age structure of the Council by the inclusion of 'youngsters to sit on their panels', not to mention conscious attempts *'to remain contemporary and "with it"'* (1968–9). The twenty-second Annual Report queries the past pattern of spending.

> No one responsible for the disbursement of money for the improvement of standards in the arts in a country would ever claim that some of the money so spent might not, with hindsight, have been better spent in some other way. ... The accounts for 1966–67 in this report are there to substantiate the Council's case that this money was well spent. (1966–7)

It would be interesting to see how much effect this kind of retrospective analysis will have on subsequent spending decisions. Without doubt, the Arts Council is performing a vital role, and it would be absurd to underestimate the contribution it has made to cultural activities. But without questioning whether or not the money was well spent, one might still ask whether or not it could in fact have been better spent some other way. Could it have been 'more cost-effective' in terms of its own objectives?

CONCLUSION

To evaluate an organization like the Arts Council is to assess the effectiveness of its policies in achieving stated aims. Since any aim can be achieved by a large number of policies, we must also take account of the costs of attaining a given degree of effectiveness; having decided on the most effective policy per unit of costs for each stated aim, there is the further problem of ordering the aims in terms of a scale of priorities.

But the whole exercise cannot even get started unless the social and cultural aims themselves are expressed in some clear form. It is not good enough to say that the arts must be diffused among new audiences. How can we possibly evaluate policies to achieve that end unless we distinguish between genuinely new audiences and additional participation of old audiences, which in turn implies definite knowledge of the composition of existing audiences? This is a small example, but we have seen many others throughout this article.

The Arts Council certainly has *objectives* – but most of them are too ill-defined to make evaluation possible. Indeed, reading the Annual Reports of the Council has proved to be a depressing experience. It is not too much to say that in 26 years of official reportage they have failed to produce a single coherent and operational statement of their aims.

NOTES

1. All subsequent references of this kind refer to the dates of publication of the Annual Reports of the Arts Council. Chairmen of the Arts Council have been: Lord Keynes (1946), economists; Sir Ernest Pooley (1946–53), barrister; Sir Kenneth Clark (1953–60), art historian and critic; Lord Cottesloe (1960–5), businessman and public administrator; Lord Goodman (1965–72), solicitor; Patrick Gibson (1972), publisher.
2. W. Baumol and W.G. Bowen, *Performing Arts: The Economic Dilemma*, New York, 1966.
3. It is not clear that this is an additional reason. Preferences on the part of one individual about another individual's consumption of the arts may be interpreted as a so-called 'consumption externality', in which case it is already dealt with under the heading of 'market failure'. For further discussion, see A.T. Peacock, 'Welfare economics and public subsidies to the arts', *Manchester School of Economic and Social Studies*, xxxvii, December 1969.
4. Earlier we quoted a statement from the 1966–7 Report to the effect that 'Artistic activity would, happily, continue without us, and the contribution we can make to promoting artistic output will always be arguable' – which appears to contradict the passage just cited. However, such inconsistencies appear throughout all the Reports.
5. Baumol and Bowen, *Performing Arts*, 92.
6. On other occasions, however, the Council has *denied* that it caters for minority tastes: 'We are not a luxury; we do not cater for a small elite out of the pockets of a protesting multitude. We supply a commodity which a great many people require and which can make a better life for a great many more once their appetite and interest has been awakened' (1966–7).
7. The fourth Annual Report said: 'It is a mistake to think that the arts must necessarily be subsidised. A great number of concerts, plays and exhibitions are and should be, self-supporting. Financial support is frequently both unnecessary and undesirable' (1951–2). But this appears to be a momentary aberration from the constant theme.
8. Eighth Report of the Estimates Committee of the House of Commons, *Grants for the Arts*, London: HMSO, 1968.
9. PEP, 'Public patronage of the arts', *Planning*, xxxi, November 1965.
10. *New Society*, 3 August 1972, 249.
11. Eighth Report of the Estimates Committee, 1968.
12. John Harris, 'Decision-makers in government programs of arts patronage: the Arts Council of Great Britain', *Western Political Quarterly*, xxii, June 1969.

REPLY TO COMMENTS*

Shortly after the appearance of our iconoclastic essay on the Arts Council's declared aims and objectives (*Encounter*, September 1973) Sir Hugh Willatt, Secretary-General of the Council, told a reporter:

> The article is an attempt to judge the Arts Council without assessing the results of the Arts Council's work. It is a criticism of our public statements and ignores what we've done. (*Guardian*, 21 August 1973).

Sir Hugh is quite correct. We limited ourselves explicitly to the Council's public statements as *a first step* in an effort to evaluate the Council's accomplishments as public patron of the arts. We will turn to what the Council has done in a forthcoming piece, and we hope eventually to be judged in the round and not simply on our preliminary skirmishes in the field.

Mr Richard Findlater in this issue [of *Encounter*, December 1973] echoes Sir Hugh's reaction. But he goes further in denying that we have done justice to what the Council has said, after which he cannot resist the temptation of implying that published pronouncements do not really matter; results are everything. As we have said, we intend to move on to results in the near future but, in the meanwhile, Mr Findlater has raised so many red herrings that an immediate response is in order.

'One flaw of the curious King–Blaug exercise', he writes, 'is that they seem to view the reports as the work of a single author, whose tactical evasions and true intentions ... will be revealed by textual and linguistic scholarship.' It is perfectly true that the reports in question span a period of 20 years which saw the Council headed by five successive chairmen. But as a matter of fact, there are glaring inconsistencies in the public statements of the Council within the lifetime of a single chairman, e.g. the statements on the ultimate value of the Council's activities. On the other hand, certain positions were steadfastly maintained despite changes in the chairmanship of the Council, not to mention the identity of the secretary-general: e.g. the policy of refusing to support jazz between 1946 and 1969. Quibbling apart, out exercise in what Mr Findlater chooses to call 'textual and linguistic scholarship' – otherwise known as 'actually bothering to read what publicly accountable bodies are forced to publish' – has demonstrated that the Arts Council is indeed committed to a definite set of objectives in terms of which it hopes presumably to be judged. This was far from obvious when we began our investigation; and it is still not obvious to many observers of the arts. Mr Findlater, for example, concedes that the size of the Council's annual grant in 1973 does warrant 'a formulation of

* First published in *Encounter*, December 1973 (written with K. King).

Cultural economics

principles', but he questions the need for such principles in past years when the annual grant was much smaller. Unfortunately, the Council does not share his strange theory of financial management. The Council's clearest statement of aims appeared in the eleventh Annual Report of 1955–6. Mr Findlater simply has not read the Annual Reports carefully enough.

When Mr Findlater turns to deeds instead of words, he is overwhelmed by the quantitative and qualitative advances in the arts in this country since the War, all of which he credits to the Arts Council, complaining only that 'the Council still does not tell us often and clearly enough *what* it is doing'. Mr Findlater thinks it is pointless to ask *why* the Council is doing what it is doing, and he is not sure precisely *what* it is doing. With friends like Mr Findlater, the Council hardly needs enemies.

Like Mr Findlater, we believe that public bodies should ultimately be judged by results but results cannot be assessed without a knowledge of intentions. If it is wrong to try to discover the intentions of a public body like the Arts Council by a careful reading of their official reports, why are such reports published at all and, by the way, published at subsidized prices?

22. Is the Arts Council cost-effective*

A careful perusal of the Annual Reports of the Arts Council, going back to 1946, leaves no doubt that the Council disburses its funds to satisfy a number of defined objectives. These may be summarized as: (a) the diffusion of the performing arts (music, opera, ballet and drama), and to a lesser extent the visual arts (museums and galleries), throughout the regions of Britain – in a phrase, 'to break the culture monopoly of London'; (b) to diffuse the performing and the visual arts among wholly new audiences; (c) to maintain and raise artistic standards in the performing arts; and (d) to encourage the emergence of new art forms as well as new creative artists.

The first question that arises is whether the Arts Council actually succeeds in achieving *any* of its avowed objectives. But that is only the first question. As all four objectives carry some weight in reaching a set of final decisions, what does the Council do when a particular decision scores high in respect of one objective but low in respect of another? After all, any decision designed to achieve multiple ends must involve some order of priorities among ends. But 'score' is a numerical term, and we have yet to demonstrate that any of the four objectives of the Council can be quantified, so as to permit us to infer after the event that a certain policy achieved one more effectively than another. Our principal task, therefore, is to show that it is at least possible to measure achievement of these objectives.

The first two aims that we listed appear to be similar. They involve the gaining of new audiences, either in London or in the provinces. Indeed, the Arts Council seems so far to have concentrated effort on regional diffusion in the belief that this will simultaneously achieve both 'vertical' (new audiences) and 'horizontal' (new regions) diffusion. But it is much easier to provide the arts for an eager audience which has been barred by distance than it is to create a new demand among members of the public who have been uninterested in consuming the arts. The Arts Council has, in fact, been far more successful in achieving a better geographical distribution of the arts than in attracting a wider cross-section of the population. There is evidence – however imperfect – that audiences all over Britain have shown themselves to be consistently homogeneous in age, education and social background. With hindsight, we may lay down the general rule that a changing composition of audiences does not

* First published in *New Society*, 3 January 1974: 7–10 (written with K. King).

come as a simple by-product of increasing provision of the arts. Only a determined policy to attract a different type of audience will achieve this.

The idea of diffusing the arts 'horizontally' to the regions is not specific enough to help us in evaluating alternative policies. 'The provinces' is too vague a term. The cost of encouraging the arts in cities, with a catchment area large enough to provide a ready-made audience, may be far less than that of providing it in small and inaccessible towns. In practice, the Council emphasizes large and medium-sized cities.

The Council, however, is then faced with deciding what form the supply should take. Regional diffusion can be achieved in two main ways, either by extensive touring by London-based companies or alternatively by the establishment of permanent arts centres. Though touring is essentially a short-term policy, and arts centres are a long-term one, the shortage of funds implies conflict between them. More and more has been spent on touring in recent years it seems; it rose to slightly more than £500,000 out of a total budget of £14 million in 1972–3. So the goal of meeting an immediate demand seems to be given priority over the aim of investing in the long-term future of the arts outside London. If supplying existing demand *is* the overriding goal, an obvious first step would be to carry out surveys to determine the catchment area per unit of expenditure. The results could then be compared to the cost of attracting the same number of people by permanent arts centres. The Council can then ask itself if the cost of gaining new audiences by concentrating expenditure on arts centres is a more effective use of funds than spending increasingly large sums of money on touring. Unfortunately, the Council has failed to survey potential demand adequately; hence it is in no position to pose these questions.

Apart from touring, there are, at present, two chief ways in which the arts are supplied outside London: (a) regional theatres and orchestras, directly subsidized by the Arts Council (£1,800,000 to theatres in 1972–3); and (b) what is done locally by the Regional Arts Associations (to which the Council gave £782,000 in 1972–3). Some local authorities also maintain their own arts departments (as well as contributing to the regional associations). This haphazard system of patronage has led both to an arbitrary division of power, and an arbitrary division of identical responsibilities. Theatres, for example, receive grants from the Arts Council, the local authorities and, to a lesser extent, private industry. Regional Arts Associations also receive money from the same three sources but they act independently of the theatres. The Council has long realized that the aim of 'horizontal' diffusion cannot be realized without more local participation and provision. The ultimate aim, therefore, remains that of local self-sufficiency. But diverse sources of patronage do not encourage an overall growth of local arts provision unless they are rationally co-ordinated. The Council has now acquired a Regional Director and money spent on the regions has sharply increased. But the present administrative structure continues to hinder the development of a comprehensive policy of promoting the arts in the regions. In short, the question of how successful the Council has been in achieving its goal of diffusing the arts to the regions, cannot be answered until the term 'diffusion' has been clarified; and until the Council has faced up to the need to base its policies on established facts, rather than on casual impressions.

Turning now to 'vertical' diffusion, the evidence continues to point overwhelmingly to an educated, middle-class audience, with a conspicuous absence of the working class. The composition of audiences cannot have changed significantly during the past 28 years of the Council's existence. Nor is there any indication that a change is in the making. Even if it were, the Council would hardly be aware of it. It has commissioned only three audience surveys in its entire history, all of which date from the late 1960s, and the only comprehensive survey of London audiences was in fact undertaken privately by two Americans.

And the Council has refused to accept what little evidence there does exist. Its 1969 *Report on Opera and Ballet* contains results of surveys carried out in Leeds and Glasgow, and at Sadler's Wells in London, which showed an average of 5 per cent of the audience to be manual workers. But the same report blithely talks of opera and ballet attracting a growing audience from a cross-section of the community: 'There is hardly a limit to audience expansion ... Ballet and dance theatre can draw an audience as large as any other branch of the theatre or cinema.'

Information about audiences is of paramount importance to the work of the Council. It is the *only* way to ascertain the success of a policy of gaining new converts. It is not simply a matter of 'head counting'. A larger audience may mean more attendances by an identical number of people. The ideal census should show not only the frequency of attendance, age, education, occupation, and distance travelled, but also the level of family income. The distribution of audiences by occupation or by social class does not necessarily reveal the ability of the consumer to pay.

Surveys should be taken at a wide range of events. Those which have so far been carried out have been limited in scope, concentrating on opera, ballet and drama. No surveys have yet been undertaken of fringe theatre, poetry readings and jazz events, all of which are being increasingly subsidized. Having discovered the composition of existing audiences, the next step is to find out more about the causes of the apparently limited appeal of the arts. It is here that in-depth interview methods, advocated by the 1969 Mann report on provincial audiences, would be most useful. It is irrational to talk of attracting new audiences, while subsidizing arts events (without further justification) which the majority refuse to attend.

With a limited budget and conflicting goals the Council must decide on the relative importance of those goals. To be cost-effective, the distribution of subsidies should then reflect these priorities. Each category of audience should be assigned weighted values according to the importance attached to attendance within that category. Audiences could then be compared to the percentage of total subsidy absorbed by each art form.

But all this presupposes a detailed specification of aims. For example, if the results of a survey showed that a major part of its subsidy was being spent on a particular art form which had limited appeal, the Council would have to ask itself if it would be a more effective use of subsidy to withdraw patronage and redirect it elsewhere. If the objective of the Arts Council is to provide the arts, regardless of who benefits, the answer would be an emphatic No. But if the Council sees its aims as reaching entirely new audiences, positive action in redirecting subsidies would be more cost-effective.

Both costs and the ability of the consumer to pay must be taken into account when allocating subsidies. Decisions on whether or not to withdraw subsidies will depend on the potential effect on demand. Obviously, such an evaluation depends on the consumer's income and the actual rate at which each set of prices is subsidized.

Take the case of subsidized theatre. To talk of average subsidy per seat is as meaningless as referring to 'the average price of a seat'. Ticket prices vary with the position of the seats in the theatre. The same level of overall subsidy is compatible with widely differing structures of ticket prices – i.e. the distribution of cheap and expensive seats in a house. The problem is to find by how much a subsidy has reduced the 'true' cost of seats of different prices. Without this, there is no way of finding out which section of the audience is benefiting most. This, together with information about audience incomes, would show what proportion of the subsidy is going to whom. It would enable the Council to discriminate more effectively in favour of specific groups.

Ticket pricing policies are still based largely on conventional rules of thumb among theatre owners and producers. The belief is widely held that further increases in ticket prices would choke off demand. Yet a recent Arts Council report on seat prices concluded that many subsidized provincial theatres had scope to raise their prices; that ticket prices had lagged behind the rise in average earnings since 1963; that middle and high-priced seats were more frequently sold out than low-priced seats; that higher ticket prices on Friday and Saturday evenings went with larger audiences; and that, in general, audiences were more responsive to events than to prices. Exactly the same phenomena were observed in London for opera, drama and concerts, with the possible exception of the most expensive seats at the Royal Opera House and at Sadler's Wells at the Coliseum. The report concludes that, 'in the provinces in particular, the grant [of the Arts Council] is used to keep certain prices below a level at which they could be kept without reducing the size of audiences; and this is the case for all the performing arts which we have examined ... In the case of the subsidized London theatres, we would certainly consider it feasible to increase the number of seats sold at middle prices.' Nevertheless, in his introduction to the report, Sir Hugh Willatt, the Secretary-General of the Council, summarizes its findings in these words: 'Although certain price increases are recommended ... the Council welcomes the fact that there is no recommendation for across the board increase' – which, while strictly correct, hardly does justice to the flavour of the report.

In general, the Council has shown little flexibility in considering alternative methods of financing the arts. At present, subsidy applications in the performing arts are based on an annual estimate of revenues. There is an unwritten rule that no application is considered if box office receipts account for less than 45–50 per cent of total costs. But the present policies of the Council appear to give producers no incentive to maximize ticket revenues. A company which shows a profit at the end of the year gets a corresponding cut in subsidy. The Council's own report on orchestral resources suggested that 'too little drive and imagination have been shown in filling the 20 per cent or more of empty seats'. Thus, few British theatres and concert halls lower ticket prices before the performance begins. This is standard practice in some American cities.

The problem of inappropriate incentives could be tackled by switching the subsidies from producers to consumers, by means of a 'ticket voucher' scheme. Theatres and concert halls would charge commercial prices, and a certain proportion of seats would be made available for a specific group (children, students, old age pensioners, trade union members), who would pay for their seats with issued vouchers. The vouchers would then be exchanged by the management for cash. Alternatively, the grant-giver could undertake to buy seats, and offer them directly to selected categories of individuals at a reduced price. This scheme has the enormous advantage of making the selection of beneficiaries as precise as possible.

A drawback of a voucher scheme – apart from possible voucher touting – is that the arts would then become far more consumer-orientated. Programmes would passively reflect, instead of actively stimulating, prevailing tastes. In the past, the Council has emphasized the need to subsidize more esoteric art. The crux of the issue, however, is not simply 'arts for the masses' versus 'arts for the elite'. The trade-off is better seen as that of spending more on inducing the uninitiated to start attending artistic events tailored to their untrained tastes, as against spending more on educating existing audiences to demand modern music and poetry. It all depends on which sector of the population the Council considers to be more important, and whether or not 'art for art's sake' is sufficient grounds for a subsidy policy.

A study, commissioned by the Northern Arts Association, to examine whether or not its youth voucher scheme was achieving its intended aims, illustrates the point. The scheme was designed to encourage young people between the ages of 15 and 21 to attend artistic events – particularly uncommitted young people who would not attend of their own initiative and in their own time. Anyone under 21 years was eligible to receive a book of vouchers. When presented at any event subsidized by the Northern Arts Association, this entitled the holder to a cut in the ticket price. The scheme was extremely popular. Demand reached some 5,000 voucher-book applications per month. But the report concluded that the goals of the scheme were not being achieved. Only 2–7 per cent of the uptake fitted the description of the idea user: 'an apprentice or working person who left school at 15, who individually obtains and chooses tickets for arts events'. Results showed that 96 per cent of the users were in full-time education, and 75 per cent attended artistic events in organized school parties. However desirable the attendance of school children may be the spending of large subsidies on a captive audience was not the express aim. In that sense, the scheme was rejected as a failure. Even voucher schemes have problems.

So much for attempts at vertical or horizontal diffusion. From its earliest days, the Arts Council has been preoccupied with its third aim, raising standards of performance. Most people feel that it is impossible to measure success here because artistic excellence is necessarily subjective. Moreover, comparison between two different productions is seen as out of the question because the differences between a badly produced and a well-produced performance makes them virtually different products.

But the issue is not how to convert subjective assessments into objective ones, but rather how to reduce the arbitrariness inherent in all aesthetic judgement. The total impact of a performance on a member of the audience can never be gauged accurately. But many of the contributory factors are purely technical. Lighting, seating, orchestral playing, the standard of acting, the amount of time spent in rehearsal, the quality of the scenery and costumes – these are all matters on which there is likely to be broad agreement among experts. 'Objective knowledge' is merely knowledge about which there is universal agreement. 'Subjective knowledge' is knowledge about which there is usually no agreement whatever. A great many aesthetic judgements fall between these two extremes. Judgements about standards of performance – rather than about the lasting value of what is being performed – tend to lie nearer the objective end of the continuum. A panel could compare two performances in terms of 'better' or 'worse'. Given the costs of producing a 'better' performance, the panel would find itself gradually working towards judgements about 'how much better' or 'how much worse'. The panel would, in fact, be gauging the quality of productions in relation to their subsidies.

The problem becomes more complicated in practice because, of course, raising standards of performance may pre-empt subsidies that could have been devoted to other objectives. The Arts Council itself certainly recognizes a conflict between the cost of raising standards and the cost of attracting new audiences. The policy of subsidizing both Covent Garden and Sadler's Wells is a case in point. Though opera sung in English is more popular, many music critics regard it as inferior to opera sung in the original language. The Council has accordingly subsidized Covent Garden to maintain high standards (£1,750,000, or 17 per cent of its budget for England in 1972–3), and at the same time has subsidized the Coliseum (£935,000 or 9 per cent), to encourage more people to go to opera. As these figures show, opera sung in the original is, unfortunately, more expensive to produce than opera in English. A given subsidy for opera can produce either a modest rise in standards at Covent Garden, or a massive increase in audience size at the Coliseum. Objective measurement does not help us here. To reach a decision, we have to rank our preferences among the two objectives. The Arts Council has never committed itself explicitly on this question. We can only infer from its respective subsidies that it gives greater weight to raising artistic standards.

The Arts Council's fourth aim – that of encouraging young artists to experiment with new art forms – has only recently come into prominence. So far, it is apparent that the Council attaches little weight to this. Only a minute fraction of expenditure at present goes on direct aid to artists, either in the form of grants to individuals or in commissions of new works. In 1972–3, the total was £126,000.

It the goal is to stimulate the emergence of new art forms, the Council might in principle evaluate the success of its policy by asking not only how many nascent art forms have been encouraged by the provision of a grant, but also how many similar ventures exist without help from the Council. If, on the other hand, the goal is rather to encourage avowedly experimental artists, we run immediately into the problem that those artists requiring financial assistance are precisely the ones who have not found public favour.

So it is very difficult to find criteria to distinguish the neglected genius from the neglected charlatan. It is simpler to earmark a set sum for such a goal, and to hope for the best. Research councils in the natural and social sciences have long been in the habit of setting aside a fraction of their budget for pure research in some critical area, the outcome of which is totally unpredictable. There is nothing wrong with this. The sum set aside for this purpose automatically provides a measure of the importance assigned to a search for answers that may well not be there. As the moment, the Arts Council devotes about 1 per cent of its budget to encouraging new art forms. Yet it emphasizes this goal in all its Annual Reports. Unless this is an area where the expenditure of small sums yields enormous results– which we doubt – this is somewhat inconsistent.

We have so far confined our argument to the Arts Council. But the debate on museum and gallery charges, which came into effect this week, highlights the danger of thinking about the arts in administrative compartments. Various arguments were used by the government to justify its decision to impose entrance charges. But the principal one was that if people were able and willing to pay for the pleasure of attending concerts and plays, they ought to be able and willing to pay for museums and galleries: there is no distinction in principle between the performing and the visual arts. Some economists, however, have argued that the analogy is not tenable. One function of prices is to ration goods and services that are in scarce supply. If entrance to the opera and theatre were free, excessive demand would almost certainly result. But free entry to museums and galleries has not led to overcrowding. So there is no reason to charge for entry.

This argument has obvious merit. But it does ignore the fact that the visual and performing arts compete with one another for resources. At present, the combined subsidies for museums and art galleries (about £30 million) exceed the Arts Council's subsidies to the rest of the arts put together. This, of course, is due to the fact that the visual arts have been quite freely provided, while box-office revenue finances approximately 45 per cent of the costs of producing the performing arts.

If we assume that the clash between private and social interests is somehow more manifest for the visual than for the performing arts, the argument implies that everyone is willing to pay taxes to guarantee the existence of museums and galleries, though no one is willing as a private citizen to pay to enter a museum of gallery. If museums and galleries were like defence – 'The more there is for you, the more there is for me; so why should I pay for it' – there would be nothing irrational in the willingness to pay taxes to support museums and galleries, while refusing to pay entry charges. But, of course, the analogy is false; and the consequences of free museums and galleries is to reduce the funds that might be devoted to supporting the performing arts.

To be sure, the role of museums and galleries in preserving what already exists is different from that of the live performing arts. But because most major museums and galleries are in London, finance for them circumscribes the diffusing of the arts throughout the regions, not to mention the stimulation of new art forms. Yet how many museums and galleries purchase acquisitions with any attention to public tastes? The tendency of prices to ration what is scarce is only one of its economic functions. Another is to reflect consumers' preferences. In that sense, there *is* an economic argument for museum and gallery charges. If the government does, in the long run, save on subsidies to museums, the money saved ought perhaps go to the performing arts because horizontal and vertical diffusion is better satisfied by spending on these than on the visual arts.

Those who are shocked by this are merely exemplifying the tendency towards compartmentalized thinking about the arts. Both the Arts Council and museum charges can only be satisfactorily discussed in terms of public patronage of the arts as a whole. And in assessing such patronage, the technique of 'cost-effectiveness analysis', 'systems analysis', 'output budgeting', 'management by objectives' – it hardly matters what we call it – is just as applicable as it is to defence, health or education, areas in which it has been successfully applied in recent years. It may be impossible to agree on the ultimate value of Stockhausen's works. But it is not impossible to agree whether a 'new music grant' to a orchestra does, or does not, gain new converts to modern music. It may be impossible to reach a national consensus on what the regions 'deserve' by way of a subsidy. But it is not impossible to reach a consensus on whether local initiative in the arts is better stimulated by an Arts Council grant to the Regional Arts Associations, or by a matching grant from the Treasury direct to local authorities. And so forth, and so forth.

If this much be granted, the rest of our case follows. Ultimate ends are a matter of value-judgements, but means to achieve ends are capable of being objectively assessed. Often, in public expenditure analysis, the difficulty is that of discovering what the goals really are. The Arts Council, however, as we have emphasized, has in fact declared its objectives, though not always with sufficient precision. But having taken the plunge of being quite explicit about its aims, the Council has failed to investigate the degree to which its grants have succeeded in achieving the stated aims. It has neatly avoided the issue of self-evaluation up to now by assuming that the arts cannot be assessed 'objectively'. This confuses aesthetic judgements with the question of measuring the consequences of disbursing funds in one way rather than in another.

23. Why are Covent Garden seat prices so high?*

INTRODUCTION

Seat prices at the Royal Opera House, Covent Garden were raised this season (September 1975) by an average of 22.5 per cent: top price seats for say, Wagner's *Ring Cycle* now cost £11, and although the cheapest seats in the house go down to 50 pence, even standing room for Wagner runs to £2. To be sure, this steep rise in seat prices is well below the British inflation rate of 25–27 per cent over the last 12 months. Nevertheless, this is the second increase at the Royal Opera House in ten months and even last year some people felt that both ballet and opera were becoming too expensive. The 1974–5 Arts Council grant to the Royal Opera House was £2.55 million and one of the purposes of that grant is to bring ballet and opera within the reach of everyone. Given that objective, we may well ask: is it really necessary to charge such high prices to produce ballet and opera of outstanding quality? What is the explanation for the persistently high levels of ballet and opera seat prices at Covent Garden? Is it due to the high fees of international stars? Is it due to the tendency to perform too many unpopular modern ballets and operas? Or is the answer to be found in the lavishness of new productions? Whatever the reason, is there no way of having the same quality of ballet and opera performances at much lower seat prices?

Our object here is to put such questions to the test. What we are going to do is play a game: suppose such and such were altered, everything else being the same – what then would be the level of seat prices? But the time we have finished playing this game, we will have a pretty shrewd idea why ballet and opera seat prices at the Royal Opera House are what they are. This does not tell us what they *should* be but it does put readers in a position to make up their own mind about seat prices.

The fun of a game lies in playing it, but for those who want to know straight away what it all adds up to, let me give away the main conclusions at the outset. We will show that it is not 'unpopular' ballets and operas, nor new productions, nor the alleged extravagance of productions that keeps ballet and opera seat prices at Covent Garden as high as they are. Any opera house combines the resources

* First published in *Journal of Cultural Economics*, **2**(1), June 1987: 1–20.

of a symphony orchestra with those of a repertory theatre and as a rough rule we can say that an opera set will usually cost as much as a ticket to a concert plus a ticket to a theatre. Nevertheless, seats at the Royal Opera House, Covent Garden cost more than seats at the English National Opera, the London Coliseum. The principal reason for this is the presence of guest stars at the Royal Opera House due to the Covent Garden policy of performing opera at international standards in the original language.

There is the further complication that the Royal Opera House also supports two ballet companies. We will demonstrate that if opera of international standing is to be available at Covent Garden the whole year round, opera seat prices have to be higher at Covent Garden than at the London Coliseum. Moreover, unless the level of the Arts Council grant keeps up with the level of inflation in Britain, seat prices at both opera houses will soon have to go higher still, in which case our only consolation will be that they have yet some way to go to catch up with the Metropolitan Opera House in New York. Seat prices could be lower at the Royal Opera House – but only if there were fewer guest artists, less opera and more ballet, or of course a larger Arts Council grant. If the use of guest artists declined, the Royal Opera House would come to duplicate the London Coliseum in so far as opera is concerned, and would thus lose what seems to me to be its unique reason for existence. And if the ratio of ballet to opera increased, it might endanger the equal partnership presently enjoyed by the Royal Opera Company and the Royal Ballet Company at Covent Garden.

My basic point is that a decision about seat prices is really a decision about the artistic policy of the Royal Opera House. We can have almost any level of seat prices we like but we cannot have the same quantity and quality of ballet and opera, whatever the level of seat prices. After reading this article, you may or may not approve of the policies of the Royal Opera House. But you will certainly know why you approve or disapprove.

THE REAL COST OF SEATS

The first question we are going to ask is: what is the true cost of a seat in the Royal Opera House? To put it differently: what is the subsidy to seat prices implied by the Arts Council grant? At first glance, the answer to that question is quite simple: all we have to do is to calculate the increase in seat prices that is required to raise the same revenue as the annual grant of the Arts Council. But surely, it will be objected right away, people would not come to the Opera House in the same numbers if seat prices were higher? True, but let us take care of that difficulty in a second round of the exercise. First, let us ask the fundamental question: how high would seat prices have to be if there were no Arts Council grant, assuming the same attendance at the same number of performances?

Seat position	No. of seats	Price schedule (£) (including VAT) A	B	C	D

HOUSE PLAN   Stage

ORCHESTRA STALLS (SIDE / SIDE, Front centre, Centre, Rear)

Seat position	No. of seats	A	B	C	D
Front centre	164	5.00	6.50	8.00	9.50
Centre & sides	202	4.50	5.80	7.20	8.70
Rear	199	3.50	4.50	5.60	6.70

STALLS CIRCLE (STAGE SIDE / STAGE SIDE, Front centre, Rear centre, Standing)

Seat position	No. of seats	A	B	C	D
Front centre	87	4.50	5.80	7.20	8.70
Rear centre & sides	117	3.50	4.50	5.60	6.70
Stage	98	2.50	3.20	4.00	4.80
Standing	43	1.00	1.30	1.60	1.80

GRAND TIER (BOXES / BOXES, Tier)

Seat position	No. of seats	A	B	C	D
Tier	138	5.00	6.50	8.00	9.50
Boxes (4 seats)	13×4	14.00	18.00	22.40	26.80

BALCONY (BOXES / BOXES, SIDE / SIDE, Centre)

Seat position	No. of seats	A	B	C	D
Centre	61	3.50	4.50	5.60	6.70
Sides	98	2.50	3.20	4.00	4.80
Boxes (4 seats)	10×4	10.00	12.80	16.00	19.20

AMPHITHEATRE (UPPER SLIPS, LOWER, SIDE, Front centre, Centre, Rear)

Seat position	No. of seats	A	B	C	D
Front centre	95	1.70	2.00	2.40	2.80
Centre & sides	310	1.40	1.70	2.00	2.30
Rear & lower slips	247	1.00	1.30	1.60	1.80
Upper slips	143	0.60	0.70	0.80	1.00

PERFORMANCES

	A	B	C	D

Madam Butterfly, Ballet performances ————————————| |

Le Nozze di Figaro, *La Clemenza di Tito*, Ballet guest performances ┘ |

Tannhäuser ————————————————————————————|

La Traviata, *Un Ballo in Maschera* ————————————————————|

Figure 23.1   Seating plans and seat prices, Royal Opera House, Covent Garden

Throughout this and all remaining calculations we will fix our attention not on current seat prices, but on those that prevailed in a typical sample period – the second half of the financial year 1974–5, ending in April 1975. We do not want to clutter the argument by attempting to predict the reaction of the audience to the new higher level of seat prices that came into effect in September 1975.

The price of an individual seat in the Royal Opera House depends on the location of that seat and on the event in question. Ballet seats in the period we are looking at were sold at two different price schedules, A and B. Opera seats, however, were sold at four different price schedules, A to D. In the booking period December 1974 to February 1975, these were the performances at various prices.

All this is terribly complicated and to simplify the presentation, we are going to select some representative seat prices in different parts of the house (see Figure 23.1): (a) 'best seats' costing at least £5 – 302 seats in Orchestra Stalls A to M and Grand Tier; (b) 'average seats' costing at least £2.50 – 238 seats in Stalls Circle Sides B and C, Balcony Boxes, and Balcony Stalls Side Blocks; and (c) 'worst seats' costing 60 pence to £1 – 163 seats in upper slips and with restricted viewing in lower slips. From now on, we will look only at those 703 seat prices, about a third of the total number of seats in the house, although of course the actual calculations are carried out on all seats.

In the current season, these representative categories are as listed in Table 23.1.

Table 23.1 Actual seat prices in selected parts of house, 1975–6 (£)

Price Schedules	Best Seats	Average Seats	Worst Seats
A	6.30	3.40	0.60
B	7.50	4.00	0.80
C	9.50	5.00	0.90
D	11.00	6.00	1.00

But in the period we are looking at, December 1974 to April 1975, they were somewhat lower (Table 23.2).

Table 23.2 Actual seat prices in selected parts of house, 1974–5 (£)

Price Schedules	Best Seats	Average Seats	Worst Seats
A	5.00	2.50	0.60
B	6.50	3.20	0.70
C	8.00	4.00	0.80
D	9.50	4.80	1.00

And now for our first calculation. How high would seat prices have to be if there were no Arts Council grant? House receipts from regular box office sales (excluding VAT) totalled £1,757,414 in the financial year 1974–5. The Arts Council grant for the same period was £2,550,000. Total income in 1974–5 was therefore the sum of these two figures, or £4,307,414 (plus another £434,131 from broadcasts, films, recordings, donations, profit on sales of programmes, food and drink, etcetera). Our problem, therefore, is to calculate the increase of seat prices that would have produced box office sales of £4,307,414 net of VAT.

Of course, seat prices can be raised in many different ways: (a) by equal *percentage* amounts across all seats; (b) by equal *absolute* amounts across all seats; (c) by raising best seats and average seats only; and (d) by raising worst seats only. Once again, to simplify the presentation of our findings, we are going to concentrate largely on the first alternative, namely, equal percentage amounts across all seats. If the Royal Opera House had raised all seat prices in 1974–5 by equal percentage amounts so as to manage without the Arts Council grant, seat prices would have been 150 per cent higher.

A crude way of estimating the subsidy to seat prices implied by the Arts Council grant is to deduct the actual seat prices ruling in December 1974 (Table 23.2) from the prices in Table 23.3. For example, we might conclude that the audience sitting in the centre of the orchestra stalls in December 1974 to hear *La Traviata* paid £9.50 for each seat, but all British taxpayers (including themselves) contributed another £14.30. Likewise, the audience in the upper slips paid £1 for a seat that really cost £2.50. This conclusion is misleading on two counts. A limited number of orchestra stalls and boxes are sold at a premium of about 45 per cent above announced box office prices. Furthermore, it has always been a house policy to keep seats in the upper and lower slips at prices which the young and the less well-off can afford, being less than the very lowest West End cinema and theatre prices. In other words, the implied Arts Council subsidy to the worst seats is almost certainly more than £1.50 and that means that it is less than £14.30 to the best seats.

Table 23.3   Hypothetical seat prices, assuming no Arts Council Grant, 1974–5 (£)

Price Schedules	Best Seats	Average Seats	Worst Seats
A	12.50	6.80	1.50
B	16.30	8.00	1.80
C	20.00	10.00	2.00
D	23.80	12.00	2.50

Note: All the figures in this and subsequent tables are rounded to the nearest 10 pence.

WIPING OUT THE DEFICIT

All this is very interesting, the reader may be saying, but why bother? So long as the Arts Council is willing to go on making its grant to the Royal Opera House – for good or for bad reasons – why calculate what seat prices would have to be if the Arts Council disappeared beneath the waves? The whole exercise may be fun, but is of no practical relevance.

On the contrary, however, the purpose of our first calculation is to provide a backdrop to all the others and to show what the Arts Council grant means in hard cash to all individuals buying a seat. Besides, the Arts Council grant has failed in recent years to keep up with the inflation of costs in the performing arts, in consequence of which the budgetary deficit of the Royal Opera House has risen since 1973 to something like 5 per cent of total receipts. Seat prices were recently raised, as we mentioned earlier, by an average of 22.5 per cent. We can now ask: what level of seat prices in 1975–6 would have wiped out the estimated deficit in the current financial year?

Assuming no audience reaction to increased prices, the answer is that seat prices would then have had to be put up in September 1975, not by 22.5 per cent, but by 35 per cent. If that increase had been spread by equal percentage amounts over all the seats in all price schedules, top prices for opera would now be £12.80 instead of £11.00, and even the worst seats for ballet would cost 80 instead of 60 pence.

AUDIENCE RESPONSE TO HIGHER PRICES

Before proceeding, we must take a moment to consider the question of attendance rates at higher prices. We have been assuming that the public would accept seat prices as high as £23.80 and would attend performances at such prices in the same numbers as before. If this assumption is false – which it almost certainly is – seat prices would have to go even higher to raise a total of £4,307,414. The question is: how high are the prices that the traffic will bear?

We can give no *precise* answer to that question. No market research can tell us how people will react to prices they have never experienced, particularly in a period when their wages and salaries, as well as the cost of living, are also going up by amounts they have never experienced. What we can ask is how they have responded in the past, and in particular whether high-priced seats have proved to be more difficult to sell than medium- and low-priced seats.

Let us take ballet and opera separately. Ballet is easier to deal with because the rate of attendance at ballet performances has remained relatively constant at 92–94 per cent over the last 4–5 years. Average box office receipts per ballet performance have crept up from £4,100 in 1972 to £5,400 in 1975, due either to increased seat prices, or to a larger number of higher-priced performances. So far at any rate, the ballet public has accepted a continuous rise in seat prices at a rate slightly above the rise in retail prices. However, the rate of increase in both seat prices and retail prices over the last 24 months makes it difficult to extrapolate recent experience to a confident prediction about future ballet attendance rates. In particular, it provides no guide to what would happen if ballet seat prices had to be increased by 150 per cent as in our first calculation.

Opera attendances raise even more difficulties. Attendance rates at opera have fluctuated wildly from year to year, ranging from 84 per cent to 93 per cent. Average box office receipts per opera performance have edged up from £5,100 in 1971 to £7,200 in 1975, but in some years seat prices went up while attendance went down. Before concluding that this is evidence of price resistance, consider the low attendance rates at certain contemporary works, despite the fact that they are sold at the lower price schedules, in contrast to the extremely high attendance rates at certain favourites, which are sold at the higher price schedules. In general, it is true to say that the higher the price schedule, the higher the proportion of seats sold. In other words, the opera public seems to be sensitive, not so much to what they are paying, but to what and of course to whom they are listening (Table 23.4).

Table 23.4   Attendance rates at selected operas, 1974–5

Title and price schedule	No. of performances	Paid admissions as % of maximum possible receipts	Average box office Receipts net of VAT (£)
Owen Wingrave (A)	5	40	1,736
Jenůfa (A)	7	51	2,330
Don Pasquale (B)	6	72	4,808
Eugene Onegin (A)	6	91	4,220
Der Rosenkavalier (B)	6	97	6,658
Tosca (C)	3	98	8,720
Wozzeck (A)	3	73	3,366
Pelléas et Mélisande (B)	5	80	5,212
Un Ballo in Maschera (D)	7	96	9,727
La Traviata (D)	6	98	9,949

Note: The operas above the break were performed in 1974 before seat prices were raised in December 1974. Those below the line were performed in 1974–5 after the price rise. Price schedule C above the break corresponds to price schedule D below.

This is only part of the story: for any particular performance, seat prices also vary between different parts of the house. Are there any signs of price resistance for the best seats? The evidence on this score is highly ambiguous. In principle, we would like to compare paid admissions for identical operas performed by identical singers before and after a price increase. Such cases are obviously hard to come by and in consequence we have to settle for a comparison which fails to match like for like.

In December 1974 average opera seat prices were raised by 10 per cent. Table 23.5 gives the percentage of empty seats in different parts of the house for certain selected operas in the 1974 booking period just *before* the price increase. And Table 23.6 gives the figures for the booking period just after the 10 per cent price increase.

Table 23.5   Percentage of unsold seats for selected operas, 1974

Title and price schedule	Orchestra stalls	Stalls circle	Grand tier	Balcony stalls	Amphi-theatre	Slips	Standing room	Total
Jenůfa (A)	49.9	53.3	50.9	46.1	28.9	69.9	100.0	46.9
Don Pasquale (B)	15.2	24.9	43.4	29.7	11.3	71.6	100.0	26.5
Eugene Onegin (A)	0.0	0.0	0.0	0.7	0.0	10.4	65.5	2.4
Der Rosen-kavalier (B)	0.0	0.1	0.2	0.0	0.0	2.4	36.0	1.0
Tosca (C)	0.0	0.0	0.0	0.0	0.0	0.0	0.0	0.0
La Clemenza di Tito (B)	0.0	0.0	2.1	1.3	0.0	2.1	48.8	1.5

Table 23.6   Percentage of unsold seats for selected operas, 1974–5

Title and price schedule	Orchestra stalls	Stalls circle	Grand tier	Balcony stalls	Amphi-theatre	Slips	Standing room	Total
Wozzeck (A)	31.9	27.1	36.4	22.6	0.0	15.6	100.0	21.4
Un Ballo in Maschera (D)	0.3	0.2	1.6	0.6	0.0	0.7	14.0	0.7
La Traviata (D)	0.0	0.0	1.2	0.0	0.0	0.0	0.0	0.1
Madama Butterfly (A)	0.3	0.1	0.7	0.0	0.0	0.0	0.0	0.3
La Clemenza di Tito (B)	11.4	6.0	20.7	9.0	0.0	20.7	74.4	10.1

If we compare attendance at Mozart's *La Clemenza di Tito* before and after the price increase, we can see evidence of unwillingness to pay higher prices.

But even this comparison is spoiled by the fact that rarely heard operas by famous composers produce an initial interest that is not always sustained in subsequent performances. On the other hand, Verdi's *La Traviata* did just as well after the price increase at price schedule D as Puccini's *Tosca* at the equivalent schedule C before prices went up. And no matter how low the price schedule is for Janacek's *Jenůfa* or Berg's *Wozzeck*, these operas were poorly attended both before and after the price increase. It is perfectly clearly, therefore, that it might be possible to raise prices even more than 10 or even 22.5 per cent if productions were entirely confined to Mozart, Verdi, Puccini, Bizet and Wagner, and particularly to the more popular operas of those composers. In short, there is no clear evidence of price resistance even for the best seats, provided the operas in question are old favourites and provided they are performed by stars. Of course, increases of 10 to 22.5 per cent are still a far cry from 150 per cent.

There are two more sources of information about possible audience reactions to higher seat prices. One of them is the rate at which seat prices at the Royal Opera House have been increasing since 1967 as compared to prices in general: the evidence shows that the public for opera, like the ballet public, has not balked at seat prices rising almost as fast as the cost of living. The other source of information is what audiences pay in other countries. If it should prove to be true that American, German and Italian audiences pay more for ballet and opera than we do, after allowing for international differences in the standard of living, it would begin to suggest that still higher seat prices might be feasible in this country once we got used to it.

As one might imagine, such comparisons are fraught with difficulties. If we look around opera houses in the world, we can certainly find some that charge much higher prices that the Royal Opera House. For example, in December 1974, when top prices at Covent Garden were £9.50, top prices at the Vienna Opera House and La Scala, Milan were £12.50 and £9.85 respectively. On the other hand, most other opera houses in the world, such as those in Brussels, Cologne, Geneva, Hamburg, Lyons, Marseille, Basel and Zurich, did not at that time charge prices higher than £5.00.

However, such facts prove very little. First of all, the audiences of these countries also have vastly different incomes. Secondly, these are opera houses differing both in size and in the proportion of seats selling at differing prices. Thirdly, many of them give special discounts to students and old age pensioners on certain evenings in the week and others raise their prices for certain special events. In an effort to get around all these difficulties, we have made a new comparison of seat prices in five different countries. We have taken seat prices in the closing months of 1974 for an average production corresponding to price schedule B at the Royal Opera House. We have calculated the weighted average seat prices for each house in pounds sterling, which is to say that we have allowed for the way different seats are distributed in each opera house.

Table 23.7   Weighted average seat price in five opera houses, 1974

Opera House	Local currency	Equivalent pounds sterling	Equivalent pounds sterling adjusted for national differences in purchasing power
Covent Garden, London	£3.50	3.50	3.50
L'Opéra, Paris	FF 50	4.30	3.60
Staats Oper, Hamburg	25 DM	4.15	2.60
La Scala, Milan	4.813 liras	3.15	3.30
Metropolitan, New York	$14.28	6.10	4.70

Source: Statistical appendix, available from the author on request.

The final results of these calculations are revealed by the last column of Table 23.7: the real price of a ballet or opera ticket was lower in Germany and higher in new York than anywhere else, with Covent Garden falling just half-way between the two, which is precisely what we would expect to find knowing that opera is heavily subsidized in Germany and lightly subsidized in the United States. Real prices at the Royal Opera House, however, were already higher in December 1974 than in Paris, Hamburg or Milan, and since then they have gone up much faster than seat prices in France, Germany and Italy (but Hamburg raised its seat prices in 1975 by 18 per cent and Basel has recently put up its prices by 40–50 per cent).

The upshot of the comparison is to show that we would have been willing to pay 35 per cent more for ballet and opera prices in 1974 if only we had the spending habits of New Yorkers; even now in 1975, we are still paying somewhat less for ballet and opera in real terms than are New Yorkers. Of course, that may be true for ballet and opera, and even for theatre and food, but the opposite is true for housing and clothing. All of which is to say that one can never really *prove* anything by international comparisons because too many things are different between different countries. Still, it is good to know that we are not the only audience in the world that is paying a lot for ballet and opera.

DOING WITHOUT INTERNATIONAL STARS

So far, all the arguments about seat prices have pointed in an upward direction. Our opening comments, however, indicated several ways in which seat prices might be reduced. We turn now to the first of these cost-cutting scenarios, involving the replacement of singers, dancers, conductors, designers and producers with an international reputation commanding relatively high world salaries by artists with a purely domestic reputation engaged at standard, British salaries.

If the Royal Opera House had carried out all its commitments for the 1974–5 season without the use of a single guest artist, it would have saved £584,000 in the first instance. On the other hand, to carry out those commitments, it would have had to increase the number of artists engaged on contract, and it is estimated that this would have cost an extra £205,000. Thus the total saving would have been only £379,000. Nevertheless, if everything else had remained the same – particularly attendances – this would have permitted a reduction in seat prices across the board in December 1974 of 21 per cent. However, the absence of guest artists would make it necessary to cancel all the higher-priced schedules, which are only feasible at the moment because they feature artists that the public cannot hear and see every day. Nevertheless, even with the use of only two price schedules, A and B, it would still have been possible to have had seat prices ranging from 45 pence to £5.95 (Table 23.8)! It is interesting to notice that the resulting structure of seat prices would then be virtually identical to those obtaining at the time at the English National Opera (ENO), the London Coliseum (Table 23.9).

Table 23.8   Hypothetical seat prices, assuming no guest artists, 1974–5 (£)

Price Schedules	Best seats	Average seats	Worst seats
A	3.90	2.00	0.40
B	5.90	2.90	0.60

Table 23.9   Actual seat prices at the ENO, London Coliseum, October–December 1974 (£)

Price Schedule	Stalls	Dress circle	Boxes	Upper circle	Balcony	Standing Dress circle Upper circle
Don Carlos	5.20 to 4.10	5.20 to 4.10	3.00 to 1.80	2.40 to 1.80	1.10 to 0.80	0.50
All others	3.20 to 2.00	3.00 to 1.90	2.00 to 1.00	1.60 to 1.00	0.90 to 0.50	0.50

Note: Current prices at the London Coliseum (October–November 1975) are higher on Saturdays than on weekdays: on weekdays they are roughly 20 per cent higher and on Saturdays they are now about 30 per cent higher than the above table.

Thus, without guest artists at the Royal Opera House there would have been little to choose between Covent Garden and the London Coliseum, except for the language of performance. In that case, it would be difficult to see why the Arts Council should give £2.5 million to the Royal Opera House and only £1.3 million to the English National Opera (which also receives £275,000 from the Greater London Council). It is true that the Royal Opera House also supports two ballet companies in addition to an opera company, but that would hardly justify the additional grant of £1.2 million. Any tendency to equalize the Arts Council grant to both houses, however, would require higher prices at Covent Garden than at the London Coliseum, and would therefore drive Covent Garden out of business in the field of opera. In short, the idea of doing without guest artists at the Royal Opera House would imply the demise of opera at Covent Garden. If that is what is wanted, here is a formula for bringing it about.

DOING WITHOUT UNPOPULAR BALLETS AND OPERAS

The use of guest artists is one explanation of why seat prices are relatively dear at the Royal Opera House. But there are several other favourite explanations. One that is frequently mentioned is Covent Garden's policy of weaving contemporary and less-popular older works into the standard repertory of 'sure winners'. As we saw earlier, operas like *Owen Wingrave*, *Jenůfa* and *Wozzeck* produce attendance rates between 40–75 per cent, while *La Traviata*, *Madama Butterfly* and *Der Rosenkavalier* are always guaranteed to fill 96–98 per cent of all seats. As a matter of fact, in the financial year 1974–5, 30 different opera products were performed over 158 evenings; average attendance was 86 per cent but of the 30 productions, seven failed to produce the average attendance rate and a further four yielded attendance rates exactly equal to the annual average. Similarly, 1974–5 saw 110 ballet performances by the Royal Ballet Company with an average attendance rate of 92 per cent, of which eight evening and two matinee performances fell below the annual average.

Suppose we now define an 'unpopular' opera or ballet event as one which produces less than 90 per cent of maximum receipts. Suppose further that we replace each of these 'unpopular' operas and ballet performances by one which can be safely predicted to yield at least 95 per cent of maximum receipts for evening performances and 90 per cent for matinees. Clearly, this would generate additional revenue which could then be applied to reduce seat prices. Given this policy of suppressing 'unpopular' events, by how much would it be possible to lower opera and ballet seat prices?

The total impact of such a policy would be minuscule: if the extra revenue were applied to all seats across the board, seat prices in December 1974 would have come down by 5.5 per cent (Table 23.10)! The reason for this is simple:

'unpopular' operas and ballets are sold at low price schedules and filling the house to maximum capacity at low prices generates very little additional revenue.

Table 23.10   Hypothetical seat prices, assuming no 'unpopular' operas and ballets, 1974–5 (£)

Price Schedule	Best Seats	Average Seats	Worst Seats
A	4.70	2.30	0.50
B	6.10	3.00	0.60
C	7.50	3.80	0.70
D	8.90	4.50	0.90

   To sum up, going back to our earlier illustration, we can say that members of the audience sitting in the orchestra stalls in December 1974 to hear *La Traviata* paid 60 pence more for their £9.50 seat than they might have done if the Royal Opera House had ruthlessly weeded out every 'unpopular' work from its repertory. This is, surely, no great price for the objectives of stimulating public taste for new and less familiar works?

DOING WITHOUT NEW PRODUCTIONS

Perhaps we do not get very far by dropping all 'unpopular' ballet and opera, but what about the idea of giving up all new productions?

   Of the 110 ballet performances and 30 opera productions in the year 1974–5, nine one-act ballets and five opera productions were either new productions or major remakes. To have dropped these would have saved the production department £427,495. On the other hand, the Royal Opera House persuaded several private donors in 1974–5 to contribute a total of £165,000 to ballet and opera, expressly for the purpose of financing new productions. These donations would have been lost within new productions because no donor likes to attach his name to a repetition of an old production. Thus, the elimination of new productions would have saved, not £427,495, but only £262,495, and this would have permitted a reduction of seat prices in December, 1974 by only 14 per cent (Table 23.11)!

   In the short run, it is perfectly possible for an opera or ballet company to retain its vitality without new productions. But in the long run, there is hardly any doubt that the failure to introduce new productions will sap the morale of singers, dancers and the orchestra. A 14 per cent reduction in seat prices, while not trivial, can hardly justify so retrogressive a step as the elimination of all new productions.

Table 23.11   Hypothetical seat prices, assuming no new productions, 1974–5 (£)

Price Schedule	Best Seats	Average Seats	Worst Seats
A	4.30	2.20	0.50
B	5.60	2.70	0.60
C	6.90	3.40	0.70
D	8.20	4.20	0.90

CUTTING DOWN ON LAVISH PRODUCTIONS

No, it is not new productions that produce high prices. It is the extravagance of new productions: the leather costumes when PVC would do, the wooden seats when papier mache could have been used, etcetera. True, or not true?

It all depends on what is meant by 'extravagance'. Without closely examining each new production to see if the costs incurred are 'really necessary', there is little we can do other than to show what would be implied by certain stated reductions in the costs of new productions. Suppose that by diligent cheeseparing, we managed to shave off 10 per cent. How far would it then have been possible to reduce seat prices across the board in 1974–5? Answer: a mere 2.3 per cent! In whatever way we twist and turn in applying this reduction to different seats, orchestra stalls would still cost £9.25 and upper slips would still sell at 53 pence. If we cut production costs ruthlessly by another 10 per cent, which would of course be much more difficult to do without affecting the quality of new productions, prices could come down another 2.1 per cent, which is still an absurdly low amount. In short, the extravagant-production argument can hardly be taken seriously.

CHANGING THE MIX OF BALLET AND OPERA

There is still another way to reduce seat prices, however, which we have so far not mentioned. We spoke earlier of the higher average attendance rate at ballet than at opera performances but we have said nothing about the contribution that an individual ballet or opera performance makes to *net* receipts, that is, gross receipts minus the extra cost of that performance. An opera like *Jenůfa* at price schedule A may produce only 51 per cent of the maximum receipts that could have been earned that evening with that price schedule, but it may nevertheless contribute more to net receipts than *Tosca*, which fills 98 per cent of the seats at price schedule B, because it is relatively cheap to produce (similarly, an

expensive international singer may more than pay his way by filling the house
at high seat prices). Thus, the replacement of ballets and operas which contribute
little to net receipts by productions which contribute a great deal to net receipts
would provide us with yet another way of cutting seat prices. Most ballet
performances make a greater contribution than opera to the net receipts of the
house, partly because they are better attended and partly because they are
cheaper to mount. Therefore, by increasing the ratio of ballet to opera
performances in an artistic season, we increase the number of evenings that make
a relatively large contribution to net receipts. The result is that we save some
receipts which can then be applied to reduce seat prices for both ballet and opera.

In 1974–5, the ratio of ballet to opera performances (excluding galas and
proms) was 40:60 – there were two ballet matinees or evenings for every three
opera performances. If we altered this ratio to 50:50, it would be necessary to
produce an extra 25 ballet performances and to cut 25 opera performances. How
much extra revenue would this generate? It all depends on which operas we cut
out and which ballets we add. We have selected a representative cross-section
of 25 operas and 25 ballet evenings produced in the year 1974–5 to illustrate
the argument (Table 23.12). These 25 opera performances contributed £33,865
to the net receipts of the house. On the other hand, the 25 ballets contributed
£101,860 to net receipts. Thus, if we replaced the former by the latter, we would
release £67,995, which could then be applied to reduce all seat prices at both
ballet and opera – by 4 per cent.

Table 23.12   Net contributions of a sample of operas and ballets, 1974–5 (£)

Title and price schedule	Net contribution per performance	Number of performances	Total net contribution
Owen Wingrave (A)	1,940	5	9,700
Madama Butterfly (A)	2,920	3	8,760
La Bohème (B)	3,560	6	21,360
Tosca (B)	1,710	4	6,840
Otello (B)	3,170	7	22,190
Ballet I (A)	3,960	12	47,520
Ballet II (A)	4,180	13	54,340

Four per cent is not very much. But why stop at a 50:50 ratio of ballet to opera
performance? If we tipped the balance in favour of ballet to achieve a ratio of
60:40 instead of 40:60, the selection of another 25 operas for removal and another
25 ballets for addition would release still more revenue, allowing us to reduce
seat prices by 6 rather than 4 per cent.

Even 6 per cent is not very impressive but the same performance ratio of 60 ballet:40 opera might in a different financial year, with a different set of opera productions, produce quite a substantial reduction in seat prices. For example, in the financial year 1975–6 it is possible to show that the removal of ten carefully selected operas, amounting to 64 opera performances, and the addition of 62 ballet performances, so as to produce a 60:40 ratio of ballet to opera, would add as much as £370,000 to net receipts (Table 23.13). This sum could be used to reduce seat prices by the fairly substantial figure of 19 per cent, which would in fact put 1975 seat prices down to the levels prevailing in 1974; alternatively, it could have been used to wipe out the whole of the current budget deficit.

Table 23.13 Hypothetical seat prices, assuming 62 more ballets and 64 fewer operas, 1975–6 (£)

Price Schedule	Best Seats	Average Seats	Worst Seats
A	5.10	2.75	0.50
B	6.10	3.25	0.65
C	7.70	4.05	0.70
D	8.90	4.85	0.80

There is of course no way of knowing whether there is a demand in London for 62 more ballet performances over a whole season, that is, two to three more performances a week. Just because ballet attendance rates are now 92 per cent, it does not follow that they would stay that way if the number of ballet performances in one year rose from 110 to 170. Nevertheless, the fact remains that a little more ballet and a little less opera would ease the financial pressures on the Royal Opera House, and would thus work to hold down seat prices.

CONCLUSION

The Royal Opera House could resort less and less to guest artists of international standing; it could lean more heavily than it already does on old favourites; it could skimp on new productions; and it could increase the number of ballet performances at the expense of opera. All these measures would tend to hold down seat prices. But without a substantial increase in its Arts Council grant, the Royal Opera House could not significantly cut seat prices unless it drastically changed its basic artistic policy.

It is not my purpose to advocate. The choice is yours. Indeed, the choice is everyone's, including people who never go to ballet or opera, because everyone is paying for ballet and opera seats.

APPENDIX

The Annual Financial Report of the Royal Opera House throws further light on these problems. The following pages are taken from the Annual Report for 1974–5.

This summary has been extracted from the published accounts for the three years to 30 March 1975. The sharp increase (25 per cent) of expenditure in 1973–4 over 1972–3 is attributable to three main factors:

1. Due to extended London seasons by both ballet companies the number of performances outside the House in UK increased substantially from 138 to 187 and foreign touring reduced from 75 to 42 performances. The net result was an adverse movement to £75,000.
2. New production expenses were exceptionally low in 1972–3 and high in 1973–4 due to the timing of new productions in relation to the financial year rather than to any variation in the workload.
3. VAT was introduced on 1 April 1973 and resulted in the loss of £153,000 in House and touring receipts for 1973–4.

The Arts Council grant for 1973–4 although up by 17 per cent on 1972–3, did not compensate for all the above items and we were obliged to bring in a guarantee of £150,000, originally intended for the three years 1973–4 to 1975–6, to balance the books. There was a further grant from the Arts Council in 1974–5 of £100,000 towards losses of House receipts due to VAT. Thus the real subsidy for the two years 1973–4 and 1974–5 can be restated as follows:

1973–4 £2,195,000 (25 per cent up on 1972–3)
1974–5 £2,650,000 (21 per cent up on 1973–4)

This puts a different complexion on the grant of £3,200,000 for the current year. In a year when inflation has been running at approximately 27 per cent and we have still further increased our touring programme, our grant has increased by only 21 per cent on the adjusted grant for 1974–5. We are still facing a backlog of about £200,000 lost receipts per annum in relation to VAT.

Referring to the summary there are two significant trends. The decrease in the number of performances in the House is a cyclic variation due to the amount of time required to mount the *Ring* at the beginning of the Season. In years when the *Ring* is not given, more performances are possible. Secondly, there is a decline in House receipts etc. (expressed as a percentage of total expenses) from 46 per cent to 38 per cent. This is partly due to the fact that seat price increases lag behind salary and wage increases, and partly due to the smaller number of performances.

Financial Report, Year ended 30 March 1975

Summary of financial results 1972–3 to 1974–5

1. Year end position

1972–3		1973–4		1974–5	
	£		£		£
Deficit b/fwd	18,000	Surplus b/fwd	(38,000)	Deficit b/fwd	171,000
Surplus for Year	(56,000)	Deficit for Year	209,000	Deficit for Year	67,000
				Special Grants	(250,000)
Surplus c/fwd	(38,000)	Deficit c/fwd	171,000	Surplus c/fwd	(12,000)

2. Expenditure/income
   Figures are shown in £000s
   (%)s relate income to total expenditure for year

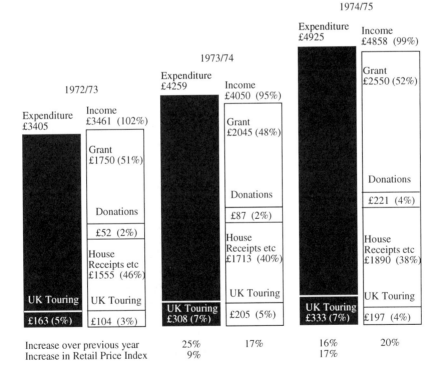

	1972/73	1973/74	1974/75
Increase over previous year		25%	17%	16%	20%
Increase in Retail Price Index		9%		17%	

3. Number of performances

	1972–3				1973–4				1974–5			
	House	London	UK	Abroad	House	London	UK	Abroad	House	London	UK	Abroad
Royal Ballet – main	127	–	–	48	117	27	–	35	109	–	31	40
Royal Ballet – touring	4	23	115	27	4	43	117	7	–	29	145	6
Royal Opera	167	–	–	–	171	–	–	–	160	–	–	–
Visiting companies	1	–	–	–	4	–	–	–	13	–	–	–
Total	299	23	115	75	296	70	117	42	282	29	176	46

4. Income and expenditure per seat sold

House

Expenditure £7.71

Premises and other costs £0.78
Front of House and Admin. £0.98
Stage and Transport £1.23
Revivals £0.51
New Prodns £0.44
Orchestra £0.82
Ballet Company £0.96
Opera Company £1.99

Income £3.52

Other £0.34
Box Office £3.18

UK Touring

Expenditure £2.59

Travel and Subsistence £0.47
Front of House and Admin. £0.25
Stage and Transport £0.28
Revivals £0.23
New Prodns £0.09
Orchestra £0.46
Ballet Company £0.81

Income £1.07

Other £0.10
Box Office £0.97

Notes
1. Touring expenditure does not include any overheads such as premises, accounting services, etc.
2. Donations towards new productions have been deducted from expenditure.

5. Average attendances

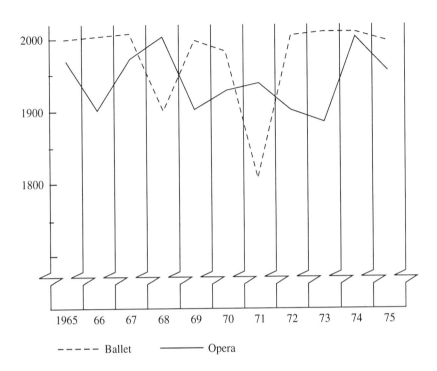

----- Ballet   ——— Opera

6. Costs of new productions (include ROH labour costs)

Ballet	1974–5 £	1973–4 £	Opera	1974–5 £	1973–4 £
The Entertainer	3,194		*La Clemenza di Tito*	45,232	
Elite Syncopations	3,951		*Das Rheingold/*		
Unfamiliar Playground	1,491		*Die Walküre*	115,913	
Four Schumann Pieces	1,859		*Faust*	83,522	
Shukumei	5,555		*Un Ballo in Maschera*	74,986	
The Four Seasons	12,820		Fees	49,455	
The Concert	3,631				
Arpège	2,208				
A Wedding Bouquet	1,670				
Fees	22,008				
	£58,387	£108,053		£369,108	£269,984

PART FIVE

Book Reviews

SECTION A

History of Economic Thought

24. Review of *The Collected Works of Walter Bagehot*, ed. Norman St John-Stevas, vols IX, X and XI: *The Economic Essays**

Bagehot is a name known to all monetary economists and to all historians of economic thought. *Lombard Street: A Description of the Money Market* (1873) must be the most frequently quoted book in the entire banking literature, and *Economic Studies* (1880) gets at least an honourable mention in all accounts of English economics between the days of Mill and Marshall. The latest edition of Bagehot's Collected Works in 13 volumes is sponsored by *The Economist* (in honour of its erstwhile editor) and edited by St John-Stevas, the author of a recent biography of Bagehot and of course the current leader of the House of Commons. The three volumes before us cover all of Bagehot's economic writings, including 106 articles written for *The Economist* which are here attributed to Bagehot for the first time. They also include a splendid new essay by Professor Sayers on 'Bagehot as an Economist' as well as an older assessment by Robert Giffen that appeared in the original, posthumous publication of *Economic Studies*. Like the rest of the *Collected Works*, these volumes are beautifully produced with helpful but unobtrusive editorial notes to identify obscure names or forgotten issues. The index is thorough and professional and there is even an index to Bagehot's epigrams (which curiously omits his funniest one: 'no real Englishman in his secret soul was ever sorry for the death of a political economist').

  Rereading *Lombard Street* is bound to be somewhat disillusioning: Bagehot's theory of central banking, with its fundamental distinction between the contrasting policies required to meet internal and external drains – lend freely on good commercial paper to meet internal drains, but do so at high interest rates so as to counter external drains – is too familiar to sustain our interest. Even his much-admired, ironic style soon begins to pall as one becomes aware that he fails to maintain any abstract argument for more than a few sentences at a time. The one chapter that can still make the modern reader sit up is the sixth, 'Why Lombard Street is Often Very Dull and Sometimes Extremely Excited', with

* First published in *Economica*, February 1979: 446–8.

its hint of a multiplier process (IX: 112), a psychological theory of the trade cycle resting on the mainspring of agricultural harvests, and abounding in such phrases as 'the excess of savings over investments' (IX: 118) – as a matter of fact, Bagehot distinguishes consistently between intended savings and intended investment (IX: 117, 118, 123–4, 274; X: 15, 25) and seems perfectly aware of their partial independence.

Professor Sayers in his introductory essay seems to share some of my misgivings about *Lombard Street* but he goes a little further to ask whether Bagehot's prescription of high interest rates in a 'panic' did not do much to aggravate slumps in subsequent years (IX: 33–4). Moreover, Professor Sayers shows that Bagehot was not as informed an observer of contemporary banking practice as is usually claimed; over and over again he was just a little out of date (IX: 35–6). In his *History of Economic Analysis*, Schumpeter likewise expresses some doubts about the reputation of *Lombard Street*: 'No doubt it is brilliantly written. But whoever turns to that book with its fame in mind will nevertheless experience some disappointment. Barring a plea for the reorganization of the management of the Bank of England and for a reform of English practice concerning gold reserves, it does not contain anything that should have been new to any student of economics.' But perhaps this judgement is unfair. Bagehot's book was addressed to Victorian businessmen, and for them it married what was at the time regarded as two irreconcilable ideas: the concept of central bank statesmanship and the philosophy of *laissez-faire*. Bagehot's *Lombard Street* did for the London money market what his *English Constitution* (1876) did for English government: it established a definite image that continued to haunt generations of readers long after the reality from which the image was drawn had faded away.

Bagehot's fragmentary and incomplete writings on the history of economic thought must, however, be judged on different grounds: they *were* directed at professional economists. His work is not easy to classify but he might be fairly described as an English historical economist (together with Cliffe Leslie, John Ingram, Arnold Toynbee and Thorold Rogers) with an unusual interest in questions of social psychology. His two essays, 'The Postulates of English Political Economy' (1876), which were considered sufficiently important by Marshall to warrant republication in 1885 with a preface by himself, started the hunt that has now gone on for 100 years for the explicit list of all the assumptions on which the deductive structure of Ricardian economics is based. Bagehot's unequivocal description of English classical economics as a valid but historically limited analysis of the heyday of capitalism (IX: 285–5) – a bourgeois piece of Marxist analysis that Marx may have read but certainly never acknowledged – still carries conviction, and his explanation of why it never proved to be a successful intellectual export (XI: 224–6) has never been improved on.

But apart from such striking observations, most of Bagehot's views on the history of economic thought were little short of banal. Adam Smith, Malthus, Ricardo and John Stuart Mill were the 'four great men' of the subject. But his Adam Smith is exclusively the Adam Smith of the *Wealth of Nations* and even here it is only Smith's view on policy questions that receive attention (IX: 299–328). Malthus is the Malthus of the *Essay on Population*, where indeed Bagehot had some sound criticisms to make (XI: 331–339), and Malthus's view on gluts are not even mentioned. In contrast to Malthus, Ricardo comes in for nothing but praise (XI: 236–7, 342–9), which is surprising in view of Bagehot's leanings towards the historical school (the essay on Ricardo, however, is unfinished). The treatment of Mill (XI: 157–4, 237, 394) is likewise focused almost solely on his social ideas and hardly begins to do justice to Mill's analytical contributions. In general, the most striking features of Bagehot's writings on the history of economic thought is the frequency with which he expresses dismay at the passing away of public interest in economics: 'It lies rather dead in the public mind. Not only does it not excite the same interest as formerly, but there is not exactly the same confidence in it' (XI: 223; also 280, 345). Remarks such as these convey the flavour of economic debates in the 1870s more vividly than the observations of any number of later observers. For this, if for no other reason, Bagehot is still worth perusing.

25. Review of *The Economics of David Ricardo*, by Samuel Hollander*

With the possible exception of Karl Marx, no great economist of the past has received so many divergent and even contradictory interpretations as David Ricardo. No sooner had he appeared on the scene but he attracted a number of ardent disciples who hailed him as the founder of a new rigorous science of political economy (Thomas de Quincey even went so far as to credit his cure from an opium addiction to the exhilarating effects of reading Ricardo). However, these were soon followed by an even larger number of detractors, who struggled, sometimes unsuccessfully, to escape from the grip of Ricardo's overwhelming influence on the economic thinking of his times. The leading economic textbook of the mid-nineteenth century, John Stuart Mill's *Principles of Economics*, paid tribute once again to Ricardo's genius, and secured his reputation with yet another generation of students. But with the onset of the 'marginal revolution' in the 1870s, Ricardo's star began to wane and many now agreed with Jevons that he had 'shunted the car of economic science on to a wrong line'. The fact that Marx hailed Ricardo as his intellectual mentor served, if anything, to accelerate the anti-Ricardian trend and even Marshall's charitable effort in his *Principles of Economics* to make the best case for him and to overlook each of his errors as the product of a clumsy style of expression failed to recuperate his declining reputation.

Ricardo has staged a comeback, however, in our own times. The turning point came with the publication of Piero Sraffa's slim masterpiece, *Production of Commodities by Means of Commodities* (1960). One of the many features of Ricardo's thinking that had puzzled generations of readers was his habit of expressing all his economic variables in terms of 'an invariable measure of value' – a hypothetical yardstick that even he himself admitted did not and could not exist as such. His trump card was 'the fundamental theorem of distribution' according to which 'profits are only low when wages are high'. Was this a proposition about the rate of profit and the rate of wages and, if so, was it true even if profits and wages were not measured in terms of the invariant yardstick? It was easy to see that it was only true on certain additional assumptions – a wage basket made up entirely of agricultural goods, labour as the only ultimately scarce

* First published as 'Marx's bourgeois mentor', *The Times Literary Supplement*, 11 April 1980.

factor of production, the absence of joint production, etc. – but the significance of the invariant measuring-rod still baffled most readers. In despair, they interpreted 'the fundamental theorem' of the inverse relation between profits and wages as a truism about relative shares of national income minus rents, thus implying that a man as clever as Ricardo wasted hundreds of pages defending a truism.

What Sraffa does in his book is to set up the Ricardian theorem in modern terms and then to show that, lo and behold, it is possible to construct a hypothetical 'money' in which to express prices such that relative prices are invariant to changes in profits and wages; therefore, a higher rate of profit must mean a lower rate of wages, and vice versa. This appears to rehabilitate Ricardo as having put his finger on a vital truth; it is possible, contrary to modern teaching, to divorce the determination of commodity prices from the determination of factor prices, and there is even a sense in which it may be said that, logically, the latter precedes the former. Coming from an author who was himself the editor of *The Works and Correspondence of David Ricardo*, Sraffa's reinterpretation of Ricardo could not be ignored.

It took little time for Marxist economists to perceive the significance of this Sraffian reading: the history of economic thought, they say, reveals two great branches, a general equilibrium branch leading down from Jevons, Walras, and even Marshall to the Samuelsons and Friedmans of today, in which all relevant economic variables are mutually and simultaneously determined, and a Ricardo–Marx–Sraffa branch in which distribution takes priority over pricing and in which economic variables are causally determined in a sequential chain starting from the real wage and hence the power relationships between capital and labour. Thus, 160 years after his death, Ricardo, that most bourgeois of all bourgeois economists, is back in business as one of the founding fathers of Marxian and radical economics. Such are the strange twists and turns of intellectual history.

The story of the chequered career of the Ricardian legacy must be continually kept in mind when reading this vast, authoritative work by Samuel Hollander, which follows on from his early work, *The Economics of Adam Smith* (1973). The introduction and the concluding chapter allude to that story; indeed they pour devastating scorn on the attempt of Sraffians to turn Ricardo into a forerunner of both Marx and Sraffa, but they do so in language that excludes not only the general reader but even economists who have not hitherto specialized in the history of economic thought. It is clearly written but so dense is the argument and so terse are the explanations that accompany the almost endless and lengthy quotations from primary sources that one's attention cannot be allowed to wander even for a moment.

After a brief introduction, we begin with 100 pages on the legacy of Adam Smith, which are designed to explain what, if any, were Ricardo's theoretical innovations. Hollander vigorously denies that there was any such thing as a Ricardian 'revolution', particularly in a methodological sense. Adam Smith, he argues, was just as abstract and deductive in his method of inquiry as Ricardo, and Ricardo must be understood as correcting and refining Smith rather than replacing him. In particular, he believed that Smith's theory of the declining rate of return on capital was untenable and he traced the error to Smith's belief that an increase in money wages is capable of raising the level of money prices. Ricardo bent all his efforts to proving that inflationary increases in wages are impossible and, moreover, that money wages only rise for one reason, namely, the increasing real cost of producing agricultural wage goods.

Ricardo's new theory of profits, and the associated concept of the invariant yardstick which he employed to demonstrate the truth of 'the fundamental theorem', take us through the next 300 pages, which make up the heart of Hollander's study. Chapter 4, which shows that Ricardo never held a so-called 'corn-model' whereby the rate of profit is first determined in purely physical terms before the question of pricing has even been raised, is Hollander at his best. The idea that such a corn-model can be read into the early Ricardo is part and parcel of the new Marxist mythology that has been created around him. There follow another 100 pages on Ricardo's monetary theories, where most of the issues raised are now distinctly old-fashioned, including another review of the debate between Ricardo and Malthus on the causes of the post-Waterloo depression, perhaps the most relentless debate ever conducted between two great economists. By page 500, we have left theory behind us and entered on an examination of Ricardo's policy proposals, with the corn-law issue and the question of the poor laws taking pride of place. A final chapter, drawing the book together and counterposing Ricardo and Sraffa, is followed by a half-dozen appendixes and an excellent bibliography of English material on and about Ricardo.

This is a very good book but not the great book on Ricardo that one might have hoped for. It is marred by a number of irritating features: it is outrageously long, and much of the length is due to nit-picking digressions that cross the t's and dot the i's of previous interpretations (for a particularly flagrant example, see Chapter 2 on 'The Law of Markets'); even if we grant the need with an author like Ricardo to document copiously his alternative versions of the same idea, nothing can excuse a text in which there are almost as many words by Ricardo as by Hollander; in the effort to defend Ricardo against virtually every charge of inconsistency and error that has ever been levelled against him, the art of sympathetic interpretation is stretched beyond all reasonable limits; and the author's ingrained habit of differentiating his own judgements from those of almost every other commentator on Ricardo, while grudgingly acknowledging in his footnotes that one or two may have been there before him, is carried to maddening lengths.

There is, moreover, at least one persistent note in Hollander's interpretation which strikes me as profoundly misleading, if not downright wrong. It has to do with the basic role of the invariable measure of value in Ricardo's system. Ricardo realized that a rise in money wages consequent upon a rise in real wages will not only distort the price structure by raising the prices of labour-intensive commodities relative to those of capital-intensive commodities but will also raise the general level of prices. To eliminate this latter effect, he measured all his prices in terms of a fictional commodity produced by a ratio of capital to labour that is a mean of the entire spectrum of capital–labour ratios in the economy, its own capital being in turn produced by a mean capital–labour ratio, and so on *ad infinitum*. This is the celebrated 'invariable measure of value'. When prices are expressed in it, we get a clear-cut Ricardian trade-off between the profit rate and the wage rate, which we nowadays label 'the factor-price frontier'.

Ricardo could have secured the same results by the heroic assumption that the capital – labour ratios in all industries are the same, so that we are faced in effect with a one-sector model, but he had laid so much emphasis on the wide variety of capital–labour ratios that actually prevail in the real world that this particular route was closed to him. He could also have arrived at the same result by simply assuming a given price level or a constant purchasing power of money, but the task of showing that there is a well-defined factor-price frontier even in a world of multiple commodities was beyond his technical competence (or for that matter the technical competence of any other economist of the period). Here then, is the key to his obsession with an 'invariable measure of value', which he incorrectly thought would support not just his theorem that profits only fall when wages rise but also the proposition that money wages only rise when there is a change in the technology of producing wage goods.

Again and again, Hollander tells us that Ricardo could have dispensed with the invariable measure, that 'the fundamental theorem of distribution' could have been proved by other means, and that he frequently took the short-cut of assuming identical factor ratios in all industries to give him the answers he looked for. But Ricardo (like Marx) never assumed identical capital–labour ratios and Hollander is unable to cite even a single sentence in support of his assertions. What he did assume is that gold, the actual unit of account in the economy, fulfils the requirements of the 'invariable measure', which is quite different assumption from that of identical factor proportions. Besides, even if he had assumed identical factor proportions, it would only have done half the job he wanted done: it would have established the inverse relationship between profits and wages. But the point is that he also wanted to prove that any change in relative prices can always be traced unambiguously to its underlying source in the changing technology of agriculture; the invariant yardstick was supposed to be invariant not only to changes in distribution but also to changes in technology. It is this second half of the search for an invariable medium of value which is constantly neglected in Hollander's discussion. In other words, all the subtleties of his reading, allowing for the nuances of Ricardo's many asides, and all the theoretical rigour of modern reformulations of Ricardo's propositions, will not save Ricardo from the charge that he was attempting to perform the impossible feat of squaring a circle using only a ruler and compass.

Hollander establishes beyond doubt that Ricardo frequently operates with a model in which wages are well above subsistence levels and in which the economy has not yet settled down to a steady state of long-run equilibrium adjustments to changes in capital and population. But to conclude from this that no definite predictions flow from the Ricardian model, that Ricardo's contribution was to create an 'engine of analysis' in which anything may happen, and that Marshall was quite right to regard him as an early but muddled forerunner of himself is, surely, something of an exaggeration? Schumpeter, writing about Ricardo's tendency to state 'strong cases' based on models with few variables and many parameters in which equilibrium adjustments are instantaneously realized, labelled it the 'Ricardian Vice'. But every experienced reader of Ricardo knows that he rarely stated his 'strong cases' without qualifying them, so that in the end we are always left wondering whether he meant them to be directly applicable to the real world.

Hollander has a field day showing that Ricardo was frequently a shrewd observer of the actual circumstances which nullified the practical implications of his abstract theorems but, in so doing, he empties out the baby with the bath-water and gives us a Ricardo so responsible, so cautious and so circumspect that his contemporaries would hardly have recognized him. Ricardo was himself inordinately fond of the verb 'predict', which appears literally hundreds of times in his writings, and he was understood at the time to be a thinker who did commit himself to definite predictions. Hollander insists that, despite the superficial appearance of pessimism, he was really an optimist about Britain's growth prospects. However, he goes so far in denying that Ricardo ever meant to place any limits on the growth potential of a closed economy 'at least within a time horizon of much interest to policy-makers' that he then has to spend three pages explaining why Ricardo chose nevertheless to adopt an analytical framework which relied so heavily on diminishing agricultural returns and the stationary state. There must be something wrong with a brand of interpretation that requires such intellectual acrobatics. The earlier argument that there is really nothing to choose between Smith's eclectic, comparative, sociological approach and Ricardo's method of abstract theorizing in terms of highly simplified models, which I personally find utterly unconvincing, is simply the other side of the coin of clearing Ricardo from any charge of ever committing the Ricardian Vice: if Ricardo and Smith are so alike, Hollander seems to be saying, the much acclaimed virtues of the latter can also be ascribed to the former.

A historian of economic thought must be concerned with what contemporaries of Ricardo made of him and not simply with what he may still be saying to us in the twentieth century. Hollander is nothing if not a dedicated historian of ideas and his view of Ricardo is therefore inevitably coloured by his reading of the early Ricardians. He argues, quite rightly in my opinion, that there was none of the rapid decline in Ricardo's authority after his death that many other commentators have discerned. Ricardo formed a school of economic opinion whose characteristic feature, according to Hollander, is the use of a special theory of value involving an invariant standard in the derivation of the inverse relationship between wages and profits. Alas, almost no one besides Mill (and later Marx) grasped the logic of this special theory of value, but they did subscribe to its chief implication, namely, that the rate of return on capital was governed by the yield of land in agriculture. It is in this latter sense that Ricardian reasoning dominated the climate of economic opinion all through the second and third quarters of the nineteenth-century. Hollander would deny this argument, which jars with his consistent belittlements of the crucial role of agriculture in Ricardo's theory of profit. The result is both to misrepresent Ricardo's meaning and to misrepresent the reception of his ideas in the heyday of classical political economy.

There is much in this book that is very well done: the delineation of the general equilibrium elements in Ricardo's thinking; the emphasis on disequilibrium adjustments in his model; the due appreciation of his awareness of demand elasticities; the acknowledgement of his perfunctory but essentially Austrian views of the nature of profits; and much more besides. But the wheat is nevertheless intermixed with chaff, and considerable pruning and editing would have done much to improve the book. Still, there can be no doubt that from now on this volume will be required reading for anyone who dares to pronounce on 'what Ricardo really meant'.

26. Review of *Main Currents of Marxism: Its Rise, Growth and Dissolution*, by L. Kolakowski[*]

This is a brilliant work, conceived on a vast scale and executed with consummate mastery, which no one with the slightest interest in the social sciences can afford to neglect. It deals with what is undoubtedly one of the most influential systems of the modern world, tracing its entire evolution first in the writings of Marx and Engels themselves and then in a steady succession of disciples, from Kautsky, Luxemburg and Bernstein to Plekhanov, Lenin, Stalin, Trotsky, Gramsci, Lukacs, Althusser, the Frankfurt School, etc. It aims not merely to survey the history of Marxism but also to provide something like a handbook of the varieties of Marxism; to achieve both objectives, the author adopts the strategy of summarizing the ideas of individual thinkers in more or less their own words, confining his critical remarks to afterthoughts. This device, so wooden in most hands, succeeds admirably in his: the reader is actually taught the strengths and weaknesses of Marxism as he goes along. The book is essentially a commentary on Marxists of all sorts and few secondary sources are mentioned; but there is an excellent bibliography attached to each volume (with some surprising omissions, however: e.g. H.B. Acton, *The Illusion of the Epoch,* and K. Popper, *The Open Society*). Not least praiseworthy in a book of such scope is the quality of the writing: the translator is to be congratulated on turning the author's Polish prose into a virile, flexible English that never betrays its foreign origins.

Professor Kolakowski knows whereof he writes. He was for many years Professor of the History of Philosophy at the University of Warsaw and, until expelled in March 1968 for political reasons, an active participant as a 'revisionist' in Marxist philosophical debates in Poland (he is now a Fellow of All Souls College, Oxford). Judged by his past writings, this work presents a final stage in his own disillusionment with the Marxist message. 'Marxism', he concludes at the end of this book,

> has been the greatest fantasy of our century ... [it] has been frozen and immobilized for decades as the ideological superstructure of a totalitarian political movement, and

[*] First published in *Economica*, February 1980: 90–2.

in consequence has lost touch with intellectual developments and social realities. The hope that it could be revived and made fruitful once again soon proved to be an illusion. As an explanatory 'system' it is dead, not does it offer any 'method' that can be effectively used to interpret modern life, to foresee the future, or cultivate Utopian projections. Contemporary Marxist literature, although plentiful in quantity, has a depressing air of sterility and helplessness, in so far as it is not purely historical. (III: 523, 529).

Professor Kolakowski denies any unitary interpretation of Marxist theory of the what-Marx-really-meant variety: Marx himself combined romantic, Promethean and rationalist motifs in a pattern that owes as much to Saint-Simon and Goethe as to Ricardo and Hegel. One of the peculiarities of Marx's thinking, which Professor Kolakowski does much to illuminate, is the way in which Marx literally banishes the is/ought distinction: for Marx there is no contradiction between describing the coming of socialism as historically inevitable and prescribing it as the unique mission of the working class; the same forces that make socialism necessary also make it desirable to the working class. But how are we to discover what workers desire? Apparently, we cannot trust the trade union movement to express the so-called 'revolutionary consciousness' of the proletariat, and so a political party must be created to express the wishes of the working class, introduced as it were from outside the labour movement. It is precisely at this point that the entire argument ceases to be an empirically testable hypothesis, becoming in fact a self-fulfilling prophecy. The acute disjunction between a theory of revolution that pins all its hopes for a social transformation on the experiences and aspirations of working people and a theory of the labour movement that decries every manifestation of spontaneous working-class organizations proved to be the Achilles heel of Marxism. It led quite naturally to Lenin's conversion of a purely theoretical 'dictatorship of the proletariat' into an entirely practical 'dictatorship of the Communist Party'.

In so excellent a general treatment, it is difficult to know what to select for special mention. Nevertheless, I would single out the remarkable chapter on the endlessly discussed theory of historical materialism (I: ch. 14) – 'in a strict form it is a commonplace'; the discussion of Engels' *Dialects of Nature* (I: ch. 15), which Professor Kolakowski shows to be at total variance with Marx's own conception of the dialectic; the treatment of Karl Kautsky, the doyen of Marxism in its golden age (II: ch. 2); the study of Georgke Plekhanov (II: ch. 14), who did more than anyone else to impose a Mickey Mouse version of Marxism on subsequent generations; the devastating analysis of Leninism (II: ch. 16–18), which Professor Kolakowski argues was a true forerunner of Stalinism – 'Leninism raised political opportunism to the dignity of a theory ... The slogan constantly met with during Stalin's dictatorship, "Stalin is the Lenin of our day", was thus entirely accurate'; the treatment of Trotsky and Trotskyism (III: ch. 5), the tragedy of a Marxist hoist with his own petard; the amazing saga of György

Lukács (III: ch. 7), who alone recaptured the tortured meaning of Marx's conception of the dialectic, providing Leninism with a better philosophical basis that Lenin himself had supplied (which naturally earned him the obloquy of the entire communist movement); the critique of Herbert Marcuse's totalitarian Utopia of the New Left (III: ch. 11); and the delicious send-up of Althusser's pretentious writings (III: 483–7).

Professor Kolakowski is a philosopher, and hence it is not surprising that he concentrates attention on the philosophical ideas of Marxists. The result is a somewhat lopsided discussion that treats Marxism as if it consisted basically of certain philosophical and political ideas to which are attached some economic ones. It is true that Marxian economics takes up two chapters in the first volume on *The Founders* (that includes some extremely pertinent remarks on the meaning of 'exploitation' in Marx; I: 332–4), and we return to the subject in the chapters on Rosa Luxemburg, Eduard Bernstein and the Austro-Marxists in the second volume on *The Golden Age*. But these make up 150 pages in a book of 1,500 pages, which is surely to distort the pivotal role of economic theory in the total Marxian schema. This would hardly matter were it not for the fact that Marxists and anti-Marxists alike are forever ignoring the fact that Marxism is fundamentally an economic theory that cannot be understood except in terms of its economic content. It must be granted that Marxian economics was virtually moribund after the publication of Rudolf Hilferding's *Das Finanzkapital* in 1910, nothing essentially new being added after that until comparatively recent times. In that sense, there is little for Professor Kolakowski to relate. Nevertheless, there are important elements in the history of Marxian economics which Professor Kolakowski either neglects altogether or mentions only in passing. There is the fact, to give only one example, that Ladislaus von Bortkiewicz, a non-Marxist, was virtually alone in realizing that Marx had failed to solve the transformation problem, without which the whole of Marxian economics is simply nonsense; Bortkiewicz indeed solved the transformation problem in 1906, but only with the aid of special and limited assumptions; thereafter the problem and Bortkiewicz's solution of it was simply forgotten until both were revived in Sweezy's *Theory of Capitalist Development* (1942) – neither Bortkiewicz nor Sweezy are mentioned by Professor Kolakowski; a perfectly general solution of the transformation problem was supplied by Francis Seton only in 1957; thus, for literally 65 years no Marxist defending *Das Kapital* knew what he was talking about (and some still do not know), because what he was defending was a theory that was logically incomplete and even inconsistent. Surely, this is one of the most extraordinary examples in the history of ideas of the members of a school being their own worst enemies?

The 'breakdown controversy' between Luxemburg, Tugan-Baranovsky, Hilferding, and Grossman, the great debate on revisionism that followed the publication of Bernstein's *Premisses of Socialism and the Tasks of Social*

Democracy (1899), and the controversies over Soviet economic policy in the 1920s deserve more extended treatments than are provided in this book. Such seminal works for Marxian economics as Maurice Dobb's *Political Economy and Capitalism* (1937) and Baran and Sweezy's *Monopoly Capitalism* (1966) do not even appear in Professor Kolakowski's survey. In short, despite the wide sweep of this splendid book, an adequate history of Marxian economics still remains to be written.

27. Review of *The Kinked Demand Curve Analysis of Oligopoly,* by Gavin C. Reid*

Invented by Sweezy and independently by Hall and Hitch in 1939 as an explanation of the apparent rigidity of industrial prices, the theory of the kinked demand curve under oligopoly has acquired a ritualistic status, being mentioned with approval by almost all current textbooks in microeconomics and industrial organization. The theory was in fact refuted by Stigler in a seminal article of 1947, which is frequently cited alongside Sweezy and Hall and Hitch as if empirical evidence against a theory actually strengthens its plausibility. I argued in *The Methodology of Economics* (1980) that the root cause of the present 'crisis' in economics is the failure of economists to practise the methodology of falsificationism which they invariably preach, and I provided a series of case studies of particular economic theories to support my contention. Had I known of this book, the theory of the kinked oligopoly demand curve would have become another case in point.

The book under review is divided into three sections: the genesis of the theory of the kinked demand curve; the analytics of the kinked demand curve (where the author breaks new grounds in an elegant exposition of the geometry and algebra of the argument); and the empirical evidence for and against the notion of kinks in the demand curve of both firms and industries under oligopoly. Since the original Stigler critique of 1947, the subject has attracted over 100 papers. The original obtuse kink of Sweezy–Hall–Hitch has been supplemented by the notion of reflex kinks, and the form of the kink has been shown to depend on the degree of capacity utilization and hence on the eagerness of firms to attract additional sales. If oligopoly may lead to kinked demand curves, oligopsony may lead to kinked factor supply curves, and this has been used by some to explain the phenomenon of labour hoarding. Doubly kinked demand curves have been explored, leading towards the theory of 'contingent demand functions' that may have kinks, gaps and cusps, depending on the capacity limitations of rival firms, the degree of product differentiation, the reaction speed of buyers, the quality of market information, etc. Most of these later developments are simply

* First published in *Economica*, May 1981: 210–11.

ignored in current textbooks, thus suggesting that the kinked demand curve of oligopoly has indeed become one of those unquestioned shibboleths of elementary economic wisdom.

According to Stigler, a firm will have reason to believe that its demand curve is kinked if its price increases go unmatched by rivals, while its price cuts are followed by rivals. In his view, therefore, an appropriate empirical test of the theory should determine whether the price history of an industry containing few firms might foster a belief on the part of a member firm in the existence of a kinked demand curve. He had little faith in asking firms what they believe and instead considered the objective market forces which ought to lead firms to believe one thing or another. This line of reasoning was contested by Efroymson, whose 1955 paper is heralded by the author as a fundamental contribution to the recent literature. Efroymson argued that a firm would attempt a unilateral price change only if it did *not* believe in the existence of a kink in its demand curve; a firm that did believe in a kink would not vary its price. Thus, objective evidence of a kink would emerge only when a firm had made a mistake in judgement. In consequence, he reinterpreted Stigler's price histories to support the notion of kinked demand curves.

Moving beyond a test of the behavioural assumptions of the theory of kinked demand curves, Stigler also attempted to test is predictive ability. His basic procedure was to compare the frequency of change in the monthly list price quotations in a collection of oligopolistic and non-oligopolistic American industries over a complete business cycle from 1929 to 1937, making use of the implied predictions that prices are less rigid for monopolies than for oligopolies, for oligopolies with price leaders than for oligopolies without dominant firms, and for oligopolies producing differentiated goods than for oligopolies producing homogeneous goods. On all these counts, his evidence refuted the hypothesis of kinked demand curves. Efroymson takes issue with Stigler's methods on all three counts, in effect denying that he had correctly specified the variable being predicted (namely, transaction rather than list prices). I can think of no more instructive example of the perennial problem of testing economic theories than this one: time and time again, it is not at all self-evident what is actually being predicted by reigning economic theories, or what are the appropriate operational counterparts of the variables being predicted.

The theory of the kinked oligopoly demand curve is not a hypothesis about price-setting, as is, for example, the theory of full-cost pricing, but a hypothesis about the conjectures of businessmen in certain market contexts. This suggests that subjective evidence is a more natural test for the theory than the objective evidence we have discussed so far. A number of questionnaire studies have been made of the beliefs of businessmen about the reactions of rivals to price changes, and these have generally tended to support the concept of kinks in demand curves even as the objective evidence has generally tended to refute it. Since then, dynamic but still untested interpretations of the kinked demand curve in terms of informational asymmetries on the part of both buyers and sellers have further clouded the picture. We are left at the end of this well-told story with the author's pointed conclusions: 'If the kinked demand curve theory is to merit the continuous attention it receives in the training of economists, there is a strong need for a great deal more empirical examination to be applied to it'.

28. Review of *Theorists of Economic Growth from David Hume to the Present*, by W.W. Rostow*

Rostow's 'stages' theory of economic growth started 36 years ago with his essay *The Take-off into Self-sustaining Growth* (1955) and the book *The Stages of Economic Growth: A Non- Communist Manifesto* (1960). Since then he has elaborated his views in some half-dozen books without, however, giving up its original message.

All countries, he argued, must pass through five well-defined stages of development, namely:

1. traditional society;
2. the preconditions for takeoff;
3. the takeoff itself;
4. the drive to maturity; and
5. the age of high mass consumption.

Of particular importance was the third stage, the takeoff, characterized as it was by three distinguishing features: a rise in productive investment from about 5 per cent of national income to at least 10 per cent; the emergence of one or more sectors as the 'leading sector'; and the drastic modification of the political framework so as to exploit the impulses emanating from the leading sector, enabling growth to be sustained.

Rostow applied this scheme to a wide range of countries, showing how each of them could be identified as falling into one of the five stages at various points in their history.

No one has ever denied that Rostow tells a good story but the problem his colleagues have had with his theory is whether it is indeed anything more than a good story.

Rostow's stage theory is certainly a convenient peg on which to hang the facts of economic development and it is perfectly capable of describing absolutely any growth path once it has taken place, but it has no real predictive power; apart from its rich interweaving of both economic and non-economic phenomena,

* First published as 'A History of the World in Five Stages', *The Financial Times*, 8 March, 1991: 3.

appropriately disaggregated to the level of individual sectors, it has no significant advantage over a number of rival descriptions of the development process.

In fact, it could be argued that the successive refinements and qualifications which Rostow has added to his original apparatus over the years have robbed it of much of its original appeal and have transformed it into a mixture of ideas so complex that no one other than Rostow himself could be trusted to handle it.

But whatever one thinks of Rostow's positive contributions, there is no doubt that his battles with his opponents have turned him into a cogent critic of orthodoxy in the field of economic development.

The present work before us therefore promises much in the way of a critical survey of two centuries of cogitation on the grand theme of *The Nature and Causes of The Wealth of Nations*, to quote the title of Adam Smith's masterpiece.

Nevertheless, and despite its considerable erudition and scholarship, this is a somewhat unsatisfactory book: for one thing it is much too long, or at least reads too slowly, because the argument is constantly interrupted by digressions and asides; for another, it is not always doctrinally accurate and, in particular, leans over backwards to be kind to the English classical school of Smith, Ricardo and Mill.

And after a simply magnificent account of Alfred Marshall's underrated ideas on growth theory in Chapter 6, one of the best chapters in the book, the presentation of successive concepts and thinkers becomes increasingly preoccupied with a slowly developing apologia for the current thoughts of one W.W. Rostow, culminating in an authoritative restatement of the Rostowian schema in Chapter 18.

The book comes to a close with an interesting penultimate chapter aptly entitled: 'What Don't We Know About Economic Growth?', but the positive effect of that is almost spoiled by a simply awful final chapter in which Rostow displays all his worst tendencies to prophesy all manner of things economic political and social, like a poor man's Nostradamus.

Classical political economy was fundamentally concerned with the mainsprings of economic growth but economic theory after the so-called Marginal Revolution of 1870 abandoned a concern with economic growth and development in favour of an interest in problems of resource allocation; in consequence, economic theory became more elegant and rigorous but at the expense of relegating such questions as population growth, technical progress and business cycles to a theoretical hinterland.

There were major contributions to our understanding of the growth in the years before the Second World War, such as those of Schumpeter, Kuznets and Colin Clark, but they made little impact on the mainstream of partial and general equilibrium analysis.

The use of devvelopment economics in the 1950s and steady-state growth theory in the 1960s finally brought the problem of economic progress back to the agenda of economists but by then the very question of why some countries are rich while others are poor was distorted by a century of theorizing unaccustomed to addressing these issues. There is indeed much wrong with the way modern economists address the problem of economic growth, as Rostow is not slow to tell us.

Rostow begins his survey with a discussion of six classical economists, treated as three contemporary pairs: David Hume and Adam Smith, Thomas Malthus and David Ricardo, and somewhat incongruously, John Stuart Mill and Karl Marx.

Most great thinkers establish their principal ideas in the third decade of their lives and Rostow shows how indeed Hume and Smith shaped their vision of economic events in the relation to Britain in the 1750s; in the same way, the theories of Malthus and Ricardo reflected the course of events observed around 1800; finally, Mill was 30 years old in 1836 and Marx was 30 years old in 1848, so that their thinking ever afterwards was essentially rooted in a pre-Victorian age.

This framework allows Rostow to demonstrate why Ricardian economics, and subsequently the whole of classical political economy handed down by Mill, was dominated by the idea of severe limits to economic growth created by scarcities of land.

It is curious that Rostow fails utterly to notice that the classical economists lived through the Industrial Revolution, or what Rostow would call the takeoff stage of economic growth, without adequately recognizing it for what it was, namely, an effective answer delivered by history against their deep-seated anxiety about the tide of human numbers running out of food.

Yes, Ricardo wrote a chapter on the 'machinery question', saying that labour-displacing machines might well lower wages and increase unemployment, and he also speculated on the question of whether landlords would be motivated to introduce land-saving improvements in farming methods but, that apart, he was silent on the great questions of technical progress.

John Stuart Mill denied Ricardo's misgivings on new machinery and noted that the great inventions of Watt and Arkwright in the 1780s had marked a fundamental turning point in the economic progress in Britain but even he, looking backwards from the vantage point of 1848, conceived of the British economy essentially as it were a single giant farm, an idea which was of course an invention of Ricardo's.

Rostow consistently overlooks the extraordinary agrarian outlook of virtually all the English classical economists and when he comes to write of Marx, who for the first time does indeed conceive of capitalism as a fully fledged industrial economy, he does not begin to do real justice to Marx's many interesting ideas about technical progress, such as his clear perception of the absolutely fundamental difference between product and process – innovations (that is, new goods and new machines) and between labour- and capital-saving innovations.

Rostow refers repeatedly to an equally important distinction between small, continuous technical improvements and large, discontinuous innovations (which he credits to Smith but which is really due to Schumpeter), but product and capital-saving innovations do not even appear in his subject index.

Classical economics was much preoccupied by 'the division of labour' and yet, I would argue, it really paid little attention to the problem of technical progress. Neoclassical economics after 1870 deliberately neglected questions of technical progress as falling outside the purview of rigorous equilibrium analysis and, in a manner still not fully understood, the revival of interest in growth problems in the recent post-war era has not succeeded in making technical progress a fully respectable subject for economists.

In short, we teach students all about demand and supply and all about unemployment and inflation but we never mention innovations, or the creative entrepreneurs who adopt them, the rate at which they are diffused throughout an industry, spreading in turn from industry to industry, and how all that goes a long way towards explaining why Japan and Germany are rich and why America and Britain are not going to be rich much longer. If Adam Smith woke up today, he would find modern economics a very strange, offbeat subject.

It is one of the tragedies of economics that economic growth is basically a function of values and attitudes – attitudes to work, thrift and enterprise, the Protestant ethic if you like. But we have almost no idea how these appropriate values and attitudes develop in particular societies at particular times, and even less how to promote them when they are not present.

'Economics', Rostow notes again and again, 'must ultimately be a biological rather than a neo-Newtonian subject'. Certainly, Newtonian equilibrium concepts have proved to be effective barriers to a proper understanding of the growth process, no doubt in part because they are irreversible, like biological processes.

We need a new dynamic economics receptive to a study of the propensities to save, to innovate and to assume economic risks but, as this book makes only too evident, such a new economics still awaits its founding father.

29. Reviews of *Robertson on Economic Policy*, ed. S.R. Dennison and J.R. Presley, and *Essays on Robertsonian Economics*, ed. J.R. Presley*

Dennis Robertson is little read these days. He was the father of the study of macroeconomic dynamics in Britain, the first to explore the relationship between saving and investment, using period analysis. But his relentless and penetrating criticisms of Keynes gave him a reputation for querulousness which he never lived down. Despite his cogent later writings on welfare economics and monetary economics and his sparkling literary style, which never left him, his reputation went into rapid decline after his death in 1963. Many of his books are now not only unread but out of print.

The purpose of these two books is to rekindle interest in his writings. The first, edited by Stanley R. Dennison and John R. Presley, contains six of Robertson's unpublished policy papers spanning the years 1956–61, together with five previously published papers ranging over the years 1937 to 1963. Selected juvenile poems and a comprehensive bibliography complete the volume. The second reprints seven essays by Presley, Charles Goodhart, Thomas Wilson, Thomas Humphrey and William Fellner on various aspects of Robertson's thought, in particular his theory of the trade cycle and his views on monetary policy. Some of these have previously appeared in obscure places, and it is good now to have them more readily to hand. It is a pity that room was not found for Paul Samuelson's somewhat disparaging essay on Robertson that appeared in the *Quarterly Journal of Economics* in 1963; or Presley's deeply appreciative essay in *Pioneers of Modern Economics in Britain*, edited by D.P. O'Brien and J.R. Presley (1981), summarizing his own book-length study of *Robertsonian Economics* (1978). Nevertheless, there is enough here to give any reader a flavour of Robertson's approach to macroeconomic issues, which was after all the object of the exercise.

Essays on Robertsonian Economics was worth doing, but I am not so sure about *Robertson on Economic Policy*. The six unpublished policy papers are not reflective of Robertson at his best and do not stand up by themselves. For those

* First published in *The Times Literary Supplement*, 12 February 1993.

who remember the 1950s like yesterday, these detailed comments on the minutiae of monetary policy may be enlightening, but for the rest of us (those under the age of 60) they are virtually unintelligible. What happened to the normal duties of an editor? Why reprint if you cannot be bothered to write editorial notes?

The introduction to *Robertson on Economic Policy* serves to remind us of the intellectual battles of the early post-war years when the strident expansionism of some of Keynes's disciples, urging the maintenance of conditions of over-full employment, gave rise in some quarters to profound fears of inflation. Such fears were frequently expressed by Robertson in the 1950s. The editors emphatically endorse Robertson's wisdom in giving priority to curbing inflation, viewing lapses from full employment as having secondary importance. Less than six months ago, such sentiments would have been applauded at No. 11 Downing Street. But since the recent U-turn in government policy, the old Keynesian agenda in which the costs of unemployment are regarded as greater than the costs of inflation, at least so long as both are in single-digit figures, has taken on a new lease of life. In short, for all the historical importance of Robertson's writings – and no one has ever matched him for his technical criticisms of the Keynesian system – his views are hopelessly out of tune with current concerns.

SECTION B

Methodology of Economics

30. Review of *The Foundations of Paul Samuelson's Revealed Preference Theory: A Study by the Method of Rational Reconstruction*, by Stanley Wong[*]

Stanley Wong has written an important book: it is important because it carefully re-examines one of the most acclaimed achievements of modern economics, Samuelson's revealed preference theory (RPT), and it does so with a methodological sophistication that is all too rare among modern commentators. Dr Wong is an out-and-out Popperian and his approach to the evaluation of scientific theories is that recommended by Popper, namely the method of rational reconstruction or the method of situational analysis: theories are interpreted as solutions to problem-situations and the task of methodology, therefore, is to reconstruct the original problem-situation and to show why the scientist in question considered his theory to be a satisfactory solution to the problem. The method of rational reconstruction allows us to separate the question of understanding a theory from that of agreeing with it, and, in addition, to separate criticisms of the problem-situation from criticisms of the adequacy of a theory as a solution to that problem-situation. Wong claims that this is the first time that the method of rational reconstruction has been applied to economics. Strictly speaking, this claim is justified. On the other hand, it is worth remembering that Popper's method is only an explicit version of an approach that many historians of economics have long employed implicitly: Stigler's famous history of utility theory, for example, is in fact an unself-conscious application of the method of rational reconstruction.

Wong's basic thesis is that Paul Samuelson has changed his mind twice in respect of the problem-situation to which RPT is addressed: in the original 1938 article, the point of RPT was to derive the main results of Hicksian ordinal utility theory without resorting to the notion of utility or indeed any other non-observable terms; in a 1948 paper, which actually christened the new approach, RPT becomes the basis for an operational method of constructing an individual's indifference map from observations of his market behaviour, thus solving a

[*] First published in the *Economic Journal*, June 1979: 478–80.

problem which appears to be incompatible with the aims of the earlier article; finally, in a 1950 paper, RPT receives yet another interpretation, namely, to explore and establish the observational equivalent of ordinal utility theory, which again seems to conflict with the objectives of the first but also with the objectives of the second paper. To add to the confusion, Samuelson has also changed his mind at least once about basic methodology: in 1938, as in the *Foundations of Economic Analysis* (1947), he was an 'operationalist', meaning one who believes that all meaningful scientific questions can only be answered through the performance of appropriate measuring operations. But by 1963 he had retreated to the more modest methodology of 'descriptivism', according to which scientific theories are merely economical descriptions rather than explanations of observable experience. RPT has been widely hailed as a landmark in the history of the theory of consumer behaviour, finally discarding all the subjective elements that have for so long dogged the economists' explanation of consumer choice. At the same time, there is general agreement that Hendrik Houthakker in 1950 proved the logical equivalence of RPT with ordinal utility theory. It is difficult to see how a RPT can claim to be both a substitute for and a complement to ordinal utility theory. Indeed, as Wong shows, RPT cannot sustain its claim of representing a new approach to the problem of consumer behaviour; nor is it possible to construct indifference curves from observable market behaviour by purely operational procedures; moreover, RPT is not an explanation but a restatement of ordinal utility theory and, like ordinal utility theory, it is not empirically falsifiable because it invokes unrestricted universal statements. The various contributions of Samuelson to RPT over a period of 25 years are mutually inconsistent and, in general, Samuelson's research programme in the revealed preference approach remains unfinished.

I am personally persuaded by Wong's case. The theory of consumer behaviour is frequently regarded as the prime example of an economic theory whose logical content has at long last been fully explored. This book will cast doubt on this presumption, which is more than enough reason for recommending it. It is a slim book (having started out as a PhD thesis at Cambridge University) but is, unfortunately, excessively repetitious. Wong's style reminds me of the popular Scottish preacher whose recipe for a good sermon ran as follows: 'First, you tells them what you are going to tell them; then you tells them; and then you tells them what you told them.' A good editor might have reduced Wong's text by 20 per cent without any loss of content.

31. Review of *The Rhetoric of Economics*, by Donald N. McCloskey*

This is a witty and provocative book about the linguistic devices economists employ to persuade their readers to believe them. It is great fun to read and one finishes it wishing it could have been longer. All this is the more remarkable in that its central thesis is untenable: McCloskey advocates a point of view that he himself violates on every other page. He leaves us in no doubt of what he is against but fails to provide a coherent account of what he is for. Nevertheless, there is much to be learned from the spirit of the book even if one discards its letter.

Economists, argues McCloskey, pay obeisance to an outmoded philosophy of science, which he labels as 'modernism', although it is usually labelled as 'logical positivism'. This matter of labels is not unimportant, for in no time at all he includes within modernism various propositions – that the assumptions of theories should never be examined for their degrees of realism; that interrogation of human subjects never yields useful experimental evidence – that have gained currency among economists but that have absolutely nothing to do with the philosophical movement known at first as 'logical positivism', and subsequently, as 'logical empiricism'. 'Modernism', McCloskey tells us, 'gleams diamond-hard from many facets, and the word can only be fully defined in use. ... It is the attitude that the only real knowledge is, in common parlance, 'scientific', that is, knowledge tested by certain kinds of rigorous scepticism.' Among the Ten Commandments of 'modernism' are such notions as that only the observable predictions of a theory matter to its truth; that facts and values belong to different realms of discourse, so that positive propositions are always to be distinguished from normative ones; that any scientific explanation of an event brings the event under a covering or universal law; and that introspection, metaphysical beliefs, aesthetic considerations, and the like may well figure in the discovery of an hypothesis but are irrelevant to its justification. Such notions, McCloskey insists, are now discarded by many professional philosophers – he cites, among others, Willard Quine, Stephen Toulmin, Paul Feyerabend and Richard Rorty. But economists have paid no attention to these reactions to 'modernism' among philosophers and continue

* First published as 'Methodology with a small m', in *Critical Review*, **9**(2), Spring 1987: 1–5.

to believe that 'ultimately' the only 'fundamental' proof of an economic assertion is 'objective', quantitative 'tests'. It is this naive belief in empirical testing as the hallmark of Truth that is the real core of 'modernism' and hence the Big Bad Wolf of McCloskey's book. 'It is hard to disbelieve the dominance of modernism in economics', he adds, *'although an objective, quantitative test would of course make it, or any assertion, more believable and would be worth doing'*. I have italicized these words because they illustrate McCloskey's schizoid attitude to empirical evidence.

On the one hand, he deplores all hints of a prescriptive methodology in a subject like economics; that is, no one is to lay down metatheoretical standards of what is to be considered a good or bad argument. On the other hand, 'an objective, quantitative test would make it, or any assertion, more believable *and* would be worth doing' (my italics). Really? Yes, it might make a proposition more believable simply if only because those unphilosophical economists tend to take quantitative tests seriously. But why would it be worth doing if it has no bearing on the validity of the assertion? And if it has at least some bearing, why are we not told what bearing it has? McCloskey ridicules the reader who believes that there are some propositions in economics that are either true or false, in which case it is difficult to see why empirical testing should ever be worth doing.

If *pre*scriptive methodology is out, what then is left of the methodology of economics? What is left is *de*scriptive methodology or what McCloskey prefers to call the study of 'rhetoric' or 'conversations'. The word 'rhetoric' has in recent years acquired a derogatory meaning but at one time (roughly up to the nineteenth century) it meant simply the ways of producing an effect on one's audience by the careful use of language; it is the art of speaking, the art of persuading people to believe what they ought to believe. McCloskey never gives a precise definition of the term 'rhetoric', but the general idea of what he is after is, surely, plain enough. Moreover, he provides a number of worked examples in the latter half of his book of rhetorical analysis, based on the writings of Paul Samuelson, Robert Solow, John Muth and Robert Fogel. These chapters make instructive reading even if one does not share what McCloskey himself calls the 'Anarchistic Theory of Knowledge in Economics'.

McCloskey implies that one can effectively divorce methodology in a prescriptive sense from methodology in a descriptive sense; in other words, one can both lay down metatheoretical standards that economists ought to follow, irrespective of whether they have actually followed these standards in the past, and one can describe how economists actually reason and argue, irrespective of what metatheoretical standards the methodologist espouses. But this is simply an eleventh commandment of 'modernism': such a rigid divorce between the two types of methodology is logically impossible. One cannot examine the language used by a scientist (or anyone else) without some selection device, some notion of what to look for, some criteria of 'good' or 'bad' language, some standards of what is to count as a telling example of, say, the belief in Truth, empirical testing, quantification, mathematical reason or whatever. Thus, any positive attempt to describe scientific activity becomes willy-nilly a form of normative methodology. Contrariwise, it is *logically* possible to lay down any number of prescriptions for 'good' science, but if these bear absolutely no relationship to what has passed as 'good' science in the past 400 years, few scientists will pay much attention to these prescriptions. To put it in a nutshell: it appears to be impossible to separate the history of science from the methodology of science – to practise one is to practise the other. But where then do we begin? We seem to be unable to approach the history of economics without a preconceived methodology of economics, however, primitive, and, similarly, we seem to be unable to consider the methodology of economics without a prior knowledge of the history of economics.

The only way out of this dilemma that I know of is that offered by the late Imre Lakatos, another modern philosopher of science.[1] He proposed to begin with a prescriptive methodology, the methodology of 'scientific research programs', and to test this methodology by consciously studying the history of science with its aid, thus making it possible to falsify the initial methodology. There have been a number of attempts to apply this Lakatosian method to economics.[2] It is too early to pronounce on its outcome, but there is little doubt that one learns a great deal about economics from these studies. This, too, is a type of rhetorical analysis but it is carried out with the aid of a consciously adopted prescriptive methodology.

The penultimate chapter of McCloskey's book. 'The Rhetoric of Significance Tests' – one of the best chapters in this book – attacks one of the worst characteristics of modern economics, namely, the confusion between significance tests and tests of substantive effects. This chapter bristles with advice on 'good' statistical practice, all of which I personally applaud. But where does such advice come from except from metatheoretical standards, otherwise known as 'methodology', that is, the logic of the methods employed by the practitioners of a subject? McCloskey is unalterably opposed to Methodology with a capital M but much in favour of methodology with a lower-case m, which seems to mean that you prescribe many little things – don't shout; be open-minded; don't resort to violence in support of your ideas; face up to the facts, such as they are; don't fall for your own rhetoric; don't pronounce on large or small without giving standards of comparison; don't confuse statistical significance with substantive significance; replay Neyman–Pearson statistical techniques with Bayesian methods; etc. – but you may not prescribe one or two big things, such as eschewing conclusions that are compatible with any and all factual evidence; always comparing one's conclusions with those of competing theories, if such exist; avoiding changes to one's theories that have no other aim but to account for an empirical anomaly, etc. Unfortunately, I fail to see a rational basis for the implied distinction between deplorable Methodology and salutory methodology.

One can imagine a rhetorical analysis of the writings of Milton Friedman on monetarism; Friedman uses some explicit and implicit literary devices that serve to account for his enormous persuasive power and, hence, his influence on modern economics. Having studies those devices, I will probably ask myself at some time whether it is actually true that control of the supply of money is the key to the control of inflation in modern, industrial economies. Silly boy, I can hear McCloskey saying, there is no such thing as truth in economics: 'Economics, like geology or evolutionary biology or history itself, is a historical rather than a predictive science.' But geology, evolutionary biology and history are retroactive sciences, that is, the validity of their propositions do depend *ex post facto* on empirical data (consider the importance of fossil evidence to the debates on Darwinian theory). Is the same true of economics? Does the validity of monetarism depend, if not on the accuracy of its future predictions, on the accuracy of its past retrodictions? Friedman did, after all, co-author a book on the *Monetary History of the United States, 1867–1960*.[3] Did he verify monetarism in terms of the historical data on the money supply? Is this an important question? Silly boy, you're doing Methodology again: off with your head!

The gist of this book was published in article form in the *Journal of Economic Literature*.[4] Bruce Caldwell and A.W. Coates, two well-known methodologists of economics, replied to the article.[5] They said everything about the article that I have tried to say about the book – expect they said it better. McCloskey counter-replied but I am unable to understand his reply. It is worth reading as a masterful use of rhetoric (in the bad sense of the word).

NOTES

1. I. Lakatos, *The Methodology of Scientific Research Programmes*, Cambridge: Cambridge University Press, 1978.
2. M. Blaug, *The Methodology of Economics; or, How Economists Explain*, Cambridge: Cambridge University Press, 1980; R.C. Maddock, 'Rational expectations macrotheory: a Lakatosian case study in program adjustment', *History of Political Economy*, 16(2), Summer 1984: 291–309; D.W. Hands, 'Second thoughts on Lakatos', ibid., 17(1), Spring 1985: 1–17; E.R. Weintraub, *General Equilibrium Analysis: Studies in Appraisal*, Cambridge: Cambridge University Press, 1985; M. Blaug, *Economic History and the History of Economics*, Brighton: Wheatsheaf Books, 1986: xviii–xix.
3. Milton Friedman and Anna Jacobson Schwartz, *A Monetary History of the United States, 1867–1960*, Princeton, N.J.: Princeton University Press, 1963.
4. D.N. McCloskey, 'The rhetoric of economics', *Journal of Economic Literature*, 21(2), June 1983: 481–517.
5. B.J. Caldwell, A.W. Coates, 'The rhetoric of economists: a comment on McCloskey', ibid., 22(2), June 1984: 575–8.

SECTION C

The Economics of Education

32. Review of *Inequality*, by Christopher Jencks *et al.**

This book amounts to nothing less than a frontal attack on the fond belief of Americans, and not only Americans, that more and better education provides a foolproof method of promoting social mobility and equalizing the distribution of income. On the contrary, argues Jencks and his colleagues at the Center for Educational Policy Research at Harvard University, even if American schools could be reformed so as to guarantee every child an equally long and equally good education, this would only alter adult incomes marginally.

This is not because genes, social class origins and neighbourhood environment determine economic success; in fact, they are shown to have little impact on earnings from employment. It is simply that the total influence of schooling on the lifetime prospects of individuals is so small and the influence of luck is so large that no conceivable educational reform could bring about discernible economic or social equality. if Americans want to equalize the distribution of income, more direct means will have to be employed.

This is a powerful book, lucidly written and persuasively argued, which will clearly take its place as a major contribution to both the economics and the sociology of education. It draws upon a wide range of American evidence from almost every available source, skilfully combing these with the aid of something known to social statisticians as 'path analysis' – the technical parts of the books ae conveniently relegated to appendices, and it must be said that they are extremely technical and difficult to follow.

Although the author has an axe to grind he rarely disguises counter-evidence and he is perfectly candid about gaps in knowledge and missing links in the argument. Nevertheless, the book suffers from a certain element of exaggeration of what I take to be an essentially valid thesis. Furthermore, Jencks appears to be satisfied with a theory of income distribution that attributes paramount significance to the play of chance, a position which is virtually indistinguishable from having no theory at all. And yet he concedes that a knowledge of certain characteristics of an individual permit us to predict his income with a 60 per cent chance of being right. Perhaps this is much less predictability than we might have

* First published as 'Environment, genotype and the luck of the rich', in *The Times Higher Education Supplement*, 22 June 1973.

hoped for, and certainly it is not enough to pin our faith on education as an instrument for achieving equality, but at least it is better than getting an answer by throwing a pair of dice.

Let me try to convey the flavour of the book's findings. The distribution of earnings in an economy is the result of a complicated interaction of variables, many of which we can only measure approximately and some of which no one has yet succeeded in measuring at all. This complex of variables does, however, have one desirable property rarely encountered in the study of social phenomena, namely, that of forming a sequential causal chain: many of the variables are clearly antecedent to others, being causes but not themselves effects.

For example, the impact of home background makes itself felt early in an individual's life, causing but not being caused by the amount and quality of schooling he or she receives. Presumably, this is also true of genetic endowment, although not everybody would agree that it is also true of IQ scores, the standard measure of that endowment. A variable like neighbourhood environment influences educational achievement both before and during school attendance, but once again the causal effect largely runs in one direction. After an individual leaves school, his earnings depend to some extent, and indeed to a considerable extent, on the occupation he enters, at which point all the previously mentioned variables act directly or indirectly to produce the observed amount of annual income received.

Since the entire process forms a temporal chain with all the causal arrows running in one direction, we can depict the cumulative impact of variables by means of 'path analysis'. (Path analysis is mathematically equivalent to analysis of variance, but its statistical interpretation is different.)

This allows us to say, for example, that father's education and father's occupation of American white non-farm males explains 43 per of the variation in IQ score taken at the age of 11; that IQ score in turn explains 45 per cent of the variation in educational attainments, that is years of schooling received, to which parental factors contributed another 36 per cent; educational attainment in turn explains 50 per cent of the variation in subsequent occupational status, which then accounts for 33 per cent of the variation in personal earnings observed in 1962; it we brought in the results of scholastic aptitude tests, these contributed an additional 15 per cent to the explanation of final earnings.

How much, then, do genes and home environment alone contribute to personal earnings? Very little, so far as we can tell, as evidenced by the fact that inequality in earnings between identical twins whether reared together or apart, as well as between brothers reared together, is almost as great as it is between random males in the population. It is, of course, questionable whether native endowment is measured successfully by any set of culture-free aptitude tests, such as an IQ, and it is even more questionable whether nature can be separated from nurture, inasmuch as unusually able children are treated differently by their own parents, thus in effect creating a different environment for themselves.

Likewise, home background characteristics are typically measured by family income, father's occupation, father's and mother's education and so forth; if what matters is the degree of achievement-motivation which parents succeed in instilling in their children and if this element is not itself highly correlated with visible signs of parental social status, we may be underestimating the impact of home background. But this is merely to say that at every point in this sort of analysis questions arise as to whether we have succeeded in measuring what we really ought to be measuring. The argument cuts both ways, however: those who have been saying that the distribution of earnings depends more on privileged upbringing and family connections than on schooling must have either ignored the American data or misunderstood it.

Jencks takes great pains to establish and measure the heritability of IQ scores *à la* Jensen and Eysenck. He notes that the data base for making generalizations about heritability is still too weak to justify precise estimates, but his best guess is that genotype explains about 45 per cent of the variance in IQ scores, that environment explains about 35 per cent, and that interaction between the two explains the remaining 20 per cent. (In a footnote, he draws attention to the fact that the relatively homogeneous environment of Britain tends to produce a larger genetic effect than has been observed in the USA.)

This a far cry from Jensen's 80 per cent nature, 20 per cent nurture, but it still leaves genes dominating environment. But this is not to say that efforts to alter the test scores of particular children by changing their environments are, therefore, bound to fail. Generalizations about heritability in populations are of little use in predicting the degree of heritability of sub-populations and even less in predicting it of individuals in sub-populations. This is the gist of Jencks's disagreement with Jensen and Eysenck. Besides, he would add, even if we succeeded in equalizing the test scores of all children, we would only make a small impact on the distribution of adult incomes.

It is time to say something about the structure of the book. The analysis begins by looking at the distribution of educational opportunities among children, in terms of availability of schools, utilization of school resources, social composition of classmates and access to privileged curricula. It turns next to the distribution of basic cognitive skills measured by standardized tests of verbal facility, reading comprehension and mathematical competence.

It is shown that genetic and environmental inequalities both play a major role in producing cognitive inequality, but the latter has very little to do with economic success in later life. This may be because standardized tests fail accurately to measure basic cognitive skills or because the skills that pay off once school is over are not so much cognitive skills as affective behavioural traits, such as punctuality and docility on the one hand, and self-reliance and perseverance on the other.

Jencks clearly favours the latter interpretation and he admits ruefully that little is known about how schools produce these non-recognitive traits, if indeed they do produce them, and even less about the value that employers seem to place on them. Schools may serve merely to select and certify those with desirable personality characteristics. Similarly, employers, unable to specify the precise skill requirements of jobs, may opt for an appropriate set of values and attitudes as reflected in the possession of an educational credential as the next best thing in deciding whether to recruit or promote an individual worker.

But all this is speculation and Jencks does little more than to look the issue boldly in the face – and then to march on. This is undoubtedly the central weakness in the book but, of course, Jencks is hardly to blame: no one has yet succeeded in presenting a coherent, empirically verified theory of the determinants of personal economic success in modern, industrialized economies. It is worth adding that the long debate on the contribution of education to economic growth remains inconclusive to this day for precisely that reason.

The next question to be examined is the distribution of educational attainments. Family background proves to have more influence on an individual's length of schooling than does genotype, exactly the opposite conclusion from the one reached earlier with respect to IQ scores. Even more significant is the finding that the influence of the family depends partly on culture and psychological factors that are independent of the standard income occupation attributes of social class. Furthermore, it is demonstrated that qualitative differences between schools play only a minor role in determining how much schooling people eventually receive.

From the distribution of years of schooling, we move to the distribution of occupational status, the distribution of job satisfaction and, finally, the distribution of income. All of these characteristics are unequally distributed in the population and each one can be only partly explained in terms of the others. The association between these various types of inequality is usually quite weak, which means that a successful effort to equalize one of them is unlikely to have much effect on the degree of inequality of another.

Jencks's final conclusion is that 'there is nearly as much income variation among men who come from similar families, have similar credentials, and have similar test scores, as among men in general. This suggests either that competence does not depend primarily on family background, schooling, and test scores, or else that income does not depend on competence.'

Jencks neatly disposes of the idea that the unequal distribution of property income is responsible for the persistent gap between rich and poor. Inherited income accounts for a small fraction of the income of the rich and there is so much social mobility that most children of the rich end up worse off than their parents. The mechanism that passes inequality from generation to generation is too weak and uncertain to explain the income inequality we observe at every point in time.

On the other hand, each extra year of elementary or secondary education boosts future income by 4 per cent, each extra year of college boosts it by 7 per cent and each year of graduate school boosts it by another 4 per cent; and these figures apply when we hold constant all differences between individuals in initial ability and family background. Thus, eliminating all social, financial and educational obstacles to college attendance, and indeed forcing everyone to have exactly the same amount of education, would somewhat reduce economic inequality among adults: it would reduce the gap between the top and the bottom fifth of all male workers from seven to one to around five to one. If we could further eliminate absolutely all environmental differences between individuals, that is, all the factors that make the incomes of brothers unequal, we would reduce the gap further from five to one to around four to one. The gap of two to one is a measure of the genetic causes of inequality acting in combination with the element of chance.

Having satisfied himself that equalizing educational opportunity would do little to make adults more equal, Jencks brings the book to a close by examining some proposals that would operate directly on income distribution. All his suggestions consist essentially of variations on the theme of an incomes policy. He proposes that the government should offer private firms financial incentives to equalize wages and even to tax firms with highly unequal pay scales. He speculates on the advantages and disadvantages of an income insurance scheme which would compensate workers whose income fell below a predicted mean and would penalize those whose incomes rose above it.

He favours free tuition and a living stipend for students, provided such funds would be financed out of a 'graduate tax' on all those who have had education beyond the age of 16. But again and again he returns to the idea that no mechanism for equalizing incomes has the slightest hope of being politically acceptable so long as Americans continue to regard the present distribution of income as the unanticipated outcome of purely private decisions that Congress neither can nor should regulate. In view of this conviction, it is strange to notice that Jencks hardly bothers to argue the merits of greater equality.

Once or twice, he resorts to the so-called law of diminishing marginal utility of income and couples it with the principle of interpersonal comparisons of utility to argue that poor people value the gain of extra income more than rich people suffer its loss. Economists will find this sort of old-fashioned utilitarianism unconvincing. There are much better arguments for equality to which many economists would subscribe. It is a pity that this book failed to explore them. If most Americans regard existing income inequalities as perfectly legitimate, it is largely because no one has ever forced them to think about either the economics or the ethics of equality.

Although *Inequality* is a book about America, containing only a few references to Sweden and Britain, it challenges assumptions held by many in this country.

For this reason alone, it would seem to be worth our careful consideration. But, in addition, it will serve to remind us, better than any book I know, how far we still have to go in educational research in Britain before we can even begin to pose the questions to which we would all dearly like to know the answer.

In fact, the only data base that may do for Britain what this book does for America is the longitudinal cohort study of J.W.B. Douglas. His cohort is now 27 years old; many of them have been employed for almost a decade and we have excellent information on their home background and school experience. It is to be hoped that Douglas will one day top his *The Home and the School and All Our Future* with a British study of inequality.

33. Review of *Schooling in Capitalist America: Educational Reform and the Contradictions of Economic Life*, by Samuel Bowles and Herbert Gintis[*]

This is a powerfully argued and richly documented book by two well-known radical economists about the impossibility of educational reform without far-reaching social and economic change. Their basic thesis is that the educational system reflects the inherent inequalities of the capitalist economy, or as they put it in their neo-Marxist jargon: 'the social relations of schools reproduce the social division of labor under capitalism'. In the style of Christopher Jencks's best-seller, *Inequality* (1972), their largely qualitative argument is buttressed by the statistical analysis of the interrelations between family origins, IQ, years of schooling and occupational status, which is hidden away in appendices lest it frighten off 'the intelligent layman' to whom this book is largely addressed. But unlike Jencks, they interlard their text with historical analyses, first of the rise of mass public education in the nineteenth century, and second of the dashed hopes of the progressive movement earlier in this century.

Jencks has concluded that the distribution of personal incomes could not be equalized by equalizing access to the education system, because schooling as such affects incomes only to a minimum degree. Bowles and Gintis concur with Jencks but they go much further: even the attempt to reduce the authoritarian tendencies in the present school system are doomed to failure because capitalism cannot survive without an obedient and subservient work force. Their largely negative critique of current effort to reform education culminates, however, in a glowing final chapter, holding out the prospects of a humane, egalitarian system of 'socialist education' consequent on the abolition of private property in the means of production. I find their arguments unconvincing on a number of levels, but I believe nevertheless that this is a book that should be read by economists and educators for its thought-provoking qualities.

There is no doubt that the authors' attack on liberal educational reformers carries a great deal of conviction: invariably, liberals argue as if the school system were outside society, as if social and economic behaviour were the product of

[*] First published in *Challenge*, **19**(3), July–August 1976: 59–61.

schooling rather than the other way around. It follows that effective educational change involves a reform programme that extends far beyond the boundaries of the formal educational system. But must we abolish capitalism in order to improve education? It is at this point in the debate that Bowles and Gintis desert the evidence and succumb to rhetoric. We can go right through this book, replacing the word 'capitalism' by 'industrial civilization, whether capitalist or communist', without in any way affecting the strength or the nature of the authors' argument.

Bowles and Gintis concede that the Soviet Union and the countries of Eastern Europe have replicated 'the relationships of economic control, dominance, and subordination characteristic of capitalism' in spite of nationalizing the means of production (pp. 57, 266), but they provide no explanation of what presumably went wrong in those countries. If collective ownership of industry does not necessarily solve the problem, we may well ask whether the real solution in fact requires collective ownership. They tell us that Cuba and China are inspiring examples of what can be done to reform education in the context of revolutionary socialism, but they also warn that 'there is no foreign model for the economic transformation we seek' (p. 266). We are thus left to infer that hierarchical authority and managerial control of the labour force is not a technical imperative of modern industry but is rather the outcome of a capitalist 'conspiracy' to divide and conquer: we can have modern industry without the concomitants of modern styles of management. This is a doubtful thesis and it is married to the even more doubtful thesis that the educational system must be a mirror-like reflection of the factory system.

I readily grant that a massive extension of profit-sharing and worker participation in the management of industry, not to mention considerable decentralization of political decision-making hand-in-hand with decentralization of the taxing power, would underwrite the Bowles–Gintis package of educational reforms – 'open enrollment, free tuition, no tracking, curriculum and evaluation procedures appropriate to all students' needs, significantly increased finances, and a critique of ideologies which celebrate the status quo' (p. 250), but there is nothing in this book which would convince the sceptic that such changes are impossible under capitalism. If socialism is a sufficiently flexible concept to allow each country to pursue its own variation on the theme of collective ownership of industry, how much more so is this true of capitalism and its theme of private ownership of industry? If we are going to concentrate all economic power in the hands of the state, including that fearful power denied even the largest of American corporations, namely, the power to deny undesirable individuals any and all means of gaining a livelihood, we need reasons better than the authors supply for nailing the flag of educational reform to the mast of socialism.

The centrepiece of the book is the demonstration that the economic value of schooling in a capitalist economy has been grossly misunderstood by economists of 'the technocratic school' (this is as near as the authors ever get to defining 'the enemy'). The widely attested association between an individual's earnings and his educational attainment is not due to cognitive skills which schooling imparts and which employers prize as indispensable to the productive process. It is due rather to certain personality traits conducive both to high grades in the classroom and to effective work performance on the job. Up to the level of high school education, these are largely traits of punctuality, persistence, concentration and obedience. In higher education, on the other hand, they are the values of independence and self-reliance within a definite framework of organizational rules and procedures. In this way, elementary and secondary education prepare the hewers of wood and the drawers of water, while college education trains the junior managers and executives.

This emphasis on affective behaviour rather than mental attainments is not the unintended by-product of schooling carried out for other purposes. So long as industry is hierarchically organized, what is required at the bottom of the job pyramid is the ability to take orders, while at the top of the pyramid what is required is the ability to give orders. Teachers are perfectly aware of this spectrum of vocational demands and hence reward students in classrooms accordingly. Employers, on the other hand, have difficulties in measuring the particular bundle of attributes required at various levels of the occupational pyramid, but past experience reveals that there is a general concordance between required behaviour and educational attainments. In that sense, educational credentials act as surrogates for qualities which employers regard as important: they predict a higher level of performance without necessarily making any direct contribution to it, particularly as they largely enforce the values and attitudes acquired before schooling begins. This scenario neatly accounts for the facts that earnings and education are positively correlated; it even explains why so many educational qualifications appear to be unrelated to the type of work that individuals eventually take up, and it certainly explains why repeated efforts to create open classrooms, untracked high schools, and curricula without assessment always fail in the face of the pervasive tendency of the labour market to stratify individuals.

This argument is not quite as revolutionary as the authors make out. Sociologists ever since Durkheim have appreciated the fact the 'socialization' is one of the principle functions of an educational system in any society. Even economists have never committed themselves to the notion that the economic value of education is due entirely to the effects of cognitive learning in schools. Writers in the human-capital tradition, for example, have viewed school as a 'black box': without pretending to know precisely what goes on in the classrooms, they have nevertheless insisted that passing through schools increases the earning power of people even if both family origins and inborn mental abilities are held constant.

Bowles and Gintis, however, deny that the pure effects of schooling outweigh the effects of family background factors, or at any rate, they seem to deny it. Actually, their own model predicting income from childhood IQ, socioeconomic background, age and years of schooling attributes a slightly greater effect to education than to family origins. It is well-known that home background does exert an independent effect on earnings – if only because unequal family incomes produce unequal capacities to purchase additional education. It is also well known that schooling as such exerts too small an effect on earnings to allow policy-makers to substantially equalize earnings solely by reductions in schooling differences among individuals. Bowles and Gintis devote a great deal of energy to a rebuttal of the IQ school (Jensen–Herrnstein and all that) but as far as most economists are concerned, this is preaching to the converted: virtually all statistical attempts to explain earnings give little weight to either childhood or adult IQ. What is at issue is the magnitude of the separate effects of IQ, home environment, years of schooling and work experience; in addition, there is disagreement about how to measure each of these variables.

Statistically speaking, only a hair's breadth divides the work of Becker, Mincer and other protagonists of human-capital theory from that of Bowles and Gintis. What Bowles and Gintis bring to the argument is a very different interpretation of the findings, which still leaves open the basic question of whether schooling merely enforces the personality traits acquired at home, or whether it actually produces these traits in certain children. Bowles and Gintis marshal a great deal of fascinating evidence that school grades tend to reward behavioural attitudes rather than mental learning (ch. 5), but measures of output without measures of input tell us little about 'value-added' in classrooms.

Although *Schooling in Capitalist America* contains occasional bits of Marxist dogma (pp. 10–11, 67–8), most of it consists of a genuinely creative attempt to develop a Marxist point of view about the interaction between schooling and the labour market, an attempt which may be as shocking to orthodox Marxists as it is to most non-Marxist readers. In the arid literature on education, one must be thankful for any book that both disturbs and provokes thought. Certainly this one does both. There are some exciting books which would be better if they were shorter. This is one which ought to have been longer. It is a tribute to the authors to say that one closes it with feelings of regret that the argument has come to an end.

34. Review of *Economics of Education: Research and Studies*, ed. George Psacharopoulos*

The economics of education as a field of study was born phoenix-like in the early 1960s out of the pioneering work of Gary Becker and Edward Denison and the promotional efforts of Theodore Schultz. In the 1970s, however, came the screening hypothesis and the associated notions of internal and segmented labour markets. At the same time, the emerging problem of stagflation in the industrialized countries and the decline in rates of economic growth in both the First and the Third Worlds sapped confidence in the power of education to promote growth, development, equality and all the other good things of life. The 1980s have seen a deepening pessimism about the importance of education and with it has come a pervasive disillusionment with the economics of education as an area of teaching and research. One might almost go so far as to say that the economics of education now lies dead in the minds of both professional economists and professional educators.

The New Palgrave: A Dictionary of Economics, published last year by Macmillan in four volumes, contains no entry for 'economics of education' and refers the reader to an essay on 'Human capital' as if the economics of education were merely another name for human capital theory, a proposition which is roughly equivalent to equating labour economics with the marginal productivity theory of wages. However, this failure of the economics of education to be recognized as a specialized field of study in an encyclopaedia that will probably remain the standard reference work on economics for the next two or three decades – and this despite the exsistence of a professional journal exclusively devoted to the subject, the *Economics of Education Review* – merely registers the general sense of boredom of economists with a subject that has remained relatively stagnant for more than a decade.

It is not difficult to find the source of this contempt for the economics of education. The simple fact is that the field has failed to deliver the goods. We are certain that education contributes to economic growth but then so do health care, housing, roads, capital markets, etcetera, and in any case we cannot quantify the growth-enhancing effects of education under different circumstances

* First published in the *Journal of Human Resources*, **14**(2), 1988: 331–5.

and we cannot even describe these effects except in the most general terms. We can measure private and social returns to educational investment but since we cannot specify, much less measure, the externalities generated by educated individuals, not to mention the consumption benefits of education, the 'social' rate of return to education is a bogus label. But even if the externalities of education were nil, it would still be true that we have been unable to separate the productivity from the screening functions of schooling and hence cannot even say what the social rate of return to education actually means. Is it cognitive knowledge or effective behavioural traits that make educated workers valuable to employers? Is it believable that we can still ask such a question, knowing that the literature does not vouchsafe a firm answer? A subject that after 25 years of study and investigation is unable convincingly to resolve at least some of these issues is not to be taken seriously. And, indeed, it is not taken seriously.

The present volume reprints 88 entries in the ten-volume *International Encyclopaedia of Education*, edited by Thorsten Husèn and Neville Postlethwaite (1985). On the whole, these entries are very well done, giving a genuine overview of the economics of education as of the mid-1980s, and the 54 contributors make up a veritable who's who in the subject. This is as sound a mini-textbook in the economics of education as we are likely to have for many years to come. But the fact remains that virtually every one of these articles could have been written in identical terms 10 or even 15 years ago; if the date of publication on the fly-page of the book were lost, only an occasional reference to recently published case studies would tell us that it had in fact been published in 1987, and not in 1977 or even in 1967. Such theoretical and empirical stagnation is to be contrasted with the explosive developments in recent years in, say, health economics, labour economics, macroeconomics, and even microeconomics. The economics of education instead rests on its oars: it does not fructify.

In come not to praise the economics of education but also not to bury it. Economists have much to say about the costing and finance of education that is relevant to current political debates in Europe and America; moreover, so long as the Vocational School Fallacy and the discredited practice of manpower forecasting are alive and well in Africa, Asia and Latin America – as unfortunately they are – the economics of education will remain a relevant field of specialization, at least for its negative messages. But there is no use in pretending that the antipathy of educators toward economists and the public disdain of economists in current controversies about education are not in part our own fault, reflecting the poor substantive achievements of the economics of education. Many, if not most, of the essays in the volume under review exhibit an alarming air of complacency about the status of the subject, which bodes ill for potential future developments.

For example, both N.L. Hicks on 'Education and Economic Growth' (pp. 101–7) and D.B. Holsinger on 'Modernization and Education' (pp. 107–10) review a number of studies that have demonstrated the correlation between measures of education and measures of economic growth but they fail to emphasize sufficiently how little we still know about the causal impact of education on either economic growth or modernization. As a case in point, much is made of studies on farmer productivity in developing countries, which conclude that additional years of formal schooling substantially raise both output per acre and output per worker, at least in modernized rural areas (see 'Farmers' Education and Economic Performance' by M.E. Lockheed, pp. 110–16). Without casting doubt on the significance of this finding so far as it goes, it is nevertheless misleading to extrapolate it to the rather different setting of large industrial enterprises in advance countries. By way of contrast, Foster writes with what seems to me to be appropriate circumspection on 'The Contribution of Education to Development' (pp. 93–100).

Likewise, there is a tendency in some of the essays to set out a long list of the pecuniary and non-pecuniary benefits of education for both educatees and society at large and to infer from this that there is underspending on education (see L.C. Solomon, 'The Range of Educational Benefits', pp. 83–93, and W.W. McMahon, 'Consumption and Other Benefits of Education' and 'Externalities in Education', pp. 129–37). But apart from the omission of an almost equally long list of negative effects of education, it is the marginal and not the total externalities of an activity that are relevant to arguments about 'market failures'; in addition the case for 'market failure' must be matched by an examination of 'government failure' before drawing conclusions about public support for education. In general, the application of standard welfare economics applied to education is never given its proper due in this volume: only two articles, namely W.W. McMahon on 'Externalities' (pp. 133–7) and J. Wiseman on 'Public Finance of Education' (pp. 436–9), are devoted to it and it is only mentioned parenthetically in one or two articles. And yet it is of crucial significance in considering all questions of educational finance and government regulation of the education industry.

Human capital theory is explained in numerous entries and extolled in many more (e.g. M. Woodhall, 'Human Capital Concepts', pp. 21–4; M.J. Bowman, 'On-the-Job Training', pp. 24–9; W.W. McMahon, 'Expected Rates of Return to Education', pp. 187–96; M. Woodhall , 'Earnings and Education', pp. 209–18; and G. Psacharopoulos, 'Earnings Functions', pp. 218–23, and 'The Cost-Benefit Model', pp. 342–7), but the failure of human capital theory decisively to disentangle the interrelationships between endowed ability, acquired ability and educational attainment is consistently underemphasized. In that respect, J.R. Behrman and P. Taubman ('Kinship Studies', pp. 291–8) stand out from all the other contributors because they argue, here as elsewhere, that rates of return on education, calculated in the usual manner, are biased upward because of omitted interactions between ability and schooling. Widening the argument, it is curious to notice how the very explanatory power of earnings functions specified in terms of human capital theory signify different things to different authors. According to Jacob Mincer, about half of the variance in the distribution of earned income is explained by variations in years of formal schooling and work experience; some see this as dramatic confirmation of human capital theory – after all, the entire distribution of an individual's earnings is being explained by two or at most three variables – while others argue that this is evidence that factors other than education and training must be important in explaining earnings differentials (cf. pp. 163, 221–2, 263).

When we add these hints of doubt to the subversive implications of the screening hypothesis, the empirical status of human capital theory seems much less secure than it appears in many entries in this book. Screening, filtering, credentialism and the like are clearly expounded by R. McNabb in 'Labour Market Theories and Education' (pp. 157–4) and D.R. Winkler provides an incisive review of the inconclusive effort to date to test the screening hypothesis ('Screening Models and Education', pp. 287–91). But the observational equivalence of human capital theory and screening models only encourages still greater caution in respect of human capital theory: the screening hypothesis *could* be true, and if it is , we have all been drawing the wrong conclusions from human capital theory.

Let me draw this review to a close by simply listing the other essays which I can recommend on pedagogic grounds: E.A. Hanushek, 'Educational Production Functions' (pp. 33–41); F. Orivel, 'Educational Technology' (pp. 42–53); L.C. Solomon, 'The Quality of Education' (pp. 53–9); S. Rosen, 'Job Information and Education' (pp. 179–82); H.G. Grubel, 'The Economics of the Brain Drain' (pp. 201–6); R.B. Freeman, 'Demand Elasticities for Educated Labor' (pp. 237–9); M.J. Bowman, 'Skill Excess and Shortage' (pp. 307–11); J.K. Hinchliffe, 'Forecasting Manpower Requirements' (pp. 315–23); and D.W. Verry, 'Education Cost Functions; (pp. 400–9). There are a surprisingly small number of weak papers and virtually no aspect of the economics of education does not get a mention somewhere in this book. I noted only one topic, or rather one feature of a topic, that was totally neglected. The famous Hansen–Weisbrod demonstration of the alleged inequitable effects of higher education subsidies is alluded to here and there (pp. 6–7, 314) but it is never adequately reviewed anywhere in the volume either in the papers on education and income distribution or in the papers on educational finance. This is very odd and even odder is the absence of any reference when the subject does appear to the intergenerational features of the who pays/who benefits? question; there have been as many as six or seven articles in recent years on education and lifetime income distribution.

The most frequently cited author in this book is not Becker, not Denison, not Schultz, but the editor, George Psacharopoulos. In part this is due to the fact that he is the author of 13 of the 88 contributory articles and is notoriously fond of citing himself. Nevertheless, even if one removes the self-citations in his prodigious entry in the Name Index, he still emerges as one of the most frequently cited writers in the economics of education. Indeed, he is the Harry Johnson of the economics of education, whose prolific output has put everyone else to shame. The preparation of *The International Encyclopedia of Education* was a herculean task in which George Psacharopoulos assumed responsibility for all articles falling within the economics of education. The result was a set of entries that has added up to a book which will serve equally for teaching purposes in departments of economics and in departments of education.

35. Review of *Bowles and Gintis Revisited: Correspondence and Contradiction in Education Theory*, ed. Mike Cole*

In 1976 Samuel Bowles and Herbert Gintis, two radical American economists, published a book entitled *Schooling in Capitalist America*. It attracted little attention from economists but it caught on immediately with sociologists, quickly becoming a classic text in the sociology of education; indeed, it is no exaggeration to say that much of the sociology of education in the Anglo-Saxon world in the past decade has been a dialogue with Bowles and Gintis. I was quite right to hail the book when it first appeared as a flawed masterpiece (*Challenge*, July/August 1976) but I totally misjudged the nature of the audience that would respond to it.

At the core of Bowles and Gintis's book was the 'correspondence principle'. In their words:

> We argued specifically that the current relationship between education and economy is ensured not through the *content* of education but its *form* ... Education prepares students to be workers through a *correspondence* between the social relations of production and the social relations of education. Like the division of labour in the capitalist enterprise, the educational system is a finely graded hierarchy of authority and control in which competition rather than co-operation governs the relations among participants, and an external reward system – wages in the case of the economy and grades in the case of schools – holds sway. This correspondence principle explains why the schools cannot a the same time promote full personal development and social equality, while integrating students into society. (p. 18).

They called it 'the correspondence principle' but they should have called it 'the reflection principle' because the argument was, not that the structure of authority and reward of schools *corresponds* to that of factories, but rather that it *reflects* that of factories. Steeped as they were in the Marxian terminology of 'base' and 'superstructure', Bowles and Gintis assumed without discussion that all educational change is the result of prior change in the economic base, and that the educational system, being an element in the superstructure of society, lacks any autonomous motion of its own.

* First published in *Economics of Education Review*, 8(3), 1989: 297–8.

However, named, 'the correspondence principle' merits serious consideration. But how much does it really explain? Most special institutions are hierarchically organised; many encourage its members/clients/participants to compete against each other for the sake of extrinsic rewards; in short, many resemble factories in these and other respects. But is this because hierarchy and competition are in fact more efficient principles for carrying out specific tasks than democratic participation and co-operation, or is it due to the dominance of the capitalist class over all aspects of the superstructure? Reading Bowles and Gintis with due attention to the problem of causal explanation reveals immediately that their thesis is so carelessly expounded as virtually to deny refutation: it is a framework for story-telling and with it one can tell almost any story one likes.

The book under review is full of criticisms of Bowles and Gintis but not on the methodological grounds just expressed. The editor, Mike Cole, in a paper reprinted from the 1983 *Sociological Review*, seems to be complaining that Bowles and Gintis are insufficiently Marxist, socialist, and in general too little concerned with the sort of 'consciousness-raising' that should characterize educational discourse; these sentiments are echoed and elaborated in a strident paper by Rachel Sharp. Peter MacDonald in one of the best essays in the book denies that the correspondence principle is much used in accounting for the rise in the nineteenth century of compulsory mass education in Canada, the United States and Britain. Others, like Michael Apple, Anne Marie Wolpe and Gloria Joseph, contend that Bowles and Gintis overemphasize social class at the expense of gender and race. There are repeated reminders of the relative and even absolute autonomy of the educational system as a social institution (pp. 9, 45, 58, 65, 71, 77, 114, 124), but little or no complaint of the very form of the argument of Bowles and Gintis. When Bowles and Gintis reply to their critics in the closing chapter of the book they merely replace 'the correspondence principle' by a new schema drawing on game theory, which is as loosely worded as was the thesis it replaced (p. 240); indeed, they revel in its indeterminacy as a source of strength (p. 243). If 'anything goes', you can never be shown to be wrong!

In general, a reading of this book induces a deep sense of depression about Marxian sociology of education. How can so many intelligent people have spent so much energy asserting that businessmen sometimes exert an overwhelming influence on schools, sometimes a certain amount of influence, and sometimes none at all; that some educational reforms are in fact due to changes in the economy but that a good deal of educational reform can only be explained by the internal momentum of the educational system? In sum, the base/superstructure metaphor applied to the production/education relationship is a dead end.

Index

absolutism in history of economics 56
Acton, H.B. 350
Ahamad, B. 209
Ahiakpor, J.C.W. 119
Alchain, A.A. 109, 271
Allen, Robert 28
Althusser, Louis 350, 352
Alum Rock Experiment 258, 261, 265
American Communist Party 4–5
Andreotti, G. 136
Apple, Michael 389
Archibald, Chris 203
Arnon, A. 122
Arrow, K.J. 72, 77, 104, 192n
   and economic methodology 160, 168, 169
   on theory 187, 188–90
art galleries, subsidies 313–14
Arts Council 285–306
   audiences 307–8, 309
   cost-effectiveness of 307–15
   goals, conflicts 293–8
   objectives 307
   and patronage 299–300
   rising costs of production 290
   role of 286–90
   subjectivity in 300–303
   subsidies to 290–293
   ticket prices 310–311
Atkinson, Anthony 163
Attwood, Thomas 118
Auden, W.H. 10
Austrian School of economics 79, 80, 87, 89, 91–3, 189
Azariadis, S. 272

Backhouse, R.E. 67, 68, 153, 171, 174
   on research programmes 189, 191, 196
Bagehot, Walter 341–3
Bailey, M.J. 272

Bank Charter Act (1844) 118, 119
Banking School on money 118–20
banks and quantity theory of money 115–16, 117–18
Baran, P. 353
Barnes, J. 218
Barr, N. 218
Barreto, H. 103, 111n
Barro, R.J. 75
Barzel, Y. 109
Bateman, Bradley 31, 40n
Bauer, Peter 15
Baumol, William 49n, 57–8, 80, 111n, 290, 291–2
   on entrepreneurship 102, 106, 109, 110
Beck, Gary 383
Becker, G. 382
behavioural traits in educational taxonomy 213–14, 276
Benassy, J.P. 75
Berhman, J.R. 385
Bernstein, Eduard 350, 352
Best, M.H. 81
Bhaskar, V.S. 75
Bianchi, M. 171, 172
Binmore, K. 172
biography
   of Keynes 26–43
   relevance of 28
   role of 27–8
Black, Max 200
Blanchard, O.J. 130
Blinder, A.S. 171
Bloom, Benjamin 213, 275–6
Boettke, P.J. 80
Böhm-Bawerk, E. von 27, 89, 101
Boland, Lawrence 131n, 153, 157
Bordo, M.D. 49n, 125, 130, 132n
Bortkiewicz, Ladislas von 352
Bowen, W.G. 291–2

Treatise on Probability (Keynes) 30–31
Trotsky, Leon 350, 351
Tugan-Baranovsky, M.I. 352
Tullock, G. 82n, 106

Un-American Activities Committee 7
uncertainty and risk 100–101
unemployment 9
  and competition 75
  indirect costs of 147–8
  and inflation 143–5
  monetary costs of 146–7
  output costs of 145–6
United Nations 15–16
Usher, A.P. 160

Vaughn, K.I. 78, 81, 91, 94n, 111n
Veblen, Thorsten 27
Verry, D.W. 386
Vickers, L.H. 117
Vickery, William 24n, 148
Voltaire, François 52
vouchers
  in Arts 311–12
  in education 216, 258–67

Wald, Abraham 168
Walker, Donald A. 28, 40n, 72, 176n
Walras, Leon 27, 62, 68, 104, 121, 168,
    345
  and general equilibrium theory 22–3,
    187–9
  on stability 71–5, 77
Walters, A.A. 167
Warming, Jens 184

The Wealth of Nations (Smith) 51–4, 67,
    96
Weber, Max 200
Weeks, J. 68
Weintraub, Roy 82n, 153, 169, 174,
    188–9
West, Edward 47n, 49n, 261
Whalley, J. 76
White, L.H. 119
Wicksell, Knut 27, 40n, 59, 89, 120–121,
    129, 132n
Wicksteed, Philip 27, 40n
Wilber, C.K. 201
Wilde, Oscar 13
Willatt, Sir Hugh 305, 311
Williams, P.L. 72
Williamson, O.E. 97
Wilson, Thomas 361
Winch, Donald 26, 41n, 48n, 50n
Winkler, D.R. 386
Winter, S.G. 81
Wiseman, Jack 261, 385
Witt, U. 81
Wolpe, Anne Marie 389
Wong, Stanley 365–6
Woodhall, M. 385
World Bank 17, 38
World Experimental Literacy Project
    (UNESCO) 17
Wright, Richard 5

Yale University 8, 9, 10, 12, 18
Youdi, R.J. 209

Zamagni, S. 190, 192n